POWER AND SEX

Scilla Elworthy PhD is Director of the Oxford Research Group, which she founded in 1982 to find out how and by whom nuclear weapons decisions are made, worldwide. She has been a consultant to UNESCO as well as research director in France for Minority Rights Group, before which she managed a self-help organization in Africa, moving agricultural surpluses to areas of starvation. The author of numerous books and reports on defence and other issues, she has a doctorate in political science, lectures in Europe, the United States, Russia, China and Japan, and appears widely on radio and television.

by the same author

The Role of Women in Peace Movements, Peace Research and the Improvement of International Relations
Who Decides? Accountability & Nuclear Weapon Decision-Making In Britain
How Nuclear Weapons Decisions Are Made
In the Dark: Parliament, The Public & NATO's New Nuclear Weapons

Scilla Elworthy

Power and Sex

A BOOK
ABOUT WOMEN

To Nancy

Remember our mutual
discovery of our goddesses
within, on Maui,
in February 1997

With my love
Scilla

ELEMENT
Shaftesbury, Dorset ● Rockport, Massachusetts
Brisbane, Queensland

Text © Scilla Elworthy 1996

First published in Great Britain in 1996 by
Element Books Limited
Shaftesbury, Dorset SP7 8BP

Published in the USA in 1996 by
Element Books, Inc.
PO Box 830, Rockport, MA 01966

Published in Australia in 1996 by
Element Books Limited
for Jacaranda Wiley Limited
33 Park Road, Milton, Brisbane 4064

Cover design by Max Fairbrother
Photograph of the author by John Hamwee
Page design by Roger Lightfoot
Typeset by ABM Typographics Ltd, Hull
Printed and bound in Great Britain by
Hartnolls Ltd, Bodmin, Cornwall

British Library Cataloguing in Publication
data available

Library of Congress Cataloguing in Publication
data available

ISBN 1–85230–788–9

To John Hamwee

Contents

Acknowledgements

Many, many people have had a hand in this book. Henrietta Wilson brought her zest and enthusiasm to it in the early stages, understood my hieroglyphics, and typed the first draft. John Hamwee took care of me while I finished the fourth draft, which he and a number of people read and commented on, including Linda Barlow, Katie Boanas, Pat Booth, Stacey Burlet, Ian Davis, Emma Dunford-Wood, Edward Elworthy, Heather Elworthy, Sissel Fowler, Pam Geggus, Deborah Gill, Mehr Gillett, Nicholas Gillett, Rob Green, Sophie Hamwee, Gaby Hock, Pauline Hodson, Rosie Houldsworth, Heather Hunt, Paul Ingram, Sean Legassick, Patricia Lewis, Joelle Mann, Margot Miller, Catherine Sherman Perry, Anne Piper, Paula Rose, Clare Scott, Richard Walters, Rob Waygood, Judy Becker Worsley, Mike Worrall and Morag Young. Felicity Wight both commented on the entire manuscript and provided the account of life in Ladakh which appears in chapter 8. Michael Maynard and his men's group brainstormed ideas for the section in chapter 11 on men with hara power, which John Hamwee drafted. I am grateful to all these people for their insight and their ideas, and for pointing out to me what I could not see – for example, how much anger there was in those early drafts. These readers taught me a lot.

After reading the manuscript, many readers continued to send me pictures, ideas, newspaper clippings and information – and that kind of involvement and support was deeply encouraging.

My daughter Polly McLean egged me on throughout, typed large sections of later drafts, and never sighed when I said for the nth time that I had finished the book. The eighth draft was read with the greatest care by Rosalind Armson, Deirdre Burton, Eva Chapman, Meriel Darby, Aimery Dunlap Smith, Gerard Fairtlough and Lisa Fairtlough. Their detailed notes were invaluable to me, and led to substantial changes.

Meredith Ramsbotham has been a godmother to the book, introducing me first to the invaluable Henrietta Wilson, and then to

Michael Mann at Element Books. It has been a delight to work with a publishing house where the contact is always personal, warm and energetic. John Baldock, my editor at Element, steered me sensitively and wisely through some difficult changes. Theresa Franklin's enthusiasm and imagination for publicizing the book is a joy. Cath Haslam and Leonie Hayler have a steadiness in handling the production schedule which gives a sense of security. Mary Clemmey was generous with her advice on publishing, as was Brian Aldiss with his on contracts. Nadine Gurr helped with some research and typing of the bibliography. Beth Wood and Pippa Hamwee read and commented on the final draft and looked after me like mothers while I was finishing it.

I am grateful to the following authors and publishers for permission to use printed material: to Marshall Rosenberg and the Center for Nonviolent Communication for excerpts from A Conversation with Marshall Rosenberg, 1992; to Parallax Press for the excerpt from Thich Nhat Hanh's The Heart of Understanding; to Janet Burroway for excerpts from Joanna Goldsworthy (ed) A Certain Age: Reflecting on the Menopause, published by Virago in 1993; to the Minority Rights Group for the drawing of an infibulated vulva from Efua Dorkenoo and Scilla Elworthy, Female Genital Mutilation: Proposals for Change, London, Minority Rights Group, International Report, 1992. Professor Nicholas Mann kindly made available the remarkable facility of the photographic collection of the Warburg Institute.

Many of the ideas in the book are now in common currency; I am deeply grateful to those who have already expressed them, and set me thinking. I have made strenuous efforts to acknowledge all of them either in the text, in the section entitled 'Additional Material and Notes', or in the bibliography. If I have omitted anyone whose ideas have been an inspiration, I shall be sad, for I value them greatly.

PART I
Introduction

I feel sick when I see power abused – businessmen awarding themselves fat pay increases, children being used for porn videos, helicopter pilots hunting down fleeing lorry drivers, girls having their genitals mutilated by older women. I feel sick and then I feel angry.

Yet I too am an abuser of power. I have caused suffering and shrugged, I have ignored my child's tears, I control and manipulate others to do what I want, I have dumped men who loved me. I have the power to hurt people and I do so.

I also feel powerless. When faced with hunger in Africa, or the intractability of generals in Serbia and Bosnia, or fish dying in polluted seas, or the man I love going off to see another woman, I feel overwhelmed. I do not know what to do.

So I want to know how to be powerful in a way which can respond effectively to these things I witness. I want to be powerful in a way which is not itself abusive. I want to be able to stand up to a bully, without becoming a thug myself. That is what this book is about.

Power is usually associated with strength, domination, rule, and ultimately military force. The misuse of this type of power has brought our world to a point where violence is endemic, where disillusion reigns, and where we are destroying our natural environment. Is another type of power possible? What would it look like? Here I describe my own experiences of researching nuclear weapons decision-making, and of introducing women and their point of view to military decision-makers. I pose the question which is one of the themes of the book: how can women and men develop another kind of power? In order to be clear what is meant by these terms, I look briefly at the concepts of power in use over recent centuries and then, by drawing on indigenous cultures, start to picture what this other type of power may be. There is then a section describing the contents of the book, who it is written for and how it is written. The Introduction ends as it begins, with a personal experience, as the serpent makes its appearance.

I have been nibbling at the subject of power for years. Biting off a little bit, chewing it over, thinking it out. I worked in South Africa for ten years, and part of that time was spent moving surplus agricultural production to areas of starvation. It was impossible not to face the starkness of power relations – not only in terms of white versus black, but also in terms of modern speed versus ancient traditions, North versus South.

When the facts about nuclear weapons finally dawned on me at the age of 37 (I was a late developer), what I wanted to know was who had the power over them: who designed and made them, who ordered them, who wrote the cheques, who deployed them, who fired them. Further, I wanted to know what these people were like, what they thought about the world, whether they were just normal people who happened to make explosive devices which could blow up the world. So I founded a research group to do just this. It grew quickly, began to publish good books and gained a substantial reputation. I was able to go and listen to nuclear decision-makers and talk to them. Now, after 15 years' research into how decisions on defence are made, I am persuaded that the way power is used in our society is a masculine way, albeit distorted. For example, almost every one of the most senior decision-makers on nuclear weapons in the USA, Russia, Britain, France and China is a man. Religious systems have been ordered by men for centuries, so has the law and so has government.

Paradoxically, the dominance of male power is not making most men happy, and certainly it is not making most women happy. Our world is a mess. We, women and men, are in the process of wrecking the planet. We have raided the earth's resources until there is almost nothing left, we have flung out toxic waste which is killing our land and our seas, we have fouled our drinking water and poisoned the air we breathe. Our spirits are dying under the weight of the trash we produce. By the time everyone possesses a mobile phone and a video game, the earth may be dead.

In the course of my research, however, I discovered something else. I discovered that those women and men who had most clarity in opposing the whole nuclear cycle were those who used an inner strength. I worked with women's groups, church groups, youth groups, medical groups and so on, putting them in touch with nuclear weapons decision-makers as individuals, so that each could hear the point of view of the other. Generally it was women who asked the simplest, straightest questions, who named names, and who were most direct and most persistent. Before the fall of the Berlin Wall, in the late 1980s, I helped to bring women leaders and parliamentarians from Eastern and Western Europe to NATO, to talk to top military and diplomatic personnel about nuclear weapons. Many of the NATO people had never had to face an informed member of the public before on the subject of nuclear weapons, let alone a woman. I watched how this epitome of a traditional hierarchial power structure was non-plussed by a group of determined, articulate, non-aggressive women.

So, could there be another kind of power, different from the kind we are used to? What is it like? What could it be like? Could it be exercised by women and by men? There are many, many questions I want answers to:

- Is there such a thing as benign power?
- Is there a kind of integrity immune to the corruptions of power?
- What is the relationship between power and responsibility?
- Can the human values of the private sphere be used in international relations?
- How can conflicts be prevented?

This book is an account of my attempts to find answers to these questions, and others. Starting from my own feelings of powerlessness, I discovered that many women and men today feel powerless: power-less to change the system which traps them in poverty, powerless to stand up to authority, powerless to defend themselves and those they love, powerless to find the meaning in their lives, powerless to stop the destruction of the earth. This book is about how power to do these things can be developed in a way that does not in turn deprive others or render them powerless.

The thing I would like to clarify right at the start is what is meant by women and men, male and female, masculine and feminine. It can really be confusing, because men have a feminine side, and women have a masculine side. But I want to be as clear as I can, so I shall try to use the words 'men' and 'women' when I mean people of those physical genders, 'male' and 'female' when I am describing things per-taining to one gender or the other, and 'feminine' and 'masculine' when I mean a type of response, a characteristic, or a way of doing things.

What this book is *not* about is the battle of the sexes. I am not inter-ested in warring about power; I am interested in both sexes learning something new. I have no wish to blame men as a sex for what indi-vidual men have done, any more than I wish to blame women as a sex for what individual women have done. What I do know is that the

domination of men in our societies over a long period, and the pre-
dominance of a distorted male way of doing things, has led to a terrible imbalance. I am deeply interested in how the female/male balance
can be re-established.

This book is not about women fighting men to gain the positions
men have and do things the way men do them, only better. That is
unimaginative, as well as being beside the point. The point is that,
when things reach a crisis, we have only really got one way of thinking about power in the West at present, and that is power through
domination and control. We have been stuck with these notions of
power for over 3,000 years. Until power itself is re-examined, we are
only dealing with one model of power. Let us have a look at what we
mean by 'power'.

What power means

A learned debate has been going on at least since Plato about what
power means. The philosopher Thomas Hobbes argued that power (or
the reputation for power) to subdue and destroy others was essential
for the security of any man's person or possessions. Only when such a
power exists, he said, can individual men realize their power to
achieve their ends. This idea is enshrined in the 'right to bear arms' in
the US constitution. Bertrand Russell defined power as 'the production of intended effects'. Max Weber and Robert Dahl both focused on
the idea of 'power over', while Talcott Parsons argued with C Wright
Mills over whether power was a general social resource or a weapon for
some groups to promote their own interests at the expense of others.
Dennis Wrong, on the same track, distinguished three forms of power:
force, manipulation and persuasion.

So, without resorting to a dictionary, it is easy to see that what
power means to most people is force, strength, influence, domination,
authority, rule – and ultimately, military force. I shall call this kind of
power *domination power*.

In our world the basic assumption is that everything can be divided
into superior and inferior, and that that which is superior is 'better'. I
recognize now that this is a method of control. The problem is that it
is thought to be the only method of control which is stable and
natural.

If it is not clear at any point who or what is superior, a competition or
contest will reveal the truth. Thus the basic way of deciding things under

patriarchy is by a power struggle. Physical coercion is there all the time under patriarchy, sometimes overt and sometimes covert. (John Rowan, 1987, page 9. B4)

Most recorded thinking on power and the use of power has been androcentric, that is, done by men and based on male values. The male norm and the human norm tend, even today, to be thought of as identical. Distorted male notions of power have become the way nations operate, and the way they assume others will respond. There is a whole set of preconceptions underlying this way of thinking, including the conviction that humans are inherently aggressive (based on the notion of original sin), and that humans are separate and independent and have no need to be responsible in a collective manner. Later in the book I shall come back to these convictions and question whether they are useful any more, whether they have any validity for us.

My own definitions of domination power are as much to do with manipulation and control as with physical force. One aspect of domination power, for example, is the ability to prevent people becoming aware of what is happening to them until it is too late for the decision to be reversed. I became fascinated that a small group of people, united around the one central idea of the enormous power of nuclear weapons, could act and do act contrary to the interests of the majority and to the interests of the planet. They do this by depriving the majority of the information they would need to wake up to what is happening.

Kenneth Boulding is one of the few Western writers, besides Stephen Lukes, who points out that beyond military power and economic power there is another kind of power. Boulding calls it integrative power. He does not give a very clear definition of it, but he talks about love, and the metaphor he uses is a hug (whereas military power is the stick, and economic power is the carrot). Many Western writers are not advanced when it comes to describing this other kind of power, so we may fruitfully turn to the traditional cultures, which know a lot about it. First the Kogi of South America, and then the Maori of Aotearoa/New Zealand.

Aluna contains everything which is past and everything that may become. *Aluna* is intelligence; it is the concentrated thought and memory which forms a bridge between the human 'spirit' and the universe, but it is also the hidden world of forces which govern the world's fertility. *Aluna* makes possible growth, birth and sexuality; it is the spiritual energy that makes things happen. If it did not, the world would be sterile. It would never have begun . . . Through concentrated thought and meditation, the Kogi enter the world of *aluna* and act there. (Alan Ereira, 1990, page 116. B11)

The marae is the place where people may stand tall. Here they are able to stand upon the Earth Mother and speak . . . While I stand here on you, Mother Earth, I feel safe, for I know that on this very place others have stood before me – my ancestors . . . Our bodies will return to you again; it is you who will guard them and use them as you will. Mother Earth, how proud we are to be your trustees during our lifetime. (Hiwi and Pat Tauroa, 1987, pages 6–11)

The elemental quality of these ancient beliefs begins to suggest what this other kind of power is like. What Kenneth Boulding is reaching for, and what ancient cultures knew, is that there is a primordial power, greater than all us little humans, which is timeless. On occasion we can touch into it, sometimes our eyes are open for a flicker of a second. It is the power of spirit, and people reach it when they go within themselves. It is neither good nor bad, light nor dark, male nor female, angel nor devil, it is all those things. It is so enormously powerful it makes armies look like ants, makes Tornado jets seem like bluebottles. And it is found inside ourselves, not outside ourselves.

The *Tao Te Ching*, the esoteric but infinitely practical book written most probably in the 6th century BCE by Lao Tsu, captures the idea in verse 37:

> The Tao never does anything,
> yet through it all things are done.
> If powerful men and women
> could concentrate themselves in it,
> the whole world would be transformed
> by itself, in its natural rhythms.
> People would be content
> with their simple everyday lives,
> in harmony, and free of desire.
> When there is no desire
> all things are at peace.

What is in the book

What this book aims to do is to unravel what this other kind of power may be, and how women and men can use it for a better world. In order to do that, it is useful to get some clues as to what life was like when feminine values *were* equal to the masculine – in the ancient goddess-worshipping cultures which flourished around the Mediterranean for thousands of years – and to learn why those cultures disappeared. The first chapter therefore describes a world in which another type of power did hold sway, a world which existed for a very long time, but so long ago that I can barely imagine it. There is no point in being nostalgic for that world, nor wanting to return to it, but as we learn more about it, it can help us deal with our present catastrophes and take us to a way of living which is far richer and more exciting. Chapter 2 is about what has happened to women since then and how women particularly have experienced powerlessness, and this is followed by a chapter on the changes going on in people today which indicate that something new and quite fundamental is taking place.

That forms the first part of the book. The second part, chapters 4–8, is about how this other kind of power can be discovered and developed in ourselves – through the body, through greater self-knowledge, through spirituality and the soul (chapters 4, 5 and 6). Chapter 7 concentrates on the split into dualistic thinking that we have come to consider normal – the polarity of good versus evil, black versus white – and how the duality can be reconciled to afford enormous new reservoirs of strength. Chapter 8 looks wider, at how this power is experienced, particularly by traditional cultures as the Great Mysterious, and how we can touch that, how we can experience it.

The third part of the book puts all of this into a practical context, describing how people use this kind of power in their daily lives, and in the outside world – in building communication, mediating, obtaining justice, defusing conflicts.

Throughout the whole book the question of sexuality keeps appearing – the question of whether physical attraction and sexiness does give a person power, an opening up of the big power issues going on when one person is attracted to another, hints of an extraordinary kind of public female sensuality in the ancient world, details of the terrifying ways in which women have been and are kept captive sexually today, learning about how the female as well as the male body can open up physically to a greater sexuality during its entire life cycle and finally, the latent power involved in perfect union. I did not design it that way; it is just the way it is – power and sex are inextricably connected. In fact, this connection was my clue to what a new kind of power might be.

The book is written for women and for men; for those for whom

feminism as currently debated is sterile and superficial; for those who
see women becoming more powerful and shudder; for those who feel
powerless on issues about which they care a great deal; for those who
would like to go into politics, but don't; for those who don't like the
way decisions are made; for those who have not found much meaning
in their lives and want it; for those aged 45 and over who feel life slipping away and are depressed; for those who feel trapped in roles, either
of aggressor or of victim, and want to get out of them; for those who
feel a hunger for inner nourishment, for something to fill the void.

It is quite difficult to talk about some of these issues without sound-
ing pious and politically correct. So before I go any further I have to
introduce you to my internal critic. He is my resident sceptic, he sits
on my shoulder and carps at me. I used to hate him, because he can be
extremely critical of almost everything I do. Now I find that he can
also be useful. What I am writing about can easily teeter over into sentimentality, and a kind of slushy reasoning which makes me feel a bit
seasick. My critic is the stabilizer. He is rational, intellectual, definitely a masculine part of me. I have the kind of mind which gets high on
ideas, and likes to jump from one to the other. He asks the sharp questions, interrupts, argues. Sometimes he makes me laugh, sometimes he
is annoying, often he is plain wrong.

This book contains a mixture of fact, experience, impression, poetry
and image – the images being just as powerful, if not more so, in
conveying meaning. Any language is rather inadequate when talking
about the spirit. I greatly want to convey the excitement of what I am
discovering, for I feel as George Fox must have done three hundred
years ago: 'All things were new; and all the creation gave another
smell unto me than before, beyond what words can utter.'

Poetry is perhaps the most appropriate medium for discussing such
matters, with the meaning coming through the cracks in the words.
The book contains myths carried down and refined through generations, and is full of stories from the lives of individuals. Many of these
stories are about men, most are about women; it is the inner power in
both that I am looking for.

This mixture of styles can be hard to follow but I ask you to bear
with it, since straight prose is punished by the core of meaning losing
its luminosity. Each chapter is introduced by an overview, which I
hope will act as a kind of map of its direction. I would like the book to
be experiential, where the reader tries things out for herself or himself,
stops and goes quiet for a few moments while reading, letting insight
drop in.

It is not written as a scholarly book. I have followed up references extensively because I wanted to check and double check the authenticity of what I was finding out, but to allow the text to flow smoothly, the references and notes showing how I arrived at what I have written are available in a chapter-by-chapter section, entitled 'Additional Material and Notes', which comes after the main text. Many of the textual references and quotes have been identified by a reference to that section in the Bibliography where the work is listed. Since in a number of instances I wanted to offer the reader descriptions of techniques or exercises which I have found useful, as well as contact addresses, there is also a section for this, entitled 'Going Further', at the end of the book.

In closing this introduction, I would like to say something about taboos. I have chosen to write about things towards which some people – women as well as men – may feel resistance. I resisted writing them down at first, until I realized that that is because they contain power – power not of the kind we are used to, but power of a different sort, which I want to explore. So I take the resistance seriously, for it is based on what we have grown up with. The new power, which is also most ancient, draws forth all sorts of taboos and prejudices. In some instances we shy away from it because we think of it as witchcraft, in others because it is about sensuality and sexuality and we have been taught to be suspicious of our bodies, in yet other cases because we have been put off 'religion' and do not distinguish it from spirituality.

I have always been a pragmatic, practical type of person. So it was hard for me, in December 1992, to admit that I was walking along a riverbank in Oxford and seeing a vast serpent in the floodwaters. Except that I knew it was a serpent; I could see it moving and snaking its way. I had to follow it. I walked along a path at the very edge of the river, and then stood watching it. Here the serpent was coiling round bends, under and over logs, swirling with phenomenal power. I knew also that it was primordial, female and endless. Her force just kept on coming. She was not going to run out. I could see her head, reared back, with a terrifying eye, the whites showing. Her main power was in her chest, broad, rounded and majestic; the scales, each exquisitely beautiful, fanned out over it in a perfect pattern, as a pheasant's do. This serpent was in charge of the deep. In the most frightening of places – deep, dank, murky water – there was nothing she was afraid of. A few minutes later I realized that for me she was the inner power response to the mess we have made of the world.

I did not ask to see this serpent. It came and I could see it. It could be argued that if I had not been in an open or 'suggestible' frame of mind, I would not have seen it. But the fact remains that I can see a serpent in the murky waters of a flooded Oxford river and at the same time be a normal, intelligent human being. These things are not mutually exclusive.

Engraving of serpent from Milton's Paradise Lost, 1866, by Gustave Doré

CHAPTER I

Before God

This culture took keen delight in the natural wonders of this world. Its people did not produce lethal weapons or build forts in inaccessible places, as their successors did, even when they were acquainted with metallurgy.

Instead, they built magnificent tomb-shrines and temples, comfortable houses in moderately-sized villages, and created superb pottery and sculptures. This was a long-lasting period of remarkable creativity and stability, an age free of strife. Their culture was a culture of art.

Marija Gimbutas, 1989

This chapter starts with a true story set in the 1960s which poses the question of what kind of power women have today. But before investigating this in more detail in chapter 2, I go back in history. The opening quotation from archaeologist Marija Gimbutas describes the goddess-worshipping cultures which are the most persistent feature of archaeological records of the Paleolithic and Neolithic ages. For many thousands of years, it seems, societies existed in which men and women shared responsibility. In these cultures, which then covered much of the globe, feminine power was valued and worshipped. The existence of such cultures came as a surprise to me. Although more information about them comes to light every day now that archaeologists and historians have by and large accepted the fact of their existence, it is still difficult for us to picture what life then was actually like. So in the following section I allow some imagination on the role of so-called temple prostitutes, who were actually priestesses. I then present different explanations of how and why these goddess-worshipping societies disappeared and were replaced by warrior monotheistic religions. The narrative returns to the issue of power and the difficulties experienced by the new rulers in gaining control of the hearts and minds of those they had suppressed. The story of Adam and Eve comes up for examination here, as well as the historical symbolic role played by the serpent. The chapter closes with a discussion of the split into dualistic thinking which followed the demise of the goddess, and how this may be a necessary part of human development, despite the harsh consequences it has had for women.

A story of power and sex

I was head-hunted as advertising and publicity manager for a retail business owned by a large company in South Africa. My final interview was with the chairman of the whole company. I took the lift to the tenth floor, and was scrutinized in turn by three secretaries, each more power-dressed than the last, before being admitted to his penthouse office. The hushed approach, the acres of carpet, the vast desk; I was duly impressed. He employed me at twice my previous salary. I was 24.

I hired my own team of five and my office suite was decorated in blue and white. Things went so well that after a while I was asked to spend six months in London promoting the shops in the English chain. I was given the chairman's flat in central London to live in.

When I had been in London for three months the chairman came over from South Africa for a series of meetings, so I vacated the flat. At the end of the first day of meetings, he said to me that there were further matters he wished to discuss over dinner. I was to collect him in the company car and take him to a restaurant in Beauchamp Place. It turned out to be a dinner for two only. Over dinner he asked me to call him Arnold and put his hand on my knee. I called him Arnold and removed his hand. In the car outside the flat he tried to kiss me and wanted me to stay the night 'because I don't know how to make my own breakfast'. I said no.

The chairman's visit included an inspection of the shops in the north of England. He instructed me to arrange a tour of the Lake District for him, prior to which he was to visit a prestigious car factory, where they were custom-building his new vehicle. On the morning of the visit, he said that I was to stand in for his wife. I found myself being addressed as Mrs Wills. Looking back, of course I should have objected, but I didn't. When we left the factory, we drove to a nearby hotel, where we were booked in as Mr and Mrs Wills.

When we were alone in a double room, I faced my employer and said that I wanted a separate room. He laughed. 'This is just an amusing situation we have got into, but never mind. A man and a woman can *perfectly* well share a room in friendship. You would be very immature if you couldn't understand that.'

'That may be so, but I'm afraid I do want my own room.'

'It'll be most embarrassing for me to ask for another room now. Please grow up a bit and then we can have a pleasant evening.'

I handed him the phone. 'If you're embarrassed, you can say that I have a cold. Please do it now.' Finally I got my own room.

The next evening, in the Lake District, he tried again to book a double room for us. When I refused, he tried to come into my room after dinner. I told him again that I did not wish to have an affair with him, nor any physical contact.

When I returned to South Africa two months later I found my department dissolved and my team dismissed. I was given a cupboard to work in. All my responsibilities had been removed and I had no work to do. After three months I resigned. My resignation was instantly accepted.

What position does this put a woman in? What options does she have?

* If she has a strong and clear idea of who she is, what her values are and what she wants, she will say publicly what has happened. There will be consequences, and she can choose either to take them or fight them. In a country where people's rights are protected and there is a legal recourse to deter sexual harassment, she could certainly bring a case against her employer.
* She can play the game. Many women do, even if the man is not attractive. Why? She may be scared. She may have dependents to support. Or she may see it as an avenue to power. One of the chairman's former secretaries, for example, rose to be the director of the retail business, and regularly received his cast-off cars. This is the same kind of power possessed by the beautiful companion of a wealthy man. To the extent that he desires her, and to the extent that she is prepared or able to manipulate, she has control over him. For attractive women, this is a simple short cut to a form of power – power by proxy. (She can get straight through to him when ministers of state have to wait. He will buy her anything she wants. She can persuade him to promote her friends and relations. She can be grand with him in grand places. His acolytes will defer to her because of her influence over him.)

* She can fall between the two, as I did. I told an unattractive, powerful man that I wanted nothing to do with him sexually, took the consequences and married an attractive, powerful man. Much of my marriage was very happy. But during it, any sense of importance that I had was not my own. It was reflected. I had no sense of self. All the sense of power that I had was through having some power over somebody powerful.

And does the woman in the second and third options really have any power? She has a kind of power as long as the man continues to desire her. But this is power over – domination power, in its way. And her power depends on his desire. How have we got to a point where a lot of the power that women have is dependent on man's desire? For many centuries now, most women in most societies have been either power-less or dependent on men for power. *But it has not always been so.*

Going back to the time of women

If we go back further to the earliest indications of how people lived, we discover that for thousands of years things were quite different. Women were then the focus and the centre of their societies, because they possessed the greatest and most mysterious power of all, the power to create new life. In the earliest times people had no idea that men played any part in procreation. They did not connect sex with childbirth. The woman apparently simply grew larger and larger and eventually produced a child. So the future appeared to depend upon women alone.

Therefore everything that was passed down seems to have been passed down through women. Continuity passed through women: sons and daughters took their names from their mother. Possessions and wealth passed from mother to child; when eventually agriculture was developed and people ceased being nomadic and settled down, the rights to use land were passed from mother to child, as well as tools and equipment and animals. And because it was the female who could create new life, it was the female who was worshipped.

The deities were all variations on one central theme – the Great Mother. In every one of the earliest settled parts of the globe we find the remains of goddess worship.

In prehistoric and early historic periods of human development, religions existed in which people revered their supreme creator as female. The

Great Goddess – the Divine Ancestress – had been worshipped from the beginnings of the Neolithic periods c 7,000BC until the closing of the last Goddess temples, about AD 500. Some authorities would extend Goddess worship as far into the past as the Upper Paleolithic Age of about 25,000 BC. (Merlin Stone, 1976, page xii. B3)

The oldest images of the Earth Mother so far discovered indeed date back as far as 25,000 BCE, into the ice age. The most famous of these are shown below:

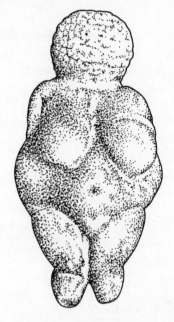 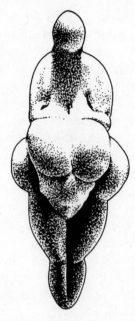

The Earth Mother of Willendorf, c c 30,000–25,000 BCE

Mammoth-ivory sculpture found at Lespugue, France c 23,000 BCE

Nearly 200 female figures have been found at dwelling sites of ice-age people from the Pyrenees in western Europe to Lake Baikal in central Siberia. This form of worship, which seems to have been more of a way of living, appears in the light of history as the worship of goddesses of many names and attributes. Historians and archaeologists like Jacquetta Hawkes, who devoted a lifetime of scholarship to understanding these cultures, suggest that they may all be recognized as one – the Mother Goddess or Great Goddess whose realm spread almost as far as Bronze Age civilization itself.

Although the goddess of the cultivators was probably at home in South-West Asia, and kept considerable power there in historic times as Inana,

Ishtar, Astarte and other divine ladies, she was to rule most powerfully and longest in the Mediterranean lands. In Asia Minor, where her images had been made over thousands of years, she rose above the surface of pre-history as the Cybele of the Phrygians and the Lydian Artemis, whose worship as a goddess of birth affronted St Paul at Ephesus. She was exceptionally powerful in the islands, notably in Cyprus where Aphrodite was to have her most famous temple, and in Malta where her name was never to be recorded, but where she was granted fine temples and was portrayed in images extraordinarily ample and voluptuous. (Jacquetta Hawkes, 1968, pages 26–7. B14)

To my mind some of the most exquisite images of her come from a group of islands known as the Cyclades. These islanders used their native marble to portray her in some examples as the abundant mother, suggesting the broad hips and full belly and squatting posture. But in others they were already seeing other aspects of the divine female, showing her tall, slender, small-breasted, and in Hawkes' words: 'with an abstract simplicity hardly to be understood again until the present time'.

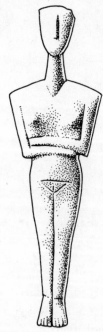

An Early Cycladic II (c2800-2300 BCE) marble female figurine

By 4000 BCE goddess figures appeared at Ur and Uruk, both situated on the southern end of the Euphrates river, not far from the Persian Gulf.

Along the Nile there are indications of the importance of the village goddess as village life became more established and Elise Boulding suggests that 'a specialised priestess class to serve cult centers would certainly have developed'. In India archaeological evidence, especially the work of Sir John Markham, reveals that before the Aryan invasions the indigenous population revered the goddess.

Over a period of many thousand years, the worship of female deities seems to have been a central spiritual practice throughout the inhabited world. The background notes for this chapter offer many more details. Since it is hard to picture what life must have been like in these cultures, it is helpful when a scholar like Sibylle von Cles-Reden brings to life the interior of the magnificent temple to the goddess in stone-age Malta:

> The Great Goddess for whom the blood of the animals flowed and the fire was lit is represented by a gigantic statue which stood in this chamber. When the site was excavated, the base and damaged lower part of a piece of statuary emerged. The statue itself must once have been about eight feet high. No other statue as big as this dating from such an early period is known in the western Mediterranean or even in the Aegean area. The exceedingly corpulent goddess seems to have been shown sitting on a stool. Her grotesque, pear-shaped legs and relatively tiny feet still protrude from under her flounced and pleated rock skirt, underneath which small human figures are sheltering. In mediaeval paintings similarly tiny Christians are to be seen kneeling at prayer in the shelter of huge Madonnas. (1961. B3)

Another temple in Malta, Hal Tarxien, has similar figurines. They enable us to visualize the goddess 'with her wide skirt, her gracious, earnest face, and her hand raised to her breast, as she once sat in her temple in the glow of the sacrificial fire'. When I visited these temples I was overcome by a sense of joy mixed with awe at how differently our ancestors had felt about the female.

Years ago I had my first taste of this when I visited a Neolithic village at Pan-p'o near Xian in China. The Chinese guide told us quite matter-of-factly that it was entirely matrilineal in organization and culture. Indeed the remains of female figurines with clear implications of worship were there to see. The remains at Pan-p'o are apparently representative of the whole Yangshao culture – defined as the earliest Neolithic culture which operated throughout the Yellow River region – and have been dated back to at least 5000 BCE using carbon-dating techniques.

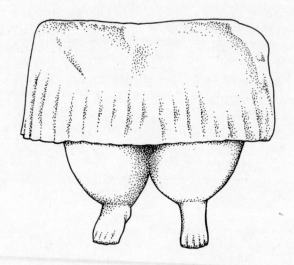

The statue of the great Earth Mother from the Tarxien temples in Malta,
c2100 BCE

Surprise

This rediscovery of our history as a human race was a total surprise to
me. I do not understand why it has not caused a revolution. I do not
understand why the newspapers have not been full of it. I would like
it to be taught in school, but because it is not I am devoting a chapter
of this book to it.

For the past 3,000 years, children have been brought up to have a
positive attitude towards male achievements and skills. These have
helped us advance in many ways, so this is justified. But this view has
not been balanced by a valuing of the female. Discovering the detail
of these ancient cultures felt, to me, like restoring the balance.

I first read about it in a book called *The Once and Future Goddess* by
art historian Elinor Gadon. Amazed and slightly incredulous, I followed up the references given in that book. I gradually unearthed fully
documented accounts of archaeological finds which indicate without
any doubt that the Goddess was worshipped throughout the
Mediterranean and Near East region for thousands of years. I checked
up to satisfy my scepticism as a researcher to find out whether any of

this evidence or its interpretation has been refuted. It has not. The only argument that I have been able to find is from Peter Ucko, who asserts that 'the accepted Mother goddess interpretation' must recognize what he sees as the logical consequences of its own assumptions, namely that there existed in prehistoric times not only a large pantheon but also a sole Father god. In a similar vein, Walter Burkert has emphasized that the discoveries of goddess figurines in Catal Huyuk do not necessarily point to a Mother goddess cult there, suggesting instead that the additional presence of some seated male figurines 'would seem to indicate a patriarchal order or perhaps a male god or even a divine couple'.

Peter Ucko's further complaint is that the Mother goddess interpretation of prehistoric figurines leaves several of their features unexplained. If this were grounds to question other archaeological interpretations, especially of early historical and prehistorical finds, then no interpretation could be attempted if it did not explain *everything*.

Having said this, some of the most notable male historians have played a role in restoring goddess religions to history. J G Frazer traced Adonis/Attis/Osiris to the legend of the Great goddess and her dying consort, symbolizing annual decay and rebirth, while Sir Arthur Evans identified Minoan iconography as representing the goddess. Joseph Needham, a distinguished biochemist who more or less single-handedly opened up Western study of Chinese science, has this to say about goddess worship:

> For hundreds, even thousands, of years before the myth of the Fall acquired its authority for the People of the Book, communities throughout the Mediterranean, Middle Eastern and Indian world worshipped a goddess, not a god. The masculine deities, including the Yahweh of the Jews, took over comparatively late, after the invention of agriculture and writing ... Many were her names and attributes, Isis, Hathor or Maat in Egypt, Ishtar or Ninlil in Babylonia, Ashtoreth in Palestine, Inanna in Sumeria. It is a sensible interpretation to associate this vision of the divine with the matrilineal institution, the mother-kinship system whereby all property was transmitted through the female line. Under those conditions paternity was not particularly important, but after patrilineal succession took over, women themselves became essentially property, and that meant inevitably the domination spoken of in the Genesis myth, as well as many other male-oriented customs, taking the name of 'morality' as such. Further light is thrown upon the Genesis myth when one realises that the serpent, *naga*, dragon, *lung*, Leviathan and all such animals, were sacred to the great goddess ... (Joseph Needham, 1979, page 22. B11)

Reading the accounts of the discoveries of the existence of the goddess from India to the Mediterranean is like reading a brilliant detective novel, but one in which the body is *me*. This is *my* history that these archaeologists and art historians are piecing together. These facts alter my outlook on life; I now know that there was a time when it was taken for granted that women would be responsible for the spiritual practices of their society, that women could be revered for their wisdom, that feminine gifts and skills – of intuition, of co-operation, of holistic thinking, of playfulness – were valued as highly as masculine gifts and skills. Knowing this has changed feminism for me personally from a *struggle to achieve* into a path. This is a path trodden before me by millions, and it is a path to integration.

Why it is a surprise

When all this began to dawn on me, my immediate response was, 'Why did no one tell me?' I had lived for half a century and been well educated, but the fact that God had been perceived as a woman for thousands of years longer than he had been perceived as a man was a total revelation. Why did I not know before?

The answer to this question is in three parts. First, all this has only been rediscovered recently. The historian Merlin Stone describes how it happened for her when the various pieces of evidence fell into place. She then understood that Ashtoreth, the despised 'pagan' deity of the Old Testament, was (despite the efforts of biblical scribes to disguise her identity by repeatedly using the masculine gender) actually Astarte – the Great goddess, as she was known in Canaan, the Near Eastern Queen of Heaven. It dawned on her that those heathen idol worshippers of the Bible had been praying to a woman god – elsewhere known as Innin, Inanna, Nana, Nut, Anat, Anahita, Istar, Isis, Au Set, Ishara, Asherah, Ashtart, Attoret, Attar and Hathor – the many-named Divine Ancestress. 'Was it merely coincidence,' she asks in the introduction to *When God Was a Woman*, 'that during all those years of Sunday school I never learned that Ashtoreth was female?'

The same author points out how so much of the evidence – the sacred artefacts of the religions which preceded monotheism – has been destroyed. She thinks that it may well have been the evident female attributes of nearly all the statues unearthed in excavations of Neolithic and early historic periods that irked the advocates of the male deity. *Most pagan idols had breasts.*

The third main reason why this information has been so slow to come to light is that until recently most archaeologists and historians have been male. Because we have not lived in a world where women are leaders of religion, prominent decision-makers, equal holders of power, we simply have not been able to imagine a world where this was so. For example, male archaeologists examining a mural showing figures holding long pointed rods conclude that they must be men wielding spears in battle, and that becomes the accepted explanation. But along comes a woman archaeologist who examines the same mural and suggests that the figures could be priests and priestesses celebrating a religious festival with willow wands. Discussion ensues. If this latter explanation fits better with the rest of the mural it is finally accepted.

The result of all this is that goddess worship has been characterized as a 'cult', whereas patriarchal monotheism is a 'religion'. Male historians of religion published and republished as recently as 1975 can still find no other way of explaining the existence of priestesses, except to refer to them as 'temple prostitutes'.

Some female writers, describing essentially the same society, see it as a world in which womens' bodies were sacred, and their sensuality a cause for celebration.

> In some instances, women not wishing to lead a chaste life or to enter into marriage spent their entire lives in the temple compounds. Such were the Vestal Virgins, who did not unite with a husband but became the 'bride' in a ritual; marriage with the king as the surrogate for a god . . . Their feminine nature was dedicated to a higher purpose, that of bringing the fertilizing power of the goddess into effective contact with the lives of human beings. (Nancy Qualls-Corbett, 1988, page 36. B10)

Based on what can be learned of Neolithic cultures, it is possible to visualize more fully what the role of priestesses may have been. Imagine, for example, the temple grounds in the morning sunshine. All is silent, except for the sound of running water. The baths in the priestesses' chambers are being filled from the stone channels which criss-cross the temple complex like an irrigation system. A handmaid in her early teens is filling a cup from the jar which contains almond oil, and she adds a few drops of the most precious essence of jasmine. She pours it into the water in the baths. The priestesses enter the chamber, shed their robes, and sink into the scented water.

They stand in the sun to dry, watching the oily droplets trickle down their bodies, through their hair, absorbing the warmth of the

spring sunshine into their bones. And then, slowly, they are dressed.
The long tiered skirts in ochre and peach; the bodice, made carefully
to fit around and under their breasts, with short sleeves; the apron,
rounded over hips and stomach. The hair is curled under the diadem
into long ringlets, tumbling down the back to the waist.

The priestesses would have been chosen by their peers for their wisdom and integrity. This shows in their bearing, tall and reflective, as
they walk slowly to the *erechtheum* next to the temple. In this chamber are the sacred serpents. Each priestess is handed two of the smaller snakes, which coil around her arms as she moves in the procession
to the sanctuary. The snakes are the most ancient symbols of the
divine, evoking awe and reverence from all. The priestesses have often
been bitten and have developed an immunity to the venom such that
it acts as a heightener of consciousness, and can assist a priestess to
attain the trance-like state essential for prophecy.

In the centre of the temple is a vast circular vat full of seed to be
blessed for the spring sowing. In deep meditation the priestesses move
into a circle round the vat, the snakes coiling over their bodies,
through their hair, and down into the vat of seed. If a priestess is bitten she may go into a trance, eyes staring, arms raised high and wide,
her handmaids swiftly removing her head-dress and robes.

Faience Snake Goddess from Knossos, c1600 BCE

The young men who have reached their peak of manhood this season
stand in an outer circle round the priestesses, watching and following
their every move. As they become erect they remove their loincloths

and step forward, turning to face the priestesses and leaning their buttocks on the rounded stone rim of the vat of seed. Each priestess moves to the young man of her choice, standing before him, arms upraised. She stands astride his legs, in contact with him, and moves slowly. When she is ready she allows herself to be entered. She moves further into trance by flexing her vaginal muscles around the penis. At this point the young man begins to move, slowly and rhythmically, using the muscles of his buttocks and thighs.

What the priestess is doing is initiating the young man into the mysteries of life, manhood and the feminine. She is giving him something precious, a knowledge that is essential to his full human being. And he is receiving.

Modern Western man's difficulty with receiving means that he has ended up seeing sex as a matter of taking, sometimes by force. In former times initiation rituals in different cultures served to mark the transition between boyhood and manhood. We have lost these traditions, and I believe we are poorer for that loss. The societies that existed around the Mediterranean in Neolithic times certainly had a much more fearless and natural emphasis on sexual life that ran through all religious expression. In Crete, for example, there is evidence of an enviable lightness of mind, a devotion to being in the moment, a passion for dancing, and no evidence of any sense of guilt or thoughts of punishment associated with sex.

What happened to the goddess?

Enter fathers

As time went by, human beings began to realize the role of the male in procreation. The earliest evidence of this awareness appears in a grey stone plaque discovered in the Neolithic shrine of the goddess at Catal Huyuk, carved there some 8,000 years ago. One side of the relief depicts the bodies of two lovers in a close embrace, the other side a woman holding an infant.

In the opinion of historians this indicates the gradual dawning of a realization that the man did have something to do with the creation of the next generation – that a child was 'his' or 'not his'. The implications for women were incalculable. It meant that men began to have a profound interest in a line, a lineage. They began to want to know which children they had fathered. And this meant one thing: they had to have control over the women they had intercourse with, in order to prevent them having intercourse with other men. Of course, these changes took place gradually, over centuries, but the result was that women became possessions of men. It meant marriage contracts and the tying down of women. It meant hideous punishments for women who dared to deviate. In some Middle Eastern societies it meant the penalty of death for a married woman, even if she was raped.

Enter weapons

Between 6500 and 5200 BCE metal objects and tools spread all over the Middle East. Soon after the first earring, the first dagger appeared, and shortly much of Europe and Asia was armed. Presumably, weapons had been used to kill animals from time immemorial; what took place now was the manufacture of metal weapons to kill human beings on a large scale.

By 1250 BCE weapons and bronze tools had spread all over Europe. Horses had been tamed in central Asia since 2500 BCE, but now men on horseback brandishing swords and spears appeared, wearing helmets and armour. This brought vast changes to the settled agricultural peoples living round the Mediterranean, in the Near and Middle East and as far as India. The big change which was to herald the end of these matrifocal societies was the notion of seizing wealth rather than creating it. This meant that every village had to build walls and learn to defend itself.

Enter armies

Warlike tribes, called by the vague term 'Indo-Europeans', came south from central Asia, through what are now Bulgaria and Greece. They were armed, fierce and worshipped male gods. Little information is available on why and how they had male deities or exactly where they came from. Over a period of 1,000 years they gradually conquered all the agricultural, female-worshipping cultures. Possibly the last southern civilization to fall to them was that of Crete, protected by sea on all sides.

So, where images of the Mother goddess had been made and venerated for over a hundred generations of peasant lives, the invaders came with their pantheon of Indo-European gods ruled by the father-figure Zeus. Zeus did not care for the dark, slow earth but ruled the sky with lightning in his hand, presiding over lesser gods and men from a mountain-top. Down below, among fields and pastures, the image of the ancient goddess dispersed into various female divinities; she could no longer be supreme.

The fall in the power of women

These three profound changes were to signal the end of the cultures which valued feminine strength. When a man realized that a child was his as well as the mother's, he no longer revered her as sole creatrix. The idea of marriage and of women as property gradually became established, and with it the necessity of female fidelity to one man. At the same time the armed tribes with male gods who invaded these societies tried to displace the sources of power which existed there. All this meant that women had to be subdued. The source of their power and identity, the female deities, had to be destroyed. There is ample evidence of this in the pages of the Old Testament, some of which is indicated in the 'Additional Material and Notes' section at the end of this book.

In Crete the great throne rooms of the Palace of Knossos were taken over by a male king, thought to have evolved from the consort of the goddess. I go into more detail of the evolution of the boy king and consort in chapter 7. This was how male rulers managed to establish their authority over the people who were still devoted to the goddess and still continued to worship her. In Anatolia burial sites have been discovered where the female figurines have had the tips of their noses or ears broken off; this desecration was thought to destroy their power.

Elise Boulding has a different interpretation of the fall in the power of women. She asserts that the organizational failure of what she calls 'matriliny' was that women did not specialize – they tended to do everything. Men responded to the asymmetry in responsibilities by inventing new patterns of social organization.

> It is one of the unlucky coincidences of history that the organisational failure of matriliny happened to coincide with the beginnings of nuclear family intimacy. (The Neolithic village provides the first evidence we have of mother-father-child dwellings.) Women's failure at that time to provide adequate role-differentiation opportunities for men, when the women were in *a position of dominance due to the temporary primacy of their productivity skills* may have led to family tensions which were played out

symbolically in the mythic and religious life of the community, but never dealt with realistically at their source . . . According to this line of reasoning the worship of the mother-goddess as the source of life flourished at the very moment, historically speaking, when women were also a source of role deprivation. (Elise Boulding 1976, my italics. B13)

Her interpretation is similar to that of Philip Slater who, studying Greek society at a later stage, argues that women's power produced a male terror of women, as well as a high achievement need in boys along with self-doubt and libidinal repressiveness. But it is clear that women's position (whether it was one of dominance we cannot say) had been as it was for many thousands of years, thus rendering it improbable that an *evolutionary* change was responsible for the comparatively sudden shift in relations between the sexes. In my view the invasion by warlike tribes from the north offers a more convincing explanation, but both explanations undoubtedly contribute to an understanding of what happened. For example, the invasion of patriarchy suggests the discovery that it was more locally efficient to raid for resources than to create one's own. This automatically meant that men were better placed to provide.

The Western creation myth

In any case, the belief in woman and the strength of the female deities was so all-pervading that conquest, laws and penalties could none of them subdue it. If open goddess worship was punished, it simply went underground and maintained its extraordinary influence, as for example in the oracle at Delphi, where the voice of the elemental feminine continued to be heard for centuries.

If goddess worship was to be displaced, something akin to its own numinous power was necessary to discredit it. One outstanding example is the creation myth in Genesis. It first reverses the idea of the female creatrix by the assertion that god made woman out of a rib taken from Adam's body. 'This one shall be called Woman, for out of Man this one was taken.' Then it blames the serpent, at that time known everywhere as the symbol of the goddess, for telling Eve to eat of the fruit of the tree of knowledge. The identification of Eve with evil became so natural in Christian thought that the serpent acquired female features, as can clearly be seen in Michelangelo's painting of *The Fall* on the Sistine Chapel ceiling.

What Eve did, and encouraged Adam to do, was to eat of the fruit of the tree (another symbol of the goddess, and present at her sanctuaries) that 'was to be desired to make one wise'. So the goddess's knowledge of wisdom is acknowledged, but it makes the male god so angry that he curses the serpent, and her, and the man, and puts them out of the Garden of Eden. This is the end of the days of peace. And the god says to the woman, 'Your desire shall be for your husband, and he shall rule over you.'

So the serpent becomes a negative symbol in the Judeo-Christian tradition, rather than the symbol of new life and transformation which it represents in most other ancient cultures. Joseph Campbell, the great historian of myth, goes further.

> What the Fall represents is indicated in the serpent. The serpent in most traditions represents the power of life to throw off death, the energy of life in the field of time. [But] when it becomes negative, life is condemned. Humans do not yield to the serpent. This has been our traditional way of interpreting this symbol, and I think it's pathological. I really do. I don't think there's any way to justify it. (Fraser Boa, 1989, page 42. B5)

Interestingly, the serpent still maintains its sacredness in some parts of the world. Today in Australia, Aboriginal people still revere the Rainbow Serpent, the giver and taker of life, who is sometimes called Kabul, sometimes Borlung, sometimes Ngalyod. In the beginning when the world was empty, the Rainbow Serpent was asleep in the ground with all the animal tribes in her belly waiting to be born. She is the mother of us all and the spirit of the land – all its beauty, all its colour. But now she is weak with anger and grief for what we are doing to this earth.

The creation myth was probably not written down until some time between the 10th and 8th centuries BCE. This information came as a shock to me, having been brought up to think it stemmed 'from about a fortnight after the beginning of the world' as Merlin Stone puts it. And yet it has had an incalculable effect on the way we in the Judaeo–Christian tradition behave and on the way we live even at the end of the 20th century. The result is that the powerful prevailing images of women today are either as temptresses or as mothers.

In other corrupted cultures things are worse: in some Islamic countries women must be entirely covered because the mere sight of their skin, their hair or their limbs would be too much of a temptation to men. In Iran the law demands the death penalty for women failing to cover themselves from head to foot, and this law is routinely enforced.

But even in the West the 'temptress' image is strong. In our newspapers, on our televisions and in our advertisements we constantly use women to seduce us into buying anything from cars to computers, from arms to alcohol.

Mother images, by contrast, are 'safe' – the Virgin Mary in every Catholic church, for example. The point is that to reach their full sanctity women have to renounce their sexuality, which is seen as the means by which they drag men down from their lofty heights. Sex and spirituality have become polar opposites in Christian teaching. For this reason most of the saints have been either virgins, martyrs, widows or married women who have taken a perpetual vow of continence. And what more effective way is there of trapping women into inadequacy than by offering us the contradiction of a virgin mother as a role model, when none of us can hope to be both! When one thinks about it, we have precious few images today of women as strong, confident and powerful. The few there are tend to be modelled on men – the Iron Lady is one. It is genuinely hard to think of a female image or role model today who is powerful, virtuous *and* sexual.

> The Goddess of unrestrained sexual love – Astarte, Ishtar, Ashtoreth Cybele – was also associated with war and death, with natural magic and primal wildness. She was also a mother, and a helper of women in childbirth. Under the Greco-Roman and Hebrew-Christian patriarchy in the West, these many aspects were separated out into the 'good woman' stereotype of the Virgin Mary, versus the 'bad woman' Eve. She was the Love Goddess, *or* the Good mother, *or* the Hag of Death, *or* the Virgin Huntress. But never again *All*. It can be hard for us to remember that the original Goddess was not a fixed dualism, but a revolving triplicity. (Monica Sjoo and Barbara Mor, 1991, page 210. B3)

The change to dualistic thinking

The creation myth was not the only great symbolic change. The second, which went with it, was the transition into dualistic thinking. This split has remained with us until this day. Our deities today can be either friendly or malicious, but they cannot be both. Except in Asia, people do not imagine, let alone worship, a divine being who destroys as well as creates, who is cruel as well as kind.

God is now only good; evil is the work of the devil. This way of thinking divisively has far-reaching implications. In our own minds we make a split between what we can tolerate about ourselves, the 'good', and what we find distasteful or 'bad', which is pressed down into an unconscious area, which some people call our Shadow. We might hide away there all sorts of unacceptable tendencies – the inclination to steal, to lie, to be cruel; they are buried away from our conscious sight where we think we can disown them. Because they are repressed, these tendencies, they have energy, they 'mean' a lot to us. But we cannot admit them in ourselves so we 'see' them outside ourselves, in other people. This is called projection. If another person has traits and characteristics which call forth strong feelings from me – I find them infuriating, disgusting, heinous – that is a fairly good indicator that that person or people has some characteristic which is actually, very secretly, mine, or that they are doing something which I want to do, deep down, but feel I cannot.

In monotheistic religions, this split or duality has often been expressed in the association of the male with the sky and with righteousness, and the female with the mundane, the earthy and the lower. Even in the highly civilized Greek culture, these attitudes existed, as expressed by the learned Pythagoras: 'There is a good principle, which has created order, light and man; and a bad principle, which has created chaos, darkness and woman.'

To bring us right up to date, here is Squadron Leader E G Jones, writing in 1993 for the *Royal United Services Institute Journal*:

> We live today, at the end of the 20th century, in a world increasingly polarised, between light and dark, between haves and have-nots, between us and them, between men and women. War seduces us in part because we continue to locate ourselves inside its prototypical emblems and identities. Men fight as symbols of a nation's sanctioned violence. Women work and weep and sometimes protest, but traditionally always as the collective 'other' to the male. (B6)

The struggles of the established churches in the Western world over the ordination of women used to puzzle me. Having been very religious as a teenager and brought up to believe that God and Jesus were just, I could not understand why the church had a problem with women priests. If men could be the servants of God, why not women? Countless exhortations in the New and Old Testaments along the lines of 'Do unto others as you would that they should do unto you' indicated plainly that women should be treated like any other human being. It was only when I realized that the problem goes back 4,000 years, to the times when women played a central role in religion, that I began to understand. It had clearly taken thousands of years of struggle to gain 'control' of the human spirit, as well as political control.

The words of the first letter of Paul to Timothy loom sternly in the back of the church's mind:

> Let a woman learn in silence with full submission. I permit no woman to teach or to have authority over a man; she is to keep silent. For Adam was formed first, then Eve; and Adam was not deceived, but the woman was deceived and became a transgressor.

The established religions are the last major institutions in the West to attempt to exclude women from positions of power. That it is they who are the last bastions against equality is not really surprising when one considers that it was in the spiritual realm that women were powerful before, that their role included their sensuality, and that it was the monotheistic religions which fought hardest to take that power away from them. The deep-rooted ambivalence of the church toward women comes through clearly in an open letter to the former Bishop of London, who is an opponent of the ordination of women, from Monica Furlong:

> You seemed to understand that we wanted much more than to see a few women ordained. What we wanted was radical change in the Church's whole attitude to women, not as a secular feminist fad . . . but to try to heal the ancient Christian split between sexuality and spirituality.
>
> What makes me think that you knew this was what it was all about is your famous remark to Dr Anthony Clare that if you saw a woman at the altar your instinct would be to take her in your arms. It was an apparently naive statement . . . But you touched the heart of the matter: that women have represented sexuality in the church, and you wanted it banned from the altar for the very reason that we wanted it present there.

The main problem with this central ambivalence over the connection between sex and the spirit, and with dualistic thinking in general, is when it is perceived only in terms of opposition, or superiority/inferiority, rather than in terms of complementarity. There is an image familiar to every schoolchild today, which goes right back to the struggle to subdue the goddess religions 3,000 years ago – St George and the dragon. Some of the oldest illustrations of the myth show that the dragon was actually the serpent, the symbol of the goddess, and the Christian St George must triumph over it.

Battles with dragons or serpents occur often in ancient Middle Eastern mythology, the best known example being that between King Marduk and the female water serpent Tiamat, in Babylon. The St George myth in turn is derived from the legend of Perseus, the Greek hero who killed the dreaded gorgon Medusa. Because he would have died merely from glancing at Medusa directly, Perseus cut off her head by looking at her reflection in his shield. Joseph Campbell says that the gorgon represents Mother Nature herself, and the more she is excluded the more terrifying she will become. Apparently the word 'gorgon' derives literally from the phrase 'the moon as it is terrible to behold'.

Mary Condren tells us that even in northern Europe symbols of the goddess were systematically co-opted and later destroyed, to be replaced by symbols of her destruction. The Irish hero Cuchulainn is apparently represented killing the serpent in several myths and images. St Patrick is credited with banishing the reptiles. She feels that the goddess was one of the hardest images for Western culture to eradicate, and that only by killing the serpent, severing the natural cycle of life and death, could dualistic patriarchal culture come into being. Killing the goddess as such was not as important as the destruction of those symbolic, political, familial and religious sources of power traditionally associated with women.

These reflections have led me to understand that inequality between men and women has not just *happened*. It came about for a reason. And the reason was that in much earlier times, especially in the realm of the spiritual, women had for centuries played an extremely prominent, central and powerful role.

Nevertheless . . .

It is possible, of course, that when they had this power, women did *not* share it – we cannot be sure. It is also possible that before the Garden of Eden story emerged, women did do something heinous. We do not know. And I realize that if I write from the basis of anger and hurt over what has happened to women, I myself reinforce the 'us' and 'them' duality referred to by Squadron Leader Jones above.

There is no reason to regard dualistic thinking as intrinsically a 'bad' thing. It can be seen as part of the dialectical model – thesis, antithesis, synthesis – and, as such, necessary to move human consciousness forward. Herbert Marcuse says that the struggle for existence was originally a struggle for pleasure: in his view culture began with people trying to achieve this, collectively. Later, however, the struggle for existence became organized in the interest of domination: the erotic basis of culture was transformed. When philosophy conceived the essence of being as *logos*, he said, it was 'already the logos of domination – commanding, mastering, directing reason – to which humans and nature were to be subjected'.

It must be recognized that the split into dualism, into 'either/or', into projection and the domination of the masculine principle, has meant an incredible speed of discovery. But our rush to discover has also had terrible effects on the earth. Over the past 800 years man has attempted to 'master' nature, to crack her secrets, tame her, penetrate her wealth, harness her forces. Since for the most part this has been done without respect and without care, we have destroyed in the process. We have left great open wounds on the country, gouging out minerals. We have killed and gone on killing every one of a species of animal or bird until there are none of that species left. We have driven ships out to sea and dumped barrels of nuclear waste to fall to the ocean bed and lie there poisoning sea life for 100,000 years. Every minute we destroy 100 acres of tropical forest. By the year 2000 one third of the earth's agricultural land will have turned to dust. There is now 25 per cent more carbon dioxide in the atmosphere than there was before the Industrial Revolution. We created the chemicals that are now destroying the ozone layer. This is evocative of what Joseph Campbell says about the gorgon representing Mother Nature herself. Perhaps the everyday reality that others once expressed through myth could now be said to be being lived out – instead of swords we have pesticides and 'progress'; instead of slaying a mythical creature, we are slaying our planet, and ourselves.

If we step right back, however, if we accept that we human beings understand very little of the whole picture, then it is conceivable that perhaps women *needed* to explore defeat, victimization and loss of power and self. Maybe men *needed* to explore the aggressor/tyrant role. Maybe, if we take a long, long, view we may see that these two lengthy polarizations had to be fully experienced before synthesis could occur.

What does all this mean for us today? It has loaded women and men with guilt for sexuality and sensuality. The emotions men have when they see women they desire have been distorted into lust – something that cannot be open, honest and frank. Instead it becomes furtive and denied, and thus of course gains enormously in the charge behind it.

When the female deity was split, when dark was separated from light, women especially became associated with temptation and 'sinful' sex. This means that women have been taught for all these hundreds of years to think of their sexuality as shameful, of their spirit as passive, of themselves as weak.

> And do you not know that you are an Eve? The sentence of God on this sex of yours lives in this age: the guilt must of necessity live too. *You* are the devil's gateway: *you* are the unsealer of that tree: *you* are the first deserter of the divine law: *you* are she who persuaded him whom the devil was not valiant enough to attack. *You* destroyed so easily God's image, man. On account of *your* desert – that is, death – even the Son of God had to die. (Tertullian c160–225 AD)

But it has to be said that women were prepared to accept this teaching. Some of us play variations of it to the hilt today. I've certainly had a go at playing the temptress; I've manipulated men; I've done false glamour; I've thought sex was sinful. Women are not innocent in this unfolding pageant. And men have suffered too – in denying women, they have denied their own internal feminine side. They too have been split. The potential wealth of their sexuality has been grievously depleted.

What this is essentially about is a loss of openness in sensuality, a loss of passion, a loss of joy and pride in our bodies. It is also a loss of connectedness in sexuality, a distancing or separation, which ends up producing a kind of arid emphasis on 'performance'.

Perhaps the most serious consequence of this change which has taken place over the last 3,000 years is that women have been oppressed. They have learned to be powerless, and men are beginning to feel powerless too. This is what the next chapter will deal with.

CHAPTER 2

Women without Power

A WORK OF ARTIFICE

The bonsai tree
in the attractive pot
could have grown eighty feet tall
on the side of a mountain
till split by lightning.
But a gardener
carefully pruned it.
It is nine inches high.
Every day as he
whittles back the branches
the gardener croons,
It is your nature to be small and cosy,
domestic and weak;
how lucky, little tree,
to have a pot to grow in.
With living creatures
one must begin very early
to dwarf their growth:
the bound feet,
the crippled brain,
the hair in curlers,
the hands you
love to touch.

Marge Piercy, 1973

Before going on to discover the sources of a new kind of power, my purpose in this chapter is to examine the painful subject of powerlessness. There are any number of candidate issues when it comes to powerlessness – abuse, torture, rape – and I have chosen to write about issues where I have some personal experience: negative body images, childbirth and motherhood, gynaecology, menopause. I also write about genital mutilation, which I have not experienced, but have spent several years learning about from African and Arab women. Genital mutilation is an example of the absolute abuse of power, because those to whom it is done are children. The chapter concludes with a section on low self-esteem as it affects powerlessness.

This chapter may be tough reading if you are a man, just as it may be if you are a woman. In order to understand about power, it is important to look at how power has been misused and distorted, as well as examining powerlessness. Many women are angry now because, having stopped being victims, they realize the extent to which they have been oppressed. Women need all their strength to get out from under, to stand up against that which has caused them suffering, and anger provides that strength. But there is a good long way to go, beyond anger. That is where the development of a new kind of power comes in.

I've had a lot of trouble with this chapter. As originally written, it came out as a catalogue of the wrongs that have been done to women. Here's my original opening paragraph:

> For 3,000 years, half the human race has been dispossessed and dominated on account only of its gender. We have moved from the situation glimpsed in the last chapter where wealth, lines of descent and rights to use of land passed only through women, to a situation where women do two thirds of the world's work, receive one tenth of the world's income and own less than one hundredth of its property.

I was angry when I first wrote the chapter, not least because the material I am writing about is the stuff of anger. Then I observed that I had written about women as victims and men as oppressors all the way through. On reflection and in rewriting it, I have learned a bit about my own anger. I needed it to free myself from what I learned as a child; I grew up in an entirely male-oriented household with four older brothers and a dominating father. I had no idea what femininity was, let alone that it had any strength.

Now that I'm learning what that strength is, the need to blame men falls away. I can see that men also have feelings of powerlessness. Men are victims too, and live with feelings of low self-esteem. I hope that what is written here can be heard and received by men. Also, and crucially, oppressors cannot oppress without victims being victims. With the exception of children, victims do have a choice (as do oppressors). One of the things victims need in order to cease being victims is a sense of their own power, and I come back to this in the next part of the book.

Women today

At this point some fashionable post-feminist will jump up and tell me
that 'victim feminism' is old fashioned, a thing of the past. Well, it
might be nice to think that in a white, Western middle-class world
there are no powerless women, but down in the street, out in the rest
of the world, just look around.

Of the world's 15 million refugees, 75 per cent are women. Today
100 million women and girls in Africa and Asia have their genitals cut
off to keep them 'under control' sexually. In the United States domestic violence is the leading cause of injury to adult women, and a rape
is committed every six minutes. Between 1970 and 1985, the number
of illiterate men in the world rose by 4 million while the number of
illiterate women rose by 54 million, according to the UN report on
women.

The status of white women in the West is better than it was, and
better than that of women in many other parts of the world. Their
educational standards have improved. Employment opportunities are
relatively better for women. One in five families in Britain is now
headed by a woman. Labour-saving devices have liberated them from
harsh domestic chores. Nevertheless the world they live in is still organized according to male beliefs and standards. Women struggling to
get to the top of male institutions, or even to survive in them, face an
appalling depletion of energy because they are continually called upon
to alter their female mode to fit the male mode of the institution.
Many intelligent women, for instance, with good political gifts, will
not go into politics because they cannot tolerate the combative nature
of our Western political system, the anti-family hours of parliaments,
the schoolboy slanging match of political debates. The women who do
go into politics say that it is a male world which is hard to change
when they are still only (with the exception of Scandinavian countries) a small percentage of elected representatives. In 1992 only five
of 1,370 chief executives of companies quoted on the London Stock
Exchange were women. Of the 650 people occupying the top decision-
making positions worldwide in the design and control of nuclear
weapons, only five are women.

The fact that women do men's jobs does not mean that men do
women's jobs. Women often end up doing two. In fact, research by
Ros Coward suggests that women are still doing 80–90 per cent of
domestic tasks. Nor has an increase in cohabiting brought a new equality to work in the home. Her evidence indicates that men's outlook,

priorities and contributions to the home have remained largely unchanged. The main difference is that men are now thought to be doing more than in previous generations. When women choose not to live with men – choose to live alone, to pair with another woman or to lead a woman-centred life with only intermittent attachments to men – it is often taken as an act of rebellion.

So what we have, still, is a way of living dictated by a deep-rooted set of values, and these are masculine values. For example, getting a big job in a company is important and is rewarded with money and honours; looking after children is not so important and is not reward-ed with money and honours. Winning and getting there first is impor-tant, more important then everyone having a good time on the way.

So how can women move into positions of power and not end up doing things the way men do? How can men make the journey from exercising the power of domination to exercising another kind of power? How can women and men develop their feminine strength? That is what this book is about.

Men today

On a psychological level, men in the West are having a tough time. The roles they have had for centuries are slipping away, with nothing much to replace them. Men used to be the breadwinners; now large numbers of women have paid jobs. Young men are suffering more from unemployment than young women. Girls are overtaking boys in vir-tually every measure of school academic performance. Eight out of ten jobs created in the closing years of the 20th century are expected to be for women. Men are no longer always the heads of the household; women are preferring to live alone or with other women. As the eco-nomic power of women grows, many men are feeling less secure. That is a fact, and it has to come into any consideration of power. That insecurity has to be addressed, or its manifestations will be more and more unpleasant.

Nobody likes to see their power base diminish. This has already begun, with women showing markedly less inclination to do chores for men in exchange for marriage. According to Shere Hite, most of the divorces in America are initiated by women, and 50 per cent of US marriages now end in divorce. Women and men are refusing to accept sexist decisions made by male judges in rape cases.

Young men are frustrated, angry, and violent – to women, to children and to themselves. One man in four in Britain is convicted of an offence by the age of 25. Young male suicides have nearly doubled in the past decade. These tragic statistics are evidence of great suffering, of a deep-rooted male discomfort, as though men were violating their own feminine side, destroying their own humanity.

In this chapter I am not going to look in detail at what men have done, or what women have done, but rather to look at what it feels like to be a woman today. Much of this concerns a woman's sexuality, her body, and her sense of herself. Some of the facts are hard to take, bu I think it's important to know what *has* happened to women and what *is* happening to them. It's as though it's necessary to go through this in order to be clear why women and men need to develop a different kind of power, rather than simply recycling the notions of power already prevalent in the world.

Negative body images

There is a nice story told by Annie Dillard. An Eskimo asked the local missionary priest: 'If I did not know about God and sin, would I go to hell?'

'No', said the priest, 'not if you did not know'

'Then why', asked the Eskimo earnestly, 'did you tell me?'

In the days of the goddess, sexuality appears to have been a cause for celebration, sensuality a source of joy, and genitals things of   beauty and reverence, portrayed everywhere in sculpture and art. In some cultures this is still so.

But, as I showed in the previous chapter, ever since the success of the Garden of Eden myth, women have carried the guilt for sexuality and been ashamed of their bodies.

I remember as a child travelling on a train and hearing two young men in the compartment sniggering over a litany of jokes they were telling each other. I don't remember the text of the jokes, but what lodged in my mind were the punchlines which revolved around the fact that female genitals smelled of fish. 'Is this true?' I asked my nine-year-old self. These kind of jokes are often based on ignorance, and ignorance often goes hand in hand with a fear of the unknown. I know now that it is not true that we smell of fish, but I never forgot. Women have become so terrified of smelling bad, especially when we have our periods, that we have been persuaded to squirt pernicious aerosol deodorant sprays into every orifice. There is a definite ambivalence in

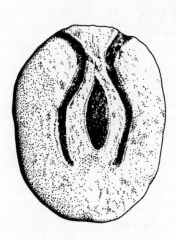

An egg-shaped stone sculpture with a vulva as flowerbud engraved on one side. (Iron Gates region of the Danube, c 6000 BCE)

A coco-de-mer, worshipped as an emblem of the vulva of the goddess (south India, 19th century)

our attitude towards our bodies. When in our daily lives we see an image of a naked female body, 99 times out of 100 it is to provoke male desire or to sell something. Almost never is it non-loaded and there simply because it is a great beauty in itself.

If I am talking about women and power, women as icons, women and powerlessness, I have to talk about fashion. Ever since the 1960s, fashion has idealized the super-thin model, with small breasts, small hips, and no belly.

> It is, at base, a powerless ideal. However vigorous the models look, how-ever powerful their lives seem, however easily they 'pick up' Hollywood stars, their bodies express a revolt against sexual maturity.
>
> The sexually immature ideal presents a body that exudes allure but is not that of a woman with adult experiences and who knows her sexuality. The sexuality suggested is that of response to the active sexuality of the man . . . It is the body waiting to be discovered rather than the body of self-discovery. (The Observer 26 September 1993)

The images we have been taught to admire are not those of strong, powerful women. Imagine how differently we would feel if magazines and hoardings glorified different images of female beauty. Contrast this, for example:

with this:

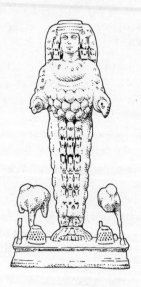

Artemis of Ephesus, 1st century BCE, Marble, 72in, Roman

The images of women that are glorified every day the world over are still an expression of a deep passivity in women. Our passion for dieting, *reducing* ourselves, is evidence of how we still seek power through attractiveness – moreover, through what the advertising and fashion world defines as attractiveness: being small, narrow, slight. Not substantial, wide, powerful. Young women especially starve themselves, sometimes literally to death, and one of the main reasons given is that they want to match the stick-thin media images of female beauty. Milham Ford comprehensive school in Oxford has the highest absentee rate in the country, due to anorexia, bulimia and other eating disorders in girls. The headmistress has no doubt what is to blame: an almost universal quest for 'model-girl thinness'. One student explains:

> We see photographs of thin, beautiful women in magazines; we see them on the catwalk on television, laughing and smiling; we know they earn millions of pounds and it says to us: if you want to do well and be happy, you've got to look like that.

Like many women, young and old, an appalling self-consciousness has haunted me always. I first remember it as a teenager. It was there all through my twenties – only assuaged when I *was* on stage, successfully. When I lived in South Africa I had a brief job as a model introducing the Mary Quant range of clothes. That assuaged it. Then it returned in force in my thirties in another guise – as a painful consciousness of my lack of place in the world. I was the anxious ego saying 'Aren't I good enough?' Gradually, as I have grown older, it has weakened. Now I just experience delight in what Germaine Greer says:

> When you are young, everything is about you. As you grow older . . . you begin to realise that everything is not about you, and that is the beginning of freedom.

I am 50 now, and my story may or may not resonate with younger women raised with a stronger sense of themselves. My father was 57 when I was born. He was so distant in his Victorian attitudes that there was no way I could get close to him. I have no memories of climbing on his knee, or of ever being carried by him. My school reports, always near the top of the class, failed to elicit any comment from him. He had several heart attacks and constant angina, so I think he must have been in pain most of the time. When I was 17 I got his permission to go out on a date with a boy. The day came and the boy turned up to collect me. I went to say goodnight to my father. 'I never said you could go out. You stay here.' I turned to my mother, I cried, but there was no relenting. The boy had to go.

When I was 18 my father died. I'm sad that he died without my being appreciated and admired by him as a woman. So I suppose that being admired by a man, were it possible, appeared to me as the height of achievement – and a turn-on, especially if he was a powerful man. I found that power sexy. Having been deprived of fatherly love and esteem, I sought it in my relationships, as many women do.

If I'm honest, what this shows is that although I didn't choose the second option in the list on page 13, I was a candidate. This option, if you remember, was to play the game when seduced by a powerful man, and use the fact that he is attracted to you. I suggested that this was a simple short cut to a form of power – by proxy. If circumstances had been different – if I had been poor, for example, or lonely, or felt more powerless than I did, or if he had been attractive – *I might have accepted*. I certainly acknowledged to myself at the time that it was the route to a new kind of power.

Very often a woman feels trapped in her situation, unable to move. Her man is violent, but she has children and no money, no training, no transport, nowhere to go. This same feeling of powerlessness can affect women whatever their economic circumstances. They have been given to understand that they depend on men. Women with so little power get a sense of power if desired by a man. The more they are desired, the more power they apparently have. And of course the less powerful they are in a worldly sense, the more they need this other power. So they do all they can to get it. They dress sexy, act like baby dolls, become seductresses. And men accuse them of being tempt-resses. And so the wheel goes round.

Menstruation

Since the invention of the Garden of Eden myth, the most important cyclical function of a woman's body, the monthly bleeding which enables her to bear a child, has been called a curse. It is something we hide. 'Hardly can be found,' said Pliny in the 1st century AD, 'a thing more monstrous than is that flux and course of theirs.' Today, Penelope Shuttle and Peter Redgrove write:

> Menstruation is regarded, not only by physiologists and many doctors, but also by some feminists, as a sickness, a blank spot, a non-event that the women must endure and would be better without, an evil time. (B1)

Many of the taboos on menstruation and menstruating women are still influential in different parts of the world today. According to Barbara Walker, the Talmud says that if a menstruating woman walks between two men, one of them will die. To this day some orthodox Jews refuse to shake hands with a woman because she might be menstruating. Traditional Brahmans ruled that a man who lay with a menstruating woman must suffer a punishment one quarter as severe as the punishment for Brahmanicide, which was the worst crime a Brahman could imagine. Persian patriarchs followed the Brahman lead in maintaining that menstruous women must be avoided like poison. They belonged to the devil; they were forbidden to look at the sun, to sit in water, to speak to a man, or to behold an altar fire. Zoroastrians held that any man who lay with a menstruating woman would beget a demon, and would be punished in hell by having filth poured into his mouth. Pliny said a menstruous woman's touch could blast the fruits of the field, sour wine, cloud mirrors, rust iron, and blunt the edge of knives. Christians inherited all the ancient patriarchs' superstitious horrors. St Jerome wrote: 'Nothing is so unclean as a woman in her periods; what she touches she causes to become unclean.' Penitential regulations laid down in the 7th century by Theodore, Bishop of Canterbury, forbade menstruating women to take communion or even enter a church. From the 8th to the 11th centuries, many laws denied menstruating women any access to church buildings. As late as 1684 it was still ordered that women in the 'fluxes' must remain outside the church door. The superstition came down to the 20th century, when a Scottish medical text quoted an old rhyme to the effect that menstrual blood could destroy the entire world:

> Oh! Menstruating women, thou'rt a fiend
> From which all nature should be closely screened.

Christian women were commanded to despise the 'uncleanness' of their own bodies, as in the Rule for Anchoresses: 'Art though not formed of foul slime? Art though not always full of uncleanness?' At the present time, just as in the Middle Ages, the Catholic Church still considers itself on firm theological ground by advancing, as an argument against the ordination of women, the notion that a menstruating priestess would 'pollute' the altar.

Negative attitudes to menstruation have not disappeared in the 20th century; now they take the form of sanitizing it. Advertising makes us feel we should all be perfectly normal and carefree during our periods. The technology of suppression – tampons, vaginal deodorants, sophisticated pain-killing and mood-altering drugs – has, together with the myth of the superwoman, created a cultural attitude that a menstruating woman is no different from one who is not bleeding. Lara Owen writes:

Tampon ads showed lithe girls in bikinis running gleefully toward the ocean and girls in tight white jeans jumping onto horses. This didn't mesh very easily with my experience of lethargy and cramps. And I knew that no one in their right mind would trust a tampon so much that they would go out for the day in white jeans. (B1)

A friend who read the draft of this section wrote to me that she now realized that she assumed that 'everyone else is much better organized than I am or has much less messy periods. I think I believe that other people *can* wear white jeans. So this kind of myth farming alienates me from other women.'

The trouble with this kind of advertising is that it is simply not true. Any woman remotely in touch with her body knows that when she is menstruating, and usually for a few days before, she feels different. And this is a part of nature that cannot be denied. If it is denied, there is a price to pay. The very fact of being trained to 'think nothing' of the cycle, to give it no place in our lives and no respect, may explain why so many women today have irregular periods, or extreme pain, cramps and depression. Crippling problems such as endometriosis (when the lining of the womb is cast off into other parts of the lower abdominal cavity) or dysmenorrhoea (severe premenstrual or menstrual symptoms) contort the lives of countless millions of women.

So the fact is that we have a lot more problems with our periods than one would guess, to see us walking around. We have colluded in a weird kind of 'king's new clothes' syndrome. We have been persuaded – nearly half the human race – to pretend that something unmentionable, like the king's nakedness, is not there, when it very much *is* there.

I say *nearly* half the human race, because in some areas a menstruating woman is still today given an entire time and space to herself in which to reap the benefits which this time, often known as 'moontime', can give. In some indigenous traditions, a menstruating woman has the potential to be more psychically and spiritually powerful than anyone, male or female, at any other time. A special hut is set aside where women can have peace and seclusion to meditate, daydream, and simply be in touch with their bodies. Fresh moss is brought in every day for them to sit on, so that their blood can return to the earth, since it is regarded as sacred and precious.

This section has been a discussion of menstruation as a curse, but of course there is a great deal that is positive about menstruation, and this will be discussed in chapter 5.

Childbirth and motherhood

All through human history, until 200 years ago, women giving birth
have been attended by women. In many countries they still are. The
expertise on childbirth, and the knowledge of the rites of passage of
women at this point in their lives, were held by midwives, sage-
femmes, wise-women. These women often served their communities
also as shamans, priestesses, healers, teachers. These were women who
had sacred knowledge. At the end of the Middle Ages in Europe, most
of them were drowned or burned at the stake as witches. Altogether,
over three centuries, approximately 9 million women and some men
were murdered (the population of Europe at that time was approximately 30 million).

> The Killer-Regeneratrix, the overseer of cyclic life energy, the personifica-
> tion of winter, and Mother of the Dead, was turned into a witch of night
> and magic. In the period of the Great Inquisition, she was considered to
> be a disciple of Satan. The dethronement of this truly formidable goddess
> whose legacy was carried on by wise women, prophetesses, and healers
> who were the best and bravest minds of the time, is marked by blood and
> is the greatest shame of the Christian Church. The witch hunt of the
> 15th–18th centuries is a most satanic event in European history in the
> name of Christ. (Marija Gimbutas, 1989. B3)

This attitude is not quite dead. As recently as 1944 a female medium
was sentenced to nine months in prison for contravening the 1735
Witchcraft Act, which was only repealed in 1951. And at the time of
the ordination of the first women into the Church of England in
March 1994, an Anglican vicar, the Revd Anthony Kennedy, was
quoted in *The Times*, of 9 March 1994 as follows: 'Priestesses should be
burned at the stake because they are assuming powers they have no
right to. I would burn the bloody witches.'

By the 18th century the medical profession, which excluded
women, began to include childbirth as part of the medical curriculum.
Dr William Cadogan wrote in 1748:

> It is with great Pleasure I see at last the Preservation of Children become
> the Care of Men of sense. In my opinion, this business has been too long
> fatally left to the management of Women, who cannot be supposed to
> have a proper knowedge to fit them for the Task, notwithstanding they
> look upon it to be their own Province.

At first only wealthy women were attended by male obstetricians;
poorer women still had midwives. In 1965 one third of all births in the

UK still happened at home, but gradually medical science and technology have taken over – by 1990 it was only one birth in a hundred. As doctors have replaced midwives, pregnancy and childbirth have come to be treated as an illness rather than as a natural function.

In Britain the pendulum is now just beginning to swing away from technology again. More and more women want to have their babies at home. Doctors, with rare exceptions, disapprove, citing the danger of being at a distance from emergency facilities, 'if anything goes wrong.' Midwives are confident that home births generally benefit both child and mother: the home atmosphere and the familiarity of the mother's own bedroom means she is more relaxed; the absence of bright lights, haste and 'efficiency' means that the baby comes from the trauma of birth into a calmer, gentler world. The Department of Health has called for women to be given a larger say in how pregnancy care is organized and has concluded that normal pregnancies can be left to midwives, but the Royal College of Obstetricians and Gynaecologists has yet to accept this.

In China today pregnant women are aborting foetuses discovered to be female with the aid of ultrasound scanning machines. This female infanticide is thought to be partly the result of government regulations penalizing families with more than one child, combined with the Chinese cultural preference for male children. It is an example of how technological advances in medicine can be abused. Since the advent of scanners in China, female infanticide has grown to such proportions that the population balance under 20 has shifted to 58 per cent boys and 42 per cent girls.

Here is my experience, of which I am not at all proud. My baby was several weeks late, induction did not work, and my husband kept putting off an overseas business trip. It came to a point where he said he had to leave next day. I was anxious to have the birth while he was in the country so I swallowed a bottle full of castor oil. Contractions started almost immediately, and he took me to the nursing home. I was put in a room by myself, my genitals were shaved, I was given an enema and left alone. I tried to do the breathing exercises I had learned. The contractions became more frequent and painful. I rang for a nurse, who said, 'I'll give you something for that, dear.' She gave me an injection and went away. The next thing I knew was the sharp pain of forceps, then I sank again to resurface briefly while I was being stitched up. Then I remember waking up in a room alone – no baby, no husband, no nobody. I screamed and screamed until they brought my baby girl to me and phoned my husband to come back to the hospital. This was 20 years ago. If I had known then what I know now, I would not have let this happen.

Incidentally, the *danse du ventre* ('womb dance') otherwise known as belly-dancing, is believed to have been practised not only as a rite through which the Mother goddess was worshipped with pelvic rocking and rippling of abdominal 'birthing' muscles, but also as a form of gymnastic childbirth preparation. In 1968 anthropologist Ashley Montagu described how it may have come about that childbirth as well as menstruation were converted from perfectly healthy natural phenomena into a handicap and a 'curse'. He felt that men project their unconscious wishes upon the screen of their society and make their institutions and their gods in the image of their desire. Their envy of woman's physiological powers causes them to feel weak and inferior, and fear is often added to jealousy. An effective way for men to protect themselves against women, as well as to punish them, is to depreciate women's capacities by depreciating their status. Women's advantages can be denied, he says, by treating them as disadvantages and by investing them with mysterious or dangerous properties.

I am struck daily by the sight of young women, straining to keep the pace of a jazzed-up, fast-food, buy-this, heavy-metal, hard-sell world, while inside them these powerful invisible moon cycles are taking place. Inside some of them, embryos are developing; for others, the care of babies and very young children in a world which is not careful of babies and young children turns what could be a daily source of joy into a daily drag. Small children's faces are at the level of the exhaust fumes of cars. Many mothers of young children in cities go through almost unbearable strain – look at their faces. The expression in the eyes, the way the mouth is set, reveal many people halfway to rage and countless others who have swallowed too much sadness.

I came across an entry in my notebook from 17 years ago, when I lived in a city in France and went to a department store to get a particular kind of lightbulb and a lampshade. I had three-year-old Polly by the hand. It was very hot in the shop. Polly was tired. The lampshades in the shop had a fitting which would not work on the lampstand I had. Were there any other kinds? A shrug. I asked where I could find light bulbs. The assistant pointed to the ceiling. We tramped to the elevator and went one floor up. The assistant had never seen a light bulb like the one in my hand. Where could I get it? 'How should I know?' Polly pulled at my dress and asked for the ninth time when we were going out of this place. I spoke sharply. She burst into tears. The assistants looked away. I picked her up and we trudged out of the shop. There was a long queue for the bus. I got tired of holding her and put her down. Someone rushing past on the pavement caught her shoulder with the edge of his briefcase. She screamed in pain. I picked her up and cuddled her. The people around turned away. Some moved away. She was still crying when we got on the bus; stony faces all around.

And I only had one child; my experience was not half as bad as what goes on every day all day in our cities for millions of parents, trying to meet the needs of young children in a world which rates their needs very low. Heather Hunt, a clinical psychologist working in a National Health Service women's project in London, says:

> It's easy to understand how feelings of powerlessness become internalized. It's hard to struggle when you're poor, exhausted with no child care and little social support. Many women are colonized by the stereotype of what motherhood ought to be and describe their sense of personal failure that their performance and feelings do not live up to the media image. (B8)

Gynaecology

Since obstetrics and gynaecology became a hospital, specialist, male preserve, the incidence of operations on women's reproductive organs has increased dramatically. By the age of 75 one in five women in Britain is wombless, and many of these operations could, it seems, have been avoided. In the USA twice as many women have hysterectomies as in Britain, in Norway half as many; some indication of confusion in medical minds?

In *Our Bodies Ourselves*, Angela Phillips and Jill Rakusen say that it is illogical to carry out a major operation on hundreds of women to prevent the occurrence of cancer or further complications in a few. If a doctor does not take the trouble to explore a woman's problems before referral to a gynaecologist, it is likely that she will be operated on simply because the consultant does not have the time (or inclination?) to discuss the matter fully.

There is that unnerving feeling that we are not supposed to argue – after all, he is the expert, the consultant. A special appointment has been made to see this important man at the hospital; the staff seem to treat him as some sort of god – 'Mr – has been delayed, you'll have to wait.' When he does arrive in a flurry of white coats and assistants, clearly *very rushed*, it is easy to be bamboozled by the terms used, by the knowledge that is apparently superior to our own. We are in a very vulnerable position: naked, legs wide apart, cold metal tools prising the vagina open – and the prodding can be very painful, even if there is nothing wrong. In these circumstances it is hard to remember that our bodies and our feelings are our best guides.

Almost every woman I know tells of fear and confusion, if not worse, in experiences with gynaecologists. One true story told by Janet Burroway speaks for the rest.

When I was forty-five my second marriage ended with the end of his fidelity. I had been happy in the marriage, he hadn't gone out looking for an affair, but it had happened, and my trust had not survived. I had already been through divorce once, and this time I handled it, on the whole, pretty well – understanding that it's harder work to leave than to be left, and that it's easier to end a good relationship than a bad one. All the same, after a month or so I began to bleed and didn't stop for three weeks.

I went to my GP, a gentle and personable intern in family practice. I wasn't willing to go back to Dr B, the ob-gyn I used to see, I explained, because he had wanted to perform a hysterectomy for no better reason than that, in his opinion, I already had children enough. When I'd told Dr B I was not willing to fool around with my psyche in that way, he'd assured me that the loss of a uterus wouldn't bother me. (*Esprit d'escalier*: Shall we cut your balls off, then?)

Now Dr GP asked what I was doing to get myself through the divorce. I was keeping busy in the evening, I said, by getting cast in a play. I was lunching with women friends and driving to the coast every other week-end to be with my younger son in his summer stock company. If I felt I was in trouble, I said, I'd go for counselling.

'People pay thousands of dollars,' he cheered me by assuring me, 'to learn how to cope like that.' All the same, for medical caution, he'd like me to see a gynaecologist. There was a new one in town, young, he probably wouldn't give me any nonsense.

At the new Dr M's, the nurse administered a haemoglobin test and stashed me in the cubicle. Dr M came in all brisk-and-clipboard, and began to take a medical history. I told him ('me and my big mouth' is the self-deprecatory phrase that comes to mind; in fact I think after all these years I am remarkably trusting, and that this is a virtue, not a lack) why I had not gone back to Dr B.

'B's a good man,' he said. 'If he wanted to take your womb out, I probably will too.' I blanched and held my tongue. When M got to the advent, in my medical history, of a second dilation and curettage, he said, 'Good lord, two D&Cs. I'm certainly going to take your womb out. I'm not going to start manipulating you with hormones now!'

'No,' I agreed, dry. 'But I don't think there's anything wrong with my womb. I think I'm under stress. I'm going through a divorce.'

'I know, you're depressed and anxious.'

'No,' I said, 'I'm not. I may be later, but at the moment I'm very active, a bit hyper. It's my usual coping pattern.'

'You're depressed and anxious,' he repeated, as the nurse came in with the test results. 'That's funny. Your blood is normal.'

'I'm sure it is,' I said. 'I think this is a normal reaction to stress, and it'll abate of its own accord.'

'I'm the doctor,' he actually said. 'I'm not interested in the total picture, just my speciality, and then we'll slot it *into* the total picture. It's very clear that what you've got here is dysfunctional bleeding, and you'll need a hysterectomy.'

Dysfunctional bleeding? Is that a diagnosis? I thought that's the symptom I came in with. Hysterectomy? We cut out my uterus to slot it into the total picture? Is that some form of medical collage? Dr M, having diagnosed and prescribed, now left me to undress for the pelvic.

I sat for a minute seething. I powerfully did not want to be touched by his immaculate hands. I had a stabbing awareness of the times in my life when I would not have been able to get mad. I thought: just now it's important for me to feel good about myself. I can't afford the luxury of decorum.

I excused myself to the nurse. 'He's made me angry, and I'm not going to have the examination. I'll tell him so myself.' I did so, with surface calm and under-rage. The doctor stayed rigid in his dignity. I was minutely mollified that he didn't charge me for the blood test.

Two days later I had a call from my ally Dr GP. 'I got to thinking about you,' he said in his pleasant way, 'and I thought maybe we ought to set up an appointment with a psychiatrist just to be sure, because, after all you must be pretty depressed and anxious.'

Bewildered, I let him make the appointment, and it was a half-hour later that I tumbled to it, how the boys' network works. This had been one of the few times in my life that I acted, clean and immediate, on anger. I wondered, then, about those two D&Cs – were they unnecessary too? – and about the thousands of wombs that were waved away, this way, from women caught more vulnerable than indignant. I wonder now, having learned that flooding is a sign of the climacteric, which stress my body was undergoing, and when the medical establishment will turn its attention to such matters.

Luckily, the following Tuesday (my bleeding having stopped by then), I was able to convince the psychiatrist that I was sane in spite of my unseemly attachment to my uterus.

Ageing and menopause

Western culture is not kind to older women. For the Czech author Milan Kundera, an elderly woman resembles a poor mechanic fruitlessly attempting to keep a small factory running. 'The more useless a woman's body becomes,' says Kundera in his novel *Immortality*, 'the more it is a body: heavy and burdensome; it resembles an old factory destined for demolition . . .

His attitude is extreme, perhaps. But for women who have depended on their looks for their identity and sense of self all their lives, the struggle to stay looking youthful is indeed a miserable one, because it is a struggle that cannot be successful. How much more sustaining it would be if instead we loved and valued the signs of age.

Menopause is a bit like the birth of a child or the death of a parent. It is a huge life change and looking back we wish someone had warned us, prepared us. But if they had, we probably wouldn't have listened.

I felt mine coming. I felt it coming in the sense that I began to feel uncomfortable – just 'not in my skin'. I was sleeping erratically, sometimes awake until three or four in the morning and then sleeping ten or eleven hours for the next two nights. I was often hot and uncomfortable in bed.

After about two weeks of this it so happened that I had an appointment to see my doctor, to talk about changing my IUD – supreme irony! She heard my symptoms and said she would do a blood test, then we would know. When I went back for the results of the test she said the follicle stimulating hormone count was high and she would be surprised if I was not menopausal.

Then the thought dawned: 'I am probably never going to have another period!' Now, like everyone I often cursed my periods when they came at an awkward time, and before I had a child I ignored them almost completely, but in later life I have grown fond of them. The routine and the rhythm are comforting. The waiting for an absent period (and previous ones had been late) was unbalancing – I felt disorientated, as though I could not get on with things until the period came and my routine was restored. So another thought dawned: 'What's it going to be like living without a cycle?' I felt very wobbly and sad.

Then I realized that what I had been having at night were night sweats – my version anyway (some people have bedclothes so drenched they have to change them). Nevertheless, it was an emotional moment to know that this was the menopause; this was *it*. 'I am no longer fertile.' I *did* feel older. I looked at younger women in a different way for a while, thinking, 'You can still do it.' Now I know that the important thing to realize is that it is not the end of sex, it is the end of childbearing. We shall come back to the subject of sex later, but the loss of the ability to conceive *does* have to be mourned, for most women, although some are delighted to experience declining fertility.

For the woman whose middle life has been devoted to child-rearing, the onset of menopause can be deeply distressing. It is like a signal that what she is good at, namely having and raising children, she can no longer do. She begins to look around a little desperately to see what she *can* do now, and the world seems to look back with a blank stare. The blankness is because the world we live in values her experience very little. We do not say to her, as we could, 'Come here, we need you now that you are free. We need all that you have learned in terms of patience, seeing the funny side, strength, stamina, compassion, not to mention 101 ways to overcome exhaustion, not to mention 101 ways to control your own power over a smaller weaker person who is driving you NUTS. You are valuable to us. You are just the kind of person we need to entrust decisions to.' We do not say that. Instead we say, 'You go off and be a nice, fairly invisible, fairly innocuous granny for the rest of your life.' This kind of thing tends to make some menopausal women depressed!

So much for Western attitudes towards women, their reproductive organs and cycles, child-bearing and motherhood. What are attitudes like in other countries?

Genital mutilation

Alice Walker, in her novel *Possessing the Secret of Joy*, writes:

> It had been done to the grandmother of our cook, she said. Many operations, when she was a girl. She couldn't have children of her own; she'd adopted Gladys, my mother's childhood companion and maid, whose own clitoris had been excised; though she had not, like her mother, been infibulated. Gladys was docile in the extreme, not legally a slave, but superbly slavish in spirit. She had no spunk. No self. This 'gentleness of spirit', as my mother called it, was always held up as exemplary and the way my mother wanted me to be. (B14)

Many women in Africa cannot bleed at all, because they have been sewn up. Following the age-old tradition of infibulation, young girls are held down without anaesthetic while the clitoris is cut off, as well as the labia minora and labia majora. The two sides of the vulva are then pinned together with catgut, or with thorns, leaving only a very small opening, preserved by the insertion of a matchstick or reed, for the passage of urine or blood. When there is a clot, the opening no longer functions and the girl's belly swells up with blood and urine, resulting in death if she is not opened up again. This practice, as well as other 'milder' versions where only the clitoris is removed, is carried on in more than 20 countries in Africa, as well as in Oman, Yemen and the United Arab Emirates.

The gravity of the mutilations varies from country to country. Infibulation is reported to affect nearly all the female population of Somalia, Djibouti and the Sudan (except the non-Muslim population of southern Sudan), southern Egypt, the Red Sea coast of Ethiopia, northern Kenya, northern Nigeria and some parts of Mali. I shall devote several pages to the subject of genital mutilation because it is a form of disempowerment of women which is still little recognized, while it affects large numbers. The most recent estimate of women mutilated is between 85 and 114 million. Globally 2 million girls a year and 6,000 per day are estimated to be at risk.

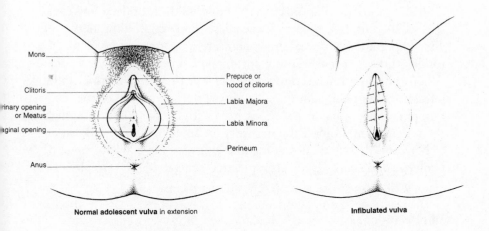

Mons

Clitoris

Urinary opening
or Meatus

Vaginal opening

Anus

Prepuce or
hood of clitoris

Labia Majora

Labia Minora

Perineum

Normal adolescent vulva in extension

Infibulated vulva

Female genital mutilation

The operations are usually performed by an old woman of the village (known as *gedda* in Somalia) or a traditional birth attendant (called *daya* in Egypt and the Sudan), using special knives (in Mali, a saw-toothed knife), razor blades, pieces of glass or scissors. In northern Nigeria and in Egypt, village barbers also carry out the task, but usually it is done by a woman; rarely, it seems, by the mother. In Mali and Senegal, it is traditionally carried out by a woman of the blacksmiths caste gifted with knowledge of the occult.

> Amina, who is Ethiopian, was nine years old when she was infibulated . . . Amina's voice trails off and her eyes glaze over. She was mutilated, she says, by her aunt, while six women held her down: 'The pain and shock is something I can't even think about, even now . . . ten years later.' Amina almost bled to death after the operation and for a long time afterwards suffered from infection and psychological trauma. (Angela Robson, 1993, p8)

The age at which the mutilations are carried out varies from area to area, and according to whether legislation against the practice is foreseen or not. It varies from a few days old (for example, the Jewish Falashas in Ethiopia and the nomads of the Sudan) to about seven years old (as in Egypt and many countries of central Africa) or to adolescence (among the Ibo of Nigeria, for instance, where excision takes place shortly before marriage, but only before the first child among the Aboh of mid-western Nigeria). Most experts are agreed, however, that the age of mutilation is becoming younger, and has less and less to do with initiation into adulthood.

In all types of mutilation, even the most 'mild' clitoridectomy (excision of the clitoris), a part of a woman's body containing nerves of vital importance to sexual enjoyment are amputated. The glans clitoridis, with its specific sensory apparatus, is a primary erogenous zone. When it has been reduced to an area of scar tissue, no orgasm can be released by its manipulation. The descriptions available of the reaction of children – panic and shock from extreme pain, biting through the tongue, convulsions, the necessity for six adults to hold down an eight-year-old, sometimes leading to fractures of the clavicle, femur or humerus, and death – indicate a practice comparable to torture.

Why is it done?

Female sexuality has been repressed in a variety of ways in all parts of the world. Female slaves in ancient Rome had one or more rings put through their labia majora to prevent them from becoming pregnant. Chastity belts were brought to Europe by the crusaders during the 12th century. Until very recently, clitoridectomy was performed as a surgical remedy against masturbation in Europe and the USA, and unnecessary genital surgery continues in the West today.

But what are the forces which motivate a mother to subject her daughters to genital mutilation, undertaking such risks? Very frequently, the reason offered by both women and men is the attenuation of sexual desire. Since the focus of this desire is clearly recognized to be the clitoris, excision is believed to protect a woman against her own oversexed nature, saving her from temptation, suspicion and disgrace, whilst preserving her chastity. Awa Thiam from Senegal writes:

> When you cut a woman's genitals, sew them up, then undo them for sex then sew them up again when the husband goes away, only to open them again for her to sleep with her husband . . . it's perfectly clear. You control the woman as you would any object.

These beliefs must be understood in the context of societies where female virginity is an absolute prerequisite for marriage, and where an extramarital relationship provokes the most severe penalties. So strong is the association of mutilation with premarital chastity that in many areas a non-excised girl (in Somalia, a non-infibulated girl) is ridiculed and often forced to leave her community, and regardless of her virginity will stand little or no chance of marriage.

Excision and infibulation are practised by Muslims, Catholics, Protestants, Copts and followers of traditional beliefs in the various countries concerned. It is believed to predate all these religions, and may have been introduced as a way of controlling female sexuality when the goddess-worshipping cultures were overthrown. Some ancient African beliefs held that each human being is endowed with two souls of different sexes. The female soul of a man was located in the penis or foreskin; in the woman the male soul was in the clitoris. Alice Walker writes: 'The dual soul is a danger; a man should be male, and a woman female. Circumcision and excision . . . are the remedy.'

Some scholars explain the practice in terms of initiation rites, of development into adulthood. In many areas (in northern Sudan, and among the Kikuyu in Kenya, the Tagouana in the Ivory Coast and the Bambara in Mali), an elaborate ceremony surrounded, and in some cases still surrounds, the event – with special songs, dances and chants intended to teach the young girl her duties and desirable characteristics as a wife and mother; with ritual rich in symbolism; with special convalescent huts for the girls, attended only by the instructress and cut off from the rest of society until their emergence as marriageable women; or simply with special clothes and food.

However, it seems that today in many of these societies the cere-monial has fallen away; both excision and infibulation are performed at a much younger age that cannot be construed as having anything to do with entry into adulthood or marriage, and the child's role in soci-ety does not change at all after the mutilation.

In the eastern areas of practice in Africa, the external female geni-tals are considered dirty. 'Their genitalia are unclean, it is said, mon-strous; its unmitigated activity frightens men and destroys crops. When erect, the clitoris challenges male authority. It must be destroyed.' In Egypt, for instance, the uncircumcised girl is called *nigsa* (unclean) and bodily hairs are removed in an effort to attain a smooth, and therefore clean, body. The same sentiment appears in Somalia and the Sudan where the aim of infibulation is to produce a smooth skin surface, and women questioned insist that it makes them cleaner. (Yet in practice infibulation clearly has the effect opposite to that of pro-moting hygiene; urine and menstrual blood, which cannot escape nat-urally, secrete and result in discomfort, odour and infection.)

Individuals interviewed in Katiola in Mali maintained that the cli-toris is ugly. However, the idea of female and male genitals being dirty or ugly is not confined to those who practise female genital mutilation. These are ideas which are deeply rooted in many areas of the world; it is the responses and practices which are different.

None of these reasons adequately explains why the central core of the custom has persisted. The most plausible explanation is that women have been persuaded, over centuries, to see their sexual impulses in terms of what suits men. This is in context of societies where marriage is the only secure future for a woman.

> Many reasons are put forward, such as religion, tradition, hygiene, but the real problem is the need to control women's sexuality, to stifle their desires and keep them like children, like people who have no responsibility for themselves, and can't be human beings in their own right . . . Excision is used to control women. (Warrior Marks, 1993)

The situation today

I began researching the subject of genital mutilation in 1978, and in 1980 edited a report published by the Minority Rights Group based on contributions from a number of African women. The response to this report was overwhelming. Not only did it receive sympathetic atten-tion from the UK and international press, but hundreds of women and men sent contributions to support those who were fighting the practice. In the wake of this interest came the formation of Women's Action Campaign Against Excision and Infibulation (WAGFEI), which carried out fact-finding missions in Africa and directed funds to small-scale projects. The report was published in French, Arabic and Italian, and copies were distributed in Africa and Europe. The first TV documentary on the subject, made with the assistance of WAGFEI, appeared in the UK in 1983.

One of the first women to join WAGFEI was Efua Dorkenoo, a professional health worker from Ghana resident in the UK. In 1982, under the auspices of the Minority Rights Group, she presented detailed information on genital mutilation to the UN Commission on Human Rights. In the same year, the World Health Organisation issued a statement that these operations should not be performed by health professionals under any circumstances. In 1983 she took the process a step further by the formation of the Foundation for Women's Health and Development (FORWARD), an independent group working to promote good health among African women, with special emphasis on education against female genital mutilation.

Opinions are divided as to whether the practice is disappearing because of legislation or social and economic changes. Esther Ogunmodede, for instance, believes that in Nigeria, Africa's most populous country, the tradition is disappearing but extremely slowly, with millions of excisions taking place. She reports that in areas where the operations are done on girls of marriageable age, they are 'running away from home to avoid the razor'.

An interesting development took place in Ethiopia during the years of civil war, which only ended in 1991. When the Eritrean People's Liberation Front (EPLF) occupied large areas from January 1977 to December 1978, among many other reforms, they categorically and successfully forbade genital mutilation and forced marriage. In fact, the reason given for the large numbers of young women in the EPLF army was that they were running away from home in other parts of Ethiopia to avoid forced marriage and the knife. Although it appears that the practice continues in remote areas, because the consciousness of Eritrean women has changed dramatically during the war years, it is easier to persuade men and women to let go of this practice.

As the subject of female genital mutilation began to be eligible at least for discussion, reports of genital operations on non-consenting females have appeared from many unexpected parts of the world. During the 1980s, women in Sweden were shocked by accounts of mutilations performed in Swedish hospitals on daughters of immigrants. In France, women from Mali and Senegal have been reported to bring an *exciseuse* to France to operate on their daughters in their apartments. In July 1982 a Malian infant died of an excision performed by a professional circumciser, who then fled to Mali. In the same year, reports appeared in the British press that excision for non-medical reasons had been performed in a London private clinic.

Since 1983, the number of educational programmes initiated to raise public awareness of the health risks associated with female genital mutilation have increased. The media have played a role in bringing the issue from the domestic to the public domain. As a result of these efforts the taboo surrounding even the public mention of the practice has at last been broken. But there is still a long, long way to go.

Low self-esteem and powerlessness

This chapter has looked at just some of the things that happen to women today; there are many other injustices and cruelties not mentioned. I have devoted several pages to genital mutilation to show the severity of what is still happening in the 1990s.

Let me now turn to the more everyday experience of Western women. Put-downs of women are more or less a pattern in our society – not only outside but inside the home as well. Shere Hite feels that women are blackmailed into silence by the labels which are applied to them if they complain (women are 'nagging' or 'difficult').

> Thus, an individual woman, no matter how strong or aware, living with these stereotypes over a period of time, can find her will steadily, slowly eroded, her self-esteem becoming something to be fought for, piece by piece, day by day, in an unending, uphill battle. (B6)

The effect of all this, plus childhood experiences, accumulates in a woman's psyche. Year in year out she absorbs this bombardment telling her that she is not clever, not comprehensible, confused, a bad driver, weak, vacillating and unable to make up her mind – in short, second-rate. She also hears words of praise, of course, but these are mostly connected with what she looks like, of the fact that she is sweet, dishy, sexy, a 'pet' or 'luv'. If she starts to assert herself, then she begins to hear herself described as difficult, strident, hysterical, boring or a nag.

For most women, this daily drip drip of belittlement erodes their confidence. One sees this in the way women constantly apologize when there is nothing to apologize about. We take the rap because we assume we must be wrong. We hesitate, are unsure. We take it out on our children. It is like a dense greyness that women carry around with them (unless they have been exceptionally lucky and been brought up by very affirmative parents, especially fathers, who taught them their self-worth). Many women live in a state of depression because of it; figures for the prescription of valium by gender attest to this. Jo Ryan suggests that the experience of being depressed can be seen as a very typically female form of distress in the sense that it is passive and socially inoffensive. It is containing, exhausting and stupefying. It exudes powerlessness and is the antithesis of activity and control. It involves self-blame, self-hatred and the collapse of self-confidence, 'an intensification of the ways in which so many women feel about themselves anyhow, their endemic low self esteem and rampant self blame'.

For me it was worst in my thirties, before I really realized what it was, and that I could do something about it. I wrote:

> I seem to be wearing so thin the tissue of my own perception that I might not exist at all. In my masochistic and miserable self examination, there is a hollow ghost, grey and filmy inside my skin – where others have entrails, no doubt. I feel as though I am gutting myself.

This is where I must introduce the concept of the animus. It is the term coined by Jung for the male personification of the unconscious in woman. It exhibits both positive and negative aspects, as does the anima, which is the equivalent phenomenon for a man. The most characteristic manifestation of the animus is in words. It comes to us as a voice commenting on every situation in which we find ourselves. Here I will confine myself to the negative side of the animus; I will deal later with the positive. In the words of Jung's wife Emma, women hear from it

> . . .a critical, usually negative comment on every movement, an exact examination of all motives and intentions, which naturally always causes feelings of inferiority, and tends to nip in the bud all initiative and every wish for self-expression. From time to time, this same voice may also dispense exaggerated praise, and the result of these extremes of judgement is that one oscillates to and fro between the consciousness of complete futility and a blown-up sense of one's own value and importance. (B8)

Yes, indeed, I know about that! But it is important to realize that all of us experience this in some way or another, and we all have to work through it if we want to become whole.

Working with a group of women in 1986 on issues of power and powerlessness, we found that several of us had built up a pattern of behaving as victims. What seemed to happen was this. All the negative messages which had damaged our self-esteem as children had become a kind of critical voice inside. This critical voice kept on at us with all the negative things that we had done, or were doing, or that we simply *were*. Then, because our view of ourselves was so weakened by all this battering, we became natural victims for a bully *outside* to pick on. It was almost a kind of unspoken collusion between us and the bully. We were vulnerable because we were bullying ourselves anyway, and the bully wanted someone to pick on, so we were natural targets.

What triggers victim behaviour in male/female relationships may be the 'poor little me' feeling. Tears are often the only things that will soften a man's heart, make him realize the *emotions* he's dealing with. That's great – getting in touch with emotions is a good first step. But 'poor me' is fatal if it gets the woman stuck in a 'weak and feeble' syndrome.

These emotions are very painful. Some people experience this lack of a sense of self as a kind of void inside, or a sense of loss. Others experience it as a kind of devouring presence, which eats up their energy. But many writers have stressed that it is only by accepting these emotions, getting down to the real deep *feelings* which are one level beneath the emotions, and working with them, that we can contact our creative potential as human beings. That is what the next chapter is about.

> Grief lays the mineral deposits in the psyche that we later mine – it is part of the foundation of our wisdom. (Lara Owen, 1993 page 77. B1)

> Most people have at some time or another, to stand alone and to suffer, and their final shape is determined by their response to their probation; they emerge either the slaves of circumstance, or in some sense captain of their souls. (Charles Raven)

CHAPTER 3

Women with Power

Our deepest fear is not that we are inadequate. Our deepest fear is that we are powerful beyond measure. It is our light, not our darkness, that most frightens us. We ask ourselves 'who am I to be brilliant, gorgeous, talented, fabulous?' Actually, who are you not to be? You are a child of God. Your playing small doesn't serve the world. There's nothing enlightened about shrinking so that other people won't feel insecure around you. We are all meant to shine, as children do. We were born to make manifest the glory of God that is within us. It's not just in some of us; it's in everyone. And as we let our own light shine, we unconsciously give other people permission to do the same. As we're liberated from our own fear, our presence automatically liberates others.

Nelson Mandela, inaugural address as President of
South Africa, 1994

In previous chapters I described a time when women and men shared power, how the power of the feminine was subdued and how this has affected women's situation today. This chapter is about the kinds of power women do have: women's growing power to do what men do, for example in the military, their economic power, their power of sexual attraction. I show how these types of power are power over, and then draw on personal experience of interviewing decision-makers to illustrate what I mean by power over. Some of this is quite funny, especially interviews with American strategic analysts. I then explore how Western women this century have developed their masculine qualities and picked up masculine notions of power. The chapter concludes with the distinction between power over and power to. This latter kind of power draws on qualities often considered female, but it is available to both women and men. Not only is it available to both sexes, it is vital to both men and women in becoming complete human beings.

The power to do what men do

In the West at least, women today have an ever-increasing power to do what men do. For several generations girls have been educated in more or less the same way as boys. We have labour-saving devices that have liberated us from the sink and the fire. We have contraception which, however flawed, does at least permit us to decide when we want to have babies. We have tampons and sanitary towels that make it possible to cope with menstruation in ways that our grandmothers would have envied. We have gradually woken up and looked at all the things men can do and we have thought: 'I could do that'. With effort and determination and skill we have overcome the barriers put in our way and done it, although often we have had to be twice as good as the male candidate to get the job. We have statutory rights to equality in most spheres. Women can be astronauts, wrestlers, fighter pilots, rugby players. With the exception of the Catholic priesthood and certain London dining clubs, women in the West can do what men can do, if they want to. Let me examine briefly the changes that have taken place in just two areas – the military and the economy.

The military

People have widely differing views on whether integration of women in the armed forces is a good or bad thing: whether women help to 'civilize' the military, or whether the military tends to 'brutalize' women. Nevertheless, in terms of sheer transition, there are some dramatic changes taking place. At the end of the Vietnam war, women composed only 1.6 per cent of US forces; in 1993 the figure was more than 11 per cent. In 1993, 7 per cent of UK forces were women, planned to rise to 10 per cent before 1998. In the 1940s, Winston Churchill always chose members of the Womens Royal Naval Service (WRENS) to record his summit meetings with Roosevelt and Stalin. He later patronizingly thanked them as 'chickens for laying so well without clucking'. In 1993 these WRENS are serving aboard warships and are being integrated with the rest of the Royal Navy. This follows a similar move by the British army in 1992, although women are still barred from front-line combat. The Royal Air Force already has its first female pilots in helicopters and transport aircraft; others are training to fly fast jets like the Tornado bomber. The British Ministry of Defence has finally realized that it is indefensible to dismiss service-women when they become pregnant; after a test case in September 1993 it is now resigned to paying out compensation totalling many millions of pounds to women who have made claims of sexual discrimination.

The economy

Only 20 years ago, lack of educational qualifications was one of the toughest hurdles for women to surmount when looking for jobs. But now girls are overtaking boys in virtually every measure of school academic performance. In 1992 in the UK for example, 45 per cent of girls, compared with 38 per cent of boys, passed five subjects in the General Certificate of Secondary Education at Grade C or above. For the first time a greater proportion of women entered higher education than men. Roughly twice as many women as men gained vocational qualifications and unemployment for male undergraduates was 15.1 per cent compared to 10.6 per cent for women.

Even though many women's jobs are part time, eight out of ten jobs created between now and the turn of the century are expected to be 'women's jobs'. The role and expectations of daughters, wives and mothers have changed profoundly. So have the prospects for sons, husbands and fathers. But, says Anna Coote of the Institute for Public Policy Research, while women have *added* the role of wage-earner to their traditional one of homemaker and carer, men have simply *lost* their breadwinning role.

Men are having a tough time today. The roles that they have had for centuries are slipping away from them. Men used to be the breadwinners: it was proof of their manhood both in their own eyes and those of women. Now large percentages of women have paid jobs. Within the last ten years, the number of women in the USA with jobs and businesses has increased so markedly that women as a group are no longer essentially economically dependent on men. This is a startling development – and one whose implications have only barely begun to take hold. Surveys have shown that although many women receive extremely low salaries (and day-care is expensive), more women than ever have enough resources to make it on their own, if they have to – even with children and even if only minimally.

Unemployment has deprived many young men of a role in life. Young women, now less likely to be unemployed than young men, have added a breadwinning role without losing that of wife and mother.

As women become less dependent on men economically they are making choices for other family systems than the traditional nuclear one. In the UK today, for example, there are 1.3 million single-parent families (one in five of all families with children), mostly headed by women; the situation in most Western countries is similar. Together with reproductive choice for women, this means that men are losing control of inheritance and reproduction.

These changes are painful. All this is very threatening to the kind of identity we have associated with being male over the past 3,000 years or so. In the face of feminism, men have felt, and do feel, insecure. Some have expressed it in writing, certainly a healthier reaction than oppression. Others have expressed it in random violence towards women.

> Thus many men are trapped, tragically, in a kind of permanent isolation and aloneness by a system which offers them 'dominance' (and says their only alternative is not equality, but 'submission'!) in exchange for holding back their feelings, keeping their emotional lives in check, suffering loneliness as they attempt to judge every situation 'rationally' – and wind up with no one to whom they can talk, really talk, about their feelings. (Shere Hite, 1993, page 311. B6)

Because this traditional kind of maleness is under threat, it is becoming exaggerated in a terrifying and soulless machismo. Young men on council estates are engaged in a 'militaristic' culture of crime, terrorizing their neighbourhoods. 'They celebrate war, force and hierarchies as ways of sorting things out', as Bea Campbell has put it. A quarter of young British males is convicted of an offence. In her 1994 Reith Lectures, Marina Warner said, 'Fear of men has grown alongside a belief that aggression – including sexual violence – inevitably defines the character of the young male'. In arcade after arcade and living rooms across the country young men spend their hours chasing monsters, zapping and slicing and chopping and head-butting. In our hi-tech world, material success seems to require aggression and macho qualities. Here is a woman speaking:

> Men's culture – that set of beliefs, attitudes and behaviour that men must develop in order to be considered *real men* – is a disconnected, violent,

demeaning, controlling culture. Inside it, men learn to lead by disempowering others, to win by defeating others, to 'think' by arguing with others.

Here is a man speaking:

> The heterosexual man grows up not learning to complain. For men, the motto is when the going gets tough, the tough get going. There's been no rewards in male socialisation for complaining about anything. You can't say you don't know how to dance, you can't ask for help at maths, you can't ask for directions.

In the UK male suicides have nearly doubled in the past decade, while female suicides have decreased. 'Growing up male is hard, very hard', says Angela Phillips, 'I began to see that, for many boys, the process of attaining manhood is a process of desensitisation, in which the openness of the small child shrinks further and further into the shell of the man.'

The power of sexual attraction and why men fear women

To read the tabloids one would think that women have enormous sexual power over men. Permeating right through every nook and cranny of our culture is the notion that women, if they are sexy enough, can do anything. Women's bodies are linked with power in advertisement after advertisement.

The story of Arnold Wills' attempt to seduce me in chapter 1 raised the possibility of a deal – an exchange of my attractiveness for his power. As I pointed out, this would have been a route to a kind of power – power by proxy. But that power would depend entirely on his desire. If (or rather when) his desire waned, I would cease to have any power.

Some analysts think that this power of sexual attraction goes deeper; that it is connected to man's primordial fear of women. They say that throughout recorded history we find evidence of this fear – the imagery of the dark, mysterious, unknown and often unknowable nature of woman. 'In many a legend do we see the hero lost for ever as he falls back into the material shadows – cave, abyss, hell'. (Simone de Beauvoir, 1984. B12)

Contemporary writers assert that man fears woman because of the awesome power his mother had over him as a child. That power, to give or withhold nourishment, to save or to abandon him, to come when he cried or ignore him, is literally one of life or death.

Denny is a Category A prisoner serving life for murder in the special
unit for violent prisoners in Parkhurst top-security prison. Bob
Johnson, consultant psychiatrist at Parkhurst, spends his working life
seeking the hurt person within the prisoner. He describes Denny as an
example of someone who was taught violence as a child. His mother
used to batter him as a matter of routine. So he grew up terrified that
she would batter him all over again, at any time. Inside he remained
convinced he was still a child. 'So', says Johnson, 'here we have a fully
grown man, a large man at that, stating that he still fears his mother,
currently aged 85, and only 5 foot 2'.

Dorothy Dinnerstein explores this view in her book *The Rocking of
the Cradle and the Ruling of the World*. She discusses how men when
they grow up do not forget that first initial experience of female power,
and spend their lives making sure it never overwhelms them again.
She says that man has magic feelings of awe and fear, sometimes dis-
gust, toward all things that are mysterious, powerful, and not himself,
and that woman's fertile body receives these projections. He therefore
tries to control this alien, dangerous nature through ritual segregation,
confinement, and avoidance. Her thesis provokes the question: but
what about the women as they grow up – don't they fear the power of
their mothers in the same way? The answer I suppose is that most
women soon have the experience of being mothers, and realize that it
does not actually feel very powerful.

It may be that these two drives – women's power of sexual attraction
and men's fear of women – combine to explain the practice of genital
mutilation discussed in the previous chapter. Perhaps women's sexuality and their power is very closely linked, and the result in some societies is that this extreme 'solution' has been attempted.

A thoughtful man I know believes that there is today a widespread
fear of women, and that it may be fear of the unknown, the mysterious, the deeper levels of consciousness and therefore the intuition. He
thinks that part of man's archetypal make-up is the need to look for
rational explanations and reasoned courses of action; if these are taken
away, a man feels lost and fearful. In the interests of his own security
he will consciously protect himself by removing the threat of the
unknown. In some ways his course of action is not unlike that of a
cornered animal; when it experiences fear it instinctively attacks the
object that makes it feel afraid, even at an archetypal level. By the
same token it is possible to see the current wave of feminism, the
revival of the goddess and modern man's uneasy predicament, as part
and parcel of the same phenomenon – a resurgence of the spiritual and
intuitive dimensions of our being.

Other men perceive women as having the power to grow life, give it birth and nurture it, all by themselves. It is expressed, this power, in the belly and breasts of adult women. In this huge, generative system, men are important only for a brief moment – during the sexual act. After that they may feel they are completely dispensable. The whole system can work without them. The other side of this coin is that men have the freedom denied to women, who are tied to the foetus and the child. So while men may feel irrelevant, they are also free.

This, coupled with the resentment men may feel after their own experience of maternal power, leaves many men today feeling powerless and irrelevant. So when they get a chance, they react by insisting on their relevance 'you can't manage without me' and on their power (with violence and abuse).

Today, however, these feelings are clearly coming closer to consciousness and expression. This means that change is taking place. Men are forming groups for self-help and mutual support and finding out what it really means to be a man.

Power *over*

Each of the three types of power which women ostensibly have – their growing power to do what men do, their economic power and their power of sexual attraction – are all perceived by our society in the masculine sense of power as *power over*. I want to go back into the personal now, and describe how I began to become aware of the pervasiveness of this notion of *power over* in a male world. During the 1980s, as I said in the Introduction, I set up a research group to discover who makes decisions on nuclear weapons. Then I helped individuals who disagree with nuclear policy to develop a dialogue with these decision-makers. At the same time, I set up a programme of interviews with top British nuclear weapons decision-makers myself. The aim was partly to understand the way they thought, and partly to introduce other ways of looking at the world. I carried out the interviews either alone or with a male colleague; tape recordings or extensive notes of the interviews were made, and the results written up.

Much of what I found out in these interviews was terrifying. When asked for scenarios of what threats were actually facing NATO in 1992, after the Cold War was clearly over, the man whose job it is to calculate numbers of NATO nuclear weapons told me:

The fact is, we haven't got a threat – we're looking pretty hard though and you can be sure we'll come up with something . . . We've adopted the 'generic' approach.

When asked what he understood by this word he said:

Well it's theoretic – not directly connected to real life. It's an academic approach. But it's not a bad threat to start with . . . In the old days it was a piece of cake – you just fed in the Soviet threat at one end, just like a fruit machine, pulled the handle, and out came all the nuclear weapons you could wish for at the other end.

At the Department of Trade and Industry in London, I asked the most senior official in charge of granting licences for weapons exports whether he had any clash of interests, as a person, between working for a department whose job is to promote trade, and seeing in the news that weapons he had licensed had killed thousands of people. He laughed suddenly and loudly, so loudly that I sat up. When the nervous heartiness had subsided, he said:

Well you couldn't really work for this department if you had moral scruples in that way. But you just don't think about it, you can't, you're too busy. If you did you'd be like the salesgirl in Woolworths who sells someone a length of flex on the assumption they want to fix a light with it, and they go off and strangle someone.

I was so taken unawares by the irrelevance of this analogy that I wasn't quick enough to point out that weapons are designed and made for killing, electric flex is not.

Some of these men are very intelligent; some simply have closed minds, and some do not tell the truth. In 1991, I had lunch with the Foreign Office man responsible for arms export policy. Since it is now generally agreed that national approaches to limiting arms export do not work, I attempted several times to discuss with him the possibilities for a co-operative, global approach to arms export control. After three tries the idea still had not got through; his point of view was entirely lodged, not just in the British position but in the particular view of the Foreign Office, as opposed, for example, to the Ministry of Defence. He told me flatly that Britain had not exported to Iran or Iraq since the beginning of the Iran/Iraq war. The Scott Inquiry has subsequently shown how untrue this statement was.

The exchanges I had with these men varied from the very intimate through the very pompous to the sad and the rather funny. Gabriel de Bellescize is French Ambassador to Aotearoa/New Zealand. After his address to a conference there in February 1992 I asked a series of questions about the new nuclear missiles which Britain may make with France, and that raised issues of testing in the Pacific. He was giving me very long-winded answers, in diplomatese. I found myself walking slowly up the aisle of the hall towards where he was standing on the podium, saying, 'Please answer my question. Please tell me what is the intended target for this new missile?' He stumbled and eventually said, 'Well, you must give your foreign minister, and mine, time to think.' The audience burst into gales of laughter, so loud that nothing more needed to be said.

Emotions are considered dangerous in this world of weapons. The chief scientist at Britain's leading weapons electronics manufacturer is a real Einstein figure – the same mane of flyaway white hair. I rather took to him. I felt he had enjoyed blowing up, in equal measure, fallacious scientific theories and stuffy committee meetings. One could be informal and say things like, 'Oh, come off it', to which he responded sometimes sharply, always quickly'. His passion is to be logical. He loves argument and taking reasoning to bits; he acknowledges that emotions get in the way and he fights this. When I asked what is wrong with emotions he was surprised, as if it was obvious:

> You *must* compartmentalise. Must keep personality out of logic. I know what you're gonna say . . . you're gonna say that upbringing and everything influences the way we think. We *have* to minimise that.

Change in individuals

Others who have entered the world of nuclear decision-makers have come to the same conclusions as myself. Carol Cohn, an American college teacher who attended a summer workshop on nuclear strategic doctrine at a distinguished US university, describes her experience as follows.

> Entering the world of defense intellectuals was a bizarre experience – bizarre because it is a world where men spend their days calmly and matter-of-factly discussing nuclear weapons, nuclear strategy, and nuclear war. The discussions are carefully and intricately reasoned, occurring seemingly without any sense of horror, urgency, or moral outrage – in fact, there seems to be no graphic reality behind the words, as they speak of 'first strikes', 'counterforce exchanges,' and 'limited nuclear war', or as they debate the comparative values of a 'minimum deterrent posture' versus a 'nuclear war-fighting capability' . . . Anyone who has seen pictures of

Hiroshima burn victims or tried to imagine the pain of hundreds of glass shards blasted into flesh may find it perverse beyond imagination to hear a class of nuclear devices matter-of-factly referred to as 'clean bombs'.

I think I had naively imagined myself as a feminist spy in the house of death – that I would need to sneak around and eavesdrop on what men said in unguarded moments, using all my subtlety and cunning to unearth whatever sexual imagery might be underneath how they thought and spoke . . . I was wrong. There was no evidence that any feminist critiques had ever reached the ears, much less the minds, of these men . . . Lectures were filled with discussion of vertical erector launchers, thrust-to-weight ratios, soft lay downs, deep penetration, and the comparative advantages of protracted versus spasm attacks – or what one military adviser to the National Security Council has called 'releasing 70 to 80 per cent of our megatonnage in one orgasmic whump.' There was serious concern about the need to harden our missiles and the need to 'face it, the Russians are a little harder than we are.' (B6)

Carol Cohn's experience with American strategic analysts was strikingly similar to mine, interviewing British decision-makers. Norman Dixon, Professor of Psychology at University College, London, thinks that today the world's fate lies in the hands of leaders who have an above-average chance of being neurotic, irrational, paranoid and egomaniacal.

A potential for destruction on a scale hitherto undreamt of lies in the hands of a few ageing individuals who, in terms of personality, motivation, and of stress and cerebral efficiency, should hardly be trusted with the weekend shopping. (B6)

One solution he offers is to confine political and military leadership to 'that half of the human race who are less likely to indulge in mass genocide – women'. That's nice of him, but completely unrealistic, and not quite to the point either. The point is that we all have to change. Women are not angels and men are not devils. It is not the case that there are some bad people out there polluting and destroying and building bombs; we all have the polluter and the destroyer and the bomb-builder inside us.

The threats to the planet stem from decisions all made separately and without consideration of their cumulative effect and without a sense of responsibility for their cumulative effect. As things are, individuals simply go on doing what they are doing, without thought for the whole. This applies whether it is decision-making on a large scale (weapons production, arms sales, toxic waste disposal) or whether it is at the level of the consumer. The wishes and desires of the individual are top priority: the good of the whole is at the bottom. In fact, the good of the whole *is* the good of the individual. And it is the individual who can change.

That is why I thought it worthwhile to develop dialogue with nuclear weapons decision-makers. However machine-like the system may seem, it is individuals who make policy, and individuals who can change it. This has been confirmed to me many times by those in the business. To quote a senior official with a lifetime in the civil service at the Department of Trade and Industry, 'In the end it's the individuals who make the difference. It can be one or two people in a department who actually set policy.' He talked about change, saying that the civil service is very good at going along in a straight line and very bad at change. 'That's why all of the Ministry of Defence is still fighting the Cold War.' (This was in 1992.) He said that in civil service departments, the key thing was individuals; departments mattered or had influence according to who was there.

In a strange way doing these interviews was fun. At the beginning, the role I was playing appealed to the masculine in me. I got big shots of adrenalin each morning when I knew I had to do an interview; it was a heady mixture of being scared and being bold. I knew my stuff. I was using my courage. I was using something my Jewish in-laws call 'chutzpah', which means a mixture of cheek and daring and going in where angels fear to tread, etc. I can get quite high on this, and have done ever since I was a child, when I was competing with boys all the time and sometimes winning. Cyrano de Bergerac was my set book at school and I was completely captivated by him, and by his white scarf as an image of daring and panache.

The masculine part of a woman

This century has seen the development of the courageous, outgoing, heroic, assertive qualities in women – qualities which are usually thought of as masculine. The masculine part of a woman is wonderful, and not to be squashed. It has, as I showed in the last chapter, a hard, dark side which one overlooks at one's peril. Even without going as far as physical violence, the dark side (for me) of this panache and courage and daring is when it is driven by the animus. The other person suddenly finds himself up against something in me that is obstinate, cold and completely inaccessible. It is apt to take the form of a sudden 'sacred' conviction – unarguable and incontestably 'true'.

Marie-Louise Von Franz says that 'such a conviction is preached with a loud, insistent voice or imposed on others by brutal emotional scenes'.

All women have an animus. It is basically influenced by the father, who endows it with its convictions – convictions that never include the personal reality of the woman herself as she really is. Von Franz goes on to say that the animus lures women away from all human relationships and especially from all contacts with real men.

In the moments when my animus gets the upper hand, he tries to judge men, and rarely has anything good to say about them. Not only can he not forgive failures and faults in real men, but he cannot see or will not admit their good qualities. He is always telling me that the perfect man, perfect lover, perfect companion, is just around the corner. He is harsh and calculating, and sees plots and conspiracies everywhere. On the positive side he gives me many strengths. He provides orderliness, rationality and discipline. He is the part of me which gets up in the morning and gets things done. He has brilliant ideas.

I painted a picture of my animus, which I saw as a huge totem pole with many faces (reproduced on page 73). I did not put in the negative, crushing, destructive faces of my animus, because I knew them well enough already (I see them daily!). What I did want to represent were the positive aspects. The top one is my *seeker of truth*, who is steady and constant and tough and will see me through whatever I have to go through on my path. The next one, with the furrowed brow, is my *thinker*. He lends me mental clarity – what Hanuman, the Hindu monkey-god, calls 'feeling judgement'. He is my strategist, lithe and agile. My *sceptic* comes next, with eyebrows raised at nearly everything. He can't bear fools and likes to look askance, question, doubt. He's wry, has a dry sense of humour, and can sometimes be ruthless. The last one is my *wise man*. He's ascetic, quiet, reflective. He is so aware of love in the world, both outside and inside himself, that finally nothing is serious. He smiles and laughs a lot.

My animus does give me courage, but courage I have to treat with care. It goes something like this. I decide I want to achieve something difficult. I am not altogether sure I am up to it, so I have to get a bit 'nerved up'. In this process of winding up I am deeply absorbed with myself and my 'task'; I am not 'in' myself but as it were 'doing to' myself, revving my engine up, so I am certainly not there for anyone else. And if and when I do achieve my goal, I can become very inflated. I have grandiose ideas about myself, expanding the (inaccurate) notion that 'I' did this. And so I cease to be able to see why

Animus

others cannot do what I have done, and I begin to tell them how to run their lives. All this reminds me uncomfortably of a recent occupant of 10 Downing Street!

This is true I think of many women who climb the ladders of our male world. They almost have to develop the same values as the men with whom they compete for places. The British House of Commons is a good example. There may now be more women MPs than before, but the culture of the place continues to be that a boys' public school, the 'prefects' putting down the 'fags', the debates degenerating into slanging matches, with nobody listening to anybody – a perverse cacophony that achieves little wisdom for the nation. Political scientist Betty Reardon thinks that success in politics as in warfare is viewed as evidence of masculinity and requires its own degree of ferocity. She finds that the political performances of the world's most powerful women show how they have to continue proving their toughness even (or especially) after they have reached the heights of power.

People who have met Mrs Gandhi and Lady Thatcher say that both women used domination power techniques as well as the terrifying aspects of the female to achieve their ends. Talk to the women who have succeeded in the world as it is today, and many will say it is no problem. They have taken on the male game, accepted the male rules, played well and won. Interview women who have become decision-makers in the world of defence; they have become indistinguishable in their views, values and attitudes from their male colleagues. Go below the surface a bit, maybe introduce the idea of using another type of power, and they will look at you oddly and say something like, 'Look, this is the real world; it's a tough world, we don't have time for vague notions like that.' Female power would automatically be assumed to be something weak. Squadron Leader Jones describes women in the armed forces thus:

> . . . many become so immersed in their male identity that women became 'the other' in their eyes; in the military they became 'one of the boys'. Often the only way for women to cope with the contradiction of being both a female and a soldier was actively to deny their connection with the feminine world. To expect such female warriors to challenge an institution in which they held such a precarious position was unrealistic.

The hardest thing for a feminist to learn about is her femininity. Yet therein lies her route to any real power. This is because real power comes from the interaction of, and the eventual union of, male and female within a person. Feminists develop their masculine sides and qualities – they need them to escape from being oppressed – but in order to be whole and powerful, they need their feminine side as well. I will explore this more fully in chapters 7 and 9.

Developing another kind of power

The question of feminism brings us back to the ways in which we see power. If I have accepted a view of the world as a tough, dangerous and threatening place, then I have to be tough, dangerous and threatening to deal with it. That is the *domination* view of power that at times I was coming face to face with in these interviews. At first I responded to it with a kind of bravado. Gradually I realized that the more centred I was, the more I was myself and not playing a role, the more each man could respond to me as a person and not as the role he was inhabiting. The chairman of a major arms manufacturer, for example, was telling me that selling weapons hopefully shortens conflict.

'But people like you sell to both sides,' I said.

'We always do strictly what the Government tells us we can do.'

'But in the Iran/Iraq war?'

'I dunno how many were killed.'

'They were sendings boys of 12.'

'Well, they were desperate. So did Hitler. I saw some of them too. They were crying.'

His face started to work, he looked down, there were tears in his eyes, and a long silence. Then all of a sudden he looked up cheerily and said, 'Where was I?'

'You were in a war.'

More agonized movements in his face. Silence. 'I'm not a warlike man you know.'

I was touched by this man's emotions. I was reached by him as a person. This gradual learning of how to be myself in the interviews – being rather than doing, responding on a human level rather than arguing and judging – became more satisfying to me and, I believe, to my interviewees. The last series of interviews I did was in 1992. After each one I sent my interviewees notes in diagram form of how our conversation had gone; in nearly all cases they responded fully, engaging with the paradoxes or contradictions I had pointed out, and in some cases making wry remarks or laughing at themselves. I felt we had both let our guards down a bit, and somehow begun to cross the huge gulf between our views of the world.

The big distinction

I want to make a distinction between the notions of *power over*, discussed earlier in this chapter in relation to women – namely their growing power to do what men do, their economic power and their power of sexual attraction – and an entirely different concept. This is *power to* and *power with*, rather than *power over*. It is the power to create, to *be* instead of to *do*. It is power *with* others which leads to co-operation rather than competition. It takes as its starting point a sense of interconnectedness with other human beings and the earth, and thus implies responsibility for them. It is available to men just as it is to women.

The problem is that distorted masculine power – what I have called domination power – has been in the ascendant in our world for several centuries. It has brought some benefits, but the extent to which it has been dominant has led to an imbalance of such proportions that the survival of the planet is at stake. The rest of this book is devoted to discovering (or rediscovering) what this other power is like, what it consists of, how it can be developed, and how it can be used.

It is as though, in striving for equality, women have been setting their sights at what is already there, and wanting that. By and large we have looked as far as what is, what exists, and gone after it: power *over*. This is like learning the lines from somebody else's play, but not considering that you could be writing it – that is, working to somebody else's agenda, not your own.

What I am suggesting now, and what others have suggested before, is that we turn our attention to what could be. Here I call on some terms from Sanskrit to help. *Upaya*, the masculine, is skilful activity. *Prajna*, the feminine, is profound cognition, it is a tool to discover wisdom. I am suggesting that we have been using the *upaya* in ourselves to achieve equality, and that now we might concentrate on using the *prajna*.

We cannot go back to the days of the goddess – we do not want to – but we can use the knowledge that the goddess was worshipped (or, if we are worried about historical evidence, the exciting myth of her worship) to change feminism from a struggle to a path. The path leads not towards liberation of the female body or the female mind, but towards liberation of another kind of power in both men and women.

Both sexes are yearning for this. Here is a young man from Walthamstow in north-east London speaking:

I've learnt that being male and being gentle don't mix. If you show vulnerability, you are picked on and attacked. I've had to remodel myself into a hard chauvinistic man to survive in my peer group. Inside though, I'm still as soft as a silkworm. I yearn for a world in which I can be myself, in which I can unlock my gentle side and get rid of the mould. It's so boring to wake up every morning and have to play the hard tough nut.

Not 'an eye for an eye'

In order to discover this inner strength, it is vital to transform our past painful experiences so that the anger from them does not turn to bitterness, leave us as victims, and prevent us discovering our real power. Jean Shinoda Bolen is Professor of Psychiatry at the University of California and she has learned from the patients she has treated about the difference between heroine and victim:

> What they felt and how they reacted inwardly and outwardly determined who they became, much more than the degree of adversity they encountered. For example, I have met people who survived childhoods full of deprivation, cruelty, beatings, or sexual abuse. *Moreover, they did not become (as might be expected) like the adults who abused them.* Despite all the bad they experienced, they felt compassion for others, both then as well as now. Traumatic experience left its mark; they were not unscathed, yet an essence of trust, a capacity to love and hope, a sense of self survived. As I surmised why, I began to understand the difference between heroine and victim. (B3)

She says that as children, each of these people somehow saw themselves as protagonists in a terrible drama. Each had an inner myth, a fantasy life, or imaginary companions. A daughter who was beaten and humiliated by her abusive father and was not protected by her depressed mother, recalled telling herself when she was a child that she was not related to this uneducated backward family, that she was really a princess who was being tested by these ordeals. Another beaten and sexually molested child escaped into a fantasy life where things were very different. A third thought of herself as a warrior.

These children thought ahead and planned how they could escape their families when they were old enough. They chose how they would react in the meantime. One said, 'I think my mind left my body. I'd go somewhere else whenever he started to touch me.' Bolen sees these children as heroines and choicemakers. They maintained a sense of themselves apart from the way they were treated. They assessed the situation, decided how they would react in the present, and made plans for the future.

The passage I have italicized in the above quotation is a clue to a vital issue: that in our history, over and over again, violence has bred violence. Those who have suffered terrible injury then go on to inflict terrible injury on others. We see this today, tragically, in the way the people of Israel, many of whom lost family, friends and faith in humanity during the Holocaust, have treated the Palestinians – herding them into camps, imposing impossible restrictions, imprisoning, beating and torturing them.

We saw in the last chapter how gravely women have suffered over 30 centuries. It is important that women do not now repeat, consciously or unconsciously, what was done to them. And as the above quotation shows, it is possible to stop the vicious cycle, to step out of the mould. So it is what happens *in* women and *in* men that matters: the growth of heart and consciousness which forms inner strength. That is what the second part of this book is about.

PART II

Hara Power: How it can be Developed

In the first part of this book I outlined a kind of power which has prevailed in our world for several thousand years – power understood as physical strength, domination, hierarchy, authority, rule, and ultimately military force. It emanates from outside a person, from armies or weapons or constituencies or god. I called this kind of power 'domination power'. This is essentially a question of having power *over* something or somebody else. I suggested another kind of power, essentially a question of power *with* others. It co-operates rather than competes. It is the power to create and accept. It resides in *being* rather than *doing*. For brevity I shall now call it 'hara power'. The word *hara* means centre of the body or centre of gravity, and is found physically in the belly, a little below the navel. Hara is the point of perfect balance in the body. It is where one can find stillness. In ancient Chinese and Japanese tradition, it is where the soul resides in the body. Japanese Master Okada puts it like this:

The Hara is the shrine of the Divine. If its stronghold is finely built so that the Divine in us can grow, then a real human being is achieved. If one divides people into ranks, the lowest is he who values his head. Those who endeavour only to amass as much knowledge as possible grow heads that become bigger and so they topple over easily, like a pyramid standing upside down . . . Next come those of middle rank. For them the chest is most important. People with self-control, given to asceticism and abstinence belong to this type. These are the men with outward courage but without real strength. Many of the so-called great men are in this category. Yet all this is not enough. But those who regard the belly as the most important part are the people of the highest rank. They have developed their minds as well as their bodies in the right way. Strength flows out of them and produces a spiritual condition of ease and equanimity. They do what seems good to them without violating any law. Those in the first category think that Science can rule Nature. Those in the second have apparent courage and discipline and they know how to fight. Those in the third know what reality is.

One of the key differences between hara power and domination power is where they come from – what their sources are, and what their direction is. Domination power comes from outside, from a sky god, from heaven, from weapons, from a straining, outstretched arm. Its movement is outwards. Hara power is receptive. It resides within. It lies in the interior – the spirit, the psyche, the body. The healthier all these are, the stronger the power. Hara power is neither specifically male nor female but is a synthesis of the two, and is available equally to men and women.

In the rest of the book I concentrate on ways in which both sexes can rediscover and develop this power, and use it. The next five chapters deal with the various routes which an individual can take in order to develop hara power: chapter 4 deals with power from self-knowledge; chapter 5 with power from within your own body; chapter 6 with power from the soul; chapter 7 with power from bringing opposites together; and chapter 8 with power from nature and from sacred knowledge. For each person the route they choose will be unique – it may combine elements from one or two or all of the above.

At this point I would like to issue a warning. People sometimes assume, when they read words like 'nature', 'sacred', 'goddess' and so on, that what it is about is in some way soft, easy, even sentimental. My experience is that quite the reverse is true. In my life I have learned to fly aeroplanes and to parachute and those things did not require anything like the fortitude it takes to know myself, to know the dark side of myself, and to develop my own power. What a person is doing in developing her or his own power is not tame. The essence of the primordial goddess is that she is *not* all sweetness and light: she is also dark and harsh. She is terrible as well as tender. That is the most important thing about her. Nature, as anyone who has witnessed an earthquake or a storm at sea knows, is not mild.

For someone raised in Western rational ways of doing things, one of the hardest changes to make is to start to rely on intuition as well as reason. We are accustomed to dismissing most of the notions and images which flash into our heads. In this work we need to learn not only to notice them but to trust them. Images are especially useful guides, and can be an extraordinary source of strength. We also need to learn to live with paradox. Things are not necessarily neat and clear-cut.

I have another warning, which concerns the time it may take to do this. Do not expect it to be quick: nothing as grand and worthwhile as the development of your power could possibly be quick. But you will feel progress quickly. In a few months you will find yourself in a situation where your power is tested, and all of a sudden you will realize that you are dealing with it differently. You will look back and say, 'I couldn't have done *that* before.' The process may also absorb quite a lot of time in your day – reflecting, writing, reading, even daydreaming. People have a habit of thinking that attending to their own muse is selfish; it is not. Give yourself the time you need.

To get an idea of hara power, there is an intriguing exercise you can do with a friend. Ask him or her to stand beside you in a relaxed fashion, arms at the side. Then with your index finger give him or her a gentle push on the breast bone; the result will be a toppling over backwards. Then ask the person to put all attention on the hara point, just below the navel, and to keep repeating internally, 'Hold one point. Hold one point.' Now again give the same gentle push with the index finger. Your friend will not move.

Becoming powerful is a task which needs great care and attention. For me it is like the opening up of a beautiful room full of treasures which has been closed and shuttered. The dust sheets must be lifted off the chairs gently, so as not to shower dust everywhere, and folded up. Floors must be swept. Then comes the wonderful moment of pulling back the curtains and throwing open the shutters and the windows, and letting the sunlight stream in. The jewel colours of the fabrics and carpets can be seen in all their glory. Deep reds, rose, coral, gold. That is me, as I uncover the power within my body and my spirit. Window-sills and tables need to be wiped with a damp cloth, so that they will shine. No sudden movements. Fresh flowers need to be brought in. There are chests full of treasures from the past: a leather-bound book with a brass clasp, old photographs in wooden frames, a wedding dress of thick cream satin and lace, stubs of old candles, an urn of ashes, cards edged with the black of mourning, a tiny stone figurine of a pregnant woman with large breasts, a glass phial of perfume, still heavy with scent, an ebony walking stick with a dagger inside the handle. Each of these is to be taken out, aired, and its story learned. When I set eyes on them, I experience a reassuring 'click' of recognition. Some are very ancient.

It takes a long time before I know all there is to know from those chests. I spend many hours in this room – at dawn, in the sunlight, at dusk, in the middle of the night. And finally I am ready for my guests, ready for them to see this room which has been hidden for so long, ready for them to see and try the strength and beauty there.

This part of the book is designed to be of use to you. It can metaphorically point to what looks like an old cardboard box in the corner and show it to be a casket. It can help pull the heavy rug off, revealing a treasure chest. It can stay while you painstakingly go through all the items, can help with a stuck window-clasp, can stand in the background reassuringly when the friends come.

So go ahead, open up and see what's inside.

CHAPTER 4

Power from Self-knowledge

There is no greater power than to understand yourself. When you get rid of your fears then you begin to be yourself. Then you can be anything, do anything. The main thing is to remember who you are every moment of your life.

Abraham Kawai'i, 1989

This chapter could have been entitled 'power from the mind': that would have made a nice neat trilogy of chapters 4, 5 and 6 – power from the mind, body and spirit. The mind is clearly a source of great power, but in the case of hara power I came to the conclusion that it is more a question of how the mind is used. We can use our minds to map out a strategy to trade on the world futures market in order to make ourselves millions and have some domination power. We can also use it to gain some knowledge of the self, of how we tick. If I do not understand myself, at least a bit, how can I understand others? If I do not understand my feelings, at least a bit, they may suddenly engulf me and I may inflict terrible damage on others. If I can become aware, if I can know and understand myself, I can give myself an essential ingredient of hara power. This chapter discusses what self-knowledge is and what it has to do with power; in the section at the end of the book entitled 'Going Further' there is a guide to how self-knowledge can be developed.

What is self-knowledge?

Self-knowledge is knowing why we do the things we do. Even before that, it is actually being aware that we do them in the first place! It is understanding and accepting our strong emotions – fear, hate, love, anger, lust, grief, joy. It is also a question of understanding what is you and what is me – why we fight and why we get on well.

Self-knowledge involves getting to know our dark side, as well as our light side – the parts we welcome as well as the parts we find most frightening and unpleasant, which we often prefer to think are not there. This dark side – the tendency to cheat or lie or steal or hurt or be dirty – is something that every one of us has. If we are not familiar with these tendencies within ourselves, then what we do is 'project' them out onto other people. If we cannot acknowledge our own darkness, we see it in others, or in a particular individual.

On the subject of projection, I remember sitting in a women's meeting and becoming gradually more and more enraged by one woman who seemed to me to be organizing everyone, bossing us about, imposing her will. I was furious. In retrospect I realize that she was doing what I wanted to do – being the boss – a tendency which I absolutely cannot accept in myself, and which to this day my conscious mind regards as *bad*.

'But surely,' says my resident sceptic, 'all this navel-gazing is just self-indulgent. It has nothing to do with power, has it?' Yes, everything. The next hundred years will determine whether life on earth is transformed into a vibrant, co-operative global community or whether it disintegrates into endless conflict and terminal destruction of our environment. The choice for positive change will not be made by governments, but will start with individual human beings who engage in their own personal transformation.

What has self-knowledge to do with power?

There are seven aspects to this question, which I will deal with one by one:

- The more we understand ourselves, the more we can understand another.
- Self-knowledge brings *personal* power as distinct from *position* power.
- Self-knowledge brings the power to *name*.
- The more we can be open and honest, the better we can communicate.
- Self-knowledge enables us to grow as big as we were meant to be.
- Guilt and blame drain us: taking responsibility gives us power.
- Feelings are vital to the future of the world.

Understanding another

Until we begin to understand ourselves, we cannot begin to understand another person. And understanding others is vital to solving problems in our lives. For example, a mother and her teenage daughter are arguing. The daughter wants to go and live with travellers and sing in a hip-hop group; she wants to give up formal education and apparently does not care about the future. Her mother is horrified; she fears that if her daughter does not finish school she will never get a job and will slide into drug abuse and homelessness. The mother's fears may be justified; the daughter's desires are very strong.

The main problem is that they are not communicating: neither can imagine what it is like to be the other, nor can they separate what is theirs and what is the other's. If the mother were to examine how much of her fear actually concerns *herself* – the fact that she left school early, never had what she regards as a proper education and now finds herself at a loss with all her children leaving, and on top of all this is worried what people will think of her having a daughter living with travellers – she might be able to distinguish between what is 'hers' in this argument, and what is really to do with her daughter in a brand new situation. The daughter, instead of seeing only her mother's opposition to her plans, could look at herself more deeply and spot what her own anxieties are. Maybe if she expressed them, whatever they are, she would be clearer and her mother would feel more empathetic. She could look at what it is she *really* wants – what her independence would be like, the nature of the freedom she seeks – and then perhaps she could begin to *feel* that freedom inside.

Hand-me-downs

It is now well-established, in countless studies, that we tend to do to our children what was done to us by our parents. We often do it quite unconsciously. In some families it is acceptable, for example, for the mother or father, coming home tired from work, to take out her or his frustrations and stress on the children. Children are slapped and shouted at. Ten to one, if there is no self-knowledge in the interim period when they are growing up, those children when they become parents will take out their frustrations on *their* children, or allow their spouses to do so. And so it goes on. One of the greatest benefits of self-knowledge is that we can put a stop to the vicious and damaging parts of our legacy. Of course there are benign parts of parenting too, which we also copy and repeat. Self-knowledge helps us to sort out what is really true for us as individuals, and to be and do the best we can.

Negotiating

A man goes into a meeting. Because he knows himself fairly well, he notices that his palms are sweaty, his throat dry, his heart pounding. He is nervous, to put it mildly. He takes himself off to the toilet, relieves himself, and breathes very deeply for a few minutes. He manages to locate the reason for the fear – it is that he will lose face, be made to look an idiot. Once he realizes this, it suddenly no longer feels so bad; he can even see the funny side. So he comes back into the meeting with a flicker of a smile on his face. The man with whom he is negotiating is sitting with arms and legs tightly crossed, the arms gripping round the top of his chest. Now because our hero is no longer so obsessed with himself, he has space to notice the stress and defensiveness of the other. By probing a bit he can find out what that stress is about, and go some way to meet it, to allay the fears of the other. So what has happened by the end of the meeting? Our hero, far from looking an idiot, is actually taking initiatives to reassure the other. The other man becomes less defensive, and the outcome is the possibility of an agreement built on trust. Without the deep breaths and the pause to understand, two frightened people would have toughed it out, and probably left with nothing more than entrenched positions.

Weakness

The more we learn about our own weakness, the stronger we shall be. This may seem paradoxical, but it is true. Everyone has so-called weaknesses, vulnerable spots, Achilles heels. The most common theme in therapy, says Carl Rogers, is: 'If you really knew me, my horrible thoughts and feelings, you couldn't accept me, and would confirm my fear that I am insane and/or hopeless.' But the more we avoid them, pretend they are not there, refuse to take them out and look at them, the more trouble they cause. Whereas if we get to know them, they become familiar and less frightening, they stop undermining us at critical moments; they can even become useful. Here is the personal experience of a college student:

I was in my final year. I was incredibly busy, not only were my final examinations coming up but I was also editing a magazine and working as a counsellor. To get everything done I had to plan every hour of my day. I went weeks without taking a day off.

Suddenly I developed arthritis in my hands and wrists. Within a week it had become difficult even to feed myself, I became very tired and depressed. I was forced to stop everything and let other people pick up the pieces. When finally in desperation I told my tutors I could not take my exams that year, they suggested I was over-reacting. I left anyway and went home extremely depressed.

I felt that if only I had been a stronger person I wouldn't have given in. Because of my weakness I had let everybody down, it felt like a terrible failure. This feeling stayed with me for months.

Later I was glad it had happened. I needed to learn that I was not super-human and that there were times in my life when I would have to put my needs first, whatever the consequences or whatever anybody thought.

The more we know about our own so-called weaknesses, the more we can feel for others. This is the beginning of compassion. It is not sympathy, where one is sorry 'for' someone, while remaining emotionally uninvolved; compassion means 'feeling with', the capacity to put oneself in the shoes of another and get a slight idea – we can never really know – what it is like to be them. In *The Power Of Myth*, Joseph Campbell explored what he calls the stages of power. He discovered several stages, ascending from the experience of being able to satisfy hunger, feeling greed, need for reproduction, then physical mastery:

> But when the centre of the heart is reached, and the sense of compassion, of participation, I *and* you are same thing. There is a whole new stage of life experience opening up – the stage of the heart. (1989. B5)

A word of caution about understanding others. Alfred Adler, a contemporary of Freud, thought that because we feel helpless and inadequate as children, some of us develop an 'inferiority complex' and some of us try to overcome this by gaining positions of authority, exerting power and domination. When I met people who exhibited dominator behaviour, who oppressed or manipulated others, I used to 'explain' this to myself in terms of these ideas – namely telling myself that underneath was a frightened child. Now I think that that may well have been true, but one is still left with the dominator behaviour to deal with, especially if the person is not interested in self-knowledge and change. Understanding another does not mean condoning what they do. Some behaviour is plain unacceptable, and boundaries have to be made clear.

Personal power and position power

Most people in our society derive their power from the position they hold. The higher the position in the hierarchy, the greater the power. In business, the chief executive or chair of the board holds power over employees; in high society, a duke would have more 'social' power than a life peer; in an army, the most senior general gives the orders. My point is that the power comes with the position, and that is why some people are driven to climb, because they feel that when they have made it to 'up there' they will be able to do what they like. People will have to do what they say, period.

Now let us look at another kind of power. The young man in question trained in law in London. He then went to South Africa and got into a lot of trouble for defending blacks against whites. He spent many years in study and reflection, learning about himself, about when he was able, when he was not, and about his spirit. He called this work 'experiments with truth'. He developed the key concept of *satyagraha*, explaining:

> Truth (*satya*) implies love, and firmness (*agraha*) engenders and, therefore, serves as a synonym for force. I thus began to call the Indian movement *Satyagraha*; that is to say, the force which is born of Truth and Love or non-violence.

Gandhi knew himself so well that he could go far beyond his own ego demands and his own needs, to concentrate on truth. This gave him enormous power. He led a poverty-stricken, unarmed and uneducated people against an imperial giant. He walked the lush carpets of the British Empire in bare feet. In a loin-cloth, Gandhi negotiated with His Majesty's ambassadors and generals. This simple personal power drove Winston Churchill nearly to apoplexy. In the House of Commons he spoke of:

> . . . the nauseating and humiliating spectacle of this one-time Inner Temple lawyer, now seditious fakir, striding half naked up the steps of the viceroy's palace, there to negotiate and to parley on equal terms with the representative of the King Emperor.

This small man held an empire to ransom – not because he had guns behind him, or because he was a king or a billionaire, but because he had the force of truth behind him, and unshakeable conviction. Gandhi knew himself well.

Self-knowledge is the bedrock of moral courage. Moral courage is what a cleaner needs to stand up to a chairman; what a commoner needs to contradict a queen; what a corporal needs, to disobey the orders of a general – if they are wrong.

Gandhi

The power to name

When we know ourselves, we are more able to see what is *actually* happening around us, as distinct from what we think is happening when we are disorientated by the fog of our own fears, hopes, prejudices, projections and expectations.

If I know a bit about myself and can recognize my emotions at work, it is much easier to see when something unjust is being done to me or to others, to put my finger on it, and then do something about it. This is the ability to *name* what is going wrong, to say, honestly, clearly and loudly, what is being done. Most people know the story of the emperor's new clothes, which is about exactly this. And remember that it was a child who said aloud that the emperor was naked, when all the grown-ups were pretending that he had sumptuous clothes on. It often takes a kind of natural child-like seeing of a situation to be able to put one's finger on what is going on, and then it takes some courage to be able to say it. Here is a true story of a young English woman travelling in South America:

I had to get my visa renewed after six months. I was living in a small Andean town – the only 'gringa' for many miles. Teaching at the university gave me unbelievable status. The immigration official told me if I slept with him I would get a new visa, otherwise I would not. He repeated this for days. Finally I told him I would tell everyone I knew in the town what kind of bargain he was trying to strike up with me. He signed along the dotted line the next day.

The essential characteristics of *naming* are that the statement must be totally accurate, and not expressed as a complaint. It must not lay blame. It must show clearly and briefly that the given picture is nonsense, a distortion or a pretence. It should be said as loudly as possible, preferably in the media if it is a public issue. The powerful effect of this is that it is telling the truth.

What this is all about is bringing into focus what is really going on. It's a very big step to take and demands courage and strength. Often this strength can come from anger. When we become aware of what is happening in our world and have worked through our feelings of despair and apathy, it is then that we become angry. Anger is a very important step on the way to courageousness. The energy of anger provides the courage to *name* it. For example, on seeing Pentagon pictures of a village in Vietnam after US soldiers had advanced through it, one of the spectators said loudly: 'Liberated village? How can that be a liberated village when the people who lived there are all dead?'

The powerful thing about all this is that because the truth is being told, people can recognize it instantly. It is the most effective way of countering information which we know to be distorted, attitudes which are patronizing, and carefully maintained secrets. And when it arouses strong emotions as a result (which it does!), don't be put off – you know that you have hit the jackpot.

These techniques appear simple, but they are not easy to apply. There is a lump in your solar plexus and your mouth is dry. A teacher from Stockwell in London had this experience:

I was driving home late one night south of the river. As I passed a lone stationary car I heard a woman screaming. She sounded frightened. There seemed to be a lot of people in the car. I decided to have a look. I drew in and looked in the mirror. I saw people struggling. I took my notebook and pen, got out, walked to the front of the car and wrote down the number. All four doors of the car opened and four men got out, one of them pushing the screaming woman out in front of him. She ran away and round a corner. I told them I had stopped to see what they were doing. The driver told me it was none of my business. I said it sounded to me as if they were hurting the woman. They laughed. I told them I had their number and I would remember their faces. I didn't recognize my own voice. I felt lucky to get away without them hurting me.

But each time we do it, the cost is less, a little less. It takes courage and conviction and practice. This *naming* it is so utterly different from what powerless people are used to doing. We are used to *wheedling* power, trying to twist things round to what we want by persuasion or manipulation – this is what happens under domination. The opposite of wheedling is taking up our own power, firmly and gently, as it is right for us to do.

Openness and honesty

It's not difficult to be open and honest when things are going well; it's when things are tough that we all tend to close up and fudge. People are afraid of expressing negativity, especially when it concerns someone who has the power to hurt, abandon or fire them. But if there is a negative feeling in me, for example, and I sit on it or deny it, I stop being real and lose contact with the other person. What is more, I will not really be available for contact until I have expressed the negativity.

So, how can I do it without alienating the other person? Here are some magic guidelines, which really work, and for which I am indebted to Jake and Eva Chapman:

1 Start by saying that you need to talk and asking for time with the other person. If it cannot be done straight away, then fix a time as soon as possible.
2 Tell the other person that you have negativity which you want to express, but that he or she *does not have to change, respond or do anything as a result of what you say*. This is the vital part. He or she simply has to receive what you say.
3 Express your negativity using the first person only; say what it is *you* feel, and do not accuse or insult, eg 'I feel furious . . .' Since this is difficult, and sticking to stage 2 is difficult as well, I find it helps to write it all down, and then cross out the blame bits.
4 If you can, find something positive and genuine to say about the other person either at the beginning or the end, and show you mean it.
5 Thank the other person for hearing you.

The payoff is in the honesty and telling the truth without blaming. The truth is an amazing liberator; put across using these guidelines, it always enables real communication to take place.

Growing into what we were meant to be

All of us have, inside, a potential person who is our true self. Self-knowledge is part of growing to be that perfect self. It is not easy. Sometimes we have to go through blackness, periods of depression or anguish on the way.

Don't fall into the trap of thinking that working on yourself is an indulgence. Many of us have been conditioned to estimate ourselves in terms of how much we give to others, and therefore think that concentrating on ourselves is selfish and detracts from our value. To my mind, there is a different meaning to the one usually understood by the maxim, 'love thy neighbour as thyself'. If you do not love yourself, how can you love other people? In fact, I am not even sure that you can have deep lovemaking with another person unless you love yourself – but that is a subject for the next chapter. To love yourself you have to know yourself. So the work on self is an essential part of growth towards power.

Marion Milner is a psychoanalyst who has written with clarity and insight on learning to be yourself. She describes one stage in her life thus:

> I had learnt that if I kept my thoughts still enough and looked beneath them, then I might sometimes know what was the real need, feel it like a child leaping in the womb, though so remotely that I might easily miss it when over-busy with purposes. Really, then, I had found that there *was* an intuitive sense of how to live.

When people become self-aware, they begin to recognize their own nature. They no longer have to struggle to convince others, and particularly themselves, that they are somebody they are not, because they are beginning to glimpse the people they really are, their true selves. When they are able to *be* their real selves, they are as powerful as anyone in the world.

In this process it is inevitable that we face the darker sides of ourselves. Men have to deal with the negative aspects of the anima, and women have to deal with their animus – the equivalent archetype in the female psyche. The animus can criticize us or others to the point of making us feel worthless. When this happens to me and I feel at the bottom, the first thing I have to tell myself is that this will pass. Take heart, because it does pass. Then I try to speak to myself in the same voice that my heart would find to encourage an oppressed, distressed friend. I say only what is true, I invent nothing, and because what I say is true I can believe it. I try to say it with utter gentleness and compassion.

In dealing with the animus, we have to lift ourselves. Energy is necessary. A woman often has to build herself up to a point of assertion and revolt against this inner critic. She has to be defiant, self-assured and contentious against the animus. What sometimes happens is that the defiance is directed against the world, when first it needs to take care of this inner tyrant.

The positive side of the animus is to provide women with drive, discipline and clarity of thought. It is also a powerfully creative force which has good ideas. Through creative activity, if we *use* the animus instead of allowing it to possess us, it can build a bridge to our true self, guiding and accompanying the movements and transformations of the soul. Here is what Marie-Louise Von Franz says:

> If she reaches who and what her Animus is and what he does to her, and if she faces these realities instead of allowing herself to be possessed, her Animus can turn into an invaluable inner companion who endows her with the masculine qualities of initiative, courage, objectivity and spiritual wisdom . . . He gives the woman spiritual firmness, an invisible inner support that compensates for her outer softness. (Jung, 1964. B5)

Establishing our strong symbol

Having a personal symbol, a symbol of our true selves and of our own inner strength, can be a powerful asset. It can be visualized whenever we are feeling intimidated or powerless. Here is a short, simple exercise to find a symbol or image of your own power.

1 Take plenty of time for this exercise in quiet undisturbed space (take the phone off the hook) and play some favourite non-vocal music if you want to.
2 Lie down or sit very comfortably and relax your body, taking plenty of time. You may like to work through the body, starting by tensing and releasing the toes and working upwards to the top of the head and the scalp, tensing and releasing the muscles as you go.
3 Focus your attention on your breath, breathing in and out slowly and deeply.
4 Imagine light being drawn into your body on the 'in' breath through the

top of your head, and on the 'out' breath radiate the light to every muscle and cell of your body. Repeat this seven times with long, deep breaths.

5 Now focus your attention on your heart or your hara or wherever you feel your 'centre' to be. Ask yourself for an image, symbol, word, picture or sound that describes your inner self, your personal power. Allow yourself whatever time you need for this to emerge and do not force it. Whatever comes up is right for you, even if you do not immediately understand it.

6 When a symbol does become clear, acknowledge it and name it.

7 Gently return to your conscious mind and awareness by flexing your toes and fingers and stretching your limbs.

8 If your image is a visual one, try to draw it – you will be surprised at the results. If it is a sound, say or sing it. Whatever it is, be comfortable with it, own it and use it. You created it. It is yours. With practice and frequent use it will become more powerful. Should an image not arise, repeat the exercise another time. The symbol may come to you later (having stimulated the imaging process) while going about your daily business, daydreaming, relaxing or in a dream.

Guilt and blame drain us; taking responsibility gives us power

When we are ashamed of something, or sorry for it, for many of us the reaction is guilt. Guilt is destructive, useless and stagnant. As Emmanuel says, guilt 'means nothing and brings all things to a stop. There is a sense of blindness, of suffocation and aloneness. The world is opaque. There is seemingly no escape.'

The other reaction is to blame somebody else, to try to shift this same destructive, stagnant force away from ourselves to another. It does not work; it hangs heavy between us, and nobody feels any better. And we do not get out of the trap. Some wise person once said to me that if I felt guilty, it meant I was going to do it again!

The *only* way out of guilt and blame is responsibility. If I feel I have done something wrong, the first thing I can do is clean my heart by honest remorse. Then I can set about doing whatever I can do to put it right. It is amazing how this changes the energy from being very heavy to being quite electric.

If on the other hand I feel that someone else has done something wrong, and I blame them for hurting or wronging me, equally the only way out is responsibility. If I am blaming, I am a victim. There is absolutely no healthy payoff for claiming victimhood. Never. Ever. Even in an abusive relationship, the most effective may to get out is first to acknowledge my role in perpetuating it. By taking responsibility, I give myself the power to get out of the situation. Learning to accept responsibility for everything that happens to me in my life is a long, hard process, but it brings me freedom and it brings me power.

Feelings are vital

I used to feel slightly vulnerable and weak when writing about female traits. So I told a friend whom I trust.

'Why?' she said 'Female is strong.'

'Why?' I asked.

'Because we know about feelings'.

'Yeah,' I said, thinking how much flak we get for being emotional women. 'Why is it strong to know about feelings?'

'Because feelings are *vital*,' she replied. 'Some people find it genuinely difficult to get in touch with their feelings. So we have to keep a bright spotlight on them, keep them always in view.'

'But men say strength lies in discovering things, producing things, inventing things. If they stopped doing that and just attended to feelings, where would we be?' I asked feebly.

Her voice dropped and became full of force. She leaned towards me then, energy roaring out of her. 'Just notice what happens when feelings are ignored, obliterated. We get Hitlers. Hitler had zero feelings.' She made an O with her thumb and middle finger and looked at me through it. 'Everything was *perfectly* efficient. The trains ran on time. Munitions factories produced magnificently. Planes zoomed into the air. And millions of people died, in terror, in cold blood, on purpose. He meant for them to die. It was planned to the last detail. He had no feelings.'

Betty Reardon's view is that self-knowledge and self-acceptance are commonly avoided by men (and, I would add, by women too) because they are afraid of not being able to stand up to judgement. She thinks that many men who resort to violence continue to believe that they are fundamentally peace-loving, and that their violence is in the name of order and justice. This notion, she feels, is absolutely disastrous in stubborn world leaders in whom more self-knowledge could well mean a greater chance for human survival.

Women have to understand how difficult it is for men to find their feelings. Many have been trained since childhood to deny feelings, been ordered not to cry, not to be afraid, not to be sentimental. I have come to realize that it is probably about as difficult for some men to understand what they are feeling as it is for me to get my head round a theorem in physics.

We have been taught to be afraid of 'behaving irrationally' or 'being sentimental'. Anne Baring and Jules Cashford say in their book *The Myth of the Goddess* that if we are moved by the prospect of the rivers and seas full of factory waste, fish and seals dying, the trees withering from acid rain, the air clouded with smog, people across the world from us starving, then this should not be written off as sentimentality. The accompanying argument that these problems are too large to do anything about is actually a familiar strategy for shrugging off inner conflict. On the contrary, the feeling of horror or regret is healthy and natural, and may reflect an awareness of belonging to a unity, in which what happens in one part of the universe affects in some way what happens everywhere else.

A capacity for change and transformation is exactly what is needed in men and in women — men and women who want to learn about their feminine sides, to recognize their feelings, to tap into the brilliant short cuts offered by intuition, to release the power of their compassion. The fundamental challenge for us all is to release ourselves from fear, for as long as fear underlies our actions or reactions, we are imprisoned in a cycle of defence and offence and the need for *power over*. The only way to release ourselves from the fear is through love – learning to love our whole selves first as a precondition to being able truly to love another — and one of the best ways to learn to love ourselves is through self-knowledge.

As we near the end of this chapter, the snake again makes its appearance. Jean Shinoda Bolen, a Jungian analyst and Clinical Professor of Psychiatry at the University of California, tells us that whenever people begin to claim their own authority, or make decisions, or become aware of having a new sense of their own political or psychic or personal power, snake dreams are common.

> The snake seems to represent this new strength. As a symbol, it represents power once held by goddesses, as well as phallic or masculine power . . .

I had not read this when I saw the serpent in the Oxford river!

The Sanskrit word *kundalini* means 'coiled up' like a snake or spring. It implies latent power or untapped potential – the possibility within each person of attaining a new and more fulfilling condition of life. It is often seen as the inner female soul in serpent shape, coiled in the pelvis, which can be induced through the proper practice of yoga to uncoil and mount through the spinal chakras towards the head, bringing wisdom. In the ancient texts the *kundalini* is referred to as a vast mass of energy – infinite power residing within. That such an infinite reservoir of energy exists is not even imagined by Western science. Those who transform this force from its latent to its active form become the dynamic genii of every age and culture. As the energy is gradually released by means of carefully supervised exercises and meditation, the individual experiences an increasing sense of well-being and liberation, moving to peak experiences.

Although the word comes from the yogic tradition, nearly all the world's major religions, spiritual paths and most ancient traditions describe something akin to the *kundalini* experience as having significance in 'divinizing' a person.

What happens in yoga or meditation may be analogous to what happens in psychotherapy, in that parts of the unconscious are being brought into awareness. As we know, a great deal of energy is tied up in keeping repressed material repressed. This energy can be released and made once more accessible when the unconscious material is brought into consciousness.

I must now stress that all tools of power, whether yoga, meditation, psychotherapy or whatever, need to be handled with the greatest of care and respect. It is characteristic of Western misunderstanding of power that some Westerners have caused themselves harm, for example, by chasing the *kundalini* experience without due preparation and understanding. These processes are safe if they are undertaken slowly and gradually, with the best guidance available. They require time, patience and perseverance. In the section at the end of the book entitled 'Going Further', I offer descriptions and references for those techniques which I have found useful.

CHAPTER 5

Power from Within the Body

It is a tradition in which the flesh, instead of being subordinated to the spirit, is recognised as the basis for life, love and worship. Sexuality and spirituality are not opposed, but reconciled.

John White, 1990

This is a chapter about the body. A good part of it is devoted to sex and sensuality and to the links between power and sex, as I develop the main themes of the book. Both men and women can find in the body a source of inner strength, not to mention delight. Being a woman I can only really describe power from within the body from a woman's point of view, but I hope that male readers will find all the sections useful. There is no particular order to the chapter, which includes sections on sexual attraction, sex and power, liberation from sexual guilt, menstruation, birth and caring, wisdom and freedom, understanding menopause, and death.

Many women are brought up to think that their body functions are at best a nuisance, at worst a curse, and to be kept firmly hidden from view. The only power we might acknowledge is the power of attraction, the power to pull men, and most of us believe that comes out of bottles, sprays and clothes shops. So how do we transform nuisance and curse into power and strength? Adrienne Rich suggests we begin to

> . . . think through the body, to connect what has been so cruelly disorganised – our great mental capacities hardly used, our highly developed tactile sense, our genius for close observation, our complicated, pain-enduring, multi-pleasured physicality . . .

Sexual attraction and power

There is a big power issue in attraction. It is worth examining briefly the different types of attraction people feel for each other, to see where and how power is involved, and whether it is power *over* or power *with*. It seems to me there are at least four types, although most actual attractions are a mixture of more than one.

General arousal/desire of the senses

This happens at parties, festivals, dances, entertainments and so on, and on warm summer evenings in delightful natural surroundings. It may happen when those around us are sexually aroused, when our imaginations have been stimulated by creative art or good news, when there is excitement of various kinds in the air. In this situation, we are ready to respond to our own or another's excitement in a general way – any partner may do. This kind of attraction is linked to the wish to touch, to stroke. As with a cat, we do not necessarily expect anything back; we just want to enjoy the beauty, to hear it purring, to have it in our lap for a time. We know quite well that after a while it will jump off and go and tear up some poor bird. James Joyce called these aesthetic/erotic experiences 'epiphanies' – the whole point being not to possess (which he called pornography) but to hold something beautiful and experience its rhythm. Assuming it does not turn into lust (which I think belongs with possession), it seems to me that power issues are probably absent here.

Craving

This is when we are magnetized to a person and we don't quite know why. That person suddenly becomes everything we desire in life: we want them as if to fill a hole in our soul. This is projection – we are putting out into someone else our own ideal internal man or woman. It can easily become infatuation. In this case, the infatuated person has as it were handed power over to the other. It makes people do extraordinary things. It is the desperate search for a lost part of the self in another. A well-known example would be Cathy and Heathcliff in *Wuthering Heights*. It is often a one-way attraction, and in spite of its initial intensity, eventually dies away unless reciprocated.

Glamour and possession

This is when a powerful or glamorous person is attractive because of the respect or awe in which others hold him or her, or because of the status to be gained by being associated with such a person – in short, domination power. This attractiveness feeds on itself: the more successful the person is in attracting others, the more attractive she or he becomes. Men compete to be seen with a woman who 'looks like a million dollars'. Women feel they will gain power by seducing a powerful man. This is seldom a calculating response; glamour can be irresistible. This kind of attraction usually leads to a wish for possession.

Possession is when we want to *own* someone, *have* them. Often when we've succeeded, we become tired, we're not interested any more; the attraction was in the challenge and the hunt. Or, in the case of many women, possession can turn into dependence, entrapment, holding on. I think that this type of attraction is an example of power *over*.

Love

This is reciprocal, equal, trusting hara power attraction. Surrender is safe. We know someone else's inner self, and we find there qualities that we want and can rely on absolutely. The feeling is one of nostalgia, of something deeply longed for, precious, familiar. This kind of attraction can mature and develop over many years and is usually nourishing to both people.

Love is the most complex of the four types of attraction, since its course never did run smooth. It needs self-sacrifice, but not too much, and gentleness, but not too much, and toughness, but not too much. Hara power, which reduces guilt and egoism, can help to get these balances right. And love can help us acquire hara power. Hara power can help the reaction to general arousal too, by liberating people from guilt, and encouraging everyone's openness and self-understanding. Its honesty and humour can defeat phoney glamour. We may be unable to help being infatuated with someone, but hara power should allow both the infatuated and the object of infatuation to understand what is going on, to see the funny side of it and to know that it is a transient state.

Domination power is obviously closely tied up with the idea of possession. It can exploit general arousal and infatuation too. But it is opposed to love, because of a fear of the letting-go which love requires, a fear of openness and equality.

Sex and power

In our Western culture the prevailing attitude to sex is to tend to treat others as objects. People settle for gratification by 'using' a partner. Pornography is an extreme example of this kind of 'object' sex, and is very isolating for those involved. I think this has come about because for a long time we have accepted a predominantly mechanistic approach to sex, that is, one which tends to separate soul and mind from body. Thus, the body may receive gratification, but the rest of the person remains distanced.

The alternative would be an approach in which the whole person – mind, body and spirit – is present in sex, and in which the body again becomes central to our daily lives in every sense, not simply tucked away and ignored except when we want gratification.

So, when sexual attraction develops into physical sexuality and lovemaking, you and I have a choice. We can approach sex as separate beings intending to remain separate, with souls and minds somewhere else, or we can approach it as an opportunity for union and wholeness. I think the two approaches correspond to the domination mode and the hara mode. In bed, I would say domination mode might manifest as follows:

* I want you to think me beautiful/sexy/desirable.
* I am using you as a means to my satisfaction.
* I am more concerned with my physical sensations than yours.
* We progress in a series of stages mounting to orgasm, and I am basically in charge.
* I keep my eyes shut and do not talk to you.
* I want you to think I am the best lover ever.
* This is a serious business.
* When I have had an orgasm, that's it and I can go to sleep.

Hara mode, by contrast, would manifest more in the following feelings and attitudes:

* I accept my body and appreciate it.
* We are very aware of each other, and find ways of checking if the other wants to continue or drift off to sleep.

* We cuddle a lot and tell each other how we feel.
* The whole thing has its funny side.
* We do not much mind whether lovemaking includes orgasm or not; it is the closeness that matters.
* Lovemaking is not a means to something, it is an end in itself.
* I am prepared to surrender, because I trust you.
* I want to become one with you, not remain as two; I want to move into the act so deeply that the actor is no more.
* We stay in the present, not in the future; we remain in the moment, going nowhere, and melt.

There is something else to say in connection with hara power and sex, and it concerns loving the self. Many of us assume that the key to sexual fulfilment lies in finding the right partner. If only the right man or woman would come along, our lovemaking would be wonderful. I doubt if this is true. I believe that the poverty or richness of my sexual experience is up to me. No one can *give* me sexual ecstasy; it comes from within. Instead of looking outside for the perfect partner, I can first simply give to myself everything that I would give to my beloved. Try it. In her book *The Art of Sexual Ecstasy*, Margot Anand explains in detail how to open yourself up to new feelings of self-acceptance and self-esteem.

> Loving yourself in this way does not mean being self-absorbed or narcissistic, or disregarding others. Rather, it means welcoming yourself as the most honoured guest in your own heart, a guest worthy of respect, a lovable companion. Your Inner Lover is not separate from yourself, nor is he or she a dreamlike phenomenon. Your Inner Lover is more like a quality, a feeling, that you can recognise in moments of joy or stillness when, deep inside yourself, you connect with a natural innocence, simplicity and spontaneity. (B10)

In chapter 7 I will return to this notion of the Inner Lover, and explore further the whole question of hara power and sexual union. Now let us look at something that runs through most people's lives like a thread from beginning to end: sexual guilt.

Liberation from sexual guilt

'Me?' you may say. 'I don't feel guilty about sex.' Well, I'm really happy if you don't. But just to be sure, try out a few questions:

* Do you ever feel bad after having had a sexual fantasy?

* Is there any erotic part of your body you do not find beautiful?
* Have you ever faked an orgasm?
* Do you have any problem making love in your parents' house?

If your answers to all these questions is an unqualified no, then you are a person blessed. If like me you answer a wobbly yes to some or all, read on. I cannot attempt to address individual backgrounds for sexual guilt; they are deep in each psyche and sometimes need skilled help to find and come to terms with. What I can do is paint a picture of how it was before we were landed with carrying this burden of sin for what is a natural instinct, and suggest some ways to put the burden down.

The naked body, in all its manifestations, used to be considered powerful and beautiful, especially the genitals. We can still find evidence of a reverence for female genitals turning up in the most unexpected of places. In old churches all over England and Ireland there are *sheela-na-gigs* – ancient stone carvings depicting a crouching woman reaching down with bold confidence and holding open her vulva.

The sheela-na-gig *from the Church of St Mary and St David, Kilpeck, Herefordshire, England*

Her origins are obscure. No one really knows what these carvings mean, but she is remembered in Ireland as the Old Woman Creatrix who gave birth to all races. *Sheela-na-gigs* are particularly welcome in the Christian context, because of their frankness, in contrast to the more usual equation of female sexuality with temptation and sin.

Mary Magdalene has been portrayed by the Church as a prostitute, a sinner who was 'forgiven' by Jesus, whereas the Gnostic Gospels show her to have been one of Jesus's disciples. In her turn, Mary Magdalene is inextricably linked to the meaning and power of black madonnas. These compelling and mysterious statues are to be found all over the world and offer us a link between Christianity, sexuality and the far more ancient belief in the black goddess.

If images are helpful, fiction is certainly helpful too. Here's a passage which took me by surprise:

> She rode bareback, always, he tells me, as we sit on a boulder in the park in the middle of an afternoon hike. She experienced orgasm while riding the horse.
>
> Are you sure? I ask.
>
> Yes, he says. She swooned. And when I asked her, she admitted it.
>
> I am speechless at the thought that any woman's pleasure might be found so easily, I stammer; so, in a sense, *carelessly*.
>
> The word you are looking for, says Pierre, is *wantonly. Loosely.* A woman who is sexually 'unrestrained,' according to the dictionary, is by definition 'lascivious, wanton and loose.' But why is that? A man who is sexually unrestrained is simply a man. (Alice Walker, 1992, page 169)

Besides absorbing and reading of course, we can do some physical liberating too. There are so many ways to do this. Simply dancing is a good start. Find somewhere where you will be undisturbed; put on whatever mood of music seems right – dreamy, haunting or a heavy pulsing beat – and just let the body do what it wants to do, being as primitive as it feels like being.

Others may prefer going deep into their bodies through yoga or t'ai chi. T'ai chi is an ancient tradition of a series of graceful, powerful movement of the entire body helping to liberate and sense the flow of energy through the body. Alternatively, some people enjoy the Alexander technique, in which a teacher shows how to make postural adjustments to liberate the full potential of the body. For me it has been yoga. I first came across the concept of the hara in yoga (exercises for strengthening the hara can be found on page 81). I like the quietness, the concentration and the feeling of stretching myself. I have learned to feel my breathing throughout my body. Simply becoming aware of parts of my body has been liberating. There is one fascinating exercise where I learned to tense and relax all three genital orifices – the urethra, the vagina and the anus – *separately*! It's amazing what this can do for a person's sexuality.

The possibilities are endless. There are now all sorts of ways of listening to, learning from and loosening up the body which come under the collective name of 'body work', and some of these are listed in the notes to this chapter.

I want to return now to the issue of weight. I touched on this in chapter 3, when discussing negative body images and the thin models which are forever before our eyes as images of female beauty. Perhaps the time has come to let the body be what it wants to be, to let it be its natural weight. To diet for health reasons is one thing; to diet to try to match an image has to be a negation of the self. Big women are big women. Dawn French has got it right:

> The point I am trying to make is that big women are sexual creatures. Big women are good at sex. There is something about weight and sex that makes it all work. Maybe it's just gravity, but it all works *well*.

She adds:

> I wanted the people who are married to fat girls or the fathers and sisters of fat girls to stop thinking of them as victims. They are people who could value themselves if, occasionally, they could be celebrated in a way that meant something to them.

Jenny Saville is a young artist aged 23. She paints women as they are, and Charles Saatchi is paying her to keep on doing it. She says that the history of art has been dominated by men, living in ivory towers and seeing women as sexual objects. She paints women as most women see themselves. She tries to catch their identity, their skin, their hair, their heat, their leakiness.

Here is a rather different picture – an example from Mexico of how life can be for women today.

> For seven days and nights during the spring Velas (Candles) fiesta in Juchitan, southern Mexico, Zapotec Indian women dance in a celebration of ancient fertility rites and to confirm their matriarchal power. The women of Juchitan are very different from their Mexican sisters. Here, it is the women and not the men who rule. They are the head of the household, they control the finances, and they dominate the men physically too. Huge and sensual, their size is a status symbol and not a reason to feel ashamed.

The women freely take lovers. One of them commented, 'Fatness is a sign of a woman's sexual energy and lack of inhibitions in bed'.

The isthmus where the Zapotec live never became part of the Spanish Empire, and this may be a reason for the survival of these traditions, including the wise women or *curandera* witches, who heal with the aid of elemental energies.

We in the West have a long way to go to reinhabit our bodies with delight and pride. Take every opportunity to learn to know and value your body more. For example, next time you are in a sunny place, with a bit of privacy, try this. It is best if you can do it in a room where the sun is streaming in through an open window or door, and where you are sure of peace and privacy. Lie down on your front with a pillow under your solar plexus, and widen your legs as far as they will go. Feel the warmth of the sun entering you; absorb its power and strength and make it your own. Feel it on your perineum (that is the strong muscle in front of the anus) and tighten that muscle and relax it. Enjoy the mystery and receptiveness of your body.

Menstruation

Barbara Walker, in the *Woman's Encyclopedia of Myths and Secrets*, takes us on a tour of the entire world through the ages with her extraordinary research on menstruation. What she has to say had my eyes popping out of my head, as it began to dawn on me that our negative attitudes to menstruation are in fact quite recent. For example, menstrual blood occupied a central position in all mother goddess cultures.

In ancient Mesopotamia, the Great Goddess Ninhursag made mankind out of clay and infused it with her 'blood of life'. Apparently she taught women to form clay dolls and smear them with menstrual blood as a conception charm, a piece of magic that underlay the name of Adam, from the feminine *adamah*, meaning 'bloody clay,' though scholars more delicately translate it as 'red earth'. According to Barbara Walker, Egyptian pharaohs became divine by ingesting 'the blood of Isis,' a soma-like ambrosia called *sa*. Its hieroglyphic sign was the same as the sign of the vulva, a yonic loop like the one on the Cross of Life. Painted red, this loop signified the female genital and the Gate of Heaven. Amulets buried with the dead specifically asked Isis to deify the deceased with her magic blood.

Later, the lives of the gods in the Greek pantheon were dependent on the power of menstrual blood. In Greece it was euphemistically called the 'supernatural red wine' given to the gods by Mother Hera in her virgin form, as Hebe. The root myths of Hinduism reveal the nature of this 'wine'. At one time all gods recognized the supremacy of the Great Mother, manifesting herself as the spirit of creation (Kali-Maya). She 'invited them to bathe in the bloody flow of her womb and to drink of it; and the gods, in holy communion, drank of the fountain of life and bathed in it, and rose blessed to the heavens.' To this day, cloths allegedly stained with the Goddess's menstrual blood are greatly prized as healing charms.

In Chinese Taoism a man could become immortal by absorbing menstrual blood, called red yin juice, from a woman's 'mysterious gateway'. Walker reports that Chinese sages called this red juice the essence of Mother Earth, the yin principle that gives life to all things. They claimed the Yellow Emperor became a god by absorbing the yin juice of 1,200 women.

In ancient societies, both East and West, menstrual blood carried the spirit of sovereign authority because it was the medium of transmission of the life of clan or tribe. Among the Ashanti, girl children are still more prized than boys because a girl is the carrier of 'blood' (*mogya*). The concept is also clearly defined in India, where menstrual blood is known as the *kula* flower or *kula* nectar, which has an intimate connection with the life of the family. When a girl first menstruates, she is said to have 'borne the Flower'.

The British goddess of flowers was Blodeuwedd, a form of the Triple Goddess associated with sacrifices of ancient kings. Welsh legend said her whole body was made of flowers – as any body was, according to the ancient theory of body formation from the blood flower.

Easter eggs, classic womb-symbols of the goddess Eostre, were traditionally coloured red and laid on graves to strengthen the dead. Walker thinks that this habit, common in Greece and southern Russia, might be traced all the way back to Palaeolithic graves and funeral furnishings reddened with ochre, for a closer resemblance to the Earth Mother's womb from which the dead could be 'born again'. Ancient tombs everywhere have shown the bones of the dead covered with red ochre. Sometimes everything in the tomb, including the walls, had the red colour. J D Evans described a well tomb on Malta filled with reddened bones, which struck fear into the workmen who insisted the bones were covered with 'fresh blood'.

Glastonbury in Somerset is the site of a conical hill long associated with the goddess. Kathy Jones, who has researched its history, describes Chalice Well, which is found at the foot of Chalice Hill,

> where the Red Waters of Birth and Menstruation flow from Her body at a constant rate of 25,000 gallons an hour and at a temperature of 52 degrees

F. Full of the iron of Her blood these are healing waters, which in the 18th century brought people in their thousands to drink and bathe in search of miracle cures. (B3)

The waters flow down through the gardens splashing into a large vesica-piscis-shaped basin, near the gate, before flowing out beneath the town, along Chilkwell Street, and to the Abbey. The vesica piscis symbol is composed of two interlocking circles, whose overlapping arcs form the vulva of the goddess. This has become an important figure in sacred architecture. In some traditions it signifies the Womb of Life, with the overlapping circles conveying the world of duality.

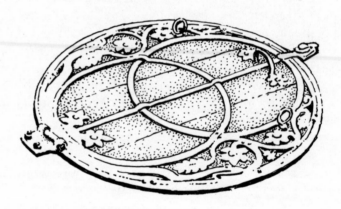

Sketch of the cover of the vesica piscis basin at Chalice Well

This ancient veneration, awe, mystery and wonder associated with menstruation has changed over recent centuries into the opposites – revulsion, horror, taboo and fear. In chapter 2, I recounted some of the taboos against menstrual blood and menstruating women and how they have developed over much of the globe. The knowledge that these taboos have not always been, and that in fact the entire human race thought quite differently about female blood for thousands of years, may help us shift our present attitudes.

There was, and there is still, something awesome and mysterious in the fact that women bleed regularly without being wounded, and without dying. Menstrual blood does not clot like other blood. When our ancestors split the powerful mother goddess idea into two, the White Goddess was pure and the Dark Goddess was the one who menstruated. It may be that now we can reclaim some of the power of the Dark Goddess in reclaiming the strengths of menstruation.

> The Dark Goddess at the red pole of a woman's nature speaks to an aspect of a woman's femininity that is self-directed, uncompromising, powerful, and impersonal. She has the audacity to focus inward rather than to relate to others. At the menstrual time the power of a woman's erotic sexuality can be used for transformation, renewal, divination, healing, and magic rather than procreation. (Demetra George, 1992, page 207. B3)

I had no idea I had such powers, until I tried an experiment. After I had read Lara Owen's book *Her Blood is Gold*, I decided that, come hell or high water, I would take the necessary space and time to give my body and my self what they needed during my next period. It wasn't easy. Since I was nearing menopause, and my periods were irregular, I couldn't plan. I had meetings scheduled in London on the second day, when I knew the flow would be heavy. Since I was brought up to 'think nothing' of my period, cancelling those meetings was especially difficult because it felt to me as though I was treating myself as *ill*, which I clearly wasn't. I was well, although I felt heavy, a band between my two hip joints felt as though it was dragging me down and in, and my focus was definitely inward.

I would normally have been dashing from train to tube, desperately locating toilets for each hourly change, gasping at the sight of stairs (I want to go upstairs on all fours when I have a period), and utterly exhausted by evening. Instead I took the day off and sat in my favourite armchair with a hot water bottle in the small of my back, my foot on a footrest, and read books. I felt magnificent sitting there. I made myself the food I liked. I didn't even disturb myself for the telephone if I didn't want to. I thought about what I did want. And I *day-dreamed*. It is not something workaholics admit to easily, daydreaming. But it was extraordinary what it produced. On days 3 and 4 of my period I sometimes fell deep in reverie, and there I found, drifting apparently out of nowhere, solutions to problems I had been tussling with for years. I had two ideas for a book I was writing, which came like shooting stars, arriving in front of me and showering golden rain around the place. Undeniably something out of the ordinary was going on.

The revelation, as Lara Owen says, is that menstruation is a source of power. She offers the following guidelines for menstruating women:

> Stay still inside and let the blood flow out. See your womb as an opening flower, full of fierce pink light, sending out a special sweet rosy energy into

the world, which cleans and nourishes. Let the beauty blood spill onto the earth. Trust the wisdom of the body's cycle. Honour it. Go with what your body wants to do. Take gentle peaceful exercise in quiet places. Listen to slow flowing water, the tinkle of a fountain in a stone-flagged square. Take a slow look and a slow movement. Turn your head gently. Stroke yourself. Let all your movements be soft and serene. Speak with gentleness. No fights. Eat simple food: grains and vegetables and broth. Nothing too rich or sweet or milky. Drink pure water, savouring the taste and clearness. Go inside, deep inside, and allow any murkiness to be seen and to flow out. A time of clearing out and of taking in. Be alert to information for the coming month. Relax. Be soft. Slow down. Open your womb, your thighs, your knees, your ankles, your toes. Open your heart. By opening, let go, let the blood flow. (B1)

Dr John Collee has calculated that in ancient societies (and today in poor countries) a woman would probably menstruate no more than 45 times in her life, because of successive pregnancies, poor nutrition and prolonged lactation. Now in the West she can expect to menstruate 450 times. Whether he is precisely right or not, the point is that we now have about ten times as much menstrual time as our ancestresses. This is a vast change, and one we can use fruitfully.

We can *choose* to find wisdom and power in bleeding, the wisdom and power of moving in cycles, like nature, instead of always at the same revs, like a machine. I am one of those people who are driven by the entirely deluded notion that they have to try and save the world. This has made me keep myself going for months and years on end at the same frenetic pace, driving myself always to write the next letter, finish the next draft, attend the next meeting, persuade the next person – and on to the next and the next. I apparently get a lot done but, I am beginning to wonder, at what cost? And what is the quality of what I do? And, most of all, where am I going to? Because *there is always more* – always more suffering to care for, always more injustice to try to stand up to, always more pain.

You will have your own areas of frenetic activity. Intense levels of energy, as Lucy Goodison points out, cannot be sustained indefinitely without dissipating or becoming destructive. She feels we need to recharge if we are to remain effective in personal or political activity. It is not difficult to 'burn ourselves out' through unremitting work. It can help to recognize the power that comes from clarity, the power that comes from resting, as well as the power that comes from using our full resources actively. There is the analogy of the bow string: if the bow is kept permanently ready to fire, the string will eventually stretch and lose its strength. In this connection the Taoist principle of *wu-wei* is very helpful. It is the way of non-action, of 'effortless effort', and places the emphasis on being rather than doing.

I shall return to the subject of burn-out at the end of chapter 10. The need for resting, for waiting, for letting go, is one that all of creation has. Men go through cycles too, and benefit from the nourishment that regular times of deep reflection can give. To move *with* our cycles, rather than *in spite* of them, must make sense when we stop and think about it. And it generates power. A straight line of activity, constantly under heavy stress, must eventually crack; whereas a cycle, which alternates between high and low pressure, which moves between different states, has flexibility and fluidity. And fluidity has a lot to do with the new kind of power we are talking about.

Birth and caring

Some women give birth to one child during their lives, some to many, and some give birth to ideas, to art, to artefacts. Some women and men are midwives to others' children and others' ideas. Some women and men care for their own children, some for the children of others, some for those who are not able to care for themselves.

None of these activities is highly valued in our society. There are prizes for the businessman of the year, the top 100 companies, best author, actor, TV programme, best documentary even, the most floral town in Britain, the most beautiful/sexy woman, the best dressed man – but who ever heard of the Marvellous Midwife of the Year, the Queen's Award Scheme for Parenting, the Creative Carer of the County, the Mighty Mum of the Municipality? Does the Prime Minister come and open the local Well Woman Clinic? All those people pushing wheelchairs on outings to the zoo – who gives them medals?

These examples serve to point out how little we even think of these talents – we assume that people should just instinctively know how to care for a child, a sick person or an elderly person. We somehow assume that care and compassion are easy. Without really thinking, we put people who care for others at the bottom of the pile, whereas the competitors get the applause, the media coverage, the attention, the valuing, the recognition.

The experience of giving birth is rich in the kinds of female strength we are interested in. Look at photographs of the faces of mothers during and after birth. They show precisely how both faces of the goddess can be found in one person – the raging howl of pain, and the tenderness so strong it reaches to the middle of you. See how the body simply takes over with its power: once contractions have started, the woman's mind becomes impotent to stop them. In giving birth, a woman has to acknowledge her body's power and surrender to it: the more she does so, the easier the birth. When she has done this, a woman has one concrete living experience of the power within her body.

It is vitally important for women to free themselves from the 'bad mother' syndrome. The weight of guilt that women carry for the needs and desires of others is already much too much, without adding the impossibility of being a perfect mother. There is by definition no such thing as a perfect mother. We could not, whatever we did, meet every one of an infant's needs. When I was beating myself up psychologically for my failures as a mother, I was much comforted by the notion that perfect mothers do not exist, and that what children thrive on is a 'good enough' mother. The change that needs to happen is for parenting to be shared, with the emphasis on 'good enough' parents, so that there is no longer the search for the perfect mother, and inevitable disappointment.

Men and childbirth

There is no doubt that some men are envious of women's power to give birth and to breast feed. A bond is being created between mother and child that a man feels he cannot emulate. Carol Cohn found evidence among nuclear scientists that suggested men's desire to appropriate from women the power of giving life.

> The bomb project is rife with images of male birth. In December 1942, Ernest Lawrence's telegram to the physicists at Chicago read, 'Congratulations to the new parents. Can hardly wait to see the new arrival.' At Los Alamos, the atom bomb was referred to as 'Oppenheimer's baby' . . . In the light of the imagery of male birth, the extraordinary names given to the bombs that reduced Hiroshima and Nagasaki to ash and rubble – 'Little Boy' and 'Fat Man' – at last become intelligible. These ultimate destroyers were the progeny of the atomic scientists – and emphatically not just any progeny but male progeny. In early tests, before they were certain that the bombs would work, the scientists expressed

their concern by saying that they hoped the baby was a boy, not a girl – that is, not a dud . . . In 1952, Teller's exultant telegram to Los Alamos announcing the successful test of the hydrogen bomb, *Mike*, at Eniwetok Atoll in the Marshall Islands, read, 'It's a boy.' The nuclear scientists gave birth to male progeny with the ultimate power of violent domination over female Nature. (B6)

There is little that can be done about the fact that a woman can conceive and give birth and a man cannot. But there is a lot that can be done, and is being done, to involve men in the process of birth and in every aspect of child-care that follows, except breast feeding. When it becomes the norm, as is rapidly happening in the West, for men to be seen proudly in charge of infants, then men's involvement with child-care will be less of a threat to those who have stood distant from it until now.

If we subscribe even mildly to the idea that the elemental power of the female body is what men most fear, then the rediscovery of that power may provoke, may already be provoking, a significant reaction among men. Some people argue that the increasing incidence of (reported) rape and violence against women is a direct result of their continuing emancipation.

The last thing our society needs is to emasculate men. We need them to be more masculine in the sense of real masculinity, masculinity which does not need to resort to violence, non-macho masculinity. We need role models of men who are heroes without killing – men like Nelson Mandela, Vaclav Havel, Bob Geldof.

The same is true with caring. Caring can be done as well by men as by women. I heard recently the story of a man called Jack who lives in Huddersfield. In his mid-thirties he married a woman who had lung cancer, aware that she was dying slowly and painfully. He gave up his job and nursed her for 35 years. When she died, he then looked after her mother.

When the carer is respectful of an individual's own movement towards health and autonomy – what Carl Rogers calls the 'self-actualizing tendency' – then there is no tendency to instruct – to *tell* the child, patient or client what to do. Simply being in such a relationship brings about change. Parents know this in their experience with children. We spend days *telling* a child not to do something, and he or she will go on doing it, overtly or covertly. And then one day when we are relaxed and in a good mood and spend time really *with* the child, actually listening to what he or she has to say, something quite different happens. The space between us changes, the child appears to blossom, *we* blossom. And in that space, merely by listening and by answering questions truthfully, we connect with the child. And the telling is no longer necessary.

Wisdom and freedom

The Crone was the third of the Triple Goddess's three aspects (maiden, mother and crone) and was usually a Goddess of Wisdom (Minerva, Athene, Metis, Sophia, and Medusa are examples). Of course, with this wisdom comes old age, and when women became objects of fear, it was the negative and frightening aspects of old age which were emphasized in depictions of the crone. So to us today the word 'crone' suggests a wrinkled, ugly, frightening hag. But the ancient belief was that post-menopausal women were the wisest of mortals because they permanently retained their wise blood.

Barbara Walker says that in the 17th century, Christian writers still insisted that old women were filled with magic power because their menstrual blood remained in their veins. This was the real reason why old women were constantly persecuted for witchcraft. The same 'magic blood' that made them leaders in the ancient clan system made them objects of fear under the new patriarchal faith.

Yes, of course, some of us do seem a bit mad in menopause. We may indeed be difficult to understand; we find it difficult to understand *ourselves*. That is because of the enormity of the transformation, which is at the same time a vast opportunity, that we are going through. The salvation, for me, has been the challenge to learn to love myself. Right now when I may to our current cultural perceptions be at my least lovable – unpredictable, insecure, jealous and wrinkly – right now is my chance to extend to myself the gifts I have been giving to others – compassion, appreciation, encouragement, humour, simple kindness.

I also need to know there's a point to it all. Lara Owen is helpful:

a post menopausal woman is wise because she has menstruated for thirty or forty years, and during that time she was a gatherer of wisdom. Now, having gathered it in, she sits on it and lets it build, fortified by the experience of her lifetime. A lifetime of garnering wisdom every month leads to a wise old age. The perpetual round of the menstrual cycle tunes a woman in to the pulse of the earth and the rays of the moon. It gives her the knowing, in her body, of the cyclical nature of all life. Now that women can realistically expect to live for at least twenty to thirty years past menopause, as a culture we have a potentially vast resource of wise women, if we would only use it. (B1)

I badly need positive images of women my age. I do not mean nice pictures of grannies looking serene and innocuous, or well-behaved grey-haired retired persons taking day trips, but images which show some of the pain, the fierceness and the power of growing older. There are not many, and Käthe Kollwitz conveys something of what I mean.

'Seed Corn Must Not Be Ground' by Käthe Kollwitz, 1942

Now, in the closing years of the 20th century, is a good time to be old. As a proportion of the population, there are more old people than ever before. In 1994 half of the English people entitled to vote were over 45; while 45 is not old, this is certainly a mature whole half of the voting population, and vast power lies in that. Life expectancy for women in the 15th century was 30 years, and reaching menopause was extremely rare. Now a significant percentage of the population of Europe and the Western world consists of women over 60. With all that combined wisdom, there is a great deal we can do.

In essence, what happens in menopause is liberation. Women are freed from child-bearing and the worry of conception. The problem is that they have been given to understand that what they go through is a disease, 'something wrong' with them. What they have not been given is support, encouragement and recognition to make one of life's three vital transitions. When the child becomes a woman this is generally welcomed, when the woman becomes a mother, this is celebrated. When the mother becomes free of her fertility, there is nothing. We are completely silent about it. In fact, we have no word at all in our language to describe her which does not have negative connotations. Even the two words 'old' and 'woman' – non-pejorative when used separately – have a definite negative ring when put together.

The reason our society thinks so little of her is directly connected with our view of power. I have shown that the kind of power a woman has in our society is to attract and fascinate men. So, when men find her less attractive, when she gets fewer of the everyday signals of interest, she feels her power going – the only power she may ever have known.

> The problem at menopause is not that the woman no longer feels sexual desire, but that her ability to arouse sexual desire in others is waning. It is her feminine power that is at stake, not her sexual capacity. (Ann Mankowitz, 1984, page 53. B8)

In fact, the sexuality of older women is the best kept secret on earth. What magazine article tells you that at 50 a woman is more sensual and more erotic than at 25? And she still has at least 25 sexually active years left, if she wants them.

> With current life expectancy, the average woman in the West has about twenty-five sexually active years in front of her after the decay of the ovaries and the ending of the fertility cycle. Women, and society, must adjust to this. We cannot go back to spending one-quarter of our lives, perhaps the sexiest time of our lives, as asexual zombies. (Monica Sjoo and Barbara Mor, 1987, page 198. B3)

Puberty, childbirth and menopause are 'gateways' when everything is changing so much in our bodies that we have the opportunity to access deeper states, to become wiser. Menopause is linked to the theme of becoming whole in the self, of having an inner understanding of the masculine and feminine principles. It's an initiation into the magical phase of womanhood, where there's a graciousness, a stillness, an integrity born of inner acceptance. We must be true to ourselves, responsible for what we take on, without expectations, making our own boundary lines clear, not deviating from our sense of our own integrity.

Understanding menopause

So it is a great moment, perhaps the greatest opportunity in a woman's life, to examine her real power and enhance it. The first step is to mourn what she has lost or is losing. The ability to bear children is a great gift, and whether or not a woman has been given or used this gift, its disappearance is a loss. If the pain is not felt and expressed it will remain.

The second step is to comprehend what is happening and be compassionate with oneself. I think this is vital – having the time (making the time) to take care of one's needs, and finding the emotional energy to understand. For example, hot flushes are very confusing. They come without warning. I felt (I didn't always look) scarlet from top to toe. And then they vanish, all for no apparent reason.

Some male doctors say hot flushes are a 'design flaw' in the female system. How dare they! Just because it is not yet clear to us what causes them, it is outrageous to treat them as a fault. I became very interested in them. It helped to have a supportive partner and female lodger, because I could talk about a hot flush as I was having it. Since they asked me questions and were equally intrigued, I was able to discover gradually that, for me at any rate, a hot flush always came up with a strong emotion behind it. It wasn't usually evident on the surface – I didn't think I was afraid, or angry, or lonely – but if I looked down deep, I found there was always something going on. And what was even more intriguing: I didn't know about these powerful emotions until I got the flush. So the flush was like a marker flag, saying 'Listen here, attend to this,' and bringing the emotion up.

For example, I had one when I was eating chips in Ealing Broadway. It happened as I was reading a sentence in a book which said, 'No money, no housing, no skills, no confidence.' I had been feeling worried that writing down my experiences seemed hopelessly middle class and out of touch with the lives of most women. I was wondering how much use this book could be. 'No confidence'! The emotion underneath the flush was fear.

So, like Chairman Mao, I began to keep a Little Red Book of hot flushes – and tried to note down most of them as soon after they happened as possible, so that I could pay proper attention to them. I found that they often occurred when I was berating myself for something – as if awakening me to the fact that I was doing it. I'm so accustomed to my inner critic that I often don't even notice it – I just assume what it is saying is fact. So I need to be made aware, or make myself aware, of the destructive part of that voice. Then I can do something about it.

Then I began to wonder whether the whole of menopause may be a cleansing process – getting rid of these negative emotions by becoming aware of them, 'flushing out' the system as it were. All this sweating must be immensely cleansing! Like a rite of passage before entering a new phase of life.

> The current obsession with staving off menopause through the use of hormone replacement therapy misses the point that there is an inherent value in ceasing to menstruate. I wonder if women need to prolong their menstrual experience because they never really had it – because they spent their periods pretending that nothing was happening. Perhaps the desire to continue to bleed is actually an unconscious attempt to complete that part of life. (Lara Owen, 1993. B1)

The third step is getting as much support as possible. I found I needed support and help. I wanted what I was going through to be acknowledged. I wanted to be properly heard. I had to ask for it, very clearly and distinctly, and then I got it.

The fourth step is to nourish oneself – one's body, mind and spirit. There are big changes going on in the body, almost a reconfiguring of its structure. So there will be more aches than usual for a while. Menopausal women need extra vitamins and extra calcium: a new diet where these needs can be met as much as possible from natural sources is a great lift in itself. Eating more raw food may be difficult at first, but it does a lot of morale boosting things besides providing vitamins – it makes the body feel energetic, makes the eyes sparkle, makes us feel a bit more in the mood to invest in a bit of our own nonsense.

Dr Caroline Shreeve's book *Overcoming the Menopause Naturally* showed me exactly how to feel better. I did what it said, and it worked. I changed my diet to include more whole foods, more raw foods and less caffeine; sorted out which vitamins and minerals I needed; took regular and proper exercise and, most important of all, gave myself the time I needed to relax, to ponder and to reflect on what was going on. The body needs taking care of in ways which might not have been considered before. A person may wish to try natural remedies and treatments which are especially helpful in menopause; some of these are described in the section 'Going Further' at the end of the book.

Women going through such a big change also need food for their minds: nourishment to help make the transition from the person you knew yourself as, to the new one. Nourishment to help find out what she is like. This may come in the form of literature – stories where the central characters are older women, as in Mary Wesley or May Sarton. There are now anthologies of writings for women going into their new age, and some are very funny.

Most of all, perhaps, we need nourishment for our souls. It is in the spirit that the real power of the older person develops. We shall discuss this further in the next chapter, but in the case of anyone in transition, it is especially important to listen for directions from inside. The spirit knows the way it needs and wants to go: if we can just be quiet and listen to it, honour it, it will tell us. But inside is where we will find our peace, and ultimately our power. I read with real excitement the last chapter of Germaine Greer's book on *The Change*, the chapter entitled 'Serenity and Power' (B1), and here is a sample:

> Even the woman whose mind and soul have been ignored by everyone, including herself, has within her the spiritual resources to make something of her new life, though she may have some difficulty in getting at them.

Ritual for transition

I'm personally a bit wary about this, because I've never designed a conscious ritual, and I have all the typical prejudices: I think it may be a bit voodooish, frightening even; it may take me into places I do not want to go; at the very least I may feel very silly dancing around in a circle. It's not surprising it's frightening, because it connects us to the dark side of our power. Nevertheless, I did design a ritual for my own menopause – which is coming and going as most menopauses do – and this is how it went.

Before the day, I prepared a beautiful full length black cloak. I invited people who have been really close to me during my transition – my daughter, my acupuncturist, the person who typed much of this book, my yoga teacher, my lodger, and several close friends who have shared my experience. Together we were 12.

Each was asked to bring what is for her a symbol of change and transformation, plus the most beautiful ribbon she could find, and the invitation explained what was to happen, so people didn't feel anxious.

The evening was a fine one in July, and we started with a drink. Then when we were ready we did a bumblebee (or brahmari) hum: simply breathing in deeply and letting the breath out slowly in a hum. After a few minutes the vibrations go right through the body, and this helps to ground everyone and get them really *there*.

Then each person brought in the names of older women, living or dead, whom they wished to honour. Each name and presence was

The ritual for transition

allowed to hang in the air for a few minutes before the next was invoked.

I then put on my cloak and talked briefly about the phases of life – what womanhood and then motherhood have meant for me, what it is from those years I was letting go of and, lastly, what I hope for and fear from the third phase.

Then each person presented what she had brought, explaining why it meant change and transformation. There was a grey and silver stone from a river in Norway, a lotus seed ready to be grown, a fired pottery vessel which made me think of alchemy, a many-coloured candle, someone's own crescent moon brooch, honey and beeswax, a cauldron to prepare flower remedies, a ceramic butterfly, a piece of amber from the Balkans, a seed from Australia which has to be burned before it can grow, and a double photograph of my daughter and me as we are now and as we were when she was four.

The ribbons were breath-taking: plum and gold and gossamer and flowers and richness of every kind and hue. They were pinned to the collar of the cloak, so when I spun round it was like a maypole (which just happens to be one of the symbols of the festival of Beltane). There is a sketch of this above. Then the cloak was reversed, so that the colours and ribbons were within, shimmering – all this richness now internal.

We ended with another bumblebee hum. Then we had a gargantuan feast, with large quantities of wine.

One-in-herself/One-in-himself

> The woman who is virgin, one-in-herself, does what she does – not because of any desire to please, not to be liked, or to be approved, even by herself; not because of any desire to gain power over another, to catch his interest or love, but because what she does is true . . . in using this term *virgin* in its psychological connotation, it refers not to external circumstances but to an inner attitude . . . The truth in the woman's action then has the tang and headiness of an intoxicating drink, while she herself is seen to be not an egotist but a personality of more profound significance.
> (M Esther Harding, 1971, pages 125–6. B13)

This possibility of being one-in-herself is usually only thought of as true for women, but I believe firmly that it is true for both sexes. Integration, self-sufficiency, internal unity is obviously true for a man too: to be 'one-in-himself' by bringing in, valuing, integrating his feminine nature. This is the opportunity to develop his connection to nature, to abundance, fecundity, great fields of corn, lightning, storms – power. It also lies in connection to the feelings. Feelings lie deeper than emotions, which are the surface manifestation. Feelings are where we attach value. When a person cries from the depth of feelings, he or she is *in* the feminine, rooted. When we are rooted, we are able to deal with the shadow, the dark side of the self. Only by facing and getting to know these nasty, unacceptable aspects of myself, and then eventually accepting them as part of myself, can I become whole.

This is a question of getting nearer and nearer to our own real nature and instinct, and being true to it. A person of integrity. It implies not seeing ourselves in relation to others, not seeing ourselves as inferior or superior. We can do this by rediscovering the significance of the goddess. And one of the ways we can do that is by means of a simple guided meditation, done with a friend. The instructions are as follows:

1 Lie down in a quiet place where you can be comfortable and undisturbed, and have your friend slowly read the following to you.
2 Imagine you are in Greece and walking up a hillside through olive trees. It is warm.
3 You reach a large temple. A woman meets you at the temple gate and asks which goddess you would like to meet, or what you desire from being there.
4 You give your request, then you enter the temple.

5 Picture what happens next. Do not censor your imagination – let it take
   its course. Possibly the goddess may give you something.
6 After ten minutes your friend gently says: 'It is time to leave now'. Bid
   farewell to those you have met, and retrace your steps out of the temple
   and back down the hillside.
7 Re-enter the room and, if you wish, tell or write down what you discovered.

What happened for me was that I walked up the hill through the olive
groves, feeling the warmth. At the temple gate I said I wanted to know
about the spiritual aspects of sexuality. I saw a huge classic temple, I
went up the white marble steps, through the columns and saw a great
empty expanse of white. In the centre was a great circle of steps, leading down to a pool. On these circular steps sat many women, talking.
As strangers approached, like me, they were welcomed. I walked down
the steps, into the pool and through it. On the other side I was met by
an older woman, her hair in a long, beautiful white plait, very like a
Quaker woman I know. She led me into the presence of what I can
only describe as a strong, honey-coloured light. In that presence I
realized what it was like to be able to be sexual without any self-consciousness, no feeling of one's own body image, no 'how am I doing?',
no presentation, no separateness, no distance. Just union – satisfaction and fulfilment. Not really another person there. And there was a
powerful honey-coloured light flowing outwards from me. I was given
two green leaves. Then it was time to leave. I went back the way I had
come. Then I drew a picture of it, and told the friends who had been
doing it with me what had happened.

> The neglect of the goddess results in a sterile, abrasive encounter with life;
> dullness and a lack of purpose creep in. A compulsive need for power
> replaces the joy of love. When feminine nature is valued, not seen as a toy
> to be played with but as an energy to be embraced, psychic life blossoms
> and becomes fruitful, bringing a new perspective. (Nancy Qualls-Corbett,
> 1988. B10)

Death

One of the things needed for true power, power which does not
depend on dominating others, is to overcome the fear of death. In our
society we fear death so terribly that we cannot bear to discuss it.
When it approaches, we talk only of medical feats and killing pain.
We do not talk about what is happening. This is in stark contrast to
what other cultures do today, and to what our forebears did.

In prehistoric times the Goddess of Death and Regeneration was deeply revered. There was a profound perception of the cycles of nature (based on the cycles of the moon and the female body) which underpinned a strong belief in the immediate resumption of life after the crisis of death. Death was not simply death; it was always death and regeneration.

There are many images in folk traditions which clearly go back to this prehistoric goddess, including the White Lady as death messenger, the goddess Freya in Norse mythology, who was mother of the dead, and the Destroyer/Regeneratrix, colourfully preserved to this day in Baltic and Slavic folk tradition. She is Baba Yaga in Russian tales, and was later degraded to a witch in the Grimms' fairy tales. In appearance she can be a beautiful woman or a nightmarish creature. Her destructive actions go back to her original control of the cyclic life power. She reminds us that we are mortal and that there is no life without death.

Traditionally, the role of women has been to deal with death, to talk about its approach, to help the dying prepare, to keep vigil with them, to hold them – and then to care for the body and to mourn. A friend of mine told me she was completely taken aback when her father died. She had no idea what she was supposed to do: where to put his body, how long it should stay in the house, what should happen to it, what she should do next. All this in the midst of her grief. Some months later she was with her husband's family in Algeria when his father died. The women from the neighbourhood instantly took over, knowing exactly what to do. Everything happened smoothly, everyone was supported, and the relatives had space to grieve fully.

If a person is really prepared for death and not afraid of it, that is power. The words may be simple, but the reality is not. Elisabeth Kubler-Ross, a doctor who has specialized in helping the dying, has discovered that there are several stages that people tend to go through when they are dying. These include denial, anger, bargaining and depression before there is finally acceptance, and then a peaceful death is possible. (B9)

As people grow older they also fear pain, humiliation and loss of wits. So even before we become ill or elderly, we need to prepare. To the Buddhist our whole life is a preparation for dying, so that we can be totally present in each moment of our life, as if it were our last. Each life has seasons in it – youth, adulthood, maturity, and dying – just as the year has spring, summer, autumn and winter. Each day has this same rhythm. In meditation, so does each moment.

CHAPTER 6

Power from Within: the Soul

We are very good at preparing to live, but not very good at living. We know how to sacrifice ten years for a diploma, and we are willing to work very hard to get a job, a car, a house, and so on. But we have difficulty remembering that we are alive in the present moment, the only moment there is for us to be alive. Every breath we take, every step we make, can be filled with peace, joy, serenity. We need only to be awake, alive in the present moment.

Thich Nhat Hanh, 1992

The previous two chapters have been concerned with the power which resides in our bodies and minds. This chapter is about the power which resides in the very essence of us – what some people call the spirit, some the soul. My purpose is to explore this, and to intrigue those who have little time in their lives for what they see in inverted commas as 'spirituality'. Again I can only speak from experience and describe what I am discovering, as many have discovered before me: each person has a unique path and will tread it in their own way. I start by clarifying what I mean by the terms 'soul' and 'spirit', and then describe how this kind of power can be found, what it is like, and what it may enable the individual to do and understand. I discuss our resistance to turning inwards, and the views of those who have no time for spirituality. The final section offers some indication of what power from within can do, for example in terms of getting beyond self-consciousness, bringing about change, finding integrity and releasing creativity.

What power from within is not

It may seem odd to start a chapter by saying what is not in it. But the words 'soul' and the 'spirit' can mean so many different things that it is as well to be clear what I am *not* talking about.

First, I am not talking about the occult, of sciences involving knowledge of the supernatural, nor of anything which is hidden or secret – mysterious, yes; secret, no. Second, I am not talking about the paranormal – about extrasensory perception, the psychic powers of mediums, table turning, telepathy or hypnotism – although I appreciate that these may be some people's experience of the spirit.

Nor, in fact, am I talking about religion. Although it goes without saying that all the great religions ultimately lead to the same fundamental truths, increasing numbers of people seem *not* to be finding what they are seeking in Western organized religion. Some feel, as Jung did, that organized religion is a defence against the deep mystery of religious experience; that it reduces everything to concepts and ideas and short circuits the transcendent experience – what Joseph Campbell calls 'the experience of deep mystery'. The path I am describing here is one which has neither creed nor dogma. Eastern religions – Buddhism, Taoism, Hinduism – provide a more accessible background to the path, perhaps because in these religions god is seen as the vehicle of elemental energy, not its source.

My own experience was to be baptized and confirmed in the Church of England, and in my teens I became deeply religious, heavily involved in church-going and my own ritual prayers every evening. When I was about 18 religion gave way to a far more worldly attitude to life, at college and later in my travels in various parts of the world. In my thirties I became passionately interested in myth, legend and fairy tale – this was partly stimulated by a Jungian analysis.

In my forties I struggled to read Christian theologians, mainly in an effort to understand the thinking of some respected churchmen who support nuclear weapons. I confess that the type of argument I encounter here is too abstruse, too jesuitical for me. I cannot hold it in my heart, only in my head (and not even there for very long). In my late forties I came to enjoy the stillness of meditation in Quaker meetings and eventually became a member of the Society of Friends.

Since then meditation has steadily become a more vital part of my life, stimulated from time to time by going on silent retreats. I have found that what I seek lies within, rather than outside. When I visit churches now, although I love the music and especially the drama of high mass, for example, I find that the liturgy can divert attention away from inner stillness.

What power from within may be

The soul, as I shall use the concept in this work, means an essence or energy which animates human life. It forms a non-material entity distinguished from, but temporarily co-existent with, a person's body. It is the 'divine essence' of the whole human being. Like Aminah Raheem, I distinguish individual soul from spirit.

> Spirit is defined as that all-encompassing, creative Order of the Cosmos which is before all beginnings and beyond all endings. Spirit has been called God, the Creator, the Tao, 'All That Is.' It is seen as the formless all-pervasive energy from which all of creation derives, including the individual soul of humankind. (B11)

Thus soul is of the individual: spirit is of the cosmos. Please do not be confused by the fact that from time to time I speak of 'spirituality' as an attribute of a person; by this I mean that person's ability to tap into the great all-encompassing never-ending spirit of the cosmos. I find that I can do this by going within. Some people call this prayer. Some call it meditation. Ardis Whitman calls it reaching for those 'luminous places in yourself'.

Those luminous places *are* there. They are very powerful. Anyone can have access to them. And today the benefits of daily reflection and meditation are becoming much more widely recognized in the West. There are many different approaches to choose from – a multitude of books, tape cassettes and meditation classes available in most towns and cities. Each individual finds his or her way to what suits best.

When we go inside, breathing and listening quietly, we find the sacred in ourselves. It is neither male nor female, it is both. It is a spring full of clear water to nourish us. Whenever I have done this, gone quiet and simply watched my breathing for a few minutes, there it is again – slipping in almost unnoticed – and then if I can stay quiet it starts to give off joy. I have tried it many times now, and it is always there, once there is quietness.

At first, when I go inside, it's very noisy: there are many things I have not done or am planning to do, lists to make, awful videos of things I have done wrong. I just have to 'go passive' on these, not try to banish them but simply look at them with my mind as an

observer. To try to 'control' them is as difficult, and as fruitless, as trying to stop a river. I must just let the river flow, but with me watching.
Most times things gradually become stiller – but sometimes this noise
persists. So be it. But when it does go still, there at the bottom of it all
is the joy, the radiating warmth. Then I can feel a smile creeping up to
my face.

Things pass

One of the greatest blessings of meditation for me so far (and I am only
a beginner) is a glimpse of the fact that the things which seem to matter to us so much at the time are transitory. They pass.

The Buddha discovered this. Through subtle, direct observation in
meditation, he found that it is possible for the conscious mind to
become aware of the minute, moment-to-moment sensations it has
and to see that they are transitory; hence there is no point in clinging
to them; hence they need not be reacted to. Simply becoming aware
of these sensations, *without judging them bad or good* and thereby call-
ing forth more reactive emotions, breaks the chain reaction.
Gradually, with practice, the habitual patterns developed in childhood
can be changed, with the consequent freeing of complexes on the
psychodynamic level.

Suffering and unhappiness can absorb great amounts of energy. A
person can become entirely immersed in pain or depression. If that
happens, the person is trapped in it. She is mesmerized by the grief,
anger or self-pity. Like a rabbit staring into the headlights, she is
unable to see anything else, unable to move to another way of being.
If, through becoming aware, she can distance herself a little, if she can
'see' herself suffering, then she can begin to work with the suffering
and transform it. Meditation is a way of becoming aware and of
loosening the power of our suffering, enabling us to move beyond it
and grow.

It works! It works both on the instantaneous level and on the
deeper level of growth. For example, if I can just catch myself in the
moment that someone is saying something critical to me, and say to
myself, 'Aha, I feel hurt' and *watch* my feeling, even for a split second,
then I am not *in* it, not caught in the emotion. The same applies to
praise, of course, and would have the effect of stopping me becoming
attached to the praise, 'believing my own press releases' and thus
prevent the embarrassing phenomenon of self-importance.

The phrase 'in the moment' is the key. It has taken me years to grasp the importance of this, of *being here now*. It is the reason why Buddhists chime bells during meditation, and why the Vietnamese monk Thich Nhat Hanh says 'Listen, listen, that wonderful sound . . . it brings me back to my true self.'

I have recently been through a time of intense pain associated with the absence of someone I love. Every time I think of him somewhere else, and that can be every few minutes or even seconds, it is like a stab. I can quickly sink into feeling worthless, old, unlovable, abandoned, afraid. Gradually I have been shown that in a strange way each stab of pain is an opportunity – a reminder that the pain is to do with devaluing *myself*, and it helps me to come back into the moment. If I come back into the moment, it becomes possible for me to recollect my value.

Of course this takes time. Of course it is distracting. But it is also deeply enlivening – the moments when I 'come back' to my own reality are shining moments. I feel more real than I have ever felt, and more alive. One could say that this is what time is *for*.

We Westerners have different ideas about time and eternity from those in the East. We tend to associate eternity with a never-ending time that continues beyond history, beyond 'the future'. We divide time into three parts – past, present and future. That division is false, said the Indian sage Osho:

> Time is really past and future. The present is not part of time. The present is part of eternity. That which has passed is time; that which is to come is time. That which is, is not time because it never passes - it is always here. The now is *always* here.

I picture this as a simple diagram:

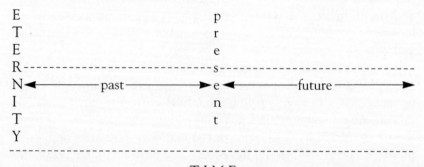

TIME

In effect, if we are able for a moment to stop ourselves thinking in terms of 'time', we give ourselves the opportunity to experience the present as it is. In the same moment we may also experience the 'timelessness' of the Eastern idea of eternity. Meditating is one way of doing this.

The advantages of meditation

Research has shown that meditation can reduce anxiety and tension while increasing alertness. It can lower blood pressure and reduce cholesterol levels, reduce insomnia and decrease dependency on drugs, cigarettes, alcohol. It can increase our awareness of emotions and the feelings which lie beneath them, and increase self-acceptance and tolerance of others. It can help us become enlightened.

Meditation is not concentration, mantra, or prayer (although for some it may include these); it is the knowing of that which is beyond thoughts and images – the power of the void. For me, my breathing space has become my refuge. Letting it be filled is sweet. Letting that space be filled is healing old hurts. The space is like garden doors opening inwards filling a room with sunlight. It nourishes the joy in me. This nourishment also comes from beauty outside, in the countryside – from blackbirds' song, from huge trees, from mist on a meadow, from lightning, from buttercups, from water in almost any form. When I'm in contact with it, actually or in my heart's eye, I can store it up so that it's there when I'm in trouble. Beauty is a balm to the bewildered.

People ask whether all this is 'just in the mind', meaning 'Do we imagine it?', 'Is it real?' The answer I think is to be found in the lives of those who do meditate. Ask them. For 2,500 years Buddhist meditators, their families, and friends, have noticed a transformation of character, a gradual movement into ease, strength and peace. How is it possible that such deep and lasting change could occur? Charlene Spretnak reports on current research in the neurophysiology of the brain, which suggests that the Buddha was not speaking metaphorically when he said it is possible to eliminate – not repress – even deeply established patterns of reaction.

> The brain and the entire nervous system are now understood to function in a state of continuous structural change insofar as the formation of the nerve pathways is plastic and dynamic. Learning and memory, for instance, are dynamic processes that sculpt and resculpt the connections between neurons. To a certain extent, we literally create the structural design of our brains by our mental processes, our habits of response. (1993. B11)

One thing is certain, the change is gradual; it cannot be forced. As we have said, the time has to be right for the snake to shed a skin; it has to be ready. If you tear the skin off a snake, you'll kill it.

Resistance

Most people experience resistance within themselves to meditating and reflecting in this way. We feel a bit silly sitting there when nothing apparently 'happens'. It's not at all like being in church where there is something going on all the time – standing up, sitting down, singing, chanting. We wonder what other people would say if they saw us. We get uncomfortable. It's these very reactions that are interesting to question and examine – to turn over in the hand like a stone. Are these ideas and habits our own? Or have they been imposed on us?

It may be that they prevent us from following our natural direction, led by intuition. It may be that they act to keep us from trusting, or even hearing, our own inner guidance. If we can gently acknowledge these fears, and see where they result from the opinions of others, then we have a choice. We can choose fear or we can choose the alternative, which is love. Love is the only response to fear that works.

We all have knots of fear – that part of us stopping us from being ourselves. If these are undone, then the kind of power available is of a different scale. Before I saw the serpent that I described in the Introduction, I had spent a weekend meditating on my fears. Physically, the main fear I have is of deep, murky water, where there are unknown, slimy creatures. In my meditation I allowed myself to sink in murky water. I felt the panic of losing all my senses – being unable to see, to smell, to hear, to breathe. The only sense left to me was of touch. As I sank to the bottom, my imagination produced the coils of a great snake down there – I touched them and they were not slimy. I came to rest on those coils. Two days later I saw the serpent in daylight on a walk in the public park in Oxford.

A few years ago I would have been unable to allow myself to imagine, let alone to admit, something like that. I would have dismissed it as valueless daydreaming. Now I realize that I am not in the least odd in having this experience. The Religious Experience Research Unit at Oxford says that at least 30 per cent of people have had experiences of this kind. Sociologist Andrew Greeley reported in a *New York Times* article that four out of ten adult Americans have had a mystical experience. We just do not talk about them, for fear of being laughed at or thought odd, or because they are precious experiences, and private.

Biochemist Rupert Sheldrake points out that most Nobel prizewinning scientists tell of how their discoveries came through a moment of enlightenment, a flash of inspiration, a 'Eureka' in the bath like Archimedes. They didn't work it out with their brains (although they did all the preparation) – it *'came'* to them. The thing is that they only feel secure enough to admit something like this *after* they have been given the Nobel Prize!

The critics of spirituality

Many people do not have strong feelings either way about spirituality; we are either interested or we are not. But others do feel strongly, and I shall now take a brief look at some of the warnings that are given against spirituality. In addition to science, these come from three unlikely quarters: feminists, Freudians and Christians.

The resurgence of spirituality among women has been viewed positively by many feminists, but others have regarded it as a waste of precious time and energy. It is considered a pleasant opiate that will keep women from facing and dealing with the 'real' issues of life, that may, in Merlin Stone's words, 'cause the believer to lie back upon her pillow in total non-action – just waiting for the will of the goddess to act itself out'.

This critique is answered by a glance at the productivity and activism of those women most engaged in the spiritual side of the women's movement. Just to examine the range and number of books which have appeared on the subject in the past 15 years is an eye-opener. Most of these authors spend their non-writing time endlessly responding to invitations to speak up and down the country. During the past few years, those women I have met who have been most active on world issues – from Bosnia, from Russia, from America, from New Zealand, from Europe – have either directly acknowledged their spiritual sources of strength, or have shown that they are open to them. Ways of acting in the world with this core element of power from within the soul will be explored in the last three chapters of this book.

An engineer friend of mine has a test for the 'validity' of any spirituality. She asks: 'Does it make this person more or less committed to shared justice?' Alas, not all spiritualities do. But those that do, really do!

Many Freudians deny any value to spirituality, regarding any interest in it as an avoidance of primal pain. Freud himself seemed to make no distinction between religion and spirituality, and says that one of the functions of psychotherapy is to get rid of religious ideas – the cured patient does not need such things. He felt that all attempts to explore spirituality were simply motivated by a desire to avoid looking at more basic and important matters, such as the Oedipus complex. People would do anything, he felt, rather than face the unpleasant aspects of their own natures.

There is indeed a general confusion around the word 'spirituality'. For many people it is synonymous with religion, and yet in reality it is *beyond* religion. It is certainly far beyond any of the dogma involved in most religions; it has nothing to say about belonging to or believing in any set of ideas. Spirituality, to me, is an aspect of the self – a capacity, a potential. Whereas popular religion, with its moral overtones, might well divert people from confronting the 'unpleasant aspects of their own natures', an essential part of any true spiritual path will involve facing the darker aspects of ourselves and transforming the suffering we encounter in the process.

When it comes to Christianity we again run into difficulties of definition – of what is acceptable to the various established Churches, and what is not. Traditional Christianity might doubt that the images and symbolism which are inextricably connected with the kind of spirituality described here are truly spiritual in the sense understood by the Church – that is, emanating from the Holy Spirit which is the spirit of God the Father. They could be considered at best irrelevant and at worst blasphemous by Roman Catholics, for example. They could be thought to distract from the concern that people need to feel for their own salvation.

The other problem for many traditional Churches is that the kind of spirituality I am talking about does not worship or recognize an exterior god, but searches for an interior truth. There are of course many Christians who *do* search for an interior truth, but the Christian Church as an institution requires acceptance and worship of its doctrines, which include the Trinity, the virgin birth, etc. I would ask, if we are filled with *prescribed beliefs* about how things are, how can we *experience* the reality of the way they really are?

What power from within does

In this section I will offer examples from my own and others' experience to try to give a flavour of what this is about. Naturally your own experience will be quite unique.

Getting beyond self-consciousness

When we are teenagers, most of us are paralysed by self-consciousness. We can only think about how mountainous and red our spots are, whether our clothes are wrong, what others are thinking of us. Our egos are ravenous for reassurance.

That's supposed to subside as we get older, but for many of us it doesn't. Going inwards to the true self gradually makes the ego less demanding. It matters less what people think of our exterior, because in our interior we are discovering what is real for us. We become authentic. This automatically means that we have a lot more room and energy to be with other people without constantly saying or thinking 'I' 'I' 'I', 'me' 'me' 'me'. So we can actually listen to them, and begin to picture and even to feel what life must be like for them. This is compassion – 'feeling with'. The world needs it badly. It's also much less tiring than self-consciousness!

Being acted through

There is a wondrous experience to be had. I have not had it very often, because my ego is still quite noisy, but I do know what it feels like. It is the feeling that it is not 'me' that is doing something, it is rather a sense of being acted 'through'. It is a bit like being a channel or pipe down which action can flow. This experience is close to the religious concept of grace, but distinct from the traditional Western understanding of grace, as it does not require belief in god or a supernatural agency. It is how power from the spirit works. It is not something I or you *organize*. It's not something *we* do. It happens through the way we *are*, our being.

My point about the ego is important because the more my ego gets in the way, or furs up the pipe with demands for strokes or other 'noise', the less I am able to allow the energy or power to come through.

Let me give an example. Like many people I have had to struggle with nervousness and self-consciousness when I give a public lecture or presentation. With practice, however, I reckoned I was getting pretty good at it – I did not perspire any more, I rarely dropped my notes, and at least I thought I *looked* fairly cool. But all this was the result of careful preparation – drafting the text, rehearsing, getting feedback, changing sentences. Then I went to do a two-day workshop on how to communicate to an audience what one really wants to communicate. I learned from those skilled teachers that what people wanted was not my carefully constructed arguments, but my *passion*. 'Throw away the notes' was the motto I went home with.

It took two years more, and the growth of a lot more trust in the spirit, before I dared. It was in February 1995, and I had to give a lecture at UNESCO in Paris. I thought there would be about 60 people there, and there were about 300. It was a full day of lectures, maybe ten in all, and all from a podium. Suddenly I realized that if I delivered the factual, reasoned message I had prepared, it would be simply more overload for tired brains. So I tore up my notes, I physically tore them up in front of everyone, and just talked from the heart. I got the impression afterwards that it was more valuable to people than my notes, because I was more in touch with what was going on in the room, and with what was needed.

Bringing about change

If you are present and fully conscious *in the moment* when something is happening, your ability to act on behalf of the larger whole is dramatically increased. Jane Roberts calls it 'the point of power in the present' – and says it is 'your only effective point of changing any aspect of your world'. The inner voice you develop, because it is authentic, has immense authority when you learn to use it outside, in the world.

Robert Woodson is president of the National Center for Neighborhood Enterprise in America. For 20 years he has been assessing which social programmes are most effective, for funding purposes. He has recently discovered that the one thing virtually all the most successful ones had in common was a strong element of spirituality. 'I am not saying the spiritually based programs always work, only that the successful programs almost always have a spiritual base,' he is quoted as saying. Woodson is not yet sure what are the implications of his insight for social service programmes, but says:

> I do know that the hunger I sense in America is not a hunger for things but a search for meaning. We don't yet have the scales to weigh the ability some people have to supply meaning – to provide the spiritual element I'm talking about . . . but I know it makes as much sense to empower those who have the spiritual wherewithal to turn lives around as to empower those whose only qualification is credentials.

Turning inwards for power teaches us the value of pausing and listening, so we start to use this in relations with other people. What happens then is that people are heard, so they can stop shouting and repeating themselves. This brings intimacy, which in turn brings trust, which means that things get done.

Here is an example. In my women's group there is no set agenda when we meet. We have a good gossip before we start but then we sit quietly for a few minutes. Then whoever is moved to speak takes up the stone which is in the middle. She keeps the stone as long as she wishes, including after she has finished speaking if she needs to. No one else may speak until they have the stone. In this way we move, each time we meet, quite quickly beyond individual concerns and on to things that concern us all. One evening a participant used her turn to speak of the case of a very violent child for whom she had professional responsibility. Because we all listened deeply to her in our hearts, we heard the pain of many thousands of disturbed children all over the country, and decided to meditate on them each day for a week at the same time. Two days later, instead of having to be locked up, the child in question was accepted by a brand new care unit which 'could have been designed for her needs.'

This example reminds me of John Donne's 'No man is an island' and the endless instances that appear all around us to show that we are interconnected, and that we can use that very awareness to bring about change.

Finding integrity

'Power corrupts', we know, and 'absolute power corrupts absolutely.' Power from within, from the spirit, on the other hand, is pure. For example, if you are really listening, you will get some surprises from your own depths, even shocks. You may not hear what your ego wants to hear. You will learn harsh lessons as well as experiencing profound joy. Going within in a serious way will lead you to your integrity. This integrity is immune to the corruption of domination power.

Think of Nelson Mandela, 28 years in a South African jail. This solitude, and what he did with it, gave him the ability to make extremely tough, often unpopular decisions. For example, five years before he was released he came to the conclusion that the time had come to begin discussions with the government. Both sides at the time regarded discussions as a sign of weakness and betrayal, and neither would come to the table unless the other made significant concessions. Mandela realized that if a dialogue was not started soon, the country would be plunged into war. Thousands if not millions of lives would be lost. Someone needed to take the first step, and from jail he did. He had to try many times before he got any response from the government. When some of his colleagues found out, they felt outraged and betrayed. But he went on.

Imagine what could happen if we were able to act with even a tiny degree of Mandela's integrity. With integrity comes freedom from fear. Finding our own integrity means finding our own completeness, tiny bit by tiny bit, daily. Saints, it has been said, are sinners who go on trying. I believe that the closer we can get to the spirit within, the more integrity we can have available to guide our every movement.

The wealth of your own creativity

Time spent with the spirit is rich in images. The images you get can be used as a means of self-help. Because they mean a lot to you (you would not have had them if they didn't), once you have recognized them and opened the door to them, they can be present to help you in all sorts of situations. My serpent, for example, comes sailing into the room whenever I am feeling at a loss (as long as I'm in the moment) and then she simply brings her strength into me, takes me into her, and I could move mountains.

In going within and getting in touch with his or her own soul, a person is literally unlocking what the real self is meant to be. That is, the self which was radiant with pure energy when that person was born, and then may have been squashed and damaged by experiences since. As we begin to touch that self, we feel joy – it's like coming home. We also feel a release of energy – that is creativity. We start doing all sorts of things we never thought we could.

> Be brave enough to live creatively. The creative is where no-one else has been. You have to leave the city of your comfort, and go into the wilderness of your intuition. You can't get there by bus, only by hard work and risk and by never quite knowing what you're doing. What you'll discover will be wonderful. What you'll discover will be yourself. (Alan Alda, quoted in Leigh and Maynard, 1993, page 23. B14)

CHAPTER 7

Hara Power and Union

Jesus said to them: When you make the two one, and when you make the inner as the outer and the outer as the inner and the above as the below, and when you make the male and female into a single one, so that the male will not be male and the female [not] be female . . . then shall you enter the Kingdom.

The Gospel of Thomas

At this point I want to address the issue of dualism first raised in chapter 1 and draw together the previous three chapters, in order to envisage the completion or wholeness of the human being. In this wholeness lies power of the kind needed to enable our species and our world to survive. I describe what has been lost in splitting off the dark side of the feminine, including our connection with nature, and how this has produced a potentially fatal imbalance leading to the destruction of our environment. We may recover balance by developing hara power, and I recap briefly how this may be done through self-knowledge and through discovering sources of power in the body and the soul. These three parts are then brought together, introducing the concept of chakras, or energy centres, in order to indicate how sexuality can bring us to wholeness. This is really the heart of the book. It shows how a hara approach to sex gives everyone more power, how we gain power by being with another and cease to need power over another. It is first discussed in the sense of lovemaking, then in terms of the inner lover, and finally in terms of relationship. Helping the individual self to be more whole in this way puts us in a position to help heal the world.

We live in a world of opposites. Polarization has become our model for thinking. In politics, for example, 'You're either for us or you're against us.' Friend or foe, we want to know. Courts decide whether people are innocent or guilty. We cling to life, we are afraid of death. In most religions, god is good and the devil is bad. Virgins are good, and whores are bad. The sacred and profane are opposed, the spiritual and the sexual cannot go together. This is probably rooted in the split between mind and body that has been fostered mainly by Western culture, in which god is masculine and mother nature – the source of nurture – is feminine.

Some feminists subscribe to this kind of dualistic thinking, asserting that feminine forces are life-giving and masculine forces are death-courting. Personally, I can't join in with this; it ascribes moral values to masculinity and femininity, making one 'bad' and the other 'good', which not only perpetuates the problem but is quite obviously false.

We do not have to live in a world of opposites

We have only lived in this world of opposites for about 4,000 years. During the preceding millennia things appear to have been quite different, in a way which is hard for us to imagine now. Deities were many-sided, as nature is, rather than one-sided. These are the deities associated with the very earliest type of worship, and they appear to have had much more energetic qualities than our present-day ones. They were more passionate, playful and ecstatic, as well as actively wrathful and destructive.

It is worth tracing how this split into thinking in opposites came about. To recap briefly what was said in chapter 1, in the beginning the Great Mother Goddess was everything, and everything was part of her, everything was sacred. No distinction was made between human beings and animals, between spirit and nature, between soul and body. This was what people in the Palaeolithic and Neolithic ages seem to have believed. It is still found in what are called (probably for that reason) 'primitive' societies.

The Moon Goddess for example was both giver of life and of all that promotes fertility, and at the same time she was the wielder of the destructive powers of nature. In this she is an ancestress of the Hindu goddess Kali, whose contradictory character is an essential quality of her divinity.

The Mother Goddess had a son in the ancient myths, and gradually he became her consort. The focus of the myth is now on the relationship between the Mother Goddess and the god, her 'son-lover' who himself becomes a god. This was the myth of Inanna and Dumuzi in Bronze Age Sumeria, Ishtar and Tammuz in Babylonia, Isis and Osiris in Egypt, Aphrodite and Adonis in Greece and Cybele and Attis in Anatolia.

In the next stage the Mother Goddess is killed by the god. This is the late Bronze Age and early Iron Age myth of Tiamat, the Mother Goddess whose corpse was split into earth and heaven by the superior power of Marduk, the sky and sun god. Creation is now seen from Marduk's perspective as the inert inanimate substance we call matter which can be shaped and ordered only by 'spirit'.

Finally, the god creates the world alone without reference to the Mother Goddess. This was the Iron Age myth of the Hebrew Yahweh, where Adam is made of clay and comes alive only when spirit is breathed into him, and Eve is made from Adam. God has by this time become pure spirit – some of which is breathed into human beings but none into animals, trees or earth itself. There is by the time of the Old Testament no relation to the Mother Goddess.

Anne Baring and Jules Cashford, whose meticulous research sheds light on this long transitional period, say that one way of understanding the long historical process of the replacing of the myth of the goddess by the myth of the god is to view it as the gradual withdrawal of humanity's participation with nature. Nature was gradually seen by humans as being less animate and more separate from them, and eventually as something to be opposed and dominated.

That is how we human beings tend to see ourselves now, except in some remaining North American and South American indigenous traditions, in parts of the Indian subcontinent, among Maori and Aboriginal peoples and among some peoples who have not yet been exposed to Western 20th century influences.

This dualistic or split way of thinking has led to societies which are materially preoccupied, spiritually impoverished, technologically possessed and pitting themselves 'against' nature.

We can nevertheless still recognize that nature is cruel as well as kind. We can also recognize that other human beings are cruel. What we find difficult to recognize is that *we* are exactly the same, *we* are cruel as well as kind. We have trouble reconciling the light in ourselves with the dark, the mean with the generous, the violent with the gentle.

The split of feminine energies into dark and light

I believe that this dualistic way of thinking is particularly evident in the way the feminine is now perceived. The wholeness of the female has gradually been lost. As I showed at the end of chapter 1, it is impossible for a woman today to be virtuous, powerful and sexual at the same time. We have as it were blacked out what was originally an essential element of the feminine – a deep dark power, sometimes cruel, sometimes destructive, but full of energy, passion and strength.

It is worth a short detour into an ancient story to illustrate this. This is the story of Medea, in all its numerous retellings. Medea is most commonly known today through the play by Euripides, and is famous for killing her children as an act of vengeance on her husband Jason. He married Medea after accepting her help in his quest to obtain the Golden Fleece from Medea's father. Jason then divorced her and married the daughter of King Creon, whereupon Medea used her strength and powers against him – presenting his new bride with a crown and veil which ignited when she put it on, burning her and her household. Most notoriously, Medea then killed her own two sons, to ensure the lasting misery and regret of Jason.

Historically, she comes well after the heyday of the goddess religions, and there is already some ambivalence about her being a decision-maker in her own life. She has come down to us portrayed as a freak. Her powers, whether used for good or evil, are somehow unnatural, they wreak havoc, and it is not proper that they are possessed by a woman.

The dramatic depiction by Euripides has now convincingly been questioned by Robert Graves. He discusses Medea's gifts for healing, indicating that Medea was responsible for curing Herakles of madness. He highlights her cunning, and her ability to take the initiative. Graves relates how she saved Jason and his crew after helping them get the Fleece, and how she overcame and killed Jason's enemy, his uncle, when the Argonauts were not bold enough to do so. Without Medea's magical powers, he would never have achieved his mission, and possibly would have died. Legend also has it that Zeus, king of the gods, fell in love with her but, perhaps uniquely among mortal women, she refused his advances.

What is interesting to us is that despite being an unusual female in Greek myths, Medea is never held up as being any sort of a role model. Her deep, dark powers make her an anomaly, an unwomanly woman, a freak of nature, an example of how women should not act.

The swing of the pendulum

Although the very early concept of the mother deity was basic space, emptiness, whole-in-herself, it must be said that she was nevertheless unreflecting, unconscious, and had no real masculine counterpart. In her day, of course, the journey to consciousness was just beginning. Later, even the Greek goddesses, in Marie-Louise Von Franz' words, 'simply personify emotional feminine reactions . . . There was infinite fertility and generosity, unstinted charity, infinite jealousy and vanity, and so on'. There was still a lack of consciousness.

Now, as a result of our dualistic way of thinking, our negating the power of the feminine, we have swung to the other extreme. Put crudely, we have now gone out of balance in the sense of too much masculine, whereas in the days of the Mother Goddess there may have been too much feminine. The last 2,000 years have seen an increasing disrespect for and destruction of the natural world, aided and hastened by technological discoveries and an impoverishment of spiritual life. We may in many ways now be more conscious and more aware, but at the same time we are cutting ourselves off from our natural world and our spiritual world. Our minds are alive, but our bodies and souls are starved and dying. We are clever, but out of balance.

We need balance because things which are dark or denied or ignored turn nasty. So if we dismiss other people as 'bad', they become enemies. If we continue to ignore the spirit, if we give ourselves no soul food, we will simply die. Experiments on animals which have been deprived of time to dream show that they soon die. If we live as though earning money and buying things are all that matters, we become robots – dead inside. If we continue to deny nature (gouging out minerals, slaughtering forests, poisoning water, contaminating soil) nature will withdraw her life-support system from us. No more eating, no more drinking, no more warmth, no more wealth.

If we continue to destroy tropical forest at our present rate, by the end of the century none will be left. It is estimated that 1.5 million species of animal and plant will become extinct over the next 25 years. Rhinos, for example, have been roaming the earth for 60 million years, while humans have been here for a mere 2.5 million; yet in 1971 there were 65,000 black rhinos in Africa and by 1994 there were just 2,300 left. At current rates of consumption, in 40 years there will be no more oil; in 60 years no more gas.

We think we can cope with feeding ourselves through artificial means, through science – but when we say 'ourselves' we mean our

Western selves, because we are already leaving most of the rest of the world to starve.

It is no longer valid to think that we are in control, that we shall be all right, no matter what we do to others. We are discovering that what we do to the rest of the world, we do to ourselves. If people in Germany sell nuclear technology to India, and that power station in India has a meltdown, people in Germany could get irradiated. Chernobyl has given us a taste of this. If people in Japan put nuclear waste into the sea as we do, there will eventually be no fresh fish for anyone to make into sushi. If people in France insist on eating straw-berries in winter, self-supporting peasants in North Africa will be turned off their land by Western agribusiness and will become economic migrants threatening the jobs of people in France. If people in Beijing insist on having one fridge per family, as people in Birmingham do, the ozone layer will be further depleted and people in Birmingham will develop skin cancer.

One could go on thus for page after page. The point is that our world is now very small, and getting smaller fast. We *have* to care what happens to others, or we will ourselves die. So we had better learn the skills we need in order to be able to do this – to care, to balance, to reconcile, to unite.

Holistic thinking

One important way to reconcile opposites and become whole is to change our way of thinking. The way of thinking which has come to dominate our culture is known as 'reductionist', so called because it attempts to solve problems by dividing the issue into smaller and smaller parts, thinking in this way to reduce the complexity of the problem. This way of tackling problems has been seen as successful because it has resulted in higher levels of material production, physi-cal well-being and comfort – so much so that there is a widespread, though often implicit, assumption that this is the best and only way to think about everything.

Here I turn to an Open University course on systems thinking which shows that, although the reductionist way of thinking *is* a powerful one, it is nevertheless limited. There are situations and prob-lems in which the reductionist approach does not work. It cannot help to cope with problems that arise as a result of complexity and inter-connectedness itself. Under these circumstances, any severing of the connections in order to make the problem simple actually removes the problem to be solved. It is necessary to take the situation as a whole, and approaches which do this are termed holistic.

So we are gradually discovering that although this reductionist method is useful for understanding the pieces, it is not very effective for fixing them, because the bigger problems are problems of the whole. Going on and on tinkering with the pieces may be good for a car, but it doesn't help the problems of a human being, or of nature or of the world. We have to develop an understanding of the whole, a holistic view.

It is perhaps useful to take the example of medicine. In a medical context, the word 'holistic' (from the Greek word *holos* meaning whole) means treating the patient as a whole, rather than concentrating on the symptoms out of context. Sickness is not understood in terms of the pathology of isolated organs, as though they were merely cogs in a machine, but rather as the dysfunction of a normally harmonious, complete living entity.

Chinese medicine never considered the mind and body as separate from each other, as Western medicine has for the last two centuries. Peter Mole, writing about acupuncture, says that this gives the two systems a fundamentally different philosophical basis which permeates to the core of their theories and practice. The Western approach has led to many extraordinary advances; for example, the remarkable developments in surgery and drug therapy. Much of the current disaffection with modern medicine amongst patients, however, stems from the limitations of this approach. It fails to recognize that the mind and spirit have an extremely powerful effect upon the body and that the human body is more than the sum of its chemistry and mechanics.

Bringing ourselves together

Now I would like to bring together what the last three chapters have said. Many writers have already said that men and women need to break free of stereotypes. What I am saying is that both women and men need to recognize and regain the dark strengths of the feminine in order to become more whole.

So far we have seen how we can use our minds to understand ourselves. We have seen the connections between self-knowledge and power, enabling us to understand others, to be clear about what is happening in our lives and to grow into the person we were meant to be.

We have also looked at our bodies, exploring how both men and women can find in the body a source of inner strength, not to mention delight. Most recently we have encountered the power which resides in the very essence of us – the soul. It showed how this kind of power may be developed and what it enables us to do in terms of releasing creativity and bringing about change.

Now I want to see how these are brought together, because body, mind and soul are not separate. Their integration brings us closer to wholeness. Being whole means being able – having the inner power to mend, heal and bring about change in whatever area we care about.

Many of the practices mentioned in the last three chapters (and described in the section 'Going Further'), such as yoga, acupuncture and meditation, work precisely towards integration. Many of them use the concept of seven basic energy centres in the body, known as chakras. This very ancient concept from Indian yogic texts is also found in Chinese theory (in Taoism in particular). These energy centres are located along the central axis, or core, of the body, in conjunction with the spinal cord. I shall use this concept of chakras to show how body, mind and soul can work together, and how power and sex can work together. In this section I have drawn on the understanding of Aminah Raheem. I start with the lowest chakra:

This is **The Root Chakra** and is situated in the centre of the base of the torso between the pubic bone and the coccyx, in the perineal floor. It is the body's foundation, its safety, the seat of physical survival. If the root chakra is strong and well developed, the person has physical strength and courage and will accept their situation rather than wishing they were somewhere or someone else; if not, there is fear for survival and physical well-being.

The Second Chakra is in the lower abdomen, between the navel and the pubis. Sensual pleasure is the focus of this chakra. This is the seat of creativity, of sexuality and of the desire for reproduction. The feelings here are of excitement: they can enliven the body completely when they are allowed to flow freely. The joy of our true uninhibited sensuality can act as a powerful impetus toward growth.

The belly is sometimes called the 'emotional brain' of the body, since feelings seem to 'grow' out of our guts. A child, especially a male child in Western culture, learns early how to repress emotions down into the belly rather than let them out into expression (in a scream, a shout, a shudder). That is why deep breathing into the belly is very releasing, and puts us in touch with our emotions. This is the most important centre of gravity for women and for men in their dealings

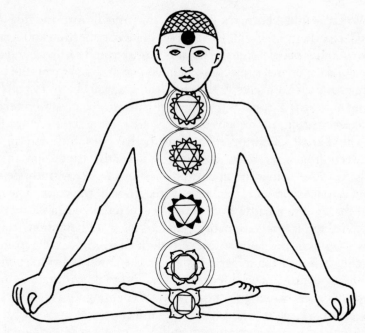

The chakras

with the world. It helps them to counterbalance the everyday ten-dency to rely on the brain for wisdom.

The Third Chakra is at the solar plexus, just above the navel. This is the seat of personal power and ego strength, mastery, control. When the issues related to this chakra have not been brought into con-sciousness and resolved, then the resulting conflict will lead to a pre-occupation with control and the exertion of power over other people.

This is where we can get in touch with our own issues of domina-tion and submission. A person with little consciousness of the third chakra may be given to a tyrannical kind of assertiveness, spending much time and effort extending areas of personal domination. Or he or she may be just the opposite: submissive and cowed. More likely it will be a case of alternating between the two, depending on the situa-tion. Such people are often labelled 'authoritarian personalities' and are given to instantly 'ranking' others as either superior or inferior. They cast others into the roles of either authority figures or underlings.

The Heart Chakra, at the centre of the sternum, is the seat of com-passion, of joy, of unconditional love and the feeling of oneness with all life. When we breathe in deep breaths to the heart, it gives us courage (*coeur* is the French for heart). Many people feel that their essence or soul lies here.

When a child is born, the heart region is usually open and free. The child experiences natural self-love, spontaneous affection and reaches toward other people. But the heart is sensitive and easily wounded. If the child experiences rejection, indifference or disapproval, the heart is hurt. If such hurts persist, the child will gradually begin to pull back from a heartfelt response and eventually develop self-protective, defensive patterns of response.

The Throat Chakra is situated at the base of the throat, midway between front and back. It is the seat of the expression of self. Whereas love is the principal expression of the heart, truth, derived from actual experience, can be delivered through the voice. The neck and throat form a pathway or bridge between the body and the head. When there is congestion here, or blockages, the emotions cannot travel up from the belly into expression; thus 'I have a lump in my throat.' It is here that a person can gain the power of having a voice, a unique identity. The throat chakra is also to do with taking in the truth of others; when we cannot accept something we say 'It sticks in my gullet', 'I can't swallow that'. The feelings associated with the developed throat chakra are tranquillity, acceptance and assurance.

The Sixth (Brow) Chakra, or third eye is situated in the centre of the forehead. It is where vision and understanding take place, and the union of opposites. It is associated with the ability to see through time and space. It is the seat of higher consciousness, discrimination, mental clarity and spiritual understanding.

The Seventh or Crown Chakra is at the top of and above the head. It is where divine guidance is received, and is the place of universal connection and transcendence. The two upper chakras do not generate emotion. They govern mental and spiritual faculties and in the yogic tradition are said to be 'beyond emotion' in the sense of being aware of emotion without being bodily involved with it. Emotion does not 'grip' or 'sway' this higher consciousness.

The traditional view is that the chakras are connected with the various glands that govern the organs and physical functioning of the body. The energy system of the chakras thus acts as a sort of interface between the spiritual energies and the physical. The flow of energy from one to the other can be blocked by emotions, thoughts or past trauma, and exercises to 'open' the chakras help develop a free flow of energy between spirit, mind and body.

If we visualize our chakras one by one, the mind gets inside the body and the spirit is nourished. We can calm and centre ourselves through them, and learn about ourselves. The concept of the chakras is useful because it helps us realize where our energy is. Life energy is channelled through the different chakras – and the one where our energy is particularly concentrated colours our reality.

At first our energy has to be in the first chakra, for survival. Once survival is assured, then a person starts to experience sexual arousal: at the instinctual level this is necessary for reproduction, but because it can be so pleasurable it holds our attention. The experience of orgasm can be the first intimation for most people of a state of transcendence. If an individual has a powerful third chakra and a strong need for control, on the other hand, then there may be problems reaching orgasm or the experience of orgasm may be short, because the controlling mind does not like the idea of surrender. And so on. So the chakras are a way, one way, of learning about and experiencing the integration of mind, body and spirit. The body then becomes a live part of our spirituality and our thinking, and vice versa. For example, when I am driving the car or reading the paper, I remain conscious of my body. When I am making love, my soul is involved and my heart is open.

Sexuality and wholeness

In chapter 5 I talked about a domination approach to sex, and a hara approach. You may remember that the attributes of a hara approach included both surrender and merging. If I take these two a bit further now, the implications are amazing. Surrender of control is essential to lovemaking which is satisfying at a deep level. This means moving from the third chakra, the seat of ego strength and control, up into the heart chakra, the seat of unconditional love and oneness. But surrender implicitly involves the dissolution of the ego – that is why we are so fearful of it, and resistant. To surrender to the other not only requires tremendous trust, but *accepting the power of the other*. If it can be done, our body, mind and spirit get what they really want, not just temporary relief of tension or a high. We know from our instincts that our bodies, minds and spirits seek fusion with another. We crave to become one, not remain as two. That's where ecstasy lies.

Now I come to the nub. These two acts, surrender and merging, have revolutionary consequences in terms of power. In this kind of lovemaking one person gains bliss, satisfaction and strength with and through another. For this kind of sex to work, a person *cannot* compete; someone else becomes a complement, necessary. And the more you are sensitive to and nourishing of this other, the more likely you are to reach that ultimate, lasting ecstasy of fusion. So, on the one hand you *gain* more power by being totally with another. On the other, you cease to *need* power over. So, in this kind of sexuality lies the end of the necessity for domination power.

This discovery stunned me. I had always been able to see, more or less, what the connection is between power and sex in a domination sense. But I never realized the full implications of the connection between *hara power* and sex. Not only does a hara approach make sexuality infinitely more satisfying, it makes ecstasy possible. Not only does it unite the body and the soul, it bridges that gap that has yawned over us for thousands of years, the gap between sexuality and spirituality. Lastly it shows us, teaches us in living reality, how we *gain* power by being with another and *cease to need* power over another.

The centuries-old gulf between sexuality and spirituality means that we have lost the ability to speak of these things openly. Listen to the ancient poetry of the sacred marriage of the goddess Inanna and her lover-king Dumuzi.

> As for me, my vulva
> For me the piled high hillock,
> Me – the maid, who will plow it for me?
> My vulva, the watered ground – for me,
> Me, the Queen, who will station the ox there?

The response is:

> Oh Lordly Lady, the King will plow it for you,
> Dumuzi, the King, will plow it for you.

And Inanna, overjoyed, says:

> Plow my vulva, man of my heart!

The inner lover

Human beings crave wholeness. You and I might spend our lives looking for the perfect other, because we have this primordial sense that union with that other will bring us bliss. And we are right. Finding the other half of ourselves will bring us bliss. But here's the twist. While this 'other half' may be personified in an actual exterior person, ultimately it is to be found inside. I may start by looking for it in sex, but more often than not that is a failure, because I am treating the other person as an object. When I am able to cease this separation, surrender to the other and to merge with him, I begin getting some clues about the ecstasy of wholeness, of union. But the ultimate other I am looking for is in myself; the man in the woman and the woman in the man. So the challenge is to develop and realize that side of me, masculine or feminine, which is dormant. (It is not necessarily the opposite to one's biological gender which is dormant; in a 'new' man, it is quite possibly the masculine which needs to be realized, and an achieving career woman may need to search for the feminine.)

When this other in myself is realized, I then have the possibility of what Jung calls the *hierosgamos – the mysterium conjunctionis*, the sacred marriage, the coming together and integration of the whole self. This is what I began to refer to in chapter 3, talking about feminists finding their feminine sides. I shall come back to it again in chapter 9.

Most of us have an ideal partner inside us, in our imagination. This is my most desired male: he is physically strong, he can carry me easily in his arms, he's joyful and full of fun and playfulness (when I meet him he picks me up and twirls me around), he makes me giddy with delight, he's able to see right into people, to take his pauses. I spent a lot of my life looking for him, *out there*. But what I have finally learned, after half a century, is that he's not out there, he's *in here*. I *am* him. Somehow I *have* these characteristics. I wouldn't know so much about them if I didn't have them.

I learned this sitting in a room with a big window facing west, late on a November afternoon as the light was leaving. There was a tree outside with knobbly branches ending in twigs which achieved an overall roundness of outline, becoming blacker against the amethyst sky. I was talking about him, and at the same time I was revelling in this tree, wondering how on an ordinary November Friday there could be this astonishing beauty. And somehow I perceived, dimly at first, that the beauty of the tree lay in the connection between it and me, in the fact that I could see it. Other people might have just walked past. That tree, that shape, against that light, might mean nothing to them but it was utterly perfect, beautiful and nourishing to me. I fed off it. It is the same with him. He makes me giddy with delight because I can see him. I know about him. *He is this to me.* I know him.

What I want to say now is that *this isn't it*. This isn't union. This recognition of the ideal other inside ourselves is a prerequisite, a stage on the way. It is blissful to find that one is this other, that one can own and liberate and use these characteristics. And that is what Joseph Campbell says – 'Follow your bliss.' Your bliss can take you there. It is the path to union. But it is not union.

Relationships

Whether or not you are making love with another person, a close relationship is an extraordinary opportunity to develop wholeness. This is true particularly when things *are not* going well, since arguments and strong emotions reveal our projections onto others. Some people are convinced that we choose a partner who presents us with precisely the same difficulties we experienced in our childhood, so that we can learn as adults to respond to those challenges and grow through them. In this scenario, our long-term partner will of course be chosen for the way he or she warms us, understands us, makes us feel wonderful.

That is what falling in love is all about. And underneath are all the *other* reasons we have chosen this person – because he or she presents to us anew the challenges that our parents originally faced us with. In a partner we may, for example, have to deal with our fear of our father, our inability to separate from our mother, our terror of being abandoned or our fury at being belittled.

We are drawn to each other because of what we know the other knows, at some unconscious level. It is always a fit with what we need in order to grow. Our invisible antennae can spot that fit across a crowded room, and we fall. And then after the period of being in love has passed, we begin to be irresistibly niggled by the other. It seems as though the other knows exactly which buttons to push and when, and we are driven to our depths. We then have a choice. We can use this as a way to learn about ourselves, and do some very painful growing up, or we can separate. If we split up, and eventually develop another relationship, we shall inevitably find ourselves faced with the same issues again, in another guise.

In other words, one of the paths to our own adultness is through a close relationship, with all its ups and downs. This is similar to the dialectical model, where opposites exist in a necessary and intimate relationship, to mirror back to each other the truth of each. Without such a dynamic there may be less chance of 'seeing' the issues and bringing them into consciousness.

On a less intimate level, we tend to go around noticing separateness and polarity: 'Oh, she's a Muslim but I'm a Christian'. 'He went to a private school, so I'm not having anything to do with him'. 'But they're *French*', etc. A lot of this is prejudice, prejudgement. It puts people into pigeon-holes and labels them. Stereotyping is the dangerous part of dualistic thinking, for it prevents us seeing people simply as fellow human beings, as people who have the same fears and hopes as we do.

The great wisdom which is available from the goddess traditions is the *relationship* between the aspects of being, not the separation. One way that this has been passed down is in the figure of Kali, the Hindu triple goddess of creation, preservation and destruction. According to Barbara Walker, Kali was the basic archetypal image of the birth-and-death Mother, simultaneously womb and tomb, giver of life and devourer of her children: the same magic portrayed in a thousand ancient religions. Her tantric title is Shakti. She is the origin of the Black Madonna mentioned in chapter 5. She is light as well as dark, violent as well as gentle, cruel as well as kind. She therefore represents life, in all its rich fullness but, because she is nature and goes through unstoppable cycles, she is also terrible and terrifying. She is capable even of devouring what she has brought forth, and re-absorbing into herself the life she gives – this is why she is tomb and death, as well as womb and life.

The goddess Kali

Marie-Louise Von Franz has the following passage in her book on fairy-tales:

> Sometimes, for instance, in the woods, or on the mountains, you see a roe-buck trying to crawl over the ice with a cancerous growth hanging from it – the other roebuck kick it aside, and it sinks, then struggles up and walks a few steps farther, dragging itself along for weeks with the cancer, until one day, thank God, it does not get up anymore. Or a fox will partially eat a swan frozen on the ice and leave it to struggle for hours and hours with a wing eaten away . . . Nature has that secret of killing in the most cruel way, and also giving birth in the most beautiful way to the most beautiful things. (B5)

Through my relationship, I have discovered this Kali side of myself – the hideous, savage, outraged destroyer. She is my shadow and she is terrible. But she is part of me, and I need to know her and to accept her.

Acceptance of ourselves is not easy to achieve on our own. We need ways of learning that we are acceptable to others, to experience that it is all right to be who we really are. I once did a weekend course at the Actors Institute in London called the Mastery. It helps people discover their creative potential through learning to express themselves. People come along with a two minute performance of any kind – a song to sing, poem to recite, speech to make – and the facilitator and group help them to work with that to express their real self. Amazing things happen. But what is most wonderful is that in that loving environment, people are able to lose their masks, to stop pretending to be someone else, and to be just as they are, symbolically naked. They end up loving each and every person who is brave enough to do that, whatever they are like, because their sheer unadorned, undefended, pretence-free basic self is so compelling. It is real. So it reaches us.

There are many ways in which we can have an experience like that, where we see others not as titles or roles or clothes or make-up or possessions, but as vulnerable human beings like ourselves. Then we will undoubtedly love them.

Even for people who have not had an experience like that and don't know what I am talking about, it is worth simply trying to notice what connects people, rather than what separates them. She may be Muslim and I a Christian, but we both have a toddler to cope with. He may have gone to quite a different school than I did, but he also has a backache, like me.

This kind of ability, to be 'in' both sides, to experience what it is like to be both sides, is the path not only to balance but to serenity. We realize that a rose is not only a rose, it is also soon to be compost, and it will be compost so that there can be a rose again next year.

The Vietnamese Buddhist monk Thich Nhat Hanh says that we are imprisoned by our ideas of good and evil. We want to be only good, and we want to remove all evil. But that is because we forget that good is made of non-good elements.

> Suppose I am holding a lovely branch. When we look at it with a non-discriminative mind, we see this wonderful branch. But as soon as we distinguish that one end is the left and the other end is the right, we get into trouble. We may say we want only the left, and we do not want the right (as you hear very often), and there is trouble right away. If the rightist is not there, how can you be a leftist? Let us say that I do not want the right end of this branch, I only want the left. So, I break off half of this reality and throw it away. But as soon as I throw the unwanted half away, the end that remains becomes right (the new right). Because as soon as the left is there, the right must be there also. I may become frustrated and do it again. I break what remains of my branch in half, and still I have the right end here.
>
> The same may be applied to good and evil. You cannot be good alone. You cannot hope to remove evil, because thanks to evil, good exists, and vice versa. (1992. B11)

Thanks to the work of archaeologists, psychologists, and anthropologists, we now know (which our grandparents did not) that separate peoples all over the world have myths and legends which are expressing the same idea in different ways. Jung found universal patterns and images in his study of the world's mythologies and religious symbols, as well as in the dreams of his patients. In other words, that there are some universal truths which humankind is experiencing; that however different we may seem, we are in fact a unity. This makes reconciliation possible in an international sense.

Where, you may ask, is the power in all this – power in the sense of how I manage in the world, how I stand up to my boss, how I help to make peace in the world instead of war. That is the business of the last part of this book. Let me recap briefly. The business of the first part was to investigate what power is. I outlined a kind of power which has prevailed in our world for several thousand years – power understood as physical strength, domination, hierarchy and ultimately military force. I called this kind of power domination power, essentially a question of having power *over* somebody or something else. I used the experiences of women to illustrate how this power is felt, while pointing out that both sexes use domination power. Towards the end of chapter 3, I introduced the notion of another kind of power – power *to* and power *with* – which I called hara power. The business of the second part of the book was to investigate ways in which both men and women can rediscover and develop this power. Chapter 4 dealt with power from self-knowledge, chapter 5 with power from the body, chapter 6 with power from the soul, and this chapter has been about the power to be gained from union, from bringing opposites together. The third part of the book will be devoted to the ways in which hara power can be used in our lives and in the world.

But first we have one more chapter – this time not about our bodies, our minds, or our souls – but about the Great Spirit, the greatest source of power there is.

CHAPTER 8

Power in the Great Mysterious

Here nature knows us. The earth knows us. We make our offerings to certain trees, certain rocks, to natural water springs, on top of hills . . . We have songs and prayers. Our history cannot be told without naming the cliffs and mountains that have witnessed our people.

Ruth Benally Yinishye, 1988

This chapter is about power of an entirely different dimension to anything that human beings can do all by themselves: it is the power inherent in the cosmos. It is power to which our ancestors had access, and to which we can have access. Since it is impossible to approach this kind of power directly, a way of describing it is through those who know about it – ancient cultures, shamans and other healers. Another way to approach this 'Great Mysterious' is through what it feels like, by way of the sacred places where it is to be found, sacred sexuality, sacred times of the year, sacred knowledge, and the sacredness to be found in some communities. One community, that of Ladakh in India, is described in some detail. The subsequent section concerns what people need to do to have access to this kind of power, namely suspension of disbelief, participation, and surrender. Lastly, I look at what getting in touch with this kind of power means in terms of living in today's world.

For the past 3,000 or 4,000 years, under patriarchal religions, we in the West have experienced a world in which God the Father has the real power. He delegates it a bit to man, to whom he gives power over animals and the earth. Power in nature does not exist. God is an idea, not a place or a feeling. Power is perceived as coming from outside, from above.

In God the Mother, the power is everywhere. Feminine creation 'brings forth from within'. Trees, rocks and ferns are quite as alive as animals and people. Power comes from the exchange of energy between beings and their deity which is all around and particularly in the earth. Some North American Indians call it the Great Mysterious. Power is within, and below. This could be shown as follows:

God the Father	Power is with God, delegated to man	Power is outside, and above
God the Mother	Power is everywhere, in the exchange of energy	Power is within, and below

During these closing years of the 20th century, some human beings are once again beginning to realize that our environment has the power of life and death over us. Our ancestors knew this, and regarded communication with their environment, and utter respect for it, as essential to survival. We on the other hand have been raised in the belief that man can and should 'conquer' nature; gouge out what we want from the earth, slaughter other species to the point where there are none left, cut down the forests which are the lungs of the earth, and poison the air and the water. We have treated the world as though it were a business in liquidation, in Herman Daly's words – a lifeless, defunct entity to be broken up and taken from. The belief is that we have been given the right to kill as we will, to use as we will, because we own nature. We have been given domination over it by God the Father.

What we are beginning to rediscover is that we can't do this and expect to survive as a species. Why? Because, although we *think* we can artificially reproduce what we have destroyed, what we *cannot* do is predict the effect on the global ecosystem of what we are doing. This is because the whole globe and everything on it is a vast and inter-related system. When we interfere with even one part that interference changes all the rest.

Chaos theory

The recent development of chaos theory in all the sciences has formally recognized the inter-related nature of the universe. Chaos theory shows how tiny alterations in a system move through the system in apparently random ways to generate widespread changes. The classic example is the conception that the effect on the surrounding air molecules of the beating of a butterfly's wings in one part of the globe might trigger off a storm halfway across the world.

Perhaps the most crucial implication of the theory is that we cannot, in principle, predict the behaviour of complex systems. It isn't simply that we do not have the mental capacity, or that our computers don't yet have the necessary processing power – it is a property of the systems themselves. What Edward Lorenz discovered, with his weather-forecasting computer models, is that the weather system is infinitely sensitive. The tiniest change in one variable can make a vast difference. For example, if the temperature today is 57.00001 degrees celsius then the result can be a weather pattern over the whole continent which would have been completely different if the temperature had been 57.00002.

Naturally there were others who were alert to these ideas at the same time as Lorenz, but his genius was to recognize that this was a property of the system itself, and not just some mistake in calculations or an error in his model. Since then, all sorts of people have tested his conclusion with all sorts of systems – including many that no-one thought were very complex at all – and have discovered the same thing.

Traditional physics used, and still uses, a model of how the world works which is a cause-and-effect model. It's a great model: it explains a lot and it enables a lot of technology to be invented. But it has a tremendous limitation. It is, by its nature, linear, sequential and necessary. 'If I put this match in a barrel of petrol fumes, then the fumes ignite and then there is an explosion' etc. In fact logic has the same ordering. 'If this is a cow, and all cows are animals, then this is an animal.' In both cases, the reasoning is linear and sequential. By 'necessary', I mean that you can't argue with the conclusion – or say that it doesn't seem like that to you; it follows inevitably from the premises.

This all works fine until you come to complex systems. Try using the cause-and-effect model to predict what will happen in a family. Try using logic to sort out arguments – as some of my academic colleagues used to insist on trying to do: they were permanently puzzled at why it didn't work!

There is another model which is well known from Eastern religions and philosophies, which is interdependence. Thich Nhat Hanh said once, 'If I clap my hands the effect is everywhere.' He talks about what he calls 'interbeing'. He even shows how you can see the whole world in a piece of paper: it is as it is because everything else is as it is. So, the new physics is adopting a model of the world which has been known to, and used by, much of humanity for a very long time.

We have already learned that the gases produced by refrigerators destroy the ozone layer. It is clear to us that the thinning of the ozone layer permits harmful ultraviolet rays from the sun to reach our bodies and give us cancer. But we continue to insist that we can control the effects of the way we as a species are living – that we shall find a technical fix. This is hubris (hubris means more than simply pride or arrogance, it means an excess of ambition or pride which ultimately causes ruin).

It is hubris because it is not one separate isolated part, one thing, that we are dealing with in these cases; it is the whole delicate, infinitely complex, inter-related billion-year-old cosmos that is at stake. How dare we – tiny specks alive on a grain of sand during a pipsqueak of a second – how dare we presume to say we have the power to fix it? That kind of power is illusory. To meet the needs of the cosmos today, another kind of power is necessary.

Have you ever been to a huge waterfall, like Niagara? Have you seen a volcano erupt? Have you seen a tree struck by lightning? What is the biggest storm you have witnessed? There you have clues, albeit tiny ones, to the power that we are talking about, the power *in* the cosmos. The earth is molten, liquid red-hot rock. Down the depth of the skin on an orange, it is there beneath us. Power. Power of an entirely different dimension to little men and women running around in white coats in a laboratory, or running around in grey suits in government offices. This is the kind of power I shall investigate now – who knows about it, what it feels like, what it requires of us, what it means.

Who knows about it?

Growing numbers of people. Here are just a few examples.

Ancient cultures

There are still some cultures alive in the 20th century designed around the core concept that the natural world is alive. Some North American and South American Indian tribes live in this way. The Kogi mentioned in the Introduction, for example, live in deliberate isolation in dense mountain jungle in Colombia. They see the world as a single living being and their whole way of life is dedicated to nurturing it. They feel that humankind has been given an immense privilege and responsibility to care for the world. They are, in short, an ecological community whose morality is wholly concerned with the health of the planet.

Shamans and witches

There are individuals all over the world rediscovering the crafts of the shaman and the witch. Anthropologist Michael Harner, who has made an extensive study of shamanism, says that today, from Zurich to Auckland, from Chicago to Sao Paulo, humans are again taking up these ancient ways of healing, divining and wisdom.

The training may take place in drumming circles or groups which meet regularly for practice and healing work. These groups are autonomous – working, as shamans have from time immemorial, independently in small communities to learn, help themselves and help others. These informal communities are part of a larger community which is now international. It has no hierarchy or dogma, for the spiritual authorities, as in tribal times, are found directly from experience by each individual shamanic journeyer.

This was a surprise to me. Shamans and witches have generally had a bad press over recent centuries. 'You bet they have,' says my resident sceptic, 'and for very good reasons. Now you've really gone too far asking people to take you seriously when you're writing about *witches* for heaven's sake.'

This is a tough one and I have to deal with my sceptic head-on. Yes, I say, we think of witches as scary old hags who cackle, frighten children and turn people into stones or frogs. And we were meant to. For four centuries the European Christian church was mobilized to crush out the remains of Western paganism. This action was eagerly supported by the European medical professions, who saw the witches (who were also herbal healers and midwives) as economic rivals. So it is not surprising that today we find it hard to overcome these centuries of conditioning. We find it hard to let down our guard against rituals, moonlight ceremonies and bonfires. When it comes to the ability to transmute from one shape to another, we denounce it as magic and back off fast.

And yet all these things are happening around us, with some extraordinary results, if we can simply open our hearts and minds to it. All we have to do as a first step is admit the *possibility* that there may be something in it.

Our prejudices about witchcraft and shamanic work mean that these sources of knowledge are still confined to the few. Today you would not consult a witch or shaman as you would your doctor! One of the reasons for this is perhaps because shamanism has been defined in terms of power, rather than in terms of healing. Our approach has been to focus on the exotic elements of shamanism – elements of drama and sorcery, rather than learning about the deep, transformational aspects of these healing arts. As Vicki Noble says, this makes sense because we do not understand transformation the way we understand power. Western observers rarely notice that shamanism has anything to do with the feminine, and yet all shamans – no matter what part of the world they are from – always work in the realm of the feminine.

Another reason is the fear we have acquired of the unknown, possibly thanks to the way in which the church has painted everything that is not Christian as being dark and fearful. It is characteristic of those who exercise domination power to try to destroy what they do not understand, because they see it as a threat. We shall come back to this question of power at the end of the chapter.

Other healers who use energy

Other kinds of healers, also practising ancient methods, know about this kind of power because they are using energy. Acupuncture has worked on this principle for thousands of years, and the Chinese word often used to denote energy is *chi*. Yoga also works with energy; in India, the word for energy is *shakti*, and it's clearly female, the female being seen as the awakener of energies. Zero-balancing is an example of a more recent use of energy pathways in the bone structure, to release and heal unease and pain.

Once we become seriously interested in energy we discover that it not only works powerfully in the human body, it also extends beyond the body, into the aura. It is but a short step from this to understanding what to ancient people was, and for some surviving ones still is, the core principle of their existence – namely that all life has energy, and that the energy from one (be it tree, dog or person) not only affects but can pass to another. Modern quantum physics has just discovered and 'proved' this, which is quite funny in a way, but also means that some unprecedented connections can now be made. Since it is now more or less respectable to subscribe to these ideas, a great deal more contact and interaction can take place between science and spirituality.

When power is everywhere, what does it feel like?

Here I want to give some examples, some tastes, of what this kind of power feels like – in sacred places, sacred sex, sacred times and experiences, sacred knowledge – as well as offering a description of a community in northern India who live in the midst of and through this kind of power.

Sacred places

When we were small, if we were lucky, we had a place we could go when things were bad: a tree house perhaps, a spot at the end of the garden or along the canal. There we were able to get sorted out, get our strength back. Perhaps, if we are lucky, we still have one: when life at the office or in the kitchen just gets too much, we have somewhere we can have a breather – a particular rosebed in the park, a favourite view which nourishes our soul, a place in the countryside where we can retreat and get strong again. In doing this we are no different from thousands of generations before us. This is our two-way spiritual communication with the awesome power of the earth. It is not nature worship; it is a personal relationship with the natural world. We derive confidence and energy from the environment we know well. To give a simple and immediate example: while I was writing this book, a helpful friend sent me some references. Here's the last paragraph of her letter:

I'm sitting in the garden at 6.45 am with the cat and a cup of tea. It's blissful. There are bees crawling up and down the foxgloves, and while I've been writing the sun has spread itself over half the garden and I can see 5 butterflies who have spread their wings wide so they can sunbathe in the warmth. Not a sound except gently murmuring birds. Another wonderful hour before I have to go inside and begin the day.

Joseph Campbell and Carl Jung shared a passion for mythology, legend and folklore, and spent time with remote peoples whose cultures had been little affected by 20th century technology. They were both struck by the groundedness which they encountered among people who lived close to the earth and its rhythms, what Campbell called 'the tremendous power which people living in the world of nature are experiencing all the time'.

A Brazilian doctor and psychiatrist, José Rosa, has become interested in the same thing. In his practice he discovered that when a person can become more physically, psychologically and mentally grounded by going into a field or forest and making contact with the earth, he or she feels joy, protection and security in the sense of being 'home'.

He decided to use this insight with individuals in psychotherapy. He took them to a retreat south-west of Rio de Janeiro – a place in the mountains by a waterfall. He helped each person search out and find a spot in nature to which he or she was instinctively drawn, and then worked with them there. By the end of the workshop, he found that the psychological work had had more power and focus than similar work done in an office. His clients seemed to have greater emotional and mental clarity, and more courage to face the truth. After further experiments he attributed this to the power they received from being in a particular spot which was right for them.

This takes us back to the connection we often had with the earth as children. As we grow up, we learn to block ourselves from our feelings and as a consequence lose our grounding. This leads us to feel insecure, and we try to resolve this by accumulating material goods and attempting to dominate nature. The harmful cycle escalates as abuse and exploitation lead to serious environmental problems, which in turn threaten our very existence. This makes us even more insecure and ungrounded. Harner concludes:

Only by coming back to the land, by respecting the Earth Mother and by making peace with Her can we break the dangerous vicious circles which threaten our existence. By becoming truly grounded we are able (both individually and collectively) to transform our society, which is in a state of crisis and disrepair. (B11)

Sacred sexuality

The idea of sex being sacred is too odd for most of us in late 20th century Europe, probably because we have become so accustomed to seeing sex in terms of 'performance' or gratification. But for our remote ancestors, for whom sex did not imply impurity, and for some existing indigenous people, ceremonial sex was and is a powerful act leading to spiritual perfection.

Monica Sjoo and Barbara Mor have reconstructed scenes from Neolithic times. They describe how the Moon Goddess was worshipped in orgiastic rites, being the divinity of matriarchal women who were free to take as many lovers as they chose. Women could 'surrender' themselves to the Goddess by making love to a stranger in her temple. As we have already seen, this has been called 'sacred prostitution' by male historians, but the word is totally misleading. This was not any kind of service to men, nor did any woman have to do this to live. It was a way for a woman to experience, for a ritual moment, a sense of fusion of masculine and feminine. The goddess comes into being 'in the moment of union' – a moment of psychic as well as sexual union. And this was one way that men could partake in her essence also, through the body of a woman.

> The rite was meant to recharge the living Goddess, and to enlarge the woman's ego-consciousness into an experience of cosmic sexual power and flow. It was a way for each woman to experience herself as 'the moon.' (B3)

Far-fetched? Well, research being carried out today has discovered neurological connections between religious or trance experience and female sexuality. A report on the work of neuropsychologist James Prescott at the Institute of Humanistic Science states:

> In women's brains there are unique neural links between the forebrain and the cerebellum, which allow sensations of physical pleasure to be directly integrated in the neocortex, or high brain centre. This explains why some women experience orgasm so intense that they enter 'religious' trance, or altered states of consciousness. And this ecstatic female orgasmic experience, in which the physical and the spiritual are fused and realized as one, is at the core of all mystical experience.

Apparently human male brains do not have these neurological connections. It is pointed out that human male sexuality has not evolved radically beyond primate sexuality, while human females, through the shift from estrous to menstrual cycles (in sharp contrast to primates), have evolved a sexual capacity that is *not* strictly for reproduction but is for affection and bonding. The researchers conclude that it is women who must take the lead in further human evolution – 'toward the integration of the conscious and the unconscious mind and to a more profound understanding of the spiritual nature of the species'.

These 'discoveries' go right to the heart of what I have been saying about female sexuality and about dualism. Originally, there was no split between matter and spirit, between body and soul. We are slowly and gradually finding our way 'back' to that connection between the sexual and the spiritual, but we are doing it in a way which hopefully will reflect something of humanity's experience on the journey. The pain and the knowledge accumulated in the collective will perhaps make of tomorrow's sacred sexuality something even richer and more ecstatic than we can imagine of yesterday.

In the meantime, as I see it, a person developing his or her feminine qualities today has to become a sort of commuter between the super-market and the shrine, between the realities of today's high street and the realities of other ways of seeing.

Sacred times

In chapter 5, I talked about the impact of ritual: how human beings need it in order to cope with life's tough experiences, and to digest life's wondrous experiences. If someone close to us dies and there is no funeral, or for some reason we do not go to the funeral, it is much harder to lay that person to rest. If people get married and they are unable to have a ceremony, a celebration and singing and dancing, they miss a dimension to their joy. In the old days country people used to celebrate the bringing in of the harvest in a big way.

In Britain certainly we have almost lost the most ancient seasonal festivals – except for the occasional maypole dance. But these mark-ings of the year, of the cycle of birth, early growth, fertility, ripening, reaping, decay, death and then rebirth again, are vital to both our psy-chic and our physical health. To our psychic health because they show us, year after year, that death is not final but part of a cycle, that every-thing comes again; this is deeply rooting and reassuring for us. To our physical health because they encourage us to allow our bodies to be in tune with the seasons – to dance all night in summer if we want to, to sleep long hours and store up energy in the winter. They also help us to understand what is going on in our lives. If we feel depressed, for example, and it is November, then we know that is not surprising:

something in us needs to die for the new growth to come in the new year.

Solar festivals

What is exciting is that some people are beginning to retrieve and reinstate the old seasonal festivals. Besides the solstices and equinoxes, there are four quarter-days which lie between them which are particularly important to the feminine in that they are connected with the earth and its cycles. I shall give the common name for them, then the Celtic, the date, and then the meaning of the festival.

Candlemass	Imbolc or Brigid	1 February	awakening spring, new life, symbolized by snowdrops.
May Day	Beltane	1 May	fertility, procreation, symbolized by dancing.
Harvest	Lammas or Lughnasad	1 August	reaping of the first corn and making of bread.
All Hallows	Samhain	1 November	death and passing on to other realms.

In 1993 on All Hallows Eve I went with my partner and stepdaughter to Avebury stone circle in Wiltshire. The site is considered to be a Neolithic centre for goddess worship, and the goddess was said to retreat into the underworld after Samhain, or All Hallows. We climbed up to the Long Barrow. This barrow is 340 feet long and seems to have been shaped in the gigantic image of the goddess, the entrance being through the birth passage and the chambers within representing her womb.

The full moon was buried behind a bank of thick cloud, and it was windy, wet and chill. I wondered if we were right to come, since my stepdaughter, then 17, was finding it freaky, and the atmosphere was certainly of a tomb: cold and dank. We crouched beneath the huge boulder which guards the entrance to the Long Barrow to light our candles. Suddenly there were voices coming from within. We advanced down the passage of boulders. To my amazement, soft flickering light was pouring out of the barrow, and within it was warmth. Where the warmth came from, I have no idea. Four or five people were meditating in the candlelight. We joined them for a while. As we went down the path when we left, others were coming up, carrying drums and flutes.

That is just one instance of the old seasonal festivals being reinstated. If you visit the other ancient sites on Beltane or Lammas, you may well find people dancing in circles, just as our ancestors did 4,000 years ago.

The particular sacred times in the lives of women, of course, are menstruation, childbirth and menopause, each one reminding her of the power in her belly or hara, and each one marking her transition into one of the three ages of woman: virgin, mother and crone. Increasingly we are rediscovering ways to celebrate these.

In the old days the ritual for the girl with her first menstruation would perhaps have been just to sit in a hut and realize what was happening to her, that she was now a vehicle of a transpersonal power. These things were happening to her beyond her own personal wishes, and it was not up to her to make decisions regarding them. As Joseph Campbell points out, one could say that life overtakes women in this way. But the transpersonal power of nature never overtakes a boy in the same way, so in the traditional societies he had to have such a powerful physical experience that he was broken into becoming a vehicle of something.

This was the reason for ceremonies of initiation – the key time when a boy makes the transition to manhood. In some societies these rituals were extremely powerful, taking young men to the limits of physical survival.

Young men of the indigenous peoples living around the upper Missouri River in the 1830s had no choice about going through this ceremony. They were first taken into a great hut and made to sit for up to five days without eating. Joseph Campbell describes how incisions were cut in their chests and wooden pegs about a foot long and two inches thick were pressed right through their pectoral muscles like skewers. Ropes were attached to the exposed ends of the pegs. More wooden skewers were then forced through their thigh and calf muscles, and heavy buffalo skulls were hung from these. He quotes a witness saying that when the pegs were being put through their muscles, these boys made a very special point of smiling and acting as though nothing was happening.

Then the boys were hung by the ropes attached to the skewers through their pectoral muscles to the roof of the hut. Each one held his medicine bag which was his special power resource. The men then beat them with long poles so that they spun around and around until finally they passed out. When all the boys were unconscious, they were dropped to the floor. As soon as they began to recover, they were grabbed by two strong men and dragged, first around the hut and then outside around the ceremonial field. This continued until the skewers were eventually pulled out from the boys' leg muscles. Then the men dropped them. By then, of course, they were almost finished. Campbell concludes:

> The point of the ritual was that the boys were to experience death. That is to say, to experience a total giving up, an experience of resting well in god, of yielding themselves to the divine power. (B5)

Interestingly, these young men said at the time, 'We have to learn to suffer in order to compensate for the suffering of our women.' As Joseph Campbell comments, life brings suffering on a woman, and the man has to match it by imposing suffering on himself.

All the old initiation rites were based on the motif of death and resurrection for very good reasons. Until their teens, young males are dependent on their parents, as children they are helpless without them. They need to break out of that psychological dependence and into an autonomous identity – their own authenticity – with the ability to have and express their own views, to be their own person. A profound experience is necessary to make and mark this change.

It is hard to find such initiations in contemporary Western life, as we saw in chapter 3. Boys drift into adulthood, often taking their boyishness with them. The Bar Mitzvah in the Jewish faith is a maturity ritual, but not an initiation rite – death is not faced. Young men today invent their own initiations, precariously and unconsciously – courting terror in all kinds of daredevil sports – but, like the experience of war, this does not work in the same way because it is haphazard and death may come by accident. For an initiation to work, the experience of possible death must be controlled and supervised by older men in full consciousness of the meaning of what is happening.

The closest I have been able to find to a powerful modern initiation for men is in *The Horned God* by John Rowan. He devotes a chapter to a detailed description of an initiation practice involving five stages of wounding, silence, healing, application and maintenance. (B4)

Death

As is clear from these accounts, probably the most powerful experience a person can have is to face death. Until only a few decades ago, women did it every time they gave birth to a child (and in many parts of the world they still do). To feel the fear of death, and go through it, and come out the other side – that changes a person profoundly. For each of us the fear is different. For one it may be a particular form of death – drowning perhaps, or suffocating. For another it may be the fear of failure – that to fail would be death. For another it may be a private monster in the form of an authority figure who struck terror into her as a child. The task is to face the fear, and not invent endless strategies to avoid it or deny its presence, to look it straight between the eyes.

Anthropologist Michael Harner did his fieldwork on the eastern slopes of the Ecuadorian Andes among the Jivaro Indians. He describes how, after many years' study, he wanted to learn how to practise shamanism the Jivaro way. Before they would teach him, he had to face death. He was taken on a trek across high mountains in thick forest for five days on foot at breakneck speed, forbidden to eat solid food, allowed little sleep, and at one point was deliberately lost by his companions and made to wander alone at night in dense forest. He was then given a powerful herbal drug.

He was awakened by a flash of lightning followed by a thunderous explosion, and jumped up in a panic. Stinging rain pelted his body as the wind ripped at his clothes. Suddenly, about 200 feet away amidst the tree trunks, he could see a luminous form floating slowly toward him. He watched, terrified, as it grew larger and larger, resolving itself into a gigantic, writhing reptilian form which floated directly toward him. Its body shone in brilliant hues of greens, purples, and reds, and as it twisted amidst the lightning and thunder it loomed towards him with a strange sardonic smile.

Remembering what he had been told by the Indians, he grabbed a stick about a foot long and desperately charged the monster with the stick outstretched before him. An earsplitting scream filled the air, and abruptly the forest was empty. The monster was gone, and all that was left behind was silence and serenity. (B11)

However sophisticated we may consider ourselves to be, we still face terrors and fear as well as joy in our lives, and huge bodily and hormonal changes have to be negotiated at certain points. We have the choice of allowing these events to pass unmarked, or of discovering through ritual the time-honoured richness they contain.

Sacred knowledge

What do witches and shamans actually know that most of us do not?

The first thing to say is that real witches and shamans go through a very long, difficult and demanding training. No weekend workshops here; rather years of trial, frustration, acute observation, setback, occasional ecstasy, a gradual mastery of oneself and learning, learning, learning. We spend a similar amount of time training for a career, but what we learn is the mastery of systems or other people, rather than mastery of ourselves.

My own experience of some tribal people is that they perceive their entire surroundings as alive, intelligent and part of themselves. Over centuries they have explored and refined a set of principles, enshrined in myth and teachings, about how it is proper to work with their surroundings to the maximum benefit of all. The medicine man or woman is usually the guardian of these principles and their application, and therefore has to be especially self-aware and disciplined.

The self-mastery is necessary to allow the person to be fully present in emergencies and dangerous situations requiring a calm, effective response. He or she becomes able to do things normally thought of as impossible.

Mircea Eliade, a much honoured scholar and historian of myth, says that shamans are the last humans able to talk with animals. People who learn to become shamans come to realize that what most people perceive as 'reality' only barely touches the grandeur, and mystery, of the universe. The same experience is recounted by those who meditate regularly and profoundly; the more I am able to get out of the prison of the little self and all its obsessions, the more I am able to perceive the astounding beauty and power around me.

The main power that shamans and other healers have, which they share with those who pursue a dedicated spiritual path, is a feeling of being held, being secure, being *safe*. This security comes from being inevitably and unquestionably a part of everything else – experiencing the self as a cell in the body of humanity; knowing that the future as well as the past is accounted for, and that they are in it, whether alive in this life or dead; and experiencing an ecstatic feeling of being cared for, part of, secure. This is reminiscent, of course, of the wonderful feeling for a child of being securely held in a mother's arms.

There is an echo of this in Michael Harner's description of the experience of trainee shamans who are not lonely, even if alone, for they have come to understand that we are never really isolated. They tend to undergo transformation as they discover the incredible safety and love of the normally-hidden universe. The cosmic love they repeatedly encounter in their journeys is increasingly expressed in their daily lives. It is as though everywhere they are surrounded by life, by family.

Sacred community

The environment in which people live can give them great power. By environment, I mean the psychological environment – not just the family, but the wider support structure, their community, where they feel at home. In Africa, people live longer than buildings; in the West, buildings last longer than people. Home to a Westerner is bricks and mortar; home to an African is a group of people and a piece of land, rather than an artificial construction. James Hillman, the psychologist who has in many ways revised modern psychology, has found that individual identity is intimately bound in the framework of community. He studied how Chinese political prisoners managed to resist signing confessions, and found that it was due to their internalized 'community' of ancestors, spirits, loved ones and all those who shared their values. Thus, even when an individual feels most alone or isolated, he or she can be surrounded by a rich interior support system.

If this is true, Hillman suggests, then the ever-increasing experience of loneliness and isolation in the world may be due in part to a loss of self, stemming from people's loss of connection with community and the identity that richly unfolds from it. We do ourselves and our communities great harm by failing to hear and honour the panoply of voices that grace our lives. Hillman suggests that:

> the heroic immovable centre is less a single monad, an inner replica of a single God, than it is a group ethos . . . Imagine them as an interior secret society or tribal unit that works in council . . . How do we observe them during the course of our days? Are we keeping our spirits alive? How do we

imagine ourselves living in such a way that we become members of the spirit world, ancestors?

It is this sense of community, built up layer by layer over years and years, which gives an individual 'rootedness'. The quotation at the beginning of the chapter is about rootedness.

Ladakh

In Ladakh, in north-western India, people still live in this way. High in the Himalaya on the western edge of the Tibetan plateau, life is dictated by the seasons – scorched by the sun in summer, the entire region freezes solid for six months in winter. Ladakh now lies in the Indian state of Jammu and Kashmir, but the region has always had close cultural ties with Tibet: the predominant religion is Tibetan Mahayana Buddhism, and architecture, mythology, medicine and music all reflect a rich Tibetan heritage. The vast majority of Ladakhis are self-sufficient farmers living in small isolated villages – bright patches of green in the stark mountainous desert. Until recent decades Ladakh remained almost totally isolated from the forces of Western industrial culture and thus the roots of social and environmental harmony remain strong.

Although deep meditation is rarely practised outside the monasteries, people spend significant periods of time in a semi-meditative state. Older people in particular recite prayers and mantras as they walk and as they work, even in the middle of conversation. A woman will pass on the path, spinning as she walks, with the Buddhist mantra 'Om mani padme hum' flowing from her lips. Recent research in the West suggests that during meditation a person enters the state of mind that perceives in wholes and patterns rather than by isolating and itemizing things. Ladakhis speak of experiencing the world through their *semba* – a cross between mind and heart. Their knowledge is gained as much from their senses and feelings as from their intellect.

When the sun casts its shadow in the right place from the *nyitho* (obelisk) that stands above each village, the sowing season begins. The astrologer chooses an auspicious day when the elements of earth and water will be matched; someone whose sign he deems favourable is chosen to sow the first seed. Next the spirits of earth and water, the *lu* or *nagas* and *sadak*, are pacified; the worms of the soil, the fish of the streams, the soul of the land. A feast is prepared in their honour and all day long monks recite prayers while no one eats meat or drinks *chang* (barley beer). In a cluster of trees at the edge of the village, where a small mound of clay bricks has been built for the spirits, milk is offered. As the sun sets, other offerings are thrown into the streams.

Manure is brought by donkeys and heaped by the fields: at dawn it is quickly spread in the furrow. At sunrise the whole family gathers, men carry the wooden plough and children lead the *dzo* (a cross between a cow and a yak) to be yoked. They set to work in a festive atmosphere, laughter and song drift back and forth across the fields, mingling with the monk's meditative chant. The *dzo* pull the plough at a dignified and unhurried pace. Behind, the sower throws the seeds and sings:

> Manjusri embodiment of wisdom, hark!
> The gods, the nagas, owner spirits of the Mother Earth, hark!
> May a hundred plants grow from one seed!
> May a thousand grow from two seeds!
> May all the grains be twins!
> Please give enough that we may worship the Buddhas and Bodhisattvas,
> That we may support the sangha and give to the poor!

Even during the harvest season when there is the most work of all, it is done at a relaxed and leisurely pace that allows an 80-year-old as well as a young child to join in and help.

Whole families work in the fields, some reaping the barley, some stacking, others winnowing the crop. Each activity has its own song. The harvest lies in golden sheaves, hundreds to a field, hardly allowing the bare earth to show through. Clear light bathes the valley with an intense brilliance. No ugly geometry has been imposed on this land, no repetitive lines. Everything is easy to the eye, calming to the soul.

The barley is threshed on a large circle of packed earth by a team of animals hitched to a central pole. Winnowing is especially graceful: two people face each other and scoop the crop into the air with wooden forks in easy rhythm. They whistle as they work, inviting the wind:

> Oh pure Goddess of the wind!
> Oh beautiful Goddess of the winds!
> Carry away the chaff!

The grain is then sifted. Before it is put into sacks, a little figure or painting of a deity is ceremoniously placed on top of the pile to bless the harvest.

In the family shrine room on the roof, monks perform ceremonies for *Skangsol* (harvest festival). Their day starts with the sun, making pyramids of barley dough decorated with butter and flour petals as offerings to the five *dharmapalas* or protective deities of Buddhism. For several days they celebrate the harvest and the start of a new cycle. Prayers are offered for the happiness and prosperity, not only of this family or village, but of every sentient being in the universe.

In the evening people gather to sing, drink and dance. A butter lamp is lit in the kitchen and garlands of wheat, barley and peas are strewn around the wooden pillars. They are served tea sitting by low tables, intricately carved with dragons and lotus flowers; flickering light illuminates frescoes on the walls, many generations old.

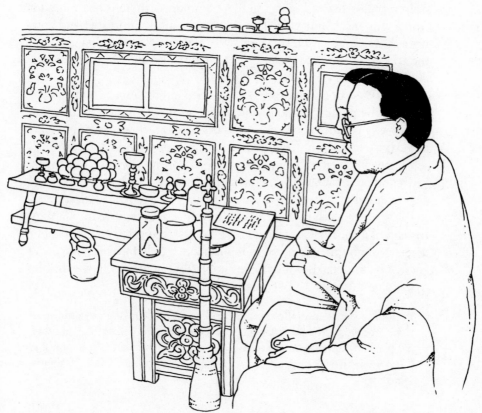

Monks celebrating harvest festival in the home of the Chungpa family, Sankar village, near Leh, Ladakh

Men wear long homespun robes, some a natural beige colour, some dyed the deep maroon of the hills. Many have a large turquoise earring and traditional hairstyle – a plait at the back with the front of their head shaved. Women wear fuller robes topped with a waistcoat of brocade, and jewellery – bracelets, rings, necklaces and dazzling *peraks*, the headdresses studded with literally hundreds of turquoises and corals snaking down their backs. For the Ladakhis there is no great distinction between work and festivity, between spirituality and attendance to the natural environment. All actions are integrated and given meaning in the cycle of existence.

There is a sense of being connected, on a spiritual and psychological level, as well as on a purely physical one. The scale is small enough for the Ladakhis to experience directly their mutual interdependence, their dependence on one another, as well as on the land. With this deep-rooted sense of belonging to a community there is less cause for fear, anger and conflict. Feeling part of a context, nurtured and connected, the sense of self is clearer. When the effect of one's actions on the whole is clear, it is easier both to feel secure and to take responsibility for one's own life.

In the West our relationships have been altered in a systematic way through the process of industrialization, with ever more sophisticated technology coming between us and the natural world. Becoming part of vastly larger socio-economic units has a profound effect on one's self-image and sense of power, as well as on one's connection to the earth and others. Our culture has shifted from values which encourage an empathetic and compassionate relationship with all that lives, towards an objectivity based on external power and manipulation. Instead of a spiritual awareness that we are connected to and dependent on the living world, there is a tendency to behave as if we stand apart. Life in Ladakh is a living example that another way is possible; that we do not have to live fragmented, powerless lives.

> If all of us, and especially the men and women occupying powerful positions, recognise the interdependence between one person and another, people and animals, animals and plants, soil and water, a happy and harmonious world can be created for all living beings. (Tashi Rabgyas, 1986)

What does this kind of power require?

The previous sections of this chapter have described some of the ways a person can get in touch with the power in the Great Mysterious. This section is a more practical one of nuts and bolts, to indicate how people can do it here and now.

Our whole training, from infancy, in modern Western societies is to be suspicious of magic. Any practices we can't explain or don't understand we condemn as superstition. Any phenomena we can't explain or don't understand are suspect, rather than a source of wonder. Mystery is the stuff of crime thrillers and detective novels, not nature. So to reach the Great Mysterious is a tough business for most of us. It includes suspension of disbelief, participation and surrender. Dostoeyevsky knew this:

> (Ivan) Love life more than the meaning of it?
> (Alyosha) Yes, certainly. Love it regardless of logic, as you say. Yes, most certainly regardless of logic, for only then will I grasp its meaning.

Suspension of disbelief

After three centuries of the age of science, we take pride in questioning everything, doubting everything until materially proven. Of course this has its advantages – without this quest for scientific proof, we would not have enjoyed the vast benefits of the discovery of penicillin, for example, as well as the physical comfort of modern life made possible by technological achievements.

But we have gone too far in this passion for proof; we have become unbalanced. It's as though we have done the ghost to death, injecting it, dissecting it, analysing it, measuring it, pouring shampoo into its eyes, bludgeoning its fingertips – without ever stepping back in awe at what a wondrous thing it is. Without according it any respect. Without even listening in case it had something to say to us. It's as though we had a pair of scales: in the left hand scale is Proof, in the right hand one is Mystery. Proof in our society weighs a ton. It is weighty. It convinces you. Mystery, on the other hand, is up there waving around in the wind, weighing nothing much. The problem is that as the tonweight of proof crashes to the floor with its profound weightiness, it lands on live things and nature and nearly obliterates them. Shortly we may starve. Meanwhile mystery has untold nourishment for us, if we will just give it some importance, pull down the scale and have a look. In that right hand scale are all the seeds of food for our souls, minute little seeds. Plant them and water them and they grow into apple trees and vines, forests of beeches, fragrant, heavy-headed dark red roses, sunflowers, corn.

So those who are scientifically or rationally minded (most of us, given our education) have a problem: to get away from the great divide set up by the scientific revolution, where mind and body wound up on opposite sides of the fence – what Morris Berman calls 'the psychic distance so central to modern cognition'. He reckons we have to abandon modern consciousness, at least temporarily, 'and this means to abandon a certain type of egoic personality structure, allowing the mind to sink into the body, as it were'.

Take the example of storytellers who assume that human beings are *not* rational, that they cannot be understood in terms of objective analysis, and that their deepest and most significant experiences are lived on a level that is largely invisible, a shadowy region where the mind and the body move in and out of each other in an infinite number of elusive combinations. Stories are a vehicle for the collective wisdom of the community, as well as for the collective unconscious. This is why when we listen to them there is often a sort of frisson as they strike a chord with our own unconscious.

Suspension of disbelief does not leave one in a woolly, indecisive state. On the contrary, it allows a work of careful, detailed feeling judgements to take place. In a mythological sense, separating the good from the bad grains is a work of patience which can neither be rushed into nor speeded up. It is, I think, what the Ladakhi mean when they speak of experiencing the world through their *semba* – a cross between mind and heart.

A wise acupuncturist who was treating me recently asked me what would it be like if my head were in the service of my heart? I was dumbfounded by the question, which indicates how unimaginable such a thing was to me. Over the weeks which followed I pondered it almost daily, until one day in meditation I finally 'saw' it. What I actually saw was an image of my own heart extending high and rose-coloured out of its usual place to about five times the height of my body. This meant that me and my mind were significantly below it. It felt extraordinary – an absolute reversal of how I have lived for 50 years. It felt warm, exciting, and a bit like coming home.

Participation

This section is short and simple. Using yoga, tai ch'i, meditation or any of a hundred techniques for allowing the mind to sink into the body, we can suspend our disbelief and then it is only a short step from this to participation, to 'being here'. This can only really be experienced, not described. It means we *become* what we are observing. If we are observing our breathing, we *become* our breath, and so on.

Surrender

Surrender is more difficult. We have used our will to get where we are. It is hard to give it up. The whole essence of being 'civilized' and 'developed' has meant seizing on technological prowess to insulate ourselves from nature. We feel that if we give this up, we might be engulfed by chaos and destruction.

We are schooled, daily and methodically, to believe that control is all important. To be in control means to be in charge, worthy of going to the top. To be in control means to have power. To be out of control carries all sorts of frightening connotations: runaway horses, inflation, violence, wildness – in short, opening up Pandora's box.

The effective alternative to being in control is consciously to surrender, to give oneself into the care of a higher power. Since we may not know exactly what this higher power is, only having a sense of it, this definitely requires courage. It is what a woman has to do in labour: an unstoppable momentum takes over, and she has no choice but to surrender to it. Surrender has a bad name too, since it is something that the defeated do in battle. Something that women do. That makes it harder for men.

Perhaps it is easier to think of it first as trust, which can be essential in order to save life. Imagine you are on one side of a huge field. You know it is densely planted with mines – the kind which explode at the slightest touch. But you have to get to the other side and there is no way round. A Buddhist nun offers to guide you through the minefield. You know she has done it a hundred times before, and knows the path like the back of her hand. You have no alternative but to trust her. You start out. With every step your trust grows. By the middle, you are entirely in her hands, you would do *exactly* as she told you. You have surrendered. By the time you reach the other side you are overwhelmed with gratitude.

Imagine you became blind. Until you were equipped with a dog or a stick you would be obliged to trust others to lead you. You would have to trust that they would not walk you into a lamp-post or off a precipice. You would have to surrender to their eyes, their judgement, their guidance. In fact, the more you surrendered, the more you would relax and the faster you would be able to go.

By contrast I now think that it is when we force things, push ourselves, 'tough it out', that we are actually endangering ourselves. Earlier I used the analogy of pulling the skin off a snake before it was ready to shed it, to illustrate the danger of forcing the pace of self-knowledge. I also know now that trying to maintain rigid control is equally deadening.

My own experience of this was in walking across the Himalaya in 1994. I was afraid that I would have neither the fitness nor the stamina to get over the high passes. At first I tried to do it by will-power, and became exhausted and desperate. Then at one point after about 14 days, when we were approaching the stiffest climbs, I discovered that if I stopped 'doing it' myself, stopped putting my effort and determination into each step, and instead simply 'let it be done', it did in fact actually do itself. From then on, when I remembered this, no effort on my part was required. I was metaphorically and actually letting go and allowing myself to be helped.

What I am talking about here is surrender to something magnificent – something infinitely wise and timeless. As solid as a rock, and more so. As powerful as a volcano, and more so. As beautiful as cherry blossom, and more so. More awesome than lightning. More endless than space. Because I have confidence in what I am surrendering to, the feeling I have as I do it is one of the greatest relief and pleasure. I am learning to surrender to the grace of the universe. It would be deeply arrogant to think I know better than it.

What does this kind of power mean, in terms of living in today's world?

Getting in touch with this kind of power inevitably brings responsibility. It makes us aware of environmental crisis, and our (so far) feeble response. Most environmental specialists agree that there is still time to reduce and halt the damage – but not a great deal of time, perhaps a decade or two. So we have the opportunity to use these tools for dealing with the crisis, more powerful tools than most of us have ever used before. Instead of rushing about this way and that, hectically issuing manifestoes and signing petitions, we can simply listen. If we listen inside, we'll know what to do. And *when* we do it, it's backed by a force far greater than our own. It works.

There are literally thousands of examples. During the Vietnam war Daniel Ellsberg, a military analyst at the Pentagon, was on his way back to the USA and his plane was delayed in Tokyo. He spent the day in a tearoom in discussion with the poet Allen Ginsberg. That conversation changed his mind about the work he was doing, and subsequent reflection changed his life, and the lives of thousands of others, when he subsequently published the Pentagon Papers, revealing the proposed bombing of Cambodia.

'That's all very well,' says my resident sceptic, 'but what about when people like that man in Waco, Texas, use black magic to lead people to their deaths?' I reply that this kind of power can be and is misused. Ask any shaman or witch and they will tell you how many precautions are taken against the abuse of these phenomenal powers. Because this power is earth-based, it can only be misused by humans to a limited degree. In other words, it could not be used on such a huge scale as for example for genocide, because it is not possible to channel it through a hierarchy. The difference between white magicians and black magicians is that the former put themselves *at the command* of divine powers, whereas the latter seek to have *command over* divine powers. The former work in a lawful, divine-moral way and therefore completely impersonally and selflessly, as the instrument of the Great Mysterious. The latter use the divine powers to satisfy egoistic ends.

To conclude this chapter, let me make a general observation. Many people in our society spend their lives trying to make money, to be successful or to achieve fame – all in order to feel better about themselves. So we have a whole maelstrom of people all wanting the same thing, and having to beat each other to get it. The result is that very few if any end up feeling satisfied. Almost all undergo stress. I have extremely competitive tendencies, and for a large part of my life was desperate to be famous, so I can feel this. But even if a person is not especially competitive, most of the hectic busy-ness of our everyday lives is an unending struggle to earn more money, to get a better job, to buy things – all in order to be happy, to have security, to feel fulfilled. What is ironic, and what these last five chapters have tried to show, is that people can get those things – security, fulfilment, feeling better about themselves – right in their own front room, quietly and without stress. What this chapter shows is that the amount of power available is literally infinite, so that the idea of competition becomes strangely pointless.

The next and final section of this book is about how this power can be used in our daily lives, in the world, to bring about change.

PART III

Hara Power: How it can be Used

The first part of this book outlined what the problem of domination power is. The second part was about how a different kind of power can be developed. Now this final part brings the other two together: it is about how that other kind of power, hara power, can be used when someone is threatened or confronted by domination power.

Chapter 9, the next chapter, is about how this power can be used by an individual confronted by domination power in a personal situation – in a relationship, in the family, at work, in the street. Chapter 10 widens the scope to examine how hara power can work in the wider world, in cases of discrimination, injustice, oppression, violence and war.

This is the point at which to recall the definitions of power referred to in the Introduction because now we're getting down to the nitty-gritty of what power means, and it is important to be clear. There is a great body of scholarship covering the last 2,000 years in which many men, and a few women, have discussed the question of power and come up with all sorts of useful broad definitions.

When the phrase 'domination power' is used in this book, something very specific is meant: the power of a person or group of people to force another person or group of people to do something against their will. I fully realize that this is, as Kenneth Boulding and others point out, only one aspect of the general nature of power. It has often been referred to as power *over*. As will be seen in chapter 11, many people think that this kind of force or coercion can only be adequately met by the same kind of force. This is exactly the issue I want to address.

Our society tends to equate power with domination, with one

person or thing exerting its will over another. The result is a zero-sum, or win-lose, game, where to be powerful means to resist the demands or influences of another, and strong defences are necessary to maintain one's advantage. This is not the way nature works. The entire planetary system has evolved over billions of years by life-forms interacting with each other in complexity, flexibility, and intelligence. Change and evolution is made possible by this very capacity to absorb new energy and information.

What these next chapters do *not* do is to examine how the misuse of power may be tamed by the setting up of institutions – parliaments, watchdogs, constitutions and so on. That is the province of others. I am staying in the terrain of the individual. I want to see how the individual can stand up to the misuse of power in a way which does not escalate violence, which works at the level of the real underlying conflict, and which may therefore be capable of creating a different kind of world.

Before starting chapter 9, I ask you to remember that this is only a page of a book with words on it – the important thing is not your reading of it, but your experience. In some systems of ancient teaching a distinction is drawn between knowledge and understanding. Knowledge is that which can be gleaned from books, it concerns facts and ideas. But to gain understanding requires knowledge and something else. The something else is referred to as being; it is to do with who a person is and what they have experienced. For example, a person could be told all about fishing, read a description of a fishing rod and so on, but would have no understanding of it until he or she had gone fishing.

The mere accumulation of ideas will not, of itself, enable you to exercise hara power. That will come in the process of trying out some of what has been outlined in chapters 4–8, in conjunction with what is suggested in the next two chapters, and perhaps following up some of the possibilities that appeal to you in the section entitled 'Going Further'. It will also come from daily noticing how you do things, and perhaps making some changes or trying out experiments; in short, the pay-off is in developing understanding rather than in accumulating knowledge.

CHAPTER 9

How do you Deal with a Bully (without becoming a thug yourself)?

Where power is, love is not.

C G Jung

The law of love will work, just as the law of gravitation will work, whether we accept it or not...The more I work at this law the more I feel the delight in life, the delight in the scheme of this universe. It gives me a peace and a meaning of the mysteries of nature that I have no power to describe.

M K Gandhi

This chapter is the first of two chapters concerned with putting hara power into action. This one is about how hara power can be used by an individual confronted with domination power in a personal situation. It examines the options available in such a situation: acquiescence, manipulation, escalation and communication. The section on communication is extensive, introducing ways of being fully present, stating feelings, being vulnerable, being direct, expecting the positive and having authority. I then address the ways in which women often tend to use power in the context of sex or in the family – types of power which are not hara power. The chapter would not be complete if it did not address the issue of violent assault: this section draws together techniques and ideas from previous chapters. Most of the examples in the chapter feature women. It goes with-out saying that men also experience difficulty in standing up to bullies in ways that are not passive, manipulatory or escalatory; and that men have to deal with domination, especially in relationships, just as women do. I hope that the examples given will speak to men too, and that male readers will stay with me to the end of the chapter, where I show how the hara concept of power is quite distinct from traditional feminism, and how men as well as women may discover this type of power.

You or I may come up against domination power, or bullying in one form or another, at any time in our everyday lives – in the home, at work, in the street, in the school playground. A survey of 7,000 children at 24 schools in the Sheffield area over a two and a half year period found that one in five children is either a victim or a bully. Jails, the military and institutions for the elderly or handicapped are fertile environments for bullying. Women are daily bullied by unwanted sexual advances. We all, men and women, know what bullying looks like and what it feels like.

Domination power is an attempt by one person to control another and to take advantage of that person's weakness. In crude form it takes advantage of physical weakness: the fact that the other is smaller, less strong, less quick or in some other way unable to resist the crude use of force. Others play on psychological weakness: the fact that the other is less assured, less cool, more anxious, more prone to guilt, readier to take the blame. So how do we deal with this? There are four main responses.

Acquiescence and passivity

Here is a type of person who gives in to a bully, or runs away. These people avoid taking responsibility for making choices, and see themselves as victims of unfairness and injustice, always finding something or someone else to blame. Many people find it difficult to accept that the 'victim' plays a part in victim/persecutor situations. Yet we only have to notice the signals that people give out. In classrooms in new Zealand/Aotearoa, teachers have found that 'victim' children actually gravitate towards bullies – they go and sit near them. They adopt 'cringe' body language, with shrunken shoulders and heads down, making as little noise as possible.

Let me give another example taken from a relationship. It is a couple who appear to be two nice liberated egalitarian people. But when things get tough, he turns into persecutor and she becomes victim. It goes like this. She raises something he has done which she thinks is wrong. He feels attacked, puts up his defences and can't hear a thing. He withdraws, goes cold. She gets panicked and tries to appease him. She ends up apologizing. He goes to sleep. In the morning she feels sad and full of self-pity. She goes into victim mode, crying inside and unable to explain what is wrong. This makes him angry. And so it goes on.

Both people in this scenario are playing roles. To end the syndrome, both need to step out of these roles. Even if only one of them can get out of role, then the tension on which the syndrome depends will be broken. For example, imagine what would happen if, when he goes cold, she did not panic, but she deliberately sought out her other sources of strength and comfort – the open air, meditation, a wise friend who helps her ground herself – in other words, if she went inside for her source of security. Then she could be calm. This would free him from the tugging – the tugging either of attack or appeasement – and he would have more choice as to what he can hear.

Let me come clean: I know about this one because the 'she' is me and the example is recent, too recent for comfort. While most of the time I don't think I behave like a victim, when I read the poem below it catches me out, and shows me the times when I do. When I am busy finding someone else to blame, I can become completely submerged in the feelings and become unable to 'see out' at all.

> Woman is born to suffer, mistreated and cheated.
> We are trained to that hothouse of exploitation.
> Never do we feel so alive, so in character
> as when we're walking the floor with the all-night blues.
> When some man not being there who's better gone
> becomes a lack that swells up to a gaseous balloon
> and flattens from us all thinking and sensing and purpose.
>
> Marge Piercy, 1973

Manipulation

Manipulation is the response of the wheeler-dealer – it attempts to get out of the situation by doing a deal with the oppressor. It cannot risk a direct response, and seeks to avoid hurt by wheedling or bargaining. The person who does it does not trust herself, or anyone else. It undermines real communication because it relies on being indirect – not naming the real issue. And it inevitably perpetuates the bully-victim syndrome.

Emotional blackmail is a good example, particularly when we use the other person's sense of guilt through which to manipulate them. We become so adept at it that we think they don't notice, and we get to a point where *we* don't even notice that we're doing it. Manipulation is one of the hardest habits to break in a relationship, for example, because until we can notice it we just keep on falling into it.

Escalation

An aggressive person is good at escalation: faced with a threatening situation, she responds with an outright attack, aiming at the other person's vulnerable points. This may stop the aggressor but it may also provoke a more aggressive response in return, developing into physical violence. The over-reaction often alienates all those around, and leaves a trail of hurt or humiliated feelings. It rarely solves things. As Martin Luther King said:

> The old law of an eye for an eye leaves everybody blind. It is immoral because it seeks to humiliate the opponent rather than win his understanding; it seeks to annihilate rather than to convert . . . Violence ends by defeating itself. It creates bitterness in the survivors and brutality in the destroyers.

The goal of the person who responds by escalation is *always* to win. Escalation is fighting fire with fire. Naomi Wolf advises women to do this, in fact makes it the title of her book: she shows how women can be as good as men at the male power game, and applauds their using vengeance, money and victory. *The Tao of Pooh* sees things rather differently:

> Never is force opposed with force; instead it is overcome with yielding. 'Flows like water, reflects like a mirror,' said Pooh, walking by.

Yes, but the big question is, how do you yield without being trampled on? The answer lies in communication.

Communication

The goal is not to win, but to address the underlying problem; not to humiliate but to settle. There are several ways of doing this: be keenly conscious of the situation, state your feelings clearly, allow yourself to be vulnerable, be direct, be your full weight, expect the positive, be aware of your authority and find the creative solution.

Be here

At the most basic level, you have to *know* that you are being bullied before you can know what to do! So the first thing to do is to become aware of what's going on. 'Ah . . . so. Here we are.' *Realize* what's happening *in the moment*. This can take a flash of a second for those who are good at being conscious. When Gandhi walked out into his garden and a gunman shot him, in the second before he died the word on his lips was 'Ram', God. When we are threatened we tend to go rigid and freeze; aggressors and oppressors often rely on this, so it is essential to get out of that and go into the moment.

Then *notice* how you feel: Afraid? Angry? Anxious? Breathless? Choking throat? Confused? Cool? Disgusted? Embarrassed? Exhausted? Guilty? Helpless? Hopeless? Hostile? Hurt? Infuriated? Intimidated? Nervous? Overwhelmed? Panicky? Puzzled? Shaky? Shocked? Suspicious? Sweaty palms? Terrified? Unconcerned? Unnerved? Unsteady? Weary? Withdrawn? Worried? I offer all these words because it's amazing what a spectrum of possible feelings there are and it's valuable to know what your reaction is.

> Take your fear as a safeguard. It is like quickness of hearing. It may make consequences passionately present to you. Try to take hold of your sensibility, and use it as if it were a faculty, like vision. (George Eliot)

At this point my resident sceptic says, 'Don't be ridiculous. Here I am under threat, and you think I'll be able to know what my *feelings* are?' I have two responses. First, yes, with a little practice, you can. Just *be here* next time you feel challenged, not necessarily in a bullying situation – it could be an interview at your child's school, an encounter with your employer or a brush with a fellow passenger on a bus or train. Secondly, what makes it worth practising is that, if you know what your feeling is, you become awake to where *you* are in this interaction, what your values are and what you want, which is the first essential part of getting to a solution. Our feelings are the messengers of our values; when we are out of touch with our feelings we are out of touch with our values.

> A big, tough samurai once went to see a little monk. 'Monk,' he said, in a voice accustomed to instant obedience, 'teach me about heaven and hell!' The monk looked up at this mighty warrior and replied with utter disdain, 'Teach you about heaven and hell? I couldn't teach you about anything. You're dirty. You smell. Your blade is rusty. You're a disgrace, an embarrassment to the samurai class. Get out of my sight. I can't stand you.'
>
> The samurai was furious. He shook, got all red in the face, was speechless with rage. He pulled out his sword and raised it above him, preparing to slay the monk.
>
> 'That's hell,' said the monk softly.
>
> The samurai was overwhelmed. The compassion and surrender of this little man who had offered his life to give this teaching to show him hell! He slowly put down his sword, filled with gratitude and suddenly peaceful.
>
> 'And that's heaven,' said the monk softly.

State your feelings

If at all possible, and if appropriate, *say* what you feel, what your reaction is. This will be totally unexpected to the aggressor. But it does take courage – we are not used to doing it and it seems to make us very vulnerable. For example, your spouse or partner might say, 'If you keep doing that I'm leaving.' You take a big deep breath. Ah . . . so. You notice that in the first instant you feel panicky, followed by a reaction of hopelessness and withdrawal. So you say, 'I feel panicky and hopeless and it's making me withdraw.' Because you are telling the truth, without topspin (ie without getting back at your partner) you are bringing honesty into the situation, being open, revealing what it is that's going on in your heart. Your partner then has information he or she did not have before: what your reality is, rather than your defence – your inside, rather than your front.

You are now in a position to get some real communication going. In a marriage or partnership, this can be done by using a process which stimulates personal growth in each person through seeing *why* they have teamed up with this particular person. One way this can be done is with a book called *Getting the Love You Want*. The author, Harville Hendrix, has discovered and put into practice a profound truth about couples: that we seek out people who represent the difficulties and challenges we had with our parents, and who offer the possibility of retrieving a disowned or lost part of ourselves. He describes how this is so in a straightforward, accessible way, and offers a programme of ten weeks' exercises which can be done at home. (B9)

I have begun this section with the example of a close relationship because that is where most of us start. But what of threatening situations at work, for example? Should we still dare to talk about our feelings? 'Surely,' says my resident sceptic, 'when the boss tells me that if I won't work overtime he'll give my job to someone who will, I can't seriously be expected to stand there and tell him I feel shocked and intimidated?' Well, yes. Because if that is the truth it is going to reach him much faster and more directly than other alternative reactions, like storming off in a fury, or putting up a show of bravado – neither of which correspond to your actual feelings. This way you become rooted into reality, and on the basis of that the other person has a chance to respond in a similar vein: he might, for example, be moved to tell you why he is in this situation of needing overtime work so badly, and then you have an opportunity to work out as equals how that can be achieved – by means of job-share or bringing in casuals or whatever.

Without being entirely conscious of what I was doing, I tried this technique out one snowy Monday morning in the Yorkshire Dales with Trish Dickinson, who has trained with Marshall Rosenberg and assists with his programme enabling communication between Israelis and Palestinians.

Trish and I were spending a long weekend with friends, walking. We had brought our dogs. Mine is a scruffy black woolly mongrel collie, quite old now and quite cowardly. Her name is Fizzy. Trish's dog, Kiri, is a young German shepherd, absolutely bursting with energy who, in my perception, had spent much of the weekend rushing at my dog, hackles raised and growling. I interpreted this as aggression, seeing that Fizzy was frightened, and several times indicated rather obtusely, by body language perhaps, that I wanted Trish to control Kiri. She interpreted it as harmless high spirits, and was unaware that I was becoming so aggravated.

By Monday morning, when Kiri bounded upstairs into our sleeping area growling, I was seething. I confronted Trish in the kitchen. What I wanted to say was something like, 'Why can't you control this crazy dog? Fizzy's spent the whole weekend terrified and I'm fed up to the back teeth. Now get your dog outside and keep her outside.' But because Trish had been telling me about her training and I'd spent part of the previous night thinking about it, I knew what I was *supposed* to say was something like, 'I can see that my dog is very scared. I find myself watching out for her the whole time and it is making me nervous and angry. In fact now I am furious. I need some peace of mind. I would like you to tie Kiri up while we're in the house, and keep her on the lead on walks.'

What I blurted out was some sort of mixture of the two and Trish, bless her, heard immediately. She really received what I had to say, was ignorant of the depth of frustration in me and was sad not to have recognized what was happening. We realized neither was winning, and in seconds we found an agreement for managing the dogs that was more satisfactory.

Be vulnerable

Doesn't the above suggest that you should be vulnerable, and isn't vulnerability the same thing as weakness? Vulnerability *hand in hand with fear* does mean weakness, and is not useful in dealing with people who are being violent. In our Western society (perhaps in all societies) this kind of vulnerability is seen as embarrassing, especially in grown people. But vulnerability *hand in hand with openness* means strength, and is most useful in dealing with bullying. This kind of vulnerability becomes possible because it's based on understanding, both of oneself (see chapter 4) and of others. As Marshall Rosenberg puts it:

> If you do open up and make yourself vulnerable and the other person comes at you with an analysis or judgment or criticism, our training teaches you to translate that judgment in somewhat the same way that a translator at the United Nations is simultaneously translating from one language into the other. We teach people how to *hear* the feelings behind the message that that person is expressing, and their unmet needs, and their request. In other words, what is that person requesting of you? (B2)

Rosenberg gives an example which took place when he was with about 170 Muslims in a mosque in a refugee camp on the West Bank. When the word got out that he was an American, one of the Muslims jumped to his feet and screamed at the top of his lungs, 'Murderer!' Rosenberg (in line with his training) managed to turn his attention to what the man was feeling, what he was needing behind that message. He was living in horrible conditions in the camp. Daily, from his point of view, he saw himself oppressed by the Israeli government, which was getting money from the American government. So he heard Rosenberg was an American and called him a murderer. So what Rosenberg did was to say out loud, 'Are you feeling angry and wanting my government to use its resources in a different way?'

The man seemed rather stunned because when people speak in the way he did, they are not used to people trying sincerely to understand what it is that they are feeling and needing. So after a moment or two, he said, 'Yes.' And then he opened up and started to tell Rosenberg the horrible conditions that existed in the camp and how painful it was for them and how infuriated the people were at the American government. Rosenberg listened. And 20 minutes later, the man was inviting him to a Ramadan dinner at his home that evening.

Ben Okri has another way of putting it:

> Maybe the new heroism of the future will have more to do with the courage to lose, in order to win; to give way, in order to gain ground; to be a little weak, in order to be invisibly strong; to live slowly, and with a low but long-lasting fire.

This approach to power and threat is all about changing the imbalance – of bully to victim – to one of equal to equal as quickly as possible. Of course, it is closely akin to the underlying principle of some of the martial arts, namely of overcoming aggression by not resisting it.

A key element of this way of being is to know your ground and stand on it, not to back down. It may seem a strange combination, being vulnerable *and* not backing down, but believe me it is powerful. It requires being very clear about what one means and what one wants. Then be absolutely firm. Susan Faludi writes about the backlash to the women's movement in the 1970s. She says that men fought it but they also absorbed it and incorporated it into their private experience; and when they saw that women wouldn't back down, many men started to make accommodations to keep the women they loved in their lives.

Be direct

Victims tend to be less direct than bullies. Victims try to appease, cajole, manipulate. Sometimes they are plain physically afraid. But often being indirect is a subtle attempt to regain power.

In her book *A Woman in Your Own Right* Anne Dickson says that it is still difficult for women to give up that indirect hold on others. 'Let him think it was his idea' is a phrase that embodies the covert attitude which many women have towards men: on the outside smiling, nodding, saying 'Yes, dear', but on the inside, treating men like little boys, and feeling very superior.

Dickson rightly points out that behind this subtle expression of patronizing contempt exists a very real fear that any other way will not work and a fear of male authority and physical power. Being direct and assertive not only provides an alternative method to this kind of tiring subterfuge, but being more real, there is a lot more energy in it for all concerned.

Here's an prime example of how directness has power. For years, Ike Turner brutalized, hit, kicked and raped his wife Tina, but she would not leave him because she had been abandoned by *her* mother and knew the pain. She endured years of injury and humiliation, until she learned to find her own strength – in fact she did it through chanting. She left Ike and made a comeback as a solo singer. Ike was crazy with rage, on cocaine, and determined that she had to come back to him. He turned up one night when she was alone in her dressing room, and put a revolver to her head. 'What are you gonna do with that, kill me?' said Tina. 'I'm not scared of you any more, Ike Turner.' Ike backed off and left.

Be your full weight

By this I mean bringing your entire presence into the situation, your strength. Feel your centre of gravity in your hara – feel the power there, built up by all your experience. Move from there; if you want to, put your hands on your belly as a pregnant woman does. Use this centre in yourself rather than your head. This may sound like nonsense but I promise you, it works. Next time you are feeling threatened or intimidated, try it. I can't really explain it but what I think happens is that one abandons the mind, and argument, and logic, and winning (where most of us do not feel on very strong ground) in favour of the place of primordial female power, where we feel on much stronger ground. When we are hara-centred an opponent or aggressor will pick up instinctive (but probably unconscious) signals that we are not to be trifled with.

If situations of threat and bullying are dealt with by brawn and brain they usually get worse, often ending up in disaster. If they can be dealt with on the level of feeling and communication, there is hope for a solution.

Before joining a women's initiative for reconciliation in former Yugoslavia in May 1994, I spent a week in Croatia working with Bosnian refugees and with Croatians who had also suffered severely from the war. I was drawn by these extraordinary women into their work of recovery and reconstruction. Emsuda Mujagic is coordinator of the organization that the women of Bosnia and Herzegovina have established in Zagreb:

> Human rights and all are just words on paper. So we women refugees set up our own organization, and women from all over the world came to support us. We want to stop the war not only in Bosnia but anywhere.

She escaped from Trnopolje concentration camp where she watched her friend Velida Mahmuljin tortured to death on high voltage wires for protesting against the war. Now Emsuda has organized 110 women to use their skills to knit sweaters and make children's clothes, which are selling well in the Netherlands. The worker gets half the sale price and half goes back to orphans in Sarajevo.

Before the war Nusreta Sivac used to be a judge in Prijedor, near Banja Luka. She was one of 36 women in the notorious Omarska concentration camp, where each day she had to clean the blood off the floor after torture sessions. She was repeatedly raped. Now as part of the refugee womens' organization, she runs a recovery project for victims of torture and rape, funded by a Norwegian foundation.

Nada Dugandzic and her husband used to have a pizzeria in Sarajevo, as well as a large flat, a car and a house in the country. Now they live with their two teenage daughters in a basement room in Croatia, but count themselves lucky because they are all alive. 'We may have lost everything but at least we haven't lost each other,' says Nada, 'so we are the ones who have to start the job of rebuilding. And forgiving.' Nada has enough energy to light a blow-torch. Her full-time job and her passion is caring for wounded Bosnians evacuated to Zagreb. She took me to visit Fikret Semenic in hospital. On 13 March 1994 a sniper's bullet entered his right temple and came out below his left ear. He is blind, deaf in one ear and has trouble eating because his jaw is smashed. Nada was determined to raise £1,500 to send him to a hospital in Antwerp where his sight in one eye could be saved. If this were achieved, he could provide for his family for the rest of his life. He had no idea how they were surviving since he last saw them.

Ten days after Pava Antunovic had her first baby, she was blown up by a hand grenade. She was in a coma for four months. Large pieces of shrapnel remained in her skull, her left foot was mutilated and there were holes in her shoulder and thighs. When Nada first visited her she could hardly speak and had no recollection of having a baby. Now she converses easily, struggles to walk, and was to be driven by Nada in a borrowed car to have an operation in Italy to remove the shrapnel.

I was awed by the endless hours of energy and care that is required to try to mend these bodies and minds, bodies and minds blown away by one second's worth of pressure on a trigger. I was imagining the sniper lining up the young Fikret in the crossed hairs of the telescopic sight of his rifle; the soldier taking the pin out of the grenade which tore Pava apart. I was remembering the jovial arms dealer I know in Manchester, who may indirectly have supplied the rifle. He says he loses no sleep because what he does is legal. I was thinking of ministers in my government insisting that British jobs depend upon the arms trade.

The Bosnian women somehow reverse this crazy chain. The way that they do it, corny though it may sound, is through love. They sit at their sewing machines and sing love songs in huge, gut-wrenching voices; they chain-smoke and tell jokes against Bosnians and howl with laughter; they set each other's hair. They have been to hell and back, they have no possessions, and yet they have love. And they look a million dollars on it.

Be your symbol

> Work of sight is done.
> Now do heart work
> On the pictures within you. (Rainer Maria Rilke, 1875–1926)

People, if you watch carefully, give off strong indications of what they expect you to think of them. A bully-power type may well walk into the room giving off a strong aura of 'I expect you to think I'm amazing.' Other people then either go along with the ego-trip or passively subscribe to it, or they challenge it. If they do that then there is a struggle, basically between two egos both wanting attention and space. They may try to manipulate the bully, by flattery or in some other way, but this does not give them any power of the kind we are talking about, because they are basically playing the same game as the bully.

Now is the time to recall your own symbol (see chapter 4) and use it.

Here is an example. I had to go and see my former husband for a discussion about money. On the way there I felt very nervous. At one point during the discussion I was feeling very small. My husband was lecturing and scolding me. Suddenly I became aware of my body posture – hunched, leaning forward, head to one side, fearful. I recalled an image I had had on the way there in the car – an image of a beautiful tall beech tree, massive, strong and full of grace. I straightened my back, dropped my shoulders, composed myself and *grew* – I must have grown visibly in my chair because his mouth dropped open and he stopped in mid-sentence. At the first opportunity I came back with a strong, clear response that carried a depth I didn't know I had.

Sketch of my beech tree

Remember that people with real power give off an extremely positive and remarkable aura. So you already have a good, strong presence of your own. You can afford to take a bit of time and take it all in. Breathe. Then get your attention off yourself and onto the other people in the room. Try not to judge. Try not to see another person as an enemy; if you do, they tend to *be* an enemy. If there is something they underestimate about you, ask yourself what it is and use your strong image to show what it is you really are like. The essential thing is to remain true to what is really you, and this is where your image of you as you really are will help. Make no mistake, the real you has a fundamental, undeniable beauty. Stay in this beauty.

People understand far, far more than merely words. From the very moment we see another person, we are collecting and processing information thousands of times a second – what they look like, their gestures, colour, facial expression, attitude, demeanour, posture, smell, approach, how near they stand to you, the speed of their movements, how consistent they are, and so on. So our bearing or demeanour is very important. It is no good saying, 'I'm an extrovert', when your arms and legs are twisted around your body. Therefore if you are feeling like a victim you will send out victim signals to a bully. If you are feeling strong you will send out signals which say 'There's no point in attacking here.'

Ninety per cent of the messages we absorb are from body language, because we are conditioned not to trust what people say. Our bearing speaks volumes, and providing we use it positively, it can be relied upon to make us feel better about what we are trying to communicate to others, and to make them take us seriously.

Expect the positive

Earlier I talked about what bullies expect us to think of them; now I want to add a note about what we expect people to think of us.

This may seem uncanny, but it is true – what we expect people to think of us, they generally do. In other words, if we *expect* them to think we are muddled, hesitant or ill-informed, they *will*. If we come into the same situation, exactly the same person with the same capabilities, but expecting people to think we are clear, fluent and knowledgeable, they will.

Once I was trying to convince a journalist to write a story about something I cared passionately about. He started questioning my facts. I grew hot under the collar and argued. He said things like, 'Well, anyone who's serious about these issues knows perfectly well that . . .' He looked down his nose at me. I went away with my tail between my legs. Afterwards, when I had recovered from the humiliation, I thought, 'I was expecting him not to take me seriously, and he didn't. I thought I was right but I expected to be found lacking.' If I had gone into the conversation *expecting* to be taken seriously and have my view respected, the interview would have taken quite a different turn.

Be aware of your authority, without being authoritarian

We confuse these two most of the time, and yet the difference is crucial.

Authoritarian people want to be obeyed. It is more important to them that *we* do what *they* want than that *they* know what *we* want.

Ultimately, they are not interested in us. They are interested in having and maintaining control.

People with authority, on the other hand, know that they know something, or can do something well. In situations where this could be useful, they offer their knowledge or skill. If their knowledge or skill is real, they receive respect for it, and have authority. They do not need to control anybody in order to continue to have the power of authority. One obvious example is when there is an accident and someone is hurt. The first doctor on the scene has instant authority, because his or her skill and knowledge are what is needed. There is no need to be authoritarian.

Bullies are always concerned with where others rank, whether others are superior to them or inferior. They rank others in a descending order of usefulness to themselves. That is the way domination power works. What a hara-powered person does is to relate to others instead of ranking them, and to see the human being instead of the title or trappings.

Find the creative solution

A creative solution is one that leaves both parties feeling good, about themselves and about the other. This seems a very tall order for the victim – having suffered he or she wants the bully to suffer too. The point is, the bully is already suffering. Ram Dass explains it well:

> If you are preoccupied with power, as I have been most of my life, then you will see relationships in power terms – you'll be afraid of being controlled or being suppressed or being dependent. Those are all power related things. And that's because your preoccupation is with power because of your feelings of inadequacy, impotence or whatever.

People who feel strong inside and good about themselves don't go around bullying others. That doesn't mean you have to feel sorry for the bully: just distanced. Don't get hooked. Don't let the bully's dismal feelings hook your dismal feelings. Making him or her suffer is no solution; nobody wins, everybody feels worse.

The co-operative solution seeks to find a common ground of need which both parties can satisfy. In order to do this it is necessary to know what each *wants*, rather than what is wrong with the other person. Marshall Rosenberg describes a couple he worked with. When he asked what it was that they were wanting from one another and not getting, the husband looked at his wife and said, 'You're totally insensitive to my needs.' She responded with the speed of light: 'That's unfair.' Rosenberg observes that so often we have the opportunity to say what we want and need from each other, but because we have not been taught *to think in terms of what we want*, we are not very skilled at saying it clearly. Instead we are practised at analysing and judging what is wrong with the other person.

So in order to get to solutions, we need to know what each needs. Bullies may appear to want other people's money, or submission, or goods, or obedience. What they in fact need may be to be heard, to feel potent, to feel strong. So in a situation of threat what is really going on may well be as follows:

> A physically or apparently strong person,
> who feels weak or impotent inside,
> trying to get something from an apparently weaker person

But we can change the interaction entirely, from one of threat to one of solution, if we can add a final line to the above:

> who is in fact strong inside.

Strong enough to hear what the bully's unmet needs are, and find a creative way to get them met.

Having examined a number of different ways to use hara power in personal situations which are stressful or threatening, I want now to tell a true story about a group of women who felt very much under threat, and decided to do something about it by going to the military headquarters of NATO to talk personally to those in charge. Although they did not do so deliberately, the group were using many of the methods of hara power. They were using inner change – changes they had begun to realize in themselves – to try to bring about change in the outer world.

During the 1980s the Cold War between East and West had heated up with the deployment by both sides of new short-range nuclear missiles in central Europe. In 1986 this group of women, who were tired of the polarization between East and West and had had enough of the millions of tax dollars being poured into armaments, decided that they would go to the NATO headquarters in Brussels and talk to decision-makers there about it. NATO is a military alliance of Western nations, controlling thousands of nuclear weapons. The women were mostly members of their national parliaments, representatives of women's organizations or women who had researched the military industry. Despite the fact that they were knowledgeable, non-combative and well known in their own countries (one was the wife of a prime minister), they had the greatest difficulty getting appointments with those they wished to see. It took a year, and a petition from members of the European Parliament, to persuade the NATO Secretary General that he had nothing to lose by talking to these women.

Finally in June 1987 they were allowed into the headquarters: the first women, other than the secretaries, cleaners and Mrs Thatcher, to cross the threshold. They went in twos and threes to see the generals and ambassadors representing their own nations, and then met with the Secretary General, who at the time was Lord Carrington. He referred to them as 'you young women who don't know anything about war'.

They were deeply alarmed by what they found: for example, that no channel of communication existed between NATO and the Warsaw Pact, and that NATO took decisions that were not even reported to the parliaments of the member countries for months or even years, and often never debated at all. They started to speak out clearly about this in their own countries: they asked questions in parliaments; and they went back to NATO in April 1988 to put direct and very specific questions to their defence ministers meeting in the Nuclear Planning Group of NATO. And they got results. A channel of communication between NATO and the Warsaw Pact was set up. A television documentary about the lack of parliamentary debate of NATO decisions was made and shown on British television.

Edouard Shevardnadze, then Soviet foreign minister, meeting women parliamentarians from Nato countries, March 1988

In March 1988 women parliamentarians from NATO countries went to Sofia in Bulgaria to meet with the then Soviet Foreign Minister, Edouard Shevardnadze, and the other Warsaw Pact foreign ministers. They talked about how mutual security could be achieved by political negotiation rather than military force.

Eight months later they again scored a first: women leaders from NATO countries invited their counterparts from behind the Iron Curtain to come to NATO headquarters to discuss defence issues with the men there. It may seem strange now, but it had never happened before that leading politicians from one of the Cold War power blocs had visited the military nerve centre of the other. NATO was extremely tense about it; nevertheless in some of the one-to-one discussions real dialogue took place, enabling each to hear the point of view of the other side. Within less than a year, the Berlin Wall fell. Over the spring and summer of 1990 the tension of the Cold War ebbed away. At the end of December 1991 the Soviet Union was dissolved and became the Commonwealth of Independent States. These women, as well as the women who camped outside the US base at Greenham Common in Britain for 12 years, the women who surrounded the Pentagon in Washington DC, and all those women and men who kept vigil at military bases in Canada, Italy, Germany and France – all these people played an important part in the ending of the Cold War.

'What part, precisely?' my resident sceptic asks. 'Surely it was the economic plight of the Soviet Union which forced Gorbachev to offer to negotiate with the Americans? Surely it was the new found confidence of the East European states which enabled them to stand up to Moscow and pull down the Berlin Wall? Surely you can't claim that holding vigils, going to NATO and talking, or camping outside military bases, had much to do with it?' I can and I do. Whether at a conscious or unconscious level, the very fact of seeing or talking to a person who calmly represents views opposite to our own affects us. Whether we acknowledge it or not, we pause. On the surface we may simply think, 'Get out of my way', but somewhere deep down a small voice says 'Oh. This person disapproves of what I am doing and cares enough to come here and show me.' You may make a joke of it, brush it off, scorn it, but it is there, lodged like a small seed in your psyche (and in some people these seeds of doubt grow very fast).

People from inside NATO, the British Ministry of Defence, the army, navy and air force have all told me this. 'News from outside like this is welcome. Visits like yours are rare. This is really the only way we get to hear new opinions.' This was said by a senior official in NATO

Defence Division, who came to talk to me in the canteen after my official talk with his superior in July 1992. And an RAF Air Commodore
whom I also interviewed in 1992 said, 'I really enjoyed this conversation . . . rarely get the chance to, er, debate these kind of issues, and,
er, as you see we don't always agree among ourselves.'

Often the quieter the protester is, the stronger the impact.
Exhortation is entirely counterproductive. It is no good lecturing people on how they 'should' take responsibility for the planet. Staking out
the moral high ground, as some in the green movement do, and as I
have done, does not achieve anything in my experience except a
rather sickly glow of righteousness. People don't respond to exhortation, and not much to anger either. But there's all the difference in the
world between 'owned' anger (which is clean) and 'dumping' or
lecturing (which is putting blame on the other person). When people
who are going about what they regard as their business (and, moreover, their duty) are faced with blame, they simply throw up defences:
nothing goes in. In nearly every case, and certainly with strangers,
blame makes people close up. What makes them open up is genuine
openness on the part of the other. Openness of course includes stating
your true feelings, being vulnerable, being direct, and being your full
weight, expecting the positive, and so on.

Power traps for women

Having looked at the various ways in which we can use communication as a response to threat, I would like to point out two of the most
common ways women exercise power. One is to do with sex and the
other to do with the family. Neither is hara power.

Sex

The biggest trap for women, when it comes to power, is sex.
Permeating right through every nook and cranny of our culture is the
idea that women have power over men if they're sexy. 'Be more beautiful if you want to be more powerful' urge the magazines. Everything
from cosmetics to cars can make you more influential, not because you
are clever or gifted, but because you're sexy.

Far from sexuality becoming less central, as the women's movement
hoped in the 70s and 80s, it seems to have become more so. Far from

using the greater equality between the sexes to determine how we want to be seen, women themselves have been reaffirming the notion that what is most important is a woman's sexual allure. Madonna, says Ros Coward, is often held up as the young woman's icon of self-defined female sexuality, but she has done nothing to challenge this traditional notion that being sexually desirable is the ultimate source of power for women.

We have been sold a dummy. And we did it ourselves, because we got stuck with the idea that power *over* men was the solution. If we want power, and if men are powerful, then the trick is to get power over them. Simple. And *stupid*. Why?

* Because that kind of power doesn't last. A wrinkle or two, and he can get himself a new woman. And if you have built up all your sense of power in being sexy, you're going to get a nasty shock as soon as you're coping with a baby, or a menopause for that matter.
* Because it is so limited. When you think of all the other kinds of power women can have – respect in their own right, the primordial power of reproduction, the power of wisdom, power in a group – it does seem rather dumb to go dressing up in fishnet stockings just to get a man to do something for you, which you could more simply do for yourself.
* Because it perpetuates the idea that men are powerful patriarchs and women are helpless victims.
* Because it gives everyone a stick to beat you with when you're not sexy any more. 'Unsexy' is one of the most demeaning insults in today's world.

The family

The simple version goes like this: men may well be powerful in the outside world, but in the home, where it counts, the woman has all the power. First we are told how important mothering is and how much power a woman has over future generations because she influences them in childhood. This may be so, but she also collects the backlash of all the frustrations small children experience with their first carers – rage, helplessness, threat of annihilation.

Secondly, the type of power a woman is supposed to have in the family is emotional power. This is quite different from either domination power or hara power. It's still in the mindset of power *over*, while apparently having something to do with passive femininity. It puts a woman in an ugly position – somewhere between a manipulator and con artist. Some women do use their power to cut men out of household and domestic involvement, even to cut them out of contact with their children. There is the story about the newspaper magnate Lord Beaverbrook – an extremely powerful man who would spend his day advising Winston Churchill and generally influencing world events – only to come home and not be allowed to enter his sitting room with his shoes on. Although she allowed others to come in shod, his wife insisted he leave his shoes at the door.

Third, power in the home is presented as something akin to power within. But it is not within the body, mind and spirit, it is within four walls. The kind of power women are assumed to have in this sense extends no further than the home, and is thus limited. This 'power' is not part of anything larger, not rooted or grounded in the Great Mysterious, for example. The result is that the 'power' of women who are confined to the home is isolated, cut off; they are not part of a great web as their ancestresses were, not part of a system of knowledge passed down from generation to generation, not part of a system of worship common to all. They receive no training in what they might do with real power if they had it; the power they do have is not used in the world. The way out is for a woman to recognize the difference between this kind of power and hara power, to develop hara power – and then to watch for the changes that will take place in her life!

Violent assault

Assault that is sudden and violent leaves little room for the communication responses discussed earlier in this chapter. If such a thing happens, the best response must be some form of physical self-defence. There are good resources now available for training and self-education in this, and some are mentioned in the section entitled 'Going Further' at the end of the book.

Many other writers have dealt with the subject of rape, from historical and sociological stand points, and in terms of survival. The aspect I would like to explore is prevention. I am interested in what attackers expect from a sexual encounter, and how victims are conditioned to behave. Some traditional advice suggests that a woman should go along with the assailant at first, 'flattering him, and even expressing sexual interest in him. Then, when the opportunity arises, the woman should resist.' This is clearly absurd. But as part of the prevailing culture, it is important to realize that we all in some way inherit these ideas, are bombarded with them from the day we are born, and even go on to perpetuate them through everyday, unrecognized actions. However, this does not mean that we cannot break free from these stereotypes.

Women in our society have been conditioned over centuries to do their utmost to attract men – to dress, walk and smile in ways that catch the eye. So what we are asking them to do is to turn all this off when they are in areas where there may be violent people. This seems to be totally contradictory. How can a girl who gets all dressed up to attract the boys at a disco, for example, suddenly turn herself into an unattractive frump to travel the dark streets to get there?

I find this a genuinely difficult problem. My inclination is to say that women do *not* have to dress, walk and smile in a certain way in order to attract men; we just have to be ourselves. And many young women today are infinitely more confident in their dress and their general being – for themselves – than my generation were. When they walk down the street they give off an air of being able to cope. The impression is that anyone who leered at them would get a sharp remark, and that they are not sexually available unless by their own choice.

This does not guarantee, of course, that they will not be attacked, and I would like to look at how the material in chapters 4, 5 and 6 may assist potential attack victims to transform themselves into non-victims. In chapter 4 I showed how the more we learn about our own weakness, the stronger we shall be. Facing and working through fears about being attacked, for example, will convert that fear into a source of strength. I described the power of 'naming'. The story about the Andean official denying a young woman her visa unless she had sex with him showed that when she named the situation – telling him she would tell the whole town about his 'bargain' – he backed down immediately. The development of a symbol for your own strength can become a vital ingredient in self-protection, because people give out so many kinds of non-verbal messages as they walk down a street.

In chapter 5 the emphasis was on finding power within the body. This depends to a large extent on valuing the functions of our bodies and centring ourselves in the hara. If you have tried the experiment where one attempts to push over someone who is well centred, you will know what strength is to be found in that centre of gravity. This centring sends out a subtle, possibly unconscious, message that attack on this person is not worthwhile.

In the case of women, liberation from sexual guilt is also essential to giving out this message. By this I mean liberation from carrying the burden of early learning that it is the female who is responsible for whatever happens sexually, that the demands of male sexuality are so imperative that men cannot control themselves and must have a release, and that it is the fault of 'provocative' women that they are in this state. This liberation shows in a woman's body and demeanour. In this connection I enjoy the mental picture of the large powerful Mexican women I referred to earlier – not a hint of sexual guilt there.

Ultimately, of course, being prepared and ready for death, if one can get to that level of serenity, means that one is not afraid in the instant of attack – and not being afraid gives time and energy to deal with the situation in ways which would otherwise not be possible. In chapter 6 I showed how this ability to be 'in the moment' can be developed. It takes time, but if a person knows his or her internal strength, this communicates itself non-verbally. If a person can be alert and aware from moment to moment, this gives a readiness to respond to whatever happens, in that instant.

Feminism and power

What I am describing is not the same thing as feminism. What I am talking about is a hara-centred way of dealing with domination power, which can just as well be done by a man as by a woman. There are many biological women who are not at all good at it, and many biological men who are. It took me a long time to struggle to this point of seeing that hara power really is *not* gender based, because I have been greatly influenced by the work of feminists, and am indebted to the feminist movement.

I would like to look now at what various strands of feminism say about domination power. Feminist writing has certainly dealt with issues of power, but less in terms of the confrontation of domination power on the world stage and more in terms of the struggle for equality, for control of women's bodies, and so on. Liberal feminism, rooted in 300-year-old traditions, believes that women in general are oppressed in so far as they suffer unjust discrimination, and that most discrimination is not mandated by the legal system but is based on custom.

Marxist thinking, with its roots 100 years ago, asserts that women are oppressed in their exclusion from wage labour, and that the continued subordination of women is in the interests of capitalism; in practice, however, traditional Marxists give low priority to struggles against male dominance. Socialist feminism, born in the 1970s, recognizes that the differences between women and men are not pre-social givens, but rather are socially constructed and therefore socially alterable.

Radical feminism, generated by the women's liberation movement of the late 1960s, struggles against male control of women's sexual and procreation capacities, the immediate goal being to regain control over women's own bodies, and in the long term to build a new society informed by radical feminist values of wholeness, trust, nurturing and sensuality. Many of their proposals for social change concern the reorganization of the so-called private sphere, and do not distinguish between this and the so-called public sphere of impersonal politics. They believe their values are appropriate to regulate all of society. This approach constitutes a sharp break with Western tradition in political theory. Machiavelli, for example, argued that it was irresponsible to apply in politics moral standards appropriate to intimate relations. He thought that betrayal, deceit and violence were necessary and justified in politics.

So it is possible to outline three stages in the revolution in women's definition of themselves and of society. Stage one began with women demanding equal rights. The next stage saw women trying to take a place in, to join, the male world. Now we are reaching the stage where women are becoming clearer about their own value system, accepting some of the values of the dominant culture but discarding others, and have more confidence that their view has validity.

Ecofeminism explores how male domination of women and domination of nature are interconnected, and the cultural and social roots that have promoted destructive relations between men and women. Some ecofeminist writers, like Rosemary Radford Reuther, go on to suggest

> . . . ways of moving forward in this work of transformative eco-justice through base communities of spirituality and resistance. In such base communities, groups of people can find local support, both for personal *metanoia*, or change of consciousness, and for sustaining a long struggle against systems of domination.

Other feminist writers have addressed the issue of power in one way or another; some of them have already been extensively referred to, and some are quoted in the section entitled 'Additional Material and Notes'. The main observation to make is that most if not all brands of feminism see the struggle as being women versus men, men being the more powerful and frequently the oppressors.

Hara power and gender

What I am saying is fundamentally different. I am positing one type of power which has become destructive to the planet and to human survival, and another type of power which can counterpose and reverse that destructive power. The first is sometimes characterized as male because it depends on qualities usually considered male, but it is not unique to men. The second is sometimes characterized as female because it depends on qualities usually considered female, but it is not unique to women. So we can have men as well as women discovering a new, and very ancient, type of power which can be used to reverse the domination power mode.

Hara power is neither male nor female. The only male/female distinction that can validly be made is in terms of direction: male power flows out through action, female power flows in through receiving. Distorted male power becomes dominating, brutal. Distorted female power becomes victimish, devious. Hara power is both male and female, but it is most accessible by going inward, which is a female direction. The evidence of the time of the goddess makes sense of the reaction away from it, towards male values. Mankind has now been going outwards for 2,000 or 3,000 years, and so has become dominated by male values. These have got out of balance and blinded us to ingoing female values. And now it makes sense that we should swing towards the inner again.

CHAPTER 10

Power and World Conflict

Concepts such as truth, justice and compassion cannot be dismissed as trite when these are often the only bulwarks which stand against ruthless power.

Aung San Suu Kyi, 1990

The power of a waterfall is nothing but a lot of drips working together.

Michael Maynard and Andrew Leigh, 1993

The focus now changes to the larger scale – this chapter explores how hara power can be used in the context of world problems. First I address the philosophy on which most international politics today is based, namely Realism, and show why it doesn't work. I then look at how imbalances of power and conflicts of interest can be met in a non-violent way, with hara power. Using plenty of examples, the various ways of working with hara power are explored, such as ju-jitsu (where the victim uses the strength of the aggressor to bring about his fall), non-violent resistance, points of leverage to use for maximum effectiveness, getting beyond the ways of thinking which produced the conflict, using and sharing information, and giving power away. Three key questions are addressed: are all conflicts two-sided? how can conflicts be prevented? and can structural conflict be solved only by structural change? The heart of the chapter lies in the final section, where the four elements of hara power in action are explained: interdependence, interconnectedness, relationship and clarity. The chapter ends with a light-hearted look at the pitfalls of working through hara power.

When faced with world problems – like hunger, overpopulation or the arms trade – are you overwhelmed by a feeling of helplessness about what you, just one person, can do about them? Take heart. That's a sane response. It's the basis for a whole new attitude to world problems. Because change at the level of the individual is more and more being recognized as essential to change in huge world systems. Here are the observations of three people who have thought hard about change from their particular perspective – one is a biologist, one a Buddhist, and one a political scientist.

> To the extent that our future survival is due to our own behaviour – our own adaptiveness – ... we have the option to *rethink* our ideas about what kinds of human behaviour and human cultural institutions *are* adaptive. (Mary Clarke, in Sandole and van der Merwe, 1993, page 50. B2)

> Basic to most spiritual traditions, as well as to the systems view of the world, is the recognition that we are not separate, isolated entities, but integral and organic parts of the vast web of life. As such, we are like neurons in a neural net, through which flow currents of awareness of what is happening to us, as a species and as a planet. In that context, the pain we feel for our world is a living testimony to our interconnectedness with it. If we deny this pain, we become like blocked and atrophied neurons, deprived of life's flow and weakening the larger body in which we take being. But if we let it move through us, we affirm our belonging; our collective awareness increases.' (Joanna Macy, 1993, page 42. B9)

> ... it is this masculine preoccupation with the public and structural that has aborted the transformative potential of most twentieth-century revolutions. It kept them as just that: a revolution, a turning of the major power wheels that failed to produce changes in the fundamental global order. Such changes remove a particular group from political power but do not make connections to changes in the interpersonal realm ... Masculine models of transformation exhibit little or no consideration of the personal and individual changes that will be required. (Betty Reardon, 1985, page 90. B6)

Before we go on to look in detail at what this means in practice, let us have a look at the alternative – the attitude which has prevailed in national and world politics for more than 400 years – which is known as Realism.

Realism

This philosophy is based on the existence of the nation state and the system of international power politics built upon it. Political communities develop separate interests, which their leaders represent and pursue. Clashes between these interests are bound to occur. In these clashes, it is the state with the greater power which will prevail. Since military force is ultimately the decisive form of power in conflict, the use or threat of force underlies the relations between states. The inevitable consequence of realist thinking is war. If conflicts are settled without the use of force, it simply indicates that both sides recognize from the distribution of power who will win. Even when power is not an overt element in conflicts, it lies beneath the surface and determines events. Consequently, states are obliged to rely on power to protect their interests. Conflicts are tests of power.

It is seen as the prime duty of political leaders to recognize these realities. What happens, therefore, is that each state or alliance sees its security as if 'from within' and seeks to protect 'our' interests and values from what is outside. Power seen this way rests on the willingness to use force.

This set of attitudes, which assumes that the others out there ('them') are vicious and will do 'us' harm unless we prevent or stop them, goes right back to the idea of original sin. It takes as its starting point that people are by nature aggressive, greedy, violent and selfish, and therefore likely to want to take what their neighbours have, by force if necessary. If 'they' are like that, then 'we' need to defend ourselves. (Of course what happens then is that 'they' see 'us' armed to the teeth, busy making new weapons, so they feel threatened and start doing the same thing, and on and on it goes – in the spiral of the arms race.)

At the heart of this way of behaving is the process of projection (described on page 29 and 99), namely, that those negative qualities which we cannot admit to in ourselves are projected out onto others. It is not 'we' who are aggressive, greedy, violent and selfish, it is 'them'. We therefore need to defend ourselves against them and have more power than them. Our present military leaders, some of whom I have interviewed at length (see chapter 3), all believe that we must defend ourselves against enemies 'out there'. Things are seen from the point of view of particular governments as if 'from within'. Security, which tends to be seen largely in military terms, means the protection of 'our' interests or values from what is outside.

Some of the greatest thinkers of this century have warned how dangerous this is. Here's Bertrand Russell:

> All war, but especially modern war, promotes dictatorship by causing the timid to seek a leader and by converting the bolder spirits from a society into a pack . . . The risk of war causes a certain kind of mass psychology, and reciprocally this kind, where it exists, increases the risk of war, as well as the likelihood of despotism. (1975. B7)

Moreover it can only be a mistake to run international relations on the basis of the power of threat. Both threat and destructive power lose potency once their legitimacy is destroyed, as the powerlessness of the USA in Vietnam and of the Soviet Union in Afghanistan demonstrated very clearly.

Why the Realist position is untenable

There are many reasons why this position is untenable, but here are two practical ones to start with:

* Those with threat power of this kind inevitably lose it. Look at what happened to all the empires. Where is the Roman Empire now? Where is the Ottoman Empire? The Spanish Empire? The British Empire? Power, in the sense in which it is used by the realists, is power for one side, not for the other. The process is therefore simply cyclical. Power *over* others tends to produce its own resistance, generating an equal and opposite force. The net result is that if a state is a 'great power' today, it will be humbled tomorrow.
* Threat power today is entirely undermined by the arms trade. The five nations which are permanent members of the United Nations Security Council are also the top five arms sellers in the world. The drive for export revenue is stronger than any other consideration in government, including caution over arming a potential enemy, as the British public have learned (after the event) in the Scott Inquiry into arms sales to Iraq. The details would be the stuff of farce, were it not for the fact that so many deaths were caused. During the Gulf War, Iraqi pilots who had actually been trained in the UK were hiding from the Royal Air Force in bomb shelters of British design; Iraqi troops were camouflaged in British-designed uniforms; Iraq had more French-made AS-30 laser guided missile systems than France herself did, and French pilots were trying to use theirs to destroy French-built Exocet Missiles in Kuwait. Ultimately France had to withdraw its own Mirage jets from the war because they were becoming confused on battle screens with the ones France had sold to Iraq. And so on.

There is another, deeper reason why the realist position is no use today, as the following parable called the Tragedy of the Commons, illustrates.

> A group of poor peasant farmers all have access to a piece of common land on which to graze their cows; say that there are ten farmers, each with six cows. The cows provide each farmer and each farmer's family with their livelihood. What is more, none of them has any private land on which to graze their cows; they only have access to the common. If the farmers all exercise self-restraint, and each puts only three cows on the land to graze, the grass will continue to grow and the cows will prosper. On the other hand, if they all put all of their cows on the land it will become overgrazed, and quite quickly it will cease to provide a livelihood for any of them. (Open University, 1991, page 28)

The Tragedy of the Commons now applies to the planet. The position of the Realist would be to say that whoever is stronger gets to graze his cows on the common, as many as he likes. He might say 'If someone else tries to push me off, just let him try. We'll see who wins', or 'Since conflict is inevitable, we'd better make sure we're on top.' That is precisely the attitude which stronger nations take today to the world's resources – oil, gas, and increasingly, water – over which many of today's wars are being fought. The problem is, of course, that the world's resources are finite, limited, non-renewable. If one nation uses force to take what it wants, then it is reasonable to expect that others will too. The obvious outcome is that there will increasingly be armed conflict over resources, and soon there will be none left for anyone.

It is no secret that the Realist way of thinking is in trouble. Arms sales are rebounding like boomerangs; the wars we do fight do not solve the problem; NATO has lost its enemy and has no idea what to do with itself; and the West with all its weapons was unable to bring peace to Bosnia.

But this problem concerns not only the military. It is a wider one concerning the way we think about the world, which we have come across in previous chapters. The ways of looking at things that we have in the past accepted as common sense really do not work any more, because we are discovering that no individual action is isolated. So how do we balance the interest of the individual with the interest of the community, the common good and, more difficult still, the good of future generations?

Ultimately, what it comes down to is this: are we willing to risk our survival as a species to defend the 'national interest'? In earlier times, the human race was not obliged to come to a decision about interde-

pendence – about our needs *and* the needs of others, about our aggression *and* others' aggression. Now we are. Now it's no longer *my* problem or *your* problem, it is *our* problem.

Hara power is the answer. As more and more attention is being paid
to it (by both women and men) it is showing how to solve imbalances
of power and conflicts of interest in a non-violent way, so that the
underlying issues of insecurity are addressed. I will start by showing
how it works in practice, in both local and international settings, and
then examine the ingredients of what it is.

Hara power in action – local and national

When our community's interests are threatened by some powerful
force – a multinational corporation, for example, or a government
department – and we have been through all the proper channels and
got no result, what do we do? There are at least three possibilities: ju-
jitsu, non-violent resistance, and using the points of leverage.

Ju-jitsu

A fundamental principle of martial arts is that if I resist or struggle
with my opponent, I risk injury or death. The best strategy is therefore
to know my opponents, anticipate their moves, and let them defeat
themselves by denying them a target. This is where the less powerful
uses the power and impetus of the more powerful to immobilize it.
Done with imagination, it can be entertaining as well as effective.

Here is an example. The residents of a subsidized welfare housing
scheme in the USA were threatened with eviction by the bank which
owned the scheme and intended to demolish the housing and build
condominiums for sale to the yuppie market. All the residents' protests
and publicity had no effect on the bank's decision. So the residents got
together, brainstormed, and came up with an idea. One Friday, each
resident, plus all the friends, relatives and supporters he or she could
muster, went to a different branch of the bank throughout the city and
stood in line to open a $5 account. Queues stretched from each teller
out into the street. All the businesses which normally banked takings
and drew wages on a Friday could not reach the tills. There was no way
the account openers could be budged – they were entirely within their
rights. The bank's business came to a standstill. After three days of this

the bank was open to negotiations with the residents, and backed off the demolition.

This story is self-explanatory. The essential power of ju-jitsu is that nobody gets hurt, yet the aggressor's action is rendered harmless in a quick and indisputable way. The victim uses the strength of the aggressor to bring this about. Several key things are required of the victim:

* Imagination. To find the right move to fit the particular aggressor requires the liberation of creative powers.
* Alertness and awareness. It is essential to be highly conscious and one step ahead of the aggressor. Koichi Tohei, the Zen aikido master, says that in defending against an attack, you must 'move when his [your opponent's] mind moves.'
* Numbers. Not always, but often, the Gulliver-like oppressor can best be dealt with by Lilliputian hordes.

Non-violent direct action

This is no wimpish negative passivity, it is an active alternative to violence which requires more courage than violence does. Gandhi's *satyagraha* in India, where tens of thousands of villagers defied the British Raj's tax on salt by drying sea water, is perhaps the best known example, followed by the women of Greenham Common. The women's peace camp kept vigil for over ten years at the gates of the US Air Force base in Berkshire where cruise missiles were located. The women talked to the soldiers and police guarding the base, invited other women to come and encircle the base (an unbroken line for 9 miles), and repeatedly cut the wire, entered the base, danced on the missile silos and painted the buildings. They achieved their goals: the cruise missiles departed, the Common was reinstated as common land, and women world-wide were empowered.

The US civil rights movement employed non-violence in such a powerful manner that racial segregation in the USA became illegal. Authentic peace-making is essentially a positive and proactive, rather than a reactive, undertaking. In 1963 Martin Luther King shocked people when he defended 'tension', 'direct action' and 'crisis creation' as legitimate activities in the movement for a more just society. He wrote from his jail cell in Birmingham:

Non-violent direct action seeks to create such a crisis and foster such a tension that a community which has constantly refused to negotiate is

forced to confront the issue . . . My citing the creation of tension as part
of the work of the non-violent resister may sound rather shocking...but
there is a type of constructive, non-violent tension which is necessary for
growth.

In fact, there can be no authentic harmony or reconciliation without
justice, and justice is seldom secured without struggle, since oppressors
do not as a rule hand over power. The base of non-violent resistance
has to be fearlessness – not only for the obvious reasons, but also in a
deeper sense. Gandhi worked this out with great clarity. He said that
when the mind is flooded with a negative emotion – most often fear –
perception is skewed and the resulting judgement is impaired. So what
he called non-violence of the mind must be used to achieve a correct
insight into any situation; only then can we separate our own emotions from it. The starting point of a *satyagraha* action is therefore the
radical wrongness of a situation, not our own emotion. The goal of
Gandhian conflict resolution is not to defeat one's opponent but to
convert him or her to seeing the rightness of one's cause.

Another example, and there are literally thousands to choose from,
comes from the Philippines. In 1974 the National Power Corporation
was trying to construct two huge hydroelectric dams along the Chico
river basin in northern Luzon. This would have rendered hundreds of
families homeless, and destroyed the priceless heritage of centuries-old
irrigation systems, not to mention the disintegration of the indigenous
culture of the Kalinga and Bontoc tribes. The people tried everything:
delegations of protest, letters, publicity. The only strategy that worked,
that stopped the reconnaissance survey, was for disrobed women to
stand in their way. Naked, the women stood in a line across the road.
The survey teams would not go past, and in this way violence was prevented.

A great deal has now been written about both the techniques and
the philosophy of non-violent resistance. Some analysts say that numbers are what count, but to me the key thing is the combination of the
'centredness' it requires (one must be well 'in one's skin' to do it successfully) and the adrenalin it produces. It's demanding, but it can also
be exhilarating.

Points of leverage for the powerless

There is a story of a motorist who, having tried everything he could to
get his car to start, finally pushed it round the corner to the garage.

The mechanic lifted up the bonnet, looked at the engine for a while and then, selecting a large hammer from his tool tray, gave it a hefty clout.

'Try it now,' he said to the owner, and it started first time.

'How much do I owe you?' asked the delighted owner.

'Ten pounds,' said the mechanic.

'Ten pounds!' exclaimed the owner, his face dropping. 'Ten pounds for just hitting it with a hammer?'

'Oh no,' said the mechanic. 'Fifty pence for hitting it with the hammer, nine pounds fifty for knowing where to hit it.'

What many powerless people do is rage, protest and complain. This may well be effective. But if there is time, sometimes it is more effective to stand back and do some research, and find out where the available energy can be focused for maximum influence; in other words, to discern the points at which change could take place if pressure were applied. This is a subject close to my heart, and I would like to illustrate it by describing the work of the Oxford Research Group.

The story starts with an experience which affected me powerfully when I was in New York in the summer of 1982 to lobby delegates at the UN Second Special Session on Disarmament. I had spent a week in the UN building depressed by the sterility of the proceedings and the entrenched positions of the participants. Then I went to Central Park for the demonstration for disarmament. A million people turned up and created such a powerful atmosphere of hope and desire for change that even the police ended up with badges all down their ties. 'This', I thought 'will change the session, get it going.'

The next day, back in the UN building, absolutely nothing had changed. The million people might never have existed. Their message had not got through. If the UN delegates could not hear the people on their doorstep, what hope was there that the men in the weapons laboratories, the ministries and the intelligence and military services could do so? Bridging that gap, the gap between the demonstrators and those who made the decisions, I thought, would be an essential step in making progress towards disarmament.

I had the idea of groups of citizens talking to decision-makers – not waving banners outside their offices, not shouting violent opposition, but sitting down and discussing the issues quietly and soberly from a background of real knowledge. I saw them not just in the West, but in all five nuclear nations, and in the nations whose governments were developing nuclear weapons too.

Over the next few months I set to work to see if it was feasible. First

I had to find out if it was possible to find out who the decision-makers were. In general I had only an intelligent lay person's knowledge about nuclear weapons, and no idea if it was possible to discover who the decision-makers were in China and the Soviet Union. After a couple of months in libraries, and somewhat to my surprise, I found that the information was fairly readily available. There were some surprises. Information about the Soviet Union came from CIA documents on open shelf in one library. The US embassy library had the agenda of meetings of joint Anglo-American committees whose existence was denied by Whitehall. But it was possible to find out who the decision-makers were, and so I started work. The Oxford Research Group began life on the kitchen table in the small cottage where I lived with my young daughter.

Over the next six months the demands of the research grew. If one wants to find out who the decision-makers are one has to find out the key positions in the decision-making structures; and to find that out one has to know which are the important organizations, and the important groups within them. And, of course, that is dictated to some extent by the relationships between those organizations. And that's only the official story. Clearly, in any complex process there will be apparently important people who nobody ever takes any notice of, and people with insignificant official positions who wield great power. So, quite quickly, some funds were raised and six researchers were hired on short-term contracts to do bits of the work. Two flew in from France and one from America; we met round the kitchen table, ate together, worked half the night, and within about six months had produced analyses of nuclear weapons decision-making in all the nuclear nations, and the emerging nations, together with biographies of the decision-makers.

It was then time to use the research, to see if the original idea of groups in dialogue with decision-makers would work. We contacted a range of voluntary groups – women's groups, peace groups, Quaker groups, professional groups, church groups, to see if they would try it out. We told the groups that each would receive a detailed information pack, which would give them the knowledge they would need to sustain an informed dialogue with a particular person, and some suggestions and ideas on how to communicate with someone remote, busy, perceived as threatening, and likely to be hostile to the approach. I also asked each of the groups to write to a decision-maker in China; it was important that the groups tackled this as a world problem and not just a British or Western one (decision-makers in the USSR were being kept for groups in America).

Most groups were fired by the idea. 'The momentum of this project carried me along,' wrote one group member. Faced with the overwhelming size of the arms race, here was a manageable task which seemed to have a chance of making a real impact.

Finally, ten groups started on a pilot project. Their experience convinced the project's funders (by now a number of national charities) to extend the project to a further 60 or 70 groups – to match the number of British decision-makers identified by the research. What happened to the 60 or 70 groups? The first thing to say is that they were an enormously varied bunch and that each of them developed its own goals. Some of them debated the ethics of nuclear weapons, others the technicalities of the reprocessing of fissile material. Some wanted to argue with the decision-maker, other simply to understand his point of view. Some presented economic arguments for converting particular factories from military to civilian products, others put forward technical arguments for the development of sophisticated defensive weapons.

There were three main outcomes of the project, none of which related only to the issue of nuclear weapons. The first and most obvious was the effect on the groups and their members. Many of them started the project feeling helpless and depressed. For them the project had an empowering effect. To some extent this was attributable to its basic concept. One member commented, after about six months: 'The hope this project has given me has counteracted the despair I felt about the arms race.' But a good deal of it was due to the expertise which group members quickly developed. It started to develop with the information in the pack supplied by the project, and was then augmented by other information gathered by group members, sometimes by expert speakers invited by a number of groups, and above all by the long, intense and sometimes fierce debates within the group about the approach they should take to their decision-maker, the questions they should ask, and the points they should make in meetings or correspondence. This process refined ideas, forced people to check their facts and sent them looking for specific pieces of information. In effect, they devised criteria of relevance as they talked; criteria which helped them to focus their efforts and attention. As they became expert they soon discovered that in their chosen area they knew as much as, if not more than, their decision-maker.

This had a powerful effect. It undermined the notion, fostered by decision-makers and often accepted by others, that all this was too complicated for ordinary members of the public and ought to be left to those in authority. Finally, the personal support which group members gave one another increased the confidence of many of them. Overall, there was a distinct change from an initial perception of powerlessness.

The second outcome was that the project brought to light some interesting aspects of accountability. The theory is that in the UK ministers are accountable to Parliament for the decisions taken by civil servants, scientists and military officers. This is an important point because the development of complex weapons systems takes as much as 10–15 years, while the average tenure of a UK Minister of Defence is about two years. In consequence it is generally accepted that many important decisions are not taken by ministers but by those with long careers in the Ministry of Defence. The theory, then, is that they are accountable to the Minister who answers for those decisions to Parliament and ultimately to the public. The groups discovered that when they addressed questions to civil servants they were told to take up the matter with the Minister; when they duly did that, they received from a junior civil servant a 'non-reply', stating government policy in the broadest terms and not answering their questions.

The third outcome should be the effect on the decision-makers and through them on the system as a whole. Of course I have no hard information on this because the conversations were confidential, but there are indications that the dialogue made some impact on some decision-makers. There is some evidence too that the project hastened an acceptance among those closely involved with defence policy of the desirability of substantial reductions in the numbers of nuclear weapons.

The Open University course on decision-making, in which a longer version of this story appears, concludes:

> When faced with a large system composed of many individuals, which is producing results you may want to change or influence, it is simply not true or realistic to believe that there is nothing that one individual can do. With a small number of allies, the effects of the decision of one individual can spread dramatically throughout the whole system, and thereby change the decisions it produces.

All the examples I have given require certain basic ways of working which are essential whenever those with less power are bringing about change. I have highlighted some of these already – for example, being aware and using your imagination – but there are five more which are equally useful:

* the means must be the same as the ends
* get beyond the way of thinking which produced the conflict
* inform yourself
* use the strengths of others
* give it away.

The means must be the same as the end

Gandhi said:

> 'Means and ends are convertible terms in my philosophy of life.' The quality of mind during an action yields the quality of mind when the goal is reached.

Herein lies a gem of a principle. It is that to arrive at your goal you must use the methods which are true to the goal. In other words your means must be of the same character and the same quality as your end. I go further: the more the methods are true to the goal, the faster and more effectively the goal will be reached. Thus, if what we are after is a world where hara power is used, then we have to use hara power to get there. And this is why we have to start with ourselves. There is not much point talking about power from interdependence and co-operation if I am denying my body, out of touch with myself and dogged by a whole host of black shadow images. So the first thing we have to do is attend to our own personal change. At the same time we can watch out for hara power initiatives and support them, while we develop our hara strength to the point where we can start our own initiative.

The story of Sister Chan Khong, a diminutive Vietnamese Buddhist nun, illustrates how a pacifist makes peace moment by moment all her lifetime, essentially becoming – being – peace. Peacefully, lovingly, in the midst of war in Vietnam, Sister Chan Khong built communes, started schools and taught in them, nursed the wounded and sick, buried the dead, and even disguised herself as the owner of a fishing boat to rescue hundreds of boat people being attacked by pirates in the sea off Thailand. At the same time, she tells of the decisions that a woman has to make – should she marry, not marry, cut off her hair, leave her family. All these deeds were tested in the hardest of circumstances during the long, escalating civil war in Vietnam. She, together with Thich Nhat Hanh and 12 other monks and nuns, maintained a position that was neither nationalist nor communist, neither North nor South. They ultimately became a means for enemies to communicate and to end the war.

Get beyond the way of thinking which produced the conflict

In most of today's wars, those who are trying to solve the problems are using the same concepts and methods that produced the war in the first place – the stale diplomacy, the shallow understanding of human nature, the futile belief in brute force.

It is not possible to solve a conflict using the same system of thought which generated it. We have to step outside that system of thought, as well as the language which defines the system to be as it is. This is why it does not work to send tired elderly Western politicians to solve the problems of former Yugoslavia. Different systems of thought, and a different kind of communication, are necessary.

'Dispute resolution' for example, is an idea which grew out of American labour management techniques and has now become a fashionable approach in US community justice schemes and increasingly in international circles. But it can all too easily end up simply being reactive to the situation it finds, rather than getting to the root of the problem. The strategy of the dispute resolver is usually dictated by those who created the problem in the first place. Thus the boat ends up being patched instead of rocked.

'Peace-keeping' has become increasingly militarized. Today six out of every seven peace-keepers is a soldier. Is this either wise or effective, when the populations where the peace is being kept have usually been terrorized, raped or beaten by men in uniforms? Many of the troops sent, although they have gone through training programmes, have received little or no instruction on inter-cultural relations, human rights, issues of power or mediation skills. For example, an elite Indonesian battalion which had been involved in the suppression of East Timor were sent to Cambodia as UN peace-keepers. There is no automatic switch inside a blue helmet that instantly turns a soldier trained for war into an indivual prepared to work non-violently and with cultural sensitivity for the resolution of conflict.

The recent fieldwork of the Transnational Foundation for Peace and Future Research makes it abundantly clear that although UN peace-keepers were in Croatia, there was no agent in charge of getting the former combatants into a process of reconciliation, structural change and peaceful coexistence. The international community has not yet found a way of preventing future violence when the peace-keepers have to withdraw. At present there are no local, regional or international efforts that aim at real peace-making – changing the structures and perceptions that led to war in the first place.

In the last paragraph I used the words 'the international community' – that does not mean some men in grey suits in Geneva or New York, it means you and me. Now is not the time to leave these issues to others, because others only have old maps, which are not proving much help in finding the way. Real change comes about when people are enabled, enable themselves, to use their thinking and their energy in a new way – using a different system of thought, different language, and having fresh visions of the future.

Even in the case of entrenched domination power systems, it is important to remember that any different action, if it is sustained, brings about change.

> Domination is a *system*, and we *are* part of it, and in that lies hope. For any system is always in delicate balance, dependent for its stability on the feedback of its parts. When the feedback changes, so does the system. At first it reacts to regain its stability, but if the new feedback is sustained, the system will be transformed. (Starhawk, 1990, page 314. B11)

This is a key point, and goes back to what was said earlier in this chapter about the importance of persistence, and in chapter 6 about gradual changes in the 'landscape' of the brain. The groups trying to communicate with nuclear decision-makers found that they had to continue, sometimes for many years, before any perceptible change took place. One British group wrote to a general for four years, receiving only the briefest of responses, until he was elevated to a seat in the House of Lords, the upper house of the British parliament. In his maiden speech he espoused, almost verbatim, the facts and arguments from their letters.

Inform yourself

One of the most frequent methods used to control people is to deprive them of information; if you don't know what's going on, you can't do anything about it; if people are keeping secrets from us, they are exerting power over us.

If we want to change something, whether it is ourselves, or the way the playgroup is run, or the world, one of the first things we need is information. The person who first said 'information is power' was not joking, nor were all the people who have said it since. To get out of a powerless situation, you need to know how to get information. Every situation is different, but here are some hints:

* Work out what you want or need to know:
    - what you want that information for
    - how you might go about getting it
    - and write it down.
* Divide the task into bite-sized pieces and share them out.
* Follow your nose, and trust your hunches as to where to start.
* If your project involves reading, seek out the writing style that you can read easily, and reject others. If an author is difficult or confusing to read, it is probably because he or she does not fully understand the subject. Ploughing through lots of written material is not obligatory; don't be afraid to ring people up and ask them questions, to ask for their help.
* Be persistent. Those holding onto the information are hoping you will give up.
* Develop a way of organizing your information. It can be as simple as a loose-leaf notebook, or it can be a whole filing cabinet or library; but if you organize it the way it seems right to you, it will start to become a friend and a key element in your power.
* Make your system look pleasing to you: if you like card index boxes or different coloured tabs, then buy them or make them. The key thing is that you should enjoy getting into your information, and not be constantly put off by it.
* If no system suggests itself to you, try a holistic way of organizing what you know. Every time you pick up a useful fact or thought, write it down on a slip from one of those yellow sticky pads one can buy. Have a great big piece of paper on your wall, and stick the yellow slips on to it. At first you can just stick them anywhere, but as you go on, you will find that you can group your yellow slips in clusters of ideas. Draw circles round these when they seem to form a whole. Then you can make connections between one circle and another, and write on the connecting line what the connection is.

One of the hidden benefits of organizing information is that one begins to see patterns. In a wonderful book called *People Power*, Tony Gibson introduces the idea of a 'neighbourhood fact bank' – numbered cards which give relevant legal, technical and financial information. They can be passed around for everyone to see, then spread out on the table, arranged and rearranged as the group works out its order of priority and so on. (B2)

A very quick way to capitalize on our strengths is to share information we already have. Think of the rare conversations we have, for example, about sex, menstruation, childbirth and pregnancy. Think of how much we learn in those conversations, and then think how little we share this information and how we let it go on being semi-taboo by not being more open about it.

Here is an example of information sharing in business. Gerard Fairtlough was the Chief Executive of Celltech, an extremely successful biotechnology company which he started from nothing. In 1989 Celltech's largest shareholder was forced to offer its shares for sale. This could have triggered a take-over bid for the whole company. The Board of Directors decided that the proper course of action was to co-operate with potential bidders for the company. It was necessary to keep this development secret from the outside world while preparations were made. Some board members felt that it should also be kept secret from employees because, as one of them put it, 'if we tell the staff it's bound to be in the *Financial Times* tomorrow'. Gerard managed to persuade the board that this was not likely, since the entire operation of the company since its inception had been based on the fact that, in his own words, 'open communication depends on trust and trust depends on open communication'. He was willing to stake his reputation on this. Everybody in the company, of whom there were then about four hundred, was given the information in confidence and kept it secret until a public announcement was made three weeks later.

Use the strengths of others

A key part of building a new kind of power lies in using the strength of others. *Dominating power seeks out the weakness of others and trades upon it, hara power looks for other people's strengths and relies on them.* It asks people what they are best at, what they like about themselves, and then enables them to make use of that.

Remarkable things happen when we use the strength of others. First, people complement each other. When one is stuck, the other can solve it. Since no-one is under the illusion that they can do everything, when they come across something they can't do, they call for help. For example, I knew two peace workers who had regular 'skeleton-in-the-cupboard' sessions: they would drag out of their filing trays the letters they did not know how to answer, or the problems they simply could not deal with, and exchange them. Sure enough, what was a complete bogey for one was no problem for the other.

In this way people's different strengths mesh together instead of competing with one another. And as a person's strength is tried, recognized and affirmed, it grows. It begins to create and have ideas itself.

This kind of power generates a greater total sum of energy, since it is not a zero sum game where one triumphs over another (what I win, you lose). It is a positive sum game, where both get more.

Perhaps I can illustrate this in a simple exercise of numbers. Imagine that each person is equal to one. When one person meets another and dominates him or her, the second person's power and energy is reduced, probably to about half, so that the sum of these two people's energy and power is one and a half. When two people meet and enter a relationship of partnership power, however, the sum of their energies would be at least two. If the peace workers mentioned above had been working on their own and not co-operatively, the chances are that many of those problem letters would have remained unanswered. As it happened they chose to go into a partnership and mesh their strengths, so that not only were those problems dealt with, but the sum of their combined energies was greater than their energies would have been if they were working on their own.

Because true power is about being able to be powerful *with* other people, it often involves compromise. This is due to the fact that real power involves being strong and being oneself on an equal footing with others, and therefore involves seeing and respecting their views even if this means that one cannot have everything one's own way. Ultimately, however, it increases everyone's power.

Give it away

When you've got it, give it away! Hara power thrives on being given away. It can be repeatedly given away and it constantly regenerates, just like love. When a second child is born, it doesn't mean the first child must be loved half as much in order to love the second. It's the same with hara power. I need only to find it within myself, and then there is an infinite amount. If I share some of it, it doesn't mean I have less. In fact it means I have more.

Because this power regenerates inside, we can give it to others. In fact, its characteristic lies in being shared. It enables others, warms them, encourages them, gives them strength. Jean Baker Miller, Director of Education at Wellesley College in Massachusetts, who has interviewed and counselled literally thousands of women, concludes:

As a result of this vast body of experience within the family as well as in the workplace and other organizations, I think most women would be most comfortable in a world in which we feel we are not limiting, but are enhancing the power of other people while simultaneously increasing our own power. Consider that statement more closely: The part about enhancing other people's power is difficult for the world to comprehend, for it is not how the 'real world' has defined power. Nonetheless, I contend that women would function much more comfortably within such a context.

This applies to men too. It is the opposite of holding onto power, which is what tyrants and bullies always do. As the old saying goes, 'In order to keep a slave in the ditch you have to stay there with him.' That is the way domination power works: we have to keep control, and the greater the power we want, the more control we have to have. It is an endless loop which lands people in ridiculous situations. It makes businesses go bankrupt, makes powerful men leave extraordinary wills, and gets lots of people killed.

Qualities like security and a sense of identity, so much craved by our society, can in fact be regenerated infinitely. The essential fact is that there is enough to go round: these are not limited resources. But there are conditions. The major one is co-operation. It is the only way in which a zero sum game can be turned into a positive sum game *at no one's expense*.

Hara power in action – international

These ways of working apply just as well when the focus shifts from the local to the international level. Now three questions arise which need a response. Are all conflicts two-sided? How can conflicts be prevented or resolved? And can structural conflict be solved only by structural change?

Are all conflicts two-sided?

To hear most protagonists in a conflict, you would think that the other side started things, carried out all the atrocities, and therefore bears responsibility for putting things right. Yet there is almost no case (except possibly where children are involved) when even the most oppressed do not bear some responsibility. What we are interested in here is how those who seem weak can assert themselves in the face of those who seem strong in such a way that further conflict is avoided, communication is established, and all end up feeling that they have got a good agreement.

Adam Curle has been writing about and practising peace-making and conflict transformation for a lifetime.

> Like everything else, peace making combines yin and yang, inner and outer, public and private. When the two are out of harmony so that yang predominates, the peace maker depends on manipulating external conditions, political manoeuvering, alternating threats and promises, the subtleties of bargain and compromise. This is the mode of a Kissinger or Metternich. It may affect the settlement of a particular dispute, but seldom establishes the deep harmony of reconciliation; it may merely eliminate the symptoms of unpeacefulness without removing their cause.
>
> When people emphasise the yin, they are attempting to change feelings and attitudes. They rely on protest, persuasion or moral pressure rather than on negotiation, political analysis or diplomacy. They usually have little impact on events.
>
> When yin and yang are harmonised, peace makers are 'as wise as serpents and as harmless as doves'; politically astute and realistic, but with a humanity wide enough to include, if they represent the victims of oppression, those they oppose. They strive for lasting peace among all contestants. (1981. B2)

Let me apply what Adam Curle says to the 'realist' approach, where international affairs are interpreted in terms of cultures, ideologies and interests in conflict – perceived as expressions of human nature itself. It is seen as the prime duty of political leaders to recognize these 'realities'. Everything is seen from the point of view of a particular government, as if 'from within'. This is a yang approach. It needs to be replaced with an approach better suited to our age, namely the 'view from above' or *transformationist* approach. This starts from the perception that the world is now faced with global problems which threaten the very survival of humankind. They include weapon proliferation and the nuclear menace, but also population growth, gross underdevelopment and environmental abuse. Unless these problems are tackled straight away they are likely to generate disorder and conflict on a massive scale. The threats are by their nature common threats and can only be overcome by a common response. They entirely eclipse sectional interest and challenge realist approaches to security. Contemporary military thinking, still structured by the Cold War and based on the traditional role of the nation state, is quite unable to cope with them – indeed itself contributes to them.

What is needed is to widen the concept of security from the interest of states to the welfare of peoples, and from the military to the economic and environmental spheres. Sustainable development must replace economic growth as the prevailing philosophy, and global security must replace national security. Instead of bloc confrontation and deterrence in Europe, the emphasis must shift to common security and disarmament. In short, political leaders must learn to see things independently of particular nations or alliances as if 'from above'.

If we believe in separateness, we are required to be strong and invulnerable, have power over others and win struggles. When we see our own interconnectedness, we realize that ultimately the triumph of the individual is a myth; we cannot prosper in isolation. This goes for nations too.

How can conflicts be prevented or resolved?

Conflict resolution has become a sort of buzz-phrase in international circles, just like peace-keeping – and each person who uses it attaches a different meaning. The UN, for example, monitors situations liable to lead to war, and the Secretary General may offer his good offices or those of his assistants to mediate. Shuttle diplomacy is the method normally used.

International diplomacy and intergovernmental negotiations, however, may not help in dealing with ethnic and minority conflicts within countries, in which parties often deny each other's legitimacy. John Burton and others have developed what they call 'second-track' diplomacy to deal with such situations. Representatives of the parties are invited to attend face-to-face discussions in an unofficial capacity. The main steps of these 'problem-solving workshops' are as follows.

1 The sponsor approaches parties and asks decision-makers to nominate representatives.
2 Representatives appear in a private capacity.
3 A panel of facilitators is formed.
4 Each participant puts his or her case. No interruptions are allowed.
5 The panel asks questions of clarification.
6 The panel identifies and states real issues, and seeks the parties' agreement to a statement of the issues.
7 The parties explore solutions.

Workshops may last several days, and may be repeated after longer time intervals. The parties do not have to make any prior commitments, nor do they reach binding agreements. The aim is to establish common ground and build understanding, which can be used later in formal negotiations between the parties. These workshops offer a rich vein of experience and suggest lessons especially in the process of moving towards agreement in locked situations.

Quaker Mediation

The Society of Friends has a long tradition of quiet mediation in violent conflicts. They tend to work along the following lines.

1 The Society of Friends appoints usually two mediators who have a concern for a particular dispute.
2 The mediators seek meetings with the leaders on both sides of the conflict.
3 They use active listening, seeking to befriend the leaders and win their trust. They aim particularly to speak to the anger, resentment, fear and guilt that affect leaders in times of conflict, and to offer another way of seeing events when perceptions are distorted.
4 The mediators shuttle between the parties, and offer to carry messages. They listen for points of agreement.
5 The aim is to reach the point where parties are willing to enter direct negotiations.

Quakers emphasize that it is essential to have a long-term concern for the conflict, and that a mediation can go on for several years. They are well aware that human beings usually work out internal conflicts in external situations. A high degree of personal fear or anger in one individual, for example, can spark an outbreak of violence. By contrast, and to exactly the same degree, self-knowledge and acceptance can lead to conflict resolution. In Adam Curle's latest book there is a moving account of how ordinary people in the conflict between Croatia and Serbia handled their own feelings as well as the stern political realities they faced.

What is emphasized in both these examples is the *kind* of communication that can most fruitfully be used in conflict prevention or in mediation; in fact it makes no difference whether it is at an international level or at the level of a parish council negotiating a boundary dispute. Here are some of the basic essential steps:

1 Make an opportunity for those who have been hurt and damaged to express their pain and outrage in a safe setting. Sometimes after a war or atrocities the focus is put on the guilty, through war crimes tribunals. It is more important to hear the voices of those who have been abused – this is the only way of healing the pain and anger which will otherwise live on to break out in revenge or in another war.

Women reporters have been particularly good at concentrating their readers' minds on the real victims of war. Many distinguished women war correspondents have refused to fit that absurd yardstick by which 'good' war reporters are judged: detachment, objectivity, the need to act as a 'neutral' observer. On the contrary, shining through their stories is passion and compassion. A good example here is Maggie O'Kane, who has written powerful, moving accounts of the wreckage of individual lives in the war in former Yugoslavia.

2 If at all possible, make time and space to envisage what peace would look like in the situation you are facing. If we have no vision of how things *could* be, of the goal, no wonder it is hard to find the path to it. So it is invaluable to sit down and imagine. Elise Boulding has developed a detailed imaging process:

> I ask participants to imagine themselves thirty years in the future, and tell them there are no weapons there. As they imagine that world, I urge them to make their fantasies graphic and detailed – see faces, smell smells, feel the roughness or smoothness of objects. I ask what kind of families, agriculture, work and government exist in their future world without weapons. When each person has a clear idea, they write it down and tell others about it. For the last step, I ask people to move back to the present, a few years at a time, and see what has to be done to create the vision. When people work backwards, they create a future history and know what steps to take to make their vision real.

3 Seek out as representatives, not necessarily the leaders but rather those who are generally respected by either side and who have little ego. In other words, the kind of people who do *not* put themselves forward to be on a committee, or want to be in the chair. In this way there is more likely to be that 'luminous clarity of mind' discussed earlier, which comes from being quiet inside, and which is so helpful in ensuring that everyone is heard. Here is an example from *Gabriela*, the umbrella organization of womens' groups in the Philippines.

> They divide a problem into primary and secondary parts, the first being what it is they must change, such as the landowner's power, lack of tools, seeds, transport, etc. The second is to organise and be able to resolve differences among the group. Everyone is trained in choosing a leader in a secret ballot. Types to reject are the 'dictator', the 'self-important', the 'Santa Claus'; the one to vote in is the democrat. Before an election, a Planning Goup is set up which includes those who wish to stand for leader. As it turns out (surprise, surprise) the first three types often have no time for this and if they do, they are barred from office if they already have a similar post, such as in a union.

4 Agree upon some rules which will help participants stay open. Marshall
   Rosenberg has been developing and teaching skills of non-violent communication for 30 years, and now works in conflict situations in 13 countries. His model for non-violent communication stresses that participants
   have to avoid criticizing, demanding and denying responsibility for their
   own thoughts, feeling and actions. Observation must stay (at least in the
   early sessions) in the first person; I must say what *I* am observing, what *I*
   am feeling, what *I* need, what *I* request.

      In the previous chapter we had the example of the dogs Kiri and Fizzy.
   Now sorting out the problems of two dogs and their owners in the
   Yorkshire Dales is not exactly an international incident. But the principle
   remains constant, and all good negotiators use it in one form or another.
   Ury and Fisher, in their now famous book *Getting to Yes*, explain how to
   move negotiators away from their 'positions' and towards their real interests and needs. It is these techniques which were responsible for the Camp
   David breakthrough between Anwar Sadat of Egypt and Menachim Begin
   of Israel.

5 In my view there is one further ingredient essential both to conflict prevention and conflict resolution, especially in larger and more complex settings. I can best express this as 'Step back at the same time as stepping forward.' It is a question of observing what is going on, watching the process,
   being conscious. For example, in the early discussions of the women's
   peace pilgrimage for Bosnia in 1994, a man kept disagreeing with or cor-
   recting one of the Bosnian women. Eventually they were interrupting each
   other and neither was listening. Somebody said, 'I notice that we're interrupting and arguing. Why don't we have a moment's quietness and just
   come back to what we're here for.' The Bosnian woman started to cry, her
   feelings began to come out, and someone fetched a guitar and began to
   sing. The whole atmosphere changed.

      This observing, seeing what is going on in the present, can usefully
   become a habit. It is exactly the same as the Buddhist notion of mindful-
   ness, and what Ram Dass calls 'being here now' (*see* pages 124 and 279).

Can structural conflict only be resolved by structural change?

In situations of structural inequality, when a person is disadvantaged
or under threat because of law or custom, then the backing of a union
or political or pressure group becomes essential. For an individual to
try to fight institutionalized injustice on her or his own is too hard.
Someone who is unfairly treated by the system can only complain or
protest using the channels provided by the system itself. So only when

that unfairness is recognized *by* the system, and complaint or redress procedures allowed or set up, can the individual get change in his or her locality.

Hugh Miall, who has made an extensive study of conflict resolution, says that in cases where unfairness is unrecognized by the system it is impossible to settle conflicts without a fundamental change in the relationship between the parties. Structural change does not always or necessarily come about through violence. The ending of apartheid, in fact, owed little to direct violent pressure. He gives other examples of mainly peaceful structural change, including the change in the status of women, brought about by the suffragettes and their successors, and the change in the status of industrial working classes, achieved by trade unions.

He goes on to say that out of this awareness comes a desire to change relationships, and that social movements for change empower their members. With this empowerment comes a possibility of confronting the defenders of the status quo with a political movement of equivalent power. Then the way may be open to a negotiated resolution, or the use of non-violent sanctions.

I agree with this as far as it goes. But running like a current beneath most of the recent women's movement for change with which I have been involved has been something else. It is like a search for another way of doing things, another way of seeing the world, another way of relating to other peoples and countries. It was beginning to be evident way back in 1979, when I was asked by UNESCO to report on women's roles in peace movements and peace research for presentation to the 1980 World Conference of the UN Decade for Women in Copenhagen. Together with other women I studied six examples of female peace initiatives – in South Africa, the Philippines, Scandinavia, New York, Cuba and Northern Ireland (this was before Greenham Common) – and we concluded:

In most cases, women have protested against the violence surrounding or threatening them, acting from *within* the system generating that violence. They have tried to change things by means of traditional political or social structures, and often the value systems underlying these structures remain unchallenged. However, at least in two cases (and likely embryonic in others) we notice something different. There is evidence of women's profound dissatisfaction with accepted value systems, and established structures. In the case of the Swedish women it is clearly verbalized; the Northern Irish women definitely felt it; many of the women active internationally for disarmament discuss it. Without in every case knowing precisely how, these

women are vitally enthusiastic to find or rediscover ways of living differently, in greater harmony with their environment, and to investigate the
roots of violence in the structure of their societies.

These last few sentences are what this book is essentially about.

The heart of the matter

Now I want to pull the ideas of this chapter together and identify the
main elements of hara power in action. I think this can be set out
under a number of headings: co-operation, interconnectedness,
responsibility and relationship, and being rather than doing, or
clarity. These nouns seem to me rather heavy and ponderous, so I'd
would prefer to use verbs: donkey-lean, link, bear, and be.

Donkey lean (co-operation)

If two people have to stand up for a long time their backs will become
very tired. If instead they were to lean in to one another, back to back,
just to that precise point where they get support without leaning *on*
each other, they can stay for hours without strain. This is what pairs of
donkeys do on steep mountain paths – they lean inwards to get support for their loads. 'That's all very well,' says my resident sceptic. 'We
all know co-operation is very nice and desirable and all that, but it's
not what people *do* . What they do is compete. Why? To win. To feel
better about themselves. To get more for their families.' But, I could
respond, we cannot all be winners. In fact, in hierarchical organizations, only one can really be top dog. To treat life as a race means 99
per cent have to be losers, or at best second or third. That cannot be
comfortable for most people. So why do we do it?

The simple answer is that everything in our present society encourages us to compete, basically because it is good for business. If I can
persuade you that your car is not new enough, your clothes are out of
date, your life will be changed by a holiday, then you might buy my
goods. But in order to get you to do that I have to trade on your insecurity. So I make you (more) insecure in order to get you to buy something (which will not actually make you feel more secure). The same
applies to changing jobs – the aim is usually to feel more secure, but
the move rarely achieves that.

A growing number of people realize that the problems facing our societies and our world cannot be solved by competition. Cannot even be approached using competition. The only way they *can* be approached is by developing ways of doing things by co-operation.

What co-operation comes from is compassion – being able to imagine what it is like to be the other person. Compassion, as we saw in Chapters 5 and 6, is located in the heart. What co-operation leads to is the greater good of all; it enables us all to survive (remember the Tragedy of the Commons?).

from 'Turning the Tide' (see page 315)

Here is a recent example of men responding in profoundly compassionate ways to the needs of others. In 1994 100,000 Rwandan refugees poured over the border into Tanzania, in an area where water was in very short supply. The Tanzanian authorities seconded water engineers, craftsmen and labourers to help. These men lived with the refugees in tents in a tense, tough environment. They worked almost without stopping for weeks on end installing water supplies and pipelines, building tanks and running pumping engines, in these vast camps full of misery, illness, hunger and fear. Jim Howard was asked by Oxfam to visit the camps and was deeply moved by their spirit. Kabeza the foreman he described as:

> very determined and inspired, driving his team day after day. These men are working hundreds of miles away from their families and home comforts and are an inspiration in such an atmosphere of despair. Their spirit showed the best of humankind set against the bloodshed and killings in Rwanda.

Link (interconnectedness)

We have already discussed this subject at some length – the idea that those with hara power know intuitively (and scientists have discovered scientifically) that we are in fact all connected. That what one group of people do in one part of the world affects others thousands of miles away. That one microgram of plutonium dropped into the Atlantic can ruin the livelihood of fishermen in Alaska. Computing networks and faxes have made these discoveries all the more actual and real for us. A Maori woman on her homestead in Aotearoa/New Zealand can now be part of a discussion on minority rights as it is taking place in London. It has even become clear that without even *doing* anything, one can affect something or somebody else merely by *observing* them (see page 287). For example, Western interest in Tibetan culture even unintentionally alters it. As Irina Tweedie says:

> The realization that every act, every word, every thought of ours not only influences our environment but mysteriously forms an integral part of the universe, fits into it as if by necessity, in the very moment we do or say or think it, is an overwhelming and even shattering experience.

So it becomes possible for the most hard-headed rationalist to begin to accept that what religious people have been saying for centuries might just be true, namely that praying works.

If these ideas are accepted, and not just accepted but lived, they do change our attitudes to the world and to other people completely. If we are brought up to know that *all* our actions have consequences for others, that we can bring about change without rushing about, and that we can affect others merely by putting our attention on them, then it *is* a different world. Some would say it's going back to the world of witchcraft, others would say it's in the realms of science fiction. I would say it's now, and it's an exciting time to be alive.

These ideas go hand in hand with an understanding of the power of the earth and the primordial creative power of the feminine. There's a coherence in them, and a strength; both an underpinning of the reasons why change is needed and a way to bring that change about.

Bear (responsibility and relationship)

It is possible that the female use of these words differs from the male. Carol Gilligan spent ten years listening to people talking about morality and halfway through she began to hear a distinction between what women and men were saying. Women's concerns were with responsibilities, men's with rights. She found that the morality of rights differs from the morality of responsibility in its emphasis on separation rather than connection, in its consideration of the individual rather than the relationship as primary.

For those using hara power, responsibility is inextricably tied up with relationship. When this different attitude is allowed to expand and develop, it has a markedly fresh and different effect on world affairs. Let us take just one example, the widespread concern over the build-up of nuclear weapons in the 1980s. If we look at a four-year period from 1982 to 1986, we find that of 34 non-violent direct actions, every single one involved people from other countries, and in most cases people from what were at the time 'enemy' countries.

In every case the theme of the action, whether it was a peace camp, a signature campaign or a conference, was concern for the collective, for the danger nuclear weapons brought not just to me or to you, but to us, our children, our future. The links formed between Soviet and American women and between women from Eastern and Western Europe have not only lasted for more than a decade, but have blossomed into educational networks and coalitions for ecological clean-up and crisis aid.

Naturally, when the issue is responsibility, the question of leadership arises. Women have real problems with this, not wanting to fall into the traps of the 'leader-led', the ego-assertive responsibility taker, and so on. Starhawk has a formulation which describes the hara power solution.

> Power-with, the influence we can exert in a group of equals, our power to shape the group's course and shift its direction, is perhaps the most fluid of all forms of power. Responsive leadership is the art of wielding power-with

in ways that foster freedom . . . I choose the term *responsive* because such leadership responds to the needs of the group and the opportunities in the environment, responds by feeling as well as by thinking and acting. A basic principle of responsive leadership is that power and responsibility work together. If you have power, you are responsible for using it in an empowering way. If you have responsibility, you need the power to meet it. (B11)

This linking of relationship and responsibility is certainly not something only women can do – it is an attitude, a world view, that we as a human race now need, and are discovering.

Be (clarity)

Where some people instantly spring into action in situations of world crisis, those with hara power tend towards intensifying their awareness. I would like to extend this further and say that the difference is between *doing* and *being*. In previous chapters we have talked about 'being here' when there is a dispute in a family or relationship; the same applies in the Security Council of the United Nations, or at a checkpoint faced by armed and angry soldiers in Bosnia.

Let's backtrack a moment to get hold of this concept again. In crises and tense situations, the individual ego is usually running about in a panic, seeking ways in which 'I' can come out of the situation alright. If, on the other hand, the ego is able to relax, it permits a luminous clarity of mind, a quality of sharp perception, to come through. That's *exactly* what is needed in crisis or power situations. The crunch is that most of us only get anywhere near it in meditation. Hence the need to practise, to train as if for the Olympics, so that we can *be here* when it is most difficult to *be here*. The great sages are the ones who have discovered how to find calm amid chaos. Their mission is not to change the world or to impose a particular truth upon others, but to live in accord with the truths they have come to understand. The power of the heart is contagious; the spirit of awareness and integrity is contagious. If we wish to have peace, we must be peace.

Potholes and pitfalls of hara power

Working through hara power is just as full of what Winnie the Pooh would call 'heffalump traps' as working in any other way. This is a section dear to my heart, as I have fallen into most of them.

Posers and Phoneys

It does not take long to realize that there are just as many of us 'on the make' in the fields of personal and spiritual growth as there are any-where else. Just as many who are pretending. Possibly more, because the spiritually lost are prone to both debasing and inflating them-selves, two sides of the same coin.

Here's just one example. In January 1994 the first public meeting was called in Croatia of a peace initiative called Through the Heart to Peace – the result of two women having had spiritual experiences inspiring them to bring women from all over the world to help end the war in Bosnia. Three hundred women came to that planning meeting. Time was given for anyone who wished to speak at the microphone. A Serbian woman poet bravely offered her song for forgiveness. People from many nations spoke. Then a young woman in flowing white clothes climbed onto the stage, paused dramatically behind the micro-phone, pointed her fingertips to the sky and then spread her arms wide. Her white shawl fell like wings from her outstretched arms. 'I invoke the energies of the archangel Michael.' Pause. 'His sacred sites are on the same latitudes as this place.' More dramatic arm gestures. 'I feel the energies of his angels moving here to bless this gathering.'

Her eyes were closed, one hand thrust dramatically towards the audience. This kind of thing continued for a little while until some irreverent souls in the audience began to grin.

The reason why this woman did not ring true was because what she was doing did not come from her hara. It was a show, whereas what other people were doing on that platform, however simple, struck a chord with others because it was real. I told my 19-year-old daughter about this incident. 'Yeah,' she said, 'that's the sort of thing gets the spirit a bad name.'

Saving the world singlehanded

I feel distinctly nostalgic about this one. For years I was driven by an inner imperative which insisted that it was up to me to do something about almost everything that was wrong in the world: refugees, apartheid, wars, nuclear weapons, nuclear power plants, torture – you name it, it was my problem. Except perhaps dolphins – there seemed to be enough people worrying about them. I felt, overwhelmingly, for people who were suffering. It seems hard to imagine that one individual can be at the same time so burdened and so inflated, but I believe it's very common. I don't want to deride it, because drives like this undoubtedly provide much of the energy and fuel which goes into change; what I do question is whether it is coming from the right place for the most profound change. My ego was most definitely involved; I needed to feel that *I* was doing something to help. There's nothing wrong with that, you might say. I agree, except that I was definitely attached to what *I* wanted the result to be. It took me a while to accept that things evolve, lots of streams feed in, and the result of lots of people's efforts may be quite different from what any of them predicted or expected. I was always *doing*, not giving myself much time for *being*. In fact not according much credit to being at all. Joanna Macy is profoundly sensible:

> Compassion, which is grief in the grief of others, is but one side of the coin. The other side is joy in the joy of others – which in Buddhism is called *mudita*. To the extent that we allow ourselves to identify with the sufferings of other beings, we can identify with their strengths as well. This is very important for a sense of adequacy and resilience, because we face a time of great challenge that demands of us more commitment, endurance and courage than we can dredge up out of our individual supply. (1993. B9)

Overwork and the activist

This is another old favourite. We become wound up in a spiral of things that have to be done – deadlines which have to be met, mailings which have to go out, contacts which have to be made, people who have to be seen, not to mention piles of material which has to be read – until we are just one mass of 'have-to's'. There is never enough money, never enough competent people to help, never enough time, and never any real satisfaction. It is all being done with the finest of intentions, and yet there's little time for joy in it. Not a lot of laughs. No time to breathe. Certainly no time to reflect, to get a bit of distance and perspective. In Thomas Merton's words:

> . . . There is a pervasive form of contemporary violence to which the idealist fighting for peace by nonviolent methods most easily succumbs: activism and overwork. The rush and pressure of modern life are a form, perhaps the most common form, of its innate violence. To allow oneself to be carried away by a multitude of conflicting concerns, to surrender to too many demands, to commit oneself to too many projects, to want to help

everyone in everything is to succumb to violence. More than that, it is cooperation in violence. The frenzy of the activist neutralizes his work for peace. It destroys his own inner capacity for peace. It destroys the fruitfulness of his own work, because it kills the root of inner wisdom which makes work fruitful. (1962. B11)

Some activists are seeing this now and giving themselves nourishment and some space. The best insist on clowns at their annual general meetings. I'm serious; the SEVA Foundation has a clown called Wavy Gravy on its board of directors, and makes anyone who uses the word 'serious' wear a Groucho Marx nose and glasses. Joy then creeps back into the work, and on its tail comes creativity, the big ideas.

Sugary good

It's not something one really *says* in peace movement circles, but I've come to the point where I do not actually want to *see* another white dove. They may well be to other people's taste, but they make me want to throw up. It's the sentimentality, I think, the notion that something sweet and white and soft will do the trick. That kind of gooey goodness just gums up the works as far as I am concerned. It keeps people naive. It's a bit like saying, 'The people out there are very hard, so we in here will be very soft.' It makes out that we are all good and they (the warmongers, arms sellers, seal killers etc) are all bad, which is just another version of 'us' and 'them' – the enemy out there. It is simply not true. We have all got crap in us as well as beauty. If we want to change, we have to step out of being either victims or holy.

> If it came to it, could we women close down a nuclear power station, dispose of its radioactive poisons in a safe, long-term method AND provide power for the nation? We cannot criticise unless we are prepared to do the most difficult jobs. (Vida Pearson, 1992, page 25. B7)

CHAPTER 11

How Hara Power Works for Men and Women

Take your practised powers and stretch them out until they span the chasm between the two contradictions . . . For the god wants to know himself in you.

Rainer Maria Rilke, 1875-1926

This final chapter pulls together the threads of the book, but it will be more than just a summing-up. It will show how the notions of power we have been living with are destructive, why we need a new kind of power and how that new view can draw on the very ancient. The prehistoric power of the feminine is briefly reviewed, especially the power inherent in female sexuality. The human journey from the Garden of Eden is described, through the struggle for development of consciousness, into the latter centuries when rationality and the masculine principle has been dominant. The rest of the chapter is devoted to what this new kind of power – hara power – can mean for us today, and why it is intimately connected with sexuality. I explore what developed hara power looks like in a woman and in a man, and in conclusion describe what hara power means to me, and how I use it.

The concept of power we have been living with is deadly

Our starting point in this book was that the world is in a mess. The statistics are by now familiar. It may take a long time, but it is clear that we will not survive, and the earth will not survive, if we go on like this.

The concept of power which has been the cause of our getting into this situation is that of domination. For several thousand years, men have been in charge of key decisions which affect the world, and even today the vast majority of these decisions are made by men. Domination power is power *over*. It is a drive which makes people compete for jobs, money, goods, security and love. It drives nations to struggle for superiority, to build or buy weapons of such destructive power that other nations are intimidated. Nations use their domination power (economic or military) to extract goods from other less powerful nations at unfair prices, to grab territory or simply to ensure the continued supply of resources considered vital for the standard of living of their people. Thus nations of the North get richer and consume more resources while those of the South get deeper into debt. It is why millions of people in the South face starvation daily. The wars which happen as a result of domination power cause millions of refugees to roam the world or fester in camps. In the process of all this, the environment steadily gets wrecked.

Even having acquired so much – nuclear weapons for security, a 'seat at the top table' of the UN, and plenty of food, warmth, cars and washing machines – people in the dominator nations are not happy. They are taking drugs and committing suicide and killing each other and becoming ill as never before. Traditional patterns of living have been wiped out; old sources of spiritual nourishment have been abandoned, there is little stability and meaning to people's lives.

In such a world view power is a zero-sum game: the more you have, the less I have; if you win, I lose. This kind of defensiveness prevents feedback. And feedback – the free circulation of information and energy – is essential to the survival of any system. Systems which lack conscious feedback, which close their perceptions to the results of their behaviour, are committing suicide. It is no longer valid to think that we are in control, that we shall be all right, no matter what we do to others. We are discovering that what we do to the rest of the world, we do to ourselves. So, if we are to survive, women and men need a new view of power.

Building on the very ancient

Earlier chapters went back 4,000 years and discovered a world where things appear to have been different, where women exercised power alongside men, where cities and towns were not fortified, where life revolved around the sacred, where the female deity was supreme. The Great Mother was worshipped under many names in the whole of what is now Europe, the Middle East and India. Reverence for her survives to this day among indigenous peoples of North and South America and in many parts of Asia. In God the Mother, the power is everywhere. Feminine creation 'brings forth from within'. Trees, rocks and ferns are quite as alive as animals and people. Power comes from the exchange of energy between beings and their deity which is all around and particularly in the earth. Some people call it the Great Mysterious.

We gathered some clues as to what this power consisted of. It was certainly to do with the primordial power of the female to create and give birth, and thus involved reverence for her body, her blood, her womb and her sexuality. Female sexuality and sensuality were considered sacred, were a central part of religious rites and were celebrated in art – in carving and painting and sculpture.

A key element of goddess worship was her wholeness – the fact that she was both light and dark, birth and death, simultaneously womb and tomb, giver of life and devourer of her children. One way that she has come down to us is in the figure of Kali, the Hindu goddess of creation, preservation and destruction. Her dark side is as cold hard winter is to the bloom of summer; it is the underworld where Persephone has to go for part of the year. It is to be found in the ferocity of nature – the way lightning fractures a great oak, the way a cyclone or an earthquake swallows lives, the way a meteor may smash into this planet and obliterate it. It is the harshness of the pronouncement of the crone, the obscurity of the oracle. Often it leaves us bewildered. It speaks a language which is hard to decipher.

This female element was apparently central to people's lives for thousands of years, until humanity began to shift. Armed tribes from the north conquered these societies, and the phenomenal power of the female was gradually subjugated. This has been done in various ways over the centuries – by splitting the wholeness of the goddess into opposites, by clamping down on female sexual energy, and by making sex sinful.

Since the myth of the Garden of Eden, woman has been the temptress leading man astray, whereas before she was the priestess offering the vital links between mind, body and soul. Clues to the ancient links between sexuality and spirituality are still found in Tantric Buddhism, Sufism, Shamanism and Gnosticism. These traditions have been destroyed or marginalized by the monotheistic religions, all of which equate female sexuality with sin. The last great struggle to destroy women's power and sexuality, defined as witchcraft, went on for 300 years in Europe. Women learned to be ashamed of their bodies and their bodily functions. Female sexuality was controlled, menstruation became a curse, wombs began to be dispensable.

One result is that women became *either* good *or* bad, whores or virgins. An overtly sexual woman, even today, cannot be a 'good' woman. And what we have lost is a powerful source of energy.

It is certainly not my view that we should try to emulate or 'go back' to the cultures described. Their importance is in the fact that they existed, and existed for so long. Understanding a bit about them, and about what has happened to women in the intervening centuries, throws an entirely new light on our problems today.

It means first that women's struggle should not be *against* men. That assumes a conflict of interests, assumes that it is a question of 'us' versus 'them' – in other words, the battle of the sexes. This merely apes the basic way of deciding things in a male-orientated society – namely by a power struggle.

Secondly it means that by identifying and developing a new kind of power, we can approach the world and its problems in a fundamentally different way. Let me crystallize what this looks like.

The new concept of power

The focus for this new kind of power is the hara; it is the seat of creativity and of sexuality. This focus makes it possible for our understanding of the world to spring from an entirely different set of premises. Instead of defining the fittest as those who 'win', we can define the fittest as those who 'fit in' with their surroundings. In place of the doctrine of original sin we can set the doctrine of original health – we can say that human beings are pure at birth and by nature fine. Instead of insisting that aggression is innate and a fact of life, we can take as our starting point that care and love are stronger forces, and more prevalent.

This takes us in an entirely different direction. Because we take a benign view of our neighbour – 'unconditional positive regard' – it becomes likely that she or he takes a benign view of us. Communication becomes possible, leading to co-operation. Because we have a sense of relatedness, rather than separateness, we feel connected to our neighbour. That sense of relatedness and interconnectedness extends to our surroundings, we feel part of the natural world, and this leads us to treat it in a responsible way. We cannot exploit and pollute what is a part of us.

This set of attitudes gives us a sense of rootedness and security. The more secure we are, the less it is necessary to fear our neighbour or covet his or her goods. These ways of being allow us greater access not only to our own higher selves, but also to the Great Mysterious – and therefore enable our lives to be rooted in sacred meaning.

Detail from Sophia, Mother Wisdom – illustration by Hildegard of Bingen
1098-1179

I want to concentrate for a moment on some of the characteristics of hara power because of their importance. The first is *awareness*. We have to know what's going on, at a deep level, and in the moment.

To step back and realize what we are doing. Chapters 6 and 9 described ways of doing this, including meditation and visualisation, becoming familiar with our feelings, being vulnerable and being direct.

The second is *communication*. The goal here is not to win, but to solve the problem: to settle, not to humiliate. Almost all the ways of dealing with a bully without becoming a thug yourself, described in chapter 9, have to do with communication.

The next is *co-operation*. What co-operation comes from is compassion – being able to imagine what it is like to be the other person – and what co-operation leads to is the greater good of all. We saw in chapter 10 how co-operation can work in practical terms to the advantage of all those prepared to undertake it.

The next characteristic is *interconnectedness*. Those developing hara power learn, as scientists are now beginning to realize, that we are all in fact interconnected and therefore interdependent. Thus hara power would act from the premise that what one group of people do in one part of the world affects others thousands of miles away. That is what chaos theory is all about. This sense of relatedness and interconnectedness means that we feel part of the natural world, rather than masters over it, and therefore means treating it responsibly.

This leads to the last characteristic, which is *responsibility*. The basic principle of responsive leadership is that power and responsibility work together. Now more than ever we have to take responsibility for our environment and begin to think long-term and globally, rather than short-term and greedily.

Power and sex

The problem with writing about all this is that the words one ends up using (like responsibility, relatedness, interconnectedness, co-operation) don't seem very exciting. They are not what my friends in the media would call sexy, whereas fights and murders and people killing each other in wars somehow *are* sexy.

But there's an irony here. Because underneath all these words, one of the sources of this new power is in sexuality. Just as the earliest religion was a sexual-spiritual religion, many people today are rediscovering the energy of their real sexuality. It is quite different from what they have been brought up to think, shockingly so. Their potential for arousal is enormous. They can have intense pleasure whenever they want, with or without a partner. Female sexuality, having been so repressed and disfigured over centuries, is beginning to regain something of its full potential.

The central theme of this book is the link between power and sex. For women sex has been connected with guilt, manipulation or false glamour. This has made it hard for them to use hara power, which depends on openness, frankness, honesty and trust. Hara power will help women to have a more grounded feeling about sex and a more joyful sexual practice.

For men sex has been connected with control, domination, aggression. This has made it hard for them to use hara power, which depends on surrender, equality, reciprocity and trust. Hara power will enrich men's sex lives. And richer sex lives will give them more hara power, to replace the domination power they must give up. Understanding the link between power and sex will result in a healthier understanding of the body and of nature.

In chapter 5 I talked about the difference between a domination approach to sex, and a hara approach, and in chapter 7 I took this further to show how surrender of control and fusion with another are essential to love-making which is satisfying at a deep level. In this kind of lovemaking we gain our bliss, our satisfaction and our strength with and through another. We gain more power by being totally with another, and we cease to need power *over*. So the end of the necessity for domination power lies in this kind of sexuality.

When people allow their sexuality and their spirituality to work together, the energy unleashed is formidable. With the exception of our modern world, sexuality has everywhere and always been a manifestation of the holy. It has long been recognized as a way into the mystery of creation, a means of knowledge. Sexuality can reveal to human beings that which is beyond themselves – in other words, the divine. The great importance we all place on sexuality may unconsciously be because it is a means of entering and knowing sacred reality.

Human beings crave union. But what we want underneath it all is a feeling of oneness, of completeness, of peace – *in ourselves*. We have a deep need to bring together the two principles, to heal the split into duality that happened so long ago. The goal of the human soul within is to create union of our own internal male and female parts.

The human journey

Maybe what I have been discovering in this book has something to do with the journey of consciousness of the human race. Perhaps human beings started off in what might be called the natural state. The early concept of the mother deity was basic space, emptiness; she was unreflecting and unconscious (that was the Garden of Eden) and she had no masculine counterpart. Then the son god emerged and through their struggles, consciousness developed, along with dualistic thinking. Humans became aware of the difference between good and evil. The masculine principle began to prevail – logical thinking, scientific inquiry, rationality and 'realism' became stronger and stronger, especially in the West.

Over the past few centuries we have gone too far this way – too far into an increasing disrespect for and destruction of the natural world, aided and hastened by technological discoveries and an impoverishment of spiritual life. People may in many ways now be more conscious and more aware, but at the same time they are cut off from the natural and the spiritual world. Our minds are alive, but our bodies and spirits are starved and dying. We may be clever, but we are out of balance.

The concept of balance has been a theme of this book. Yin and yang is a concept of balance. So are the pairs of dark and light, masculine and feminine, assertiveness and surrender, ancient and modern. And the triad of mind, body and spirit. The concept of the chakras is a concept of balance. People need survival, sensuality, compassion, toughness, truth, mental clarity and spirituality – all of these and in the right balance. For each situation each person must find his or her own balance, and a lifetime of learning is the only way to approach this ideal. We have to learn to live with paradox and uncertainty. We have to be able to balance certainty and doubt. The emphasis in this book has been on experimentation, on trying things for yourself, on making them your own and on continuous learning.

It seems to me that what has been happening in the 20th century is that women have been developing their masculine qualities: getting out and exploring and exercising their talents in the world and fighting for equality and obtaining their rights. This is admirable and fine. Nevertheless what is needed now is the development of their feminine strength and the feminine strength of men. The world needs both sexes to develop this new kind of power. Hara power is synthesis, not thesis or antithesis. It is in this combination of the inner and the outer, of the spiritual and the sexual, of change in the self and change in the structure, of yin and of yang, that our future and our survival lie.

The problem of attaining *balanced* manhood has troubled human societies since time immemorial, hence the complexity and variety of initiation rites across the globe. To learn what he must learn, the son must leave what he already knows – separation from the mother is crucial. Some of these rites test men physically to the point of death. In the West we have abandoned such rites, with the exception of surrogates like dangerous sports and military service, which fail dismally because they omit the spiritual underpinnings – support from older, experienced men making it possible for the initiates to gain value from their experience.

The problem remains of how to enable boys to become men without insisting on aggression as the defining characteristic of heroism and power. Patriarchy has only recently begun to crumble, and new descriptions of manhood are still hard to find.

The man with hara power

A man with hara power wants to know the patterns of the world, to understand himself and to experience his connection with the eternal. This is his life's most serious work. He is permanently challenged by his own problems and those of others and of the world, but because he has learned how to learn, he meets problems with flexibility and receptiveness.

His power does not come from any position he may hold, but from within. He needs neither a gun nor God the Father on his side. He knows that he cannot harm others without harming himself. He cares little for material acquisition or appearances and would give up a fortune to preserve forests, lakes and animals.

He is compassionate about the suffering of others, and so brings out the best in those he lives and works with. He takes responsibility and exercises leadership not from any desire for self-aggrandisement, but because he recognizes that using his own talents to the full will encourage those around him to do the same. He liberally bends the rules to meet different situations.

His impulse is to discover and to innovate. In the past, scientific knowledge and technological invention has often been driven by a desire to dominate or control: men with hara power relate their enquiring instinct to a sense of responsibility and respect for the natural world. They are curious about and accepting of strange new phenomena, cultures and experiences.

When hara power is developed in a man, his masculinity has a solidity about it, a presence in the body to balance the activity of the mind. He consults his body rather than simply using it. He tries to give it what it wants, rather than pushing it to its limits. He learns from it, and certainly finds it beautiful. As a lover he is gentle, sensitive, and moves into the act so deeply that the actor is no more. He values being as much as doing.

He lives and works with women on the basis of equality and respect. He is stable. He loves to play, values children for what they can teach him, and willingly cares for them. He is sustained by the natural environment, and spends as much time outside as he can. He is able to seek help when he does not know. He doesn't have to be certain, but he does have to be brave.

This is where the hero comes in. He knows that if he can find what he is supposed to do, who he is supposed to be, and thus become his real self, he need not fear any change. He may lose his job, may suffer periods of disappointment or grief, but his eye on the eternal will give such events the perspective of opportunities to learn more about himself and to become more effective in what he does.

The woman with hara power

This kind of woman has learned to rely on the messages of her body and the knowledge of her self. She listens to her body carefully, and allows herself to go deeply into its feelings: from this she gains insight for what she needs to do and how to do it. She has strong internal images, which she does not dismiss but absorbs and examines for their indications of her situation and of the path she may best take.

All this gives her power to go out in the world in her own way. She does not feel obliged to curb her intuition about what needs to be done: she values her creative instincts and acts upon them. This gets her past the criticism she experiences, enabling her not to fight those who put her down, but work with them. People feel safe with her because she stands with her feet planted in the earth.

Her power comes from within. She uses it only in the light of her certainty that everything in the world is interconnected, and that her every action affects others and the earth. She can be very fierce. What saves her from burn-out is her spiritual knowledge: she has realized that she is not the centre of everything. That gives her freedom.

She has patience and stamina gained from caring for children – her own or those of others' – and the sense of ordinariness that one gets when a small person has just burped all over one's shoulder. Call this humility or whatever, it does bring a sense of perspective into life, and usually a sense of the funny side of it all. The stamina and sense of being related to what is quite basic and ordinary give her the strength to go on caring and rebuilding, again and again.

She is profoundly creative: her blood and her womb are valued, being part of her life giving powers. Her sexuality grows and develops all through her life, giving her insight into the state of being where oneness is experienced, where she is one-in-herself, where there is no boundary between herself and all else that is.

She finds self-knowledge and understanding through her cycles and her connection with the earth. Her ear is to the ground. Sometimes she appears to be destructive, chaotic, irrational – at the very least inconsistent and unpredictable. This is her nature and part of her strength.

She becomes wiser as she gets older, and becomes more essential to her community, not less. She knows that death is only part of a never-ending cycle, and is not afraid of it.

Personal postscript

As can be seen from the Bibliography, many other people are writing about what I am writing about, in different ways. Do not passively accept what I say. Put it into practice, try it, and see if it works for you. In other words, the payoff in reading this book is not the accumulation of knowledge, but the development of your own understanding, your own certainty.

I would like to end with a note about what hara power means to me, and how I use it in my life. A good current example is the writing of this book. When I had finished the fourth draft, I sent it to about 30 men and women who had kindly agreed to read it and give me their comments. Now I hoped, as I suppose most writers do, that these readers would phone up more or less instantly, fainting with amazement at my extraordinary accomplishment, and tell me that reading it had changed their lives. I was wrong. Some manuscripts came back with outrage scribbled on every other page. There was anger and hurt. People thought it humourless and turgid. There was also joy and delight, and real discovery apparent in readers' comments – but those weren't the ones I had to deal with.

The ones I had to deal with eventually showed me how much anger I had in me, and had put in the book, anger against the system of domination which has so subjugated the feminine spirit. First I had to sit down and actually recognize the anger. Once I saw it, I saw it on almost every page of the first part of the book. My ego was offended that I, such a wise woman, could be so askew. Then I had to sit quietly and confront the anger. I managed to take it down from my head into my heart, where I could attend to the roots of it; I held it there, and re-experienced the personal losses which had produced it. I suppose that took several weeks, and by the end I had absorbed and changed the destructive parts of the anger. Then I changed the book, chapter by chapter, and as I did so I learned something about myself on almost every page. Much of what I learned came from readers' comments; I am grateful to every one of those people.

That is something of what hara power means to me. Now I shall try and describe how I use it. The first example is internal, the second out in the world. Recently I went to a five-day retreat. When I tried to meditate, a stream of banal images kept appearing, and my loftiest thoughts were somewhere at the level of which dog food to buy. I spent two days struggling with a turmoil of feelings, mostly connected with not receiving the love I wanted. Suddenly it dawned on me that, after all the time I have spent in the past year thinking about this, I know a lot about the kind of love I want. So why not try and give it to myself?

The following day was to be a day of complete silence, and there was nothing in the world that I had to do, like working or cleaning or washing up. No mail would arrive and no phone would ring. So why not devote the entire day to myself, to giving myself the love I wanted? It seemed oddly risky. Critical voices started talking about 'people who love themselves'. But I saluted them and started out. I was really kind to myself. I paid *full attention* to myself. I dwelt on my better qualities rather than those that make me cringe. I forgave myself at every turn. I looked in the mirror at myself and liked what I saw. I took care of my needs.

By the end of the morning I experienced a welling-up of lightness in my chest, and a sort of tingling all down my breast-bone. And from that moment I have been able, some of the time, to 'see' myself – to step back as it were from my feelings and see them, almost at arm's length. This means that for at least a few moments I am not 'in' the feeling. So if necessary I am able to take care of it without acting on it, for example without *being* hurt or angry or whatever it is I am feeling. It goes like this: I observe how I am, so then I know what I feel, so then I know what I need, so then if appropriate I can ask for it.

I have no idea what the connection is, or even if there is one, between giving oneself love and being able to 'see' oneself; but I do know how valuable the ability is. It means that less energy goes into my own moods and more into what's going on in the world.

The other example happened when I was in Bosnia. Two courageous Bosnian women were trying to negotiate with three different armies to obtain passes for 150 people to get through the lines and into the besieged city of Sarajevo, bringing support and help. The negotiations involved reaching an army commander in East Mostar, the Muslim part of the city which had been shelled to rubble. The women asked me to go with them. They talked their way through the UN checkpoint and we crossed the rickety metal girders thrown across the river in place of the 15th century bridge, which had been blown up. We passed people queuing for water at one of the only taps still working, and down devastated streets to the War Presidency. This was guarded by soldiers who looked angrily at us as we asked permission to enter. The face of the one in charge showed the misery and harshness of the months of fear he had been through. I could not understand what was being said, so I was just standing there, watching and cogitating. For some reason, an image of a red rose came into my mind. So I mentally picked it up and put it in his heart. At that point his face broke into a smile and he let us in. Now I do not know how much that had to do with the rose and how much it had to do with what my Bosnian friends were saying to him. But when we were waiting upstairs to see the commander, his secretary came out and handed me four red roses. To this day I do not know where they came from.

Additional Material and Notes

This section is intended to provide supplementary information to the main text. It includes further stories where relevant, even poetry and pictures, as well as references for those authors I have quoted or found useful. The purpose is to give more background to the ideas in the book and to make clear how they were arrived at. Where I refer to publications listed in the Bibliography, only the authors and publication dates are given here. Full details are provided in the Bibliography.

Introduction
Page 2.
In 1982 I founded the Oxford Research Group to carry out research into how and by whom nuclear weapons decisions are made in each of the nuclear nations. The Group enjoys the support of charities and foundations in Britain and the USA, and the European Parliament. It is an independent, multi-disciplinary team of 12 researchers and support staff, whose policy is to make accurate information available on a process often cloaked in secrecy. It has published on all stages of nuclear weapons production in the former Soviet Union, the USA, Britain, France and China, examining the roles and assumptions of all involved, from scientists to intelligence analysts, from politicians to defence contractors. Among many published titles are the following: Scilla McLean, 1986, (B6); Hugh Miall, 1987, (B6); Patrick Burke, 1988, (B6). This last book contains biographies of some 650 nuclear weapons decision-makers worldwide. The interviews with those who design and deploy nuclear weapons were written up as 'The Assumptions of Nuclear Weapons Decision Makers' in Barnett & Lee, 1989, (B6).
Pages 4-6. What power means
The paragraph on what power means in traditional terms has been drawn from the following: Bertrand Russell, 1975, pages 186–7, (B7); Max Weber, 1978, (B14); Robert Dahl, 1957, (B7); Dennis Wrong,

1979, (B7). The quotation in the next paragraph is from John Rowan, 1987, page 9, (B4).

On the subject of the journey of human development, and whether human beings are or are not innately aggressive, I was intrigued to discover the work of Mary Clark, who is a biologist. She challenges the Western view of 'progress' as being based on widely held but erroneous beliefs about evolution generally.

> One is the notion that Darwin's ideas about natural selection and survival of the fittest imply 'winning' in a giant competition for scarce resources: food, nesting sites, mates. Such an interpretation argues that individuals and cultures that fall by the wayside are 'less fit' because they lose out to 'superior' persons or societies. Indeed, defining the 'fittest' as those who 'win' allows us to justify the most pathological social institutions of Western society. (Mary Clark, 'Symptoms of cultural pathologies: A hypothesis' in Dennis Sandale & Hugo van der Merwe, 1993, pages 48–9. B2)

She does not deny that competition occurs in nature, but asserts that it is a far from complete explanation of fitness. We would do better to think of fitness in much broader terms as 'fitting in' with one's surroundings. As C G Simpson says:

> To generalize that natural selection is over-all and even in a figurative sense the outcome of struggle is quite unjustified . . . Struggle is sometimes involved, but it usually is not, and when it is, it may even work against rather than toward natural selection. Advantage in . . . reproduction is usually a peaceful process in which the concept of struggle is really irrelevant. It more often involves such things as better integration into the ecological situation . . . more efficient utilization of food, better care of the young, elimination of intra-group discords . . . that might hamper reproduction, [and] exploitation of environmental possibilities that are not the objects of competition or are less effectively exploited by others. (C G Simpson, 1949, pages 221–2. B14)

What Clark shows is that human beings have a set of 'needs' not experienced by other primates. These are the needs that arise out of self-awareness and self-consciousness – the need for sacred meaning and the need for social bonding. These are the needs to which our 'survival of the fittest' (dominator power) way of behaving cannot respond.

Both Stephen Lukes (1986, B7) and Kenneth Boulding (1990, B7) see power in its widest meaning, as potential for change, as:

> . . . the search for the sources of change – the access points, the winning coalitions, the pivots, the levers, the bastions, the weak links . . . by means

of which desired social changes may be brought about, or prevented. (Stephen Lukes, 1986, page 15. B7)

The translation of the *Tao Te Ching* that is used here is that by Stephen Mitchell, published by Macmillan in 1989.

Pages 6-9. What is in the book

On the subject of stories about women, Carol Christ has this to say:

> Women's stories have not been told. And without stories there is no artic- ulation of experience. Without stories a woman is lost when she comes to make important decisions in her life. She does not learn to value her struggles, to celebrate her strengths, to comprehend her pain. Without sto- ries she is alienated from those deeper experiences of self and world that have been called spiritual or religious. She is closed in silence. (C Christ, 1980. B11)

I am indebted to Nancy Qualls-Corbett for the germ of the idea of resistance to taboos in the introduction to her book *The Sacred Prostitute*, 1988.

The experience with the serpent happened some months before I had begun to read about the goddess, and to realize that the snake or serpent is her symbol and the symbol in many traditions for primordial energy and continual creation.

Chapter 1

Page 11.

The Marija Gimbutas quotation at the head of the chapter is from *The Language of the Goddess*, 1989, page 321, (B3).

Pages 13-14.

At the end of the seduction story, I make the point that much of the power that women have is dependent on man's desire. It is of course quite relevant to argue that no-one has power over another without the other accepting that power. I am indebted to Paul Ingram for pointing this out and for referring me to *The Legitimation of Power* by David Beetham (1991, B7). Part of the process of re-empowering is learning to say no.

Pages 14-17. Going back to the time of women

The information about matrifocal societies is drawn from Merlin Stone, 1976, (B3), page xii to whom I owe the quotations about the Divine Ancestress; from Elinor Gadon, 1989, (B3), page 6; from

Jacquetta Hawkes & Leonard Woolley, 1963, (B14), pages 199, 204, 213–14; and from Jacquetta Hawkes, 1963, (B14), pages 26–27, to whom I owe the long quotation describing the art of the Cyclades. I recommend chapter 2 of Merlin Stone's book and chapters 3 and 4 of Elinor Gadon's, as well as the amazing illustrations.

The Neolithic village at Pan-p'o in China, is described in *The Continuity of China* Vol 1, 1982, page 160. At the site that is now known as Jericho, in Palestine:

> Various finds point to an active religious life. Female clay figures with their hands raised to their breast resemble idols of the mother goddess which were later so widely disseminated in the Near East. (Sibylle von Cles-Reden, 1961. B3)

In Elise Boulding's view, it is possible that priestesses in Catal Huyuk (in what is now Turkey) presided over three types of rites – rites of giving birth, rites of marriage and funerary rites. The number of cultic objects found indicates that a substantial amount of ritual activity was going on and that the priestess may have had a full-time occupation. (Elise Boulding, a former Professor of Sociology at the University of Colorado and consultant to UNESCO, is author of *The Underside of History,* 1976, a work of extraordinary scholarship which tells the other half of history.)

About 1,000 megalithic tombs still remain in Ireland, many of which carry the symbols of the goddess.

> The menhir is the Goddess. That a menhir is the epiphany of the Owl Goddess we know from prehistoric stelae in Southern France, Spain, and Portugal. The Goddess's intimacy with stone is also witnessed in historical times. Great Artemis was called 'the stony one' and Mesopotamian Ninhursaga, 'Lady of the stony ground.' In folk memories, the menhir is the abode of Irish Brigit and Baltic Laima (Fate) as late as the 20th Century. (*See* G E Daniel & O G S Crawford, 1957. B3)

Megalith builders are now thought to have been goddess worshippers.

Many believe that all gods and goddesses have their origins in Kali the Dark Mother, triple goddess of creation, preservation and destruction. This is how she is described in the Nirvana Tantra:

> Compared with the vast sea of being Kali, the existence of Brahma and the other gods is nothing but such a little water as is obtained in the hollow made by a cow's hoof. Just as it is impossible for a hollow made by a cow's hoof to form a notion of the unfathomable depths of a sea, so it is impossible for Brahma and other gods to have a knowledge of the nature of Kali.

This description is from Philip Rawson, 1973, page 184, (B10), and is taken from Barbara Walker, 1983, page 490, (B5).

Goddess religions appear to have extended right across the Pacific. Rita Gross, Professor of Comparative Studies in Religion at the University of Wisconsin-Eau Claire, studied the role of Aboriginal women in Australian and Melanesian religions. She recalls:

> The scholars all told me that in these religions, men are regarded as sacred while women are regarded as profane and unclean and had no significant religious life.

> Nevertheless, I couldn't help but notice that the actual data of Australian and Melanesian religions recounted myths in which women originally held power and taught men all the religious rituals; only later, according to these myths, did men steal power and knowledge from the women. The actual data also included numerous rituals in which men imitated female physiological processes, even though they also excluded women from participation in those rituals. Something seemed not quite to add up. (Rita M. Gross, 1993, page 292. B11) (Rita M. Gross, 'Tribal Religions: Aboriginal Australia' in Arvind Sharma (ed), 1987, pages 41–2 has a summary of that literature and its refutation. B11)

Pages 18-20. Surprise

The authors who question the worship of a mother goddess in prehistoric times include Peter Ucko, who asserts, in rather strangled language, that it cannot be proved, except in the Near East.

> It has been shown that only for the Near East is there conclusive early historical evidence of the worship of a Mother Goddess primarily concerned with fertility. It may be argued for the interpretation of prehistoric figurines from this region that it is legitimate to approach such an investigation predisposed to accept that this later Mother Goddess worship may be relevant to the modelling of small anthropomorphic figurines. (Peter Ucko, page 414. B3)

Another is Andrew Fleming, author of 'The Myth of the Mother Goddess' in *World Archaeology* Vol 2, October 1969, pages 247–61, (B3). This is mainly an objection to the view of prehistorians that the great megalithic tomb builders of western Europe were devotees of the goddess, but does not offer any evidence to refute it.

The Walter Burkert quotation is from *Greek Religion Archaic and Classical*, 1985, page 12, (B11).

Pages 20-23. Why it is a surprise

Here are two other passages from Merlin Stone's introduction to *When God was a Woman:*

> Most of the information and artefacts concerning the vast female religion, which flourished for thousands of years before the advent of Judaism, Christianity and the Classical Age of Greece, have been dug out of the ground only to be reburied in obscure archaeological texts, carefully shelved away in the exclusively protected stacks of university and museum libraries. Quite a few of these were accessible only with the proof of university affiliation or university degree . . . In the difficulties I encountered gathering material, I could not help thinking of the ancient writing and statuary that must have been intentionally destroyed. Accounts of the antagonistic attitudes of Judaism, Christianity and Mohammedanism (Islam) toward the sacred artefacts of the religions that preceded them revealed that this was so, especially in the case of the goddess worshipped in Canaan (Palestine).

> The bloody massacres, the demolition of statues (ie pagan idols) and sanctuaries are recorded in the pages of the Bible following this command by Yahweh: 'You must completely destroy all the places where the nations you dispossess have served their gods, on high mountains, on hills, under any spreading tree; you must tear down their altars, smash their pillars, cut down their sacred poles, set fire to the carved images of their gods and wipe out their name from that place.' (Deuteronomy 12:2,3.) There can be little doubt that the continuous attacks, as recorded in the Old Testament, destroyed much precious and irretrievable information.

As women in increasing numbers have become historians, they have begun to recognize that history is not necessarily objective fact (*see* Catherine Hall, 1992. B6). Here is Mary Condren's opinion:

> History is not the objective science it was once thought to be but a particular form of power and knowledge, involving the manipulation of academic and political resources and serving to ensure the dominance of certain groups. (Mary Condren, 1989, page xxiii. B3)

In *The Living World of the Old Testament* (1978, page 141. B11) Bernard Anderson tells us:

> A prominent feature of this Canaanite cult was sacred prostitution. In the act of temple prostitution the man identified himself with Baal, the woman with Ashtart. It was believed that human pairs, by imitating the action of Baal and his partner [sic] could bring the divine pair together in fertilising union. (B11)

I am also indebted to Bernard Anderson for the information that the Hebrew language has no word for goddess.

The description of vestal virgins is from Nancy Qualls-Corbett, 1988, page 36, (B10).

Page 23. What happened to the Goddess?

The description of the plaque at Catal Huyuk is from Merlin Stone, 1976, page 154, (B3).

The sentences describing the spread of weapons and fortification of villages are based on Elise Boulding, 1976, pages 171 and 172, (B13).

Page 24. Enter weapons

I should qualify my phrase 'the end of matrifocal societies', since some still exist, for example on the island of Belau in the Pacific. Belau is a matrilineal society, where inheritance is through the female line. See *Daughters of the Pacific* by Zohl de Ishtar, available from 3/164 Annandale Street, Annandale, NSW 2038, Australia.

The description of patriarchal invaders and the father god Zeus is based on Jaquetta Hawkes, 1968, page 30, (B14).

Pages 25-6. The fall in the power of women

In the Old Testament, there are plenty of references to the worship of the Baals and the Ashtartes (Judges 2:13;10:6; I Samuel 7:4; 12:10) which was punished by the jealous god Yahweh. Baal was the male deity, and his consort was in some areas referred to as Baalat, a name widely given to the Great Mother.

> If Israel was to grow as a nation-state, with all the entailed military and political trappings, goddess religions would have to be overthrown. Allegiance would have to be to one god, Yahweh, and the central symbolism of the new religion would be based on Promise and History rather than on the Life and Cyclical Regeneration represented by the Serpent. (Mary Condren, 1989, page 11. B3)

Some writers, like Bernard Anderson, see the conflict between the monotheistic religion and the goddess as a conflict between obedience and sex:

> In Canaanite religion, sex was elevated to the realm of the divine . . . The gods were sexual in nature and were worshipped in sexual rites . . . According to Israel's faith, on the other hand, the power of the divine was disclosed in the sphere of history – that is, in the wonder of a non-recurring event (the Exodus) which was at once the sign of God's deliverance of his people from servitude and the call to obey his will within a covenant community. (Bernard Anderson, 1978. B11)

Philip Slater's argument is presented in *The Glory of Hera*, 1968, (B5).
Pages 26-8. The western creation myth
The serpent has been found all round the Mediterranean as a representative or symbol of the goddess. As long ago as 1930, Sir Arthur
Evans wrote: 'Accumulating evidences are now before us of the survival of the cult of a Snake goddess at Knossos itself and in other parts
of Crete . . .' (Evans, 1930, page 507. B14)

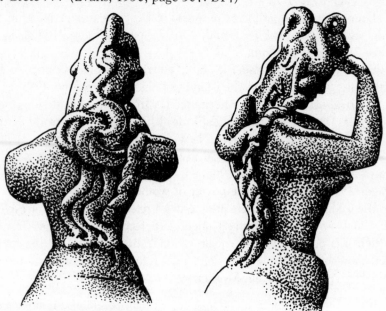

The upper part of a Minoan bronze figure, showing triple coil of snakes

Figurative links between snakes and the goddess were also widespread
in ancient cultures other than those based around the Mediterranean.
Mary Condren writes:

> The symbol of the Serpent was the one most widely used to represent or
> adorn the Goddess of the ancient Near East or to depict, or mediate, the
> relationship between goddesses and human culture. In Egypt and
> Mesopotamia, according to the evidence derived from scarabs, scaraboids,
> and seals, the Serpent was an emblem of life. In Sumerian mythology, the
> Goddess Ninhursag was the goddess of creation. Known as Nintu, she was
> 'the Lady who gave birth.' One of her common images was that of a
> Serpent. (Mary Condren, 1989. B3)

She cites the following: A L Frothingham, 1911, pages 349–77, (B3);
A L Frothingham, 1915, pages 13–23, (B3); George Roux, 1964, page
69, (B14); Joseph Campbell, 1974, pages 281–301, (B5); M Esther

Harding, 1971, pages 52–54, (B13); Monica Sjoo & Barbara Mor, 1987, pages 100, 155, 268, (B3); Riane Eisler, 1987, pages 21, 86–87, (B3); K Joines, 1974, page 20, (B5); Kramer *The Sumerians* page 122; S H Langdon, 1931, page 91, (B5); Edith Porada, 'Remarks on Mitannian (Hurrian) and Middle Assyrian Glyptic Art' in *Akkadica* 13, 1979, pages 2–15; and Briggs Buchanan, 'A Snake Goddess and Her Companions: A Problem in the Iconography of the Early 2nd Milennium BC' in *Iraq* 33, 1971, pages 1–18.

I am indebted to Oodgeroo Noonuccal and Kabul Oodgeroo Noonuccal for information about how Aboriginal people still revere the serpent; see *The Rainbow Serpent*, 1988, (B5).

For references to the tree as another symbol of the goddess, see Merlin Stone, 1976, pages 214–216, (B3), Joseph Needham, 1979, (B11), and many others.

The Garden of Eden creation tale apparently drew upon and usurped previous myths. Robert Graves, in *Adam's Rib*, page 1 tells us that, in contrast to the belief that Genesis was a factual recording,

> Textual researches show that the Creation legend in Genesis i.1 to ii.3 was written by a post-Exilic priest who lived at Jerusalem not later than the end of the fifth century BC; he was familiar with the legends of the Terrestrial Paradise, the Fall...

Bernard Anderson, 1978, pages 19, 422, (B11), and Mary Condren, 1989, page 11, (B3), put the writing down of the creation myth a little earlier than Robert Graves.

The reference to the Michelangelo painting of Eve and the serpent is from Marina Warner, *Alone of all Her Sex; the Myth and Cult of the Virgin Mary*, London, Picador, 1985, (B14). For this observation I am indebted to Nancy Qualls-Corbett, 1988, page 44, and on her page 46 I picked up the extraordinary Pythagoras quote. (B10)

The British Parliamentary Human Rights Group published a report in November 1994 detailing torture, oppression and executions of Iranian women under the rule of the mullahs.

The reference to sex and spirituality as polar opposites in the Christian church is drawn from Mary Condren, 1989, page 5, (B3).

Pages 28-31. The change to dualistic thinking
On the transition into dualistic thinking Lucy Goodison writes:

> The old Cretan female symbols are either co-opted, or become discredited: a familiar process whereby the gods of the old religion become the devils of the new religion. The process reflects a historic shift, begun in the

Mycenaean age, towards a society in which one half of the population, the women, are politically inferior to the other half. The repercussions of this shift in the symbolic plane can be seen not only in the division of male gods from female gods, but also in the separation of sky from earth, of mind from body, of spirituality from sexuality . . . From this early Greek geometric period onwards, European culture ceases to offer the imaginative vocabulary for any human being, female or male, to experience themselves as whole and undivided. (Lucy Goodison, 1992, page 343. B10)

Marija Gimbutas points out how the goddess combined both positive and negative qualities:

The 'Fertility Goddess' or 'Mother Goddess' is a more complex image than most people think. She was not only the Mother Goddess who commands fertility, or the Lady of the Beasts who governed the fecundity of animals and all wild nature, or the Frightening Mother Terrible, but a composite image with traits accumulated from both the pre-agricultural and agricultural eras. During the latter she became essentially a Goddess of Regeneration, ie a Moon Goddess, product of a sedentary matrilinear community, encompassing the archetypical unity and multiplicity of the feminine nature. She was giver of life and all that promotes fertility, and at the same time she was the wielder of the destructive powers of nature. The feminine nature, like the moon, is light as well as dark. (Marija Gimbutas, 1982, page 152. B3)

Hinduism is one religion where deities with destructive as well as creative powers are worshipped. For example, the Hindu deity named Ardha-Nari Nateswar, half of whom symbolizes the female, in terms of creation and sustenance, and half of whom symbolizes the male, in terms of creative destruction.

Two Jungian analysts, writing about the sacred marriage of goddess and god, are helpful on the subject of projection.

In individual psychology a radical and permanent split in the psyche between 'good things' and 'bad things' is generally interpreted as a sign that the natural growing of the psyche has been arrested by something that could not be accepted as it was not placed in a wider framework that would render it intelligible and so tolerable. Then a way is sought to heal the split, so that the intolerable feeling that conflicts with the established view of the world is not repressed into unconsciousness and subsequently projected and discovered outside in the figure of a person or a group of people who are seen as an enemy threatening the conscious position. (Anne Baring & Jules Cashford, 1991, page 668. B3)

The wider implications of this idea help to explain conflict and war.

Western thought is profoundly dual, which is to say that in the West difference is more important than similarity. Put another way, distinction is more important than equivalence, division than solidarity. Such a valorization is a necessary component of a morality that exists to confer superiority on one group or caste of humans; their superiority rests upon their difference from other humans. The philosophical problem of the Either/Or, as Kierkegaard referred to it, is therefore largely a factitious problem, in which philosophers attempt to synthesize or reconcile oppositions that are created primarily by their own categorizations. We are told that a thing is either A or not A, and logically these categories are exclusive. But such division is not intrinsic in reality, in which elements flow into each other and possess similar properties. (Marilyn French, 1985, page 500. B7)

On dualistic mentality, Carol Christ & Judith Plaskow have this to say:

Dualistic mentality opposes soul, spirit, rationality, and transcendence to body, flesh, matter, nature and immanence . . . Classical dualism also became the role model for the oppression of women when the culture-creating males identified the negative sides with women over whom they claimed the right to rule. (Christ & Plaskow, 1979, page 5. B11)

Squadron Leader E G Jones's paper is 'Women in Combat – Historical Quirk or the Future Cutting Edge?', 1993, (B6).

The Monica Furlong letter appeared in The *Independent*, 25 November 1993.

The link of the St George myth with Perseus is found in the *Cassell Encyclopedia of Myths and Legends*, 1992, page 156. Medusa is the negative aspect of the goddess Athena:

On her breastplate Athena wore a symbol of her power – a goatskin decorated with the gorgon's head, the head of Medusa. This was a monster with serpents instead of hair, whose terrifying appearance turned to stone anyone who gazed on it.

This description is from Jean Shinoda Bolen, 1985, page 101, (B3), who on page 262 also quotes Erich Neumann as saying that 'the power of the Great Mother is too overwhelming for any consciousness to tackle direct'.

The Perseus story in turn has echoes of the story of how the archer god Apollo gained control of the powerful oracle at Delphi.

Sources state that the site at Delphi was originally a shrine of Earth, where a dragoness, or snake held sway. The shrine centred on a sacred round stone called the omphalos, the word means 'navel', 'recalling the importance of the stone-belly connection in the Bronze Age. The Homeric hymn to Apollo tells how he wiped out this shrine:

'Whoever met [the dragoness] the day of doom carried him away, until Lord Apollo, who shoots from afar, fired a strong arrow at her . . . and darkness covered her eyes.'

If myths are thought to epitomise political trends, a clearer metaphor of the male takeover could hardly be found. The new male sky-and-sun authority . . . violently defeats the old earth-based, female centred religion based on the belly-stone and symbolised by the dragoness or snake. The snake, previously revered, becomes monstrous, a symbol of everything in the old religion which has to be rejected, one of the first major symbols to be thoroughly discredited. From the role it plays in Greek history it is clear that control of the Delphic oracle was an important political weapon, too powerful and influential a weapon perhaps to be left in control of women, and it is likely that the transition from female to male control of prophecy was a period of struggle, expressed poetically in the battle of Apollo with the snake. (Lucy Goodison, 1992, page 347. B10)

See also Vicki Noble, 1991, page 49, (B3).

In the struggle for supremacy one of the weapons has been to debase female strength.

Constricted, the joy of the feminine has been denigrated as mere frivolity; her joyful lust demeaned as whorishness, or sentimentalized and maternalized; her vitality bound into duty and obedience. This devaluation produced ungrounded daughters of the patriarchy, their feminine strength and passion split off, their dreams and ideals in the unobtainable heavens, maintained grandly with a spirit false to the instinctual patterns symbolized by the queen of heaven and earth. It also produced frustrated furies. (Sylvia Brinton Perera, 1981, page 20. B3)

The uncompromising attitude of the Vatican on the issue of birth control is the clearest possible statement of the wish (of the Catholic church) to continue to control women's bodies and their sexuality. It is failing. Sixty-six per cent of the British Catholic population use contraception, and all the Pope can hope to do is set up a form of disobedience in people's hearts. And just when the Church of England is beginning to relax its attitudes to women, the Vatican re-emphasizes what Marina Warner calls 'doctrinal justification for excluding women and discarding women and despising women.' This justification is based on selected parts of the Bible, and the assertion that Jesus's disciples were male. This assertion is not borne out in the Gnostic gospels which portray women as Jesus's close and trusted companions.

Clare Short MP is more forthright than Marina Warner:

> The Pope's a silly old fool. I'm one of the millions who were brought up as a Catholic and who've rejected the church. One of the major reasons is that the church's teaching on contraception is a joke. I saw the Vatican recently decreeing that if you're a woman in Bosnia and likely to be raped, then you would be allowed to take contraception. It's a bad joke. I feel very sorry for all the poor Catholic couples who deeply want to be loyal to their church, and for whom this question causes real agony. You have these men, these priests, who, if they are to be believed, have never had sex in their lives, and they're telling the rest of the world how to have sex. It's tragic.

Both Marina Warner and Clare Short were quoted in the *Guardian*, 5 June 1993.

I must admit, Clare's first sentence shook me. Having been very religious as a teenager, I would never have dared say anything remotely like that about the Archbishop of Canterbury. But this is another shock that women go through – what Merlin Stone calls 'the bolt of lightning syndrome'. When she was sitting in her small room in Oxford, finally typing the manuscript of *When God Was A Woman*, after years of research and studying the excavation sites and museums of the Near East, she suddenly found herself thinking that a bolt of lightning was about to strike her dead as she typed. It was fear, fear of questioning and challenging early religious training.

> When I suggested to the women I knew that each of the traditional religions in which we had been raised had played a major part in keeping women in a second class position, and that people had once thought of God as female, I encountered what I now call 'the bolt of lightning syndrome'. It was fine to challenge husbands and corporations, media and government, but one simply did not question the churches or God. (From *Return of the Goddess: From Ancient Belief to Modern Attitudes*, Canadian Broadcasting Corporation programmes designed and narrated by Merlin Stone.)

This brings me back to the strength of the emotions which surge beneath issues of power for women and for men. Back in the 1960s, 1970s, and to an extent in the 1980s, feminists were full of rage. But now there is a change of attitude. Most women seem to be past rage; they simply cast off or shed what no longer matters to them, what no longer holds any authority. Nancy Kline says she has rejected fury – 'It means you're still a victim' – in favour of solutions (the *Observer*, 5

September 1993). This is easy to say but hard to do. Getting to know my own anger and trying to transform it was and is extremely hard work.

Pages 31-3. Nevertheless . . .
The piece from Marcuse which I paraphrase is to be found in *Eros and Civilisation*, 1955, page 114, (B14).

The statistics are from Joni Seager, 1990, (B6). There is a Native American teaching that encapsulates the wisdom and respect with which indigenous people have regarded the earth. It says something to the effect that cutting down trees is like cutting the hair off our mother's head, cutting open the earth is like cutting open her body.

I am indebted to Rosalind Armson for three observations in this chapter. The first concerns the discovery that it was more efficient to raid for resources than grow them. The second concerns how women are trapped in inadequacy by being offered the Virgin Mary as role model. Third, à propos St George and the dragon, Armson is intrigued by the notion that St Patrick brought Christianity to Ireland and also expelled all the snakes from Ireland. There was of course Celtic Christianity in Ireland 'long before Patrick showed up and dragged Ireland into the Roman obedience'. Her hypothesis (she's never had an opportunity to check it) is that snakes represent the goddess worship that co-existed with Celtic Christianity. 'What Patrick actually did was to impose Catholic orthodoxy by suppressing the goddess worship that had previously been tolerated by the much more creation-centred Celtic Christians.'

Chapter 2

Page 34.
The poem 'A work of artifice' is from Marge Piercy, 1973, page 3, (B14).
Pages 35-7. Women today
The well-known statistics in the second paragraph are from *The United Nations Report*, 1980.

The statistics on chief executives of companies are from the National Institute of Economic and Social Research, 1993. Those in the fourth paragraph are from Efua Dorkenoo and Scilla Elworthy, 1992, page 11, and United Nations, 1992, (B1). The research by Ros Coward is published as *Our Treacherous Hearts*, 1993, (B12).

On women choosing to live alone, see Thelma Jean Goodrich, *Women and Power: Perspectives for Family Therapy*, W W Norton & Company, New York, 1991, page 27, (B12).

Pages 37-8. Men today

For more detail see chapter 3, and the *Statistical Bulletin on Women in Post-Compulsory Education*, Department for Education, December 1993. Shere Hite's statistics are to be found in *Women as Revolutionary Agents of Change*, 1993, page 311, (B6). Official figures from the Home Office, released in November 1993, show that between 1982 and 1992 there was an 83 per cent rise in suicides in England and Wales among 15–24-year-old men.

Pages 38-42. Negative body images

The Annie Dillard story is from *A Pilgrim at Tinker's Creek*, Harper & Row, New York, 1974, page 122, cited in Charlene Spretnak, 1993, page 94, (B11).

Ambivalence in our attitude to women's bodies is best illustrated by writers like Simone de Beauvoir, 1984, Margaret Mead, 1978, and H R Hays, 1966.

The quote about schoolgirls copying supermodels is from the *Observer*, 4 December 1994.

The Germaine Greer quotation is from *The Change*, 1992, page 423, (B1).

Pages 42-4. Menstruation

The quotation at the beginning of the section on menstruation is from Penelope Shuttle & Peter Redgrove, 1980, page 30. (B1)

The list of menstrual taboos is from Barbara G Walker, 1983, pages 641–5, (B5).

The quotation about tampon ads is from Lara Owen, 1993, page 14, (B1). Penelope Shuttle and Peter Redgrove (1980, page 281) quote research figures of up to 100 per cent for incidence of premenstrual stress among women.

Pages 45-8. Childbirth and motherhood

For a full account of witch-burning, see Monica Sjoo & Barbara Mor, 1987, pages 298–314, (B3). See also Elise Boulding, 1976 (B13), and Penelope Shuttle & Peter Redgrove, 1980, pages 208–37, and Julia O'Faolain & Lauro Martines, 1973. The quotation in the section on witch-burning is from Marija Gimbutas, 1989, page 319, (B3).

On the issue of women having babies at home, there are signs of change in the UK. In August 1993 the Department of Health published a report, *Changing Childbirth*, which called for women to be given a larger say in how pregnancy care is organized.

The intriguing insight into belly-dancing is from *Mamatoto – a celebration of birth*, 1991, (B14). The quotation which follows this is from a male anthropologist, Ashley Montagu, whose views are expressed in *The Natural Superiority of Women*, 1968, page 22, (B14).

The piece about the pain we see around us every day is based on Charlene Spretnak, 1993, page 33. Heather Hunt's comments on powerlessness and motherhood are from her paper presented at the First International Seminar for Mental Disorders of Women, Rome, June 1988, page 3, (B12).

Pages 48-50. Gynaecology

The reference to unnecessary operations on women's reproductive organs is from Angela Phillips & Jill Rakusen, 1986, page 185, (B1). Germaine Greer writes: 'No human organ has been so often operated on as the uterus and yet doctors do not agree if and when to perform hysterectomy. "When in doubt cut it out" is the policy generally followed, but even then surgeons and gynaecologists cannot agree whether to leave the ovaries or take them out.' (1992, pages 180–1. B1)

Janet Burroway's story is to be found in the anthology edited by Joanna Goldsworthy, 1993, pages 13–15, (B1).

Pages 52-58. Genital mutilation

Alice Walker wrote *Possessing the Secret of Joy* in 1992 and it was hailed by the media. For example, the *Daily Telegraph* said: 'Walker's delicate narrative gifts have never been better displayed, her depiction of the unbearable never so unflinchingly believable.' The novel has already had an effect in making the subject known and discussed, and if it were made into a film with the same success as *The Colour Purple* it could play a crucial role in eradicating the practice.

For the data on genital mutilation see *Warrior Marks*, a film directed by Pratibha Parmar and shown on Channel 4 television's *Critical Eye*, 14 October 1993; Fran Hosken, *Women's International Network News*, Vol 18, No 4, Autumn 1992; Dr Nahid Toubia, *Female Genital Mutilation: a Call for Global Action*, Women Inc, New York, 1993, quoted in Efua Dorkenoo, 1994, (B1); and Efua Dorkenoo and Scilla Elworthy, 1992, (B1), available from Minority Rights Group, 379 Brixton Road, London SW9 7DE, who kindly gave permission for use of the illustration.

The story about Amina is from Angela Robson, 'Torture, not culture' in *AIBS Journal* September/October 1993, page 8.

Awa Thiam, of the Senegal Commission for the Abolition of Sexual Mutilation, spoke on *Warrior Marks*, Channel 4 television, 14 October 1993.

The quote about the dual soul is from Alice Walker, 1992, page 167, (B14), and that about the erect clitoris challenging male authority is from *Warrior Marks*, as is the next one about the need to control women's sexuality.

Efua Dorkenoo became co-author of the Minority Rights Group report, and revised it for new editions in 1983, 1985 and 1992. Some of the information she presents is deeply depressing. More reports have emerged of female genital mutilations taking place in the Western world. Programmes which had once seemed so promising, in Sudan and Somalia, for example, have now collapsed as both countries have succumbed to political repression and warfare. In those countries where work continues, economic restructuring programmes have placed severe pressure on projects which work to improve the lives of women and children. Resolutions and proclamations from governments and international agencies have as yet had few positive effects on the lives of ordinary women.

However, there are some signs of positive change. In some countries, programmes in women's health, welfare and education continue, while prominent members of government and the community have spoken and acted against the practice. Urban educated Africans are beginning to reject the operation for their children while men are choosing to marry uncircumcised women. In the UK, community education schemes and sensitive, appropriate child protection measures have helped to prevent mutilation taking place. Some of the African immigrants and refugees involved will return to Africa and will take back a positive message and practical skills to their compatriots. In 1993 a UK doctor was struck off the medical register for agreeing to perform genital mutilation.

Esther Ogunmodede's article 'Female Circumcision in Nigeria' appears in Efua Dorkenoo & Scilla Elworthy, 1992, page 32, (B1). Her findings confirm Fran Hosken's assertion that operations are being done at earlier and earlier ages, in order that the children should be 'too young to resist'. Fran Hosken does not think that the custom is dying out, and she has the best published range of information concerning all the countries where the practice is known. She was one of the first and most insistent western women to write about it. She published *The Hosken Report: Genital and Sexual Mutilation of Females* in 1982. Efua Dorkenoo's most recent book is *Cutting the Rose*, 1994, (B1).

Pages 58-60. Low self-esteem and powerlessness

The quotation about the slow erosion of self-esteem is from Shere Hite, 1993, page 266, (B6).

Jo Ryan's observations on female depression are from her Pam Smith Memorial Lecture, Dept of Applied Social Science, Polytechnic of North London, 1983, quoted in Heather Hunt's paper. (See above, p.267.)

The Emma Jung quotation is from *Animus and Anima*, 1978, page 20, (B8).

The final quotation is from Charles E Raven, *A Wanderer's Way*, London, 1928. Raven was Regius Professor of Divinity at Cambridge 1932–50.

Chapter 3

Pages 62-65. The power to do what men do
The data on women in the armed forces is derived from various sources including Squadron Leader E G Jones, 1993, page 37, (B4).

The data on girls' academic performance is from the *Statistical Bulletin on Women in Post-Compulsory Education*, Department for Education, December 1993, and the comment on women's jobs is from Anna Coote, 'Boys who can't grow up', *Independent on Sunday*, 14 November 1993, and from her paper to the Institute for Public Policy Research Conference, November 1993.

For 20 years a large American poll, the Yankelovich Monitor, has asked its subjects to define masculinity.

> And for 20 years, the leading definition, ahead by a huge margin, has never changed. It isn't being a leader, athlete, Lothario, decision-maker, or even just being 'born male'. It is simply this: being a 'good provider for the family'. (Susan Faludi, 1992, page 87. B12)

The survey referred to on women's economic independence is from Shere Hite, 1993, page 376, (B6).

The two quotations about the violence of young men are from Bea Campbell at the Institute for Public Policy Research Conference, November 1993, and Marina Warner's second Reith Lecture, *Boys will be Boys*, broadcast on Radio 4 on 2 February 1994.

The 'woman speaking' is Nancy Kline, 1993, page 14, (B7). The 'man speaking' is Warren Farrell, author of *The Myth of Male Power: Why Men are the Disposable Sex*, Fourth Estate, London, 1994, interviewed by Ruth Picardie for the *Independent*, 28 January 1994.

Angela Phillips is author of *The Trouble with Boys*, Pandora, London, 1993.

Pages 65-67. The power of sexual attraction and why men fear women
Bob Johnson's description of Denny comes from 'Knowing Why', 1993, (B9).

I am indebted to John Baldock for the observations on men's fear of women as fear of the deeper levels of consciousness, and to John

Hamwee for the observations on the power of women's generative system and men's feelings of irrelevance.

Pages 67-69. Power over

The interviews with decision-makers were written up as 'The Assumptions of Nuclear Weapons Decision Makers' by Scilla Elworthy, John Hamwee and Hugh Miall in Barnett & Lee, 1989, and in Scilla Elworthy, *British Nuclear Weapons Policy: why it has not changed with the end of the Cold War*, unpublished PhD thesis, (B6).

A nice thing happened after the meeting with De Bellescize. A very strong Maori woman, Pauline Tangiora of Rongomaiwahine, who had opened the conference with a traditional Maori welcome, went up to the ambassador and presented him with a book on the effect of nuclear testing on the peoples of the Pacific. She then insisted on the traditional Maori sign of friendship – a *hongi* – which involves rubbing noses.

Pages 69-71. Change in individuals

Carol Cohn's experience is written up in 'Sex and Death in the Rational World of Defense Intellectuals', 1987, (B6).

The Norman Dixon quotation is from *Our Own Worst Enemy*, 1976, pages 203–36, (B6). A little later I use the word 'ego'. This word means many different things to different people, so the most sensible thing I can do is to say what it means to me. I see it as the part of me which is primarily interested in my success, my advancement – and ultimately, my survival.

Pages 71-4. The masculine part of a woman

Marie-Louise Von Franz wrote a chapter entitled 'The Process of Individuation' in C G Jung, 1964, (B5).

Betty Reardon's views on women in politics come from *Sexism and the War System*, 1985, page 33, (B6).

The quotation about a woman in the forces becoming 'one of the boys' is from Squadron Leader Jones, 1993, page 35, (B6).

Pages 75-6. The big distinction

The young man from Walthamstow is Iain, aged 16, interviewed by David Cohen for the *Observer*, 19 September 1993.

Pages 76-7. Not 'an eye for an eye'

The Jean Shinoda Bolen quotation is from *Goddess in Everywoman*, 1987, pages 278–9 (B3).

Part II

Pages 79-82.

With regard to the use of the word 'hara', Barbara Walker has this to say:

> From the root *har* came Hara, Hebrew for both a holy mountain and a pregnant belly; Hariti or Hairaiti, the 'Lofty Mountain' of paradise in both pre-Vedic Dravidian and Old Iranian cosmology; and Harmonia, a 'daughter of Aphrodite', a bringer of peace, one of the functions of the holy harlot . . . She was married to Cadmus. (Barbara Walker, 1983, page 374. B5)

Incidentally, when Harmonia died and she and Cadmus went to paradise, they were both transformed into serpents. Walker thinks that they were assimilated to the male-and-female, perpetually entwined serpents of the Hermetic caduceus, whose meaning was life. This is a fine indication of how hara power is not only available to men and women but is essential to harmony and balance between the male and female parts of ourselves.

Chapter 4

Kawai'i is a Hawaiian *kahuna*, meaning 'Keeper of the Secrets'. The *kahuna* practise sacred healing techniques dating back 10,000 years.

Pages 83-4. What is self-knowledge?

The passage about the next hundred years determining whether life on earth is transformed or not draws on Josè Stevens, 1994, page xi, (B9).

Pages 85-7. Understanding another

The Carl Rogers quotation is from *On Personal Power*, 1986, page 231, (B7). The story of the student with arthritis is told in *The Power Pack*, an empowerment package for women prepared by nine women in 1988. Being a multi-media package, it was a daunting prospect for a publisher, and has not yet been published.

Pages 88-9. Personal power and position power

The Gandhi quotation is from M K Gandhi, 1983, pages 109–10, (B2), cited in Charlene Spretnak, 1993, page 64, (B11).

Pages 89-91. The power to name

What is meant here by the expression *the power to name* in my sense is slightly different from what is intended by Mary Daly in *Beyond God the Father*, 1973, (B12). She is concerned more with the power of naming what was in her view stolen from women.

The stories about the Englishwoman in South America and the woman in the car are told in *The Power Pack*, an unpublished multimedia empowerment package for women.

Pages 92-4. Growing into what we were meant to be

If I have paid a lot of attention to the animus, it is because, in Jolande Jacobi's words:

> ... In consequence of the patriarchially oriented development of our western culture, the woman tends to think that the masculine as such is more valuable than the feminine, and this attitude does much to increase the power of the Animus. (1975 page 117. B8)

The Marion Milner quotation is from Joanna Field, 1987, (B9), and the Marie-Louise Von Franz one is from C G Jung, 1964, page 194.

There is a paragraph from Demetra George about the Dark Goddess destroying the old and forcing us to change, which occurred to me as helpful in coping with the difficulties of growing into the person we were meant to be:

> Because we do not understand the dark, we see the destructive activity of the Dark Goddess as negative and evil. This is a fundamental mistake. Through the vehicle of crisis, the Dark Goddess does destroy the old. This forces us to change, and thus urges us forward to a new life. Without her there would be no motivation and challenge to the growth of awareness. In the end what we have dreaded as her malice turns out to be part of the vital process needed to transform our lives into something of greater value and meaning.' (Demetra George, 1992, page 229. B3)

Page 94. Guilt and blame drain us . . .

For more on dealing with guilt, see Pat Rodegast & Judith Stanton, 1987 and 1989. (B11)

On the subject of taking responsibility in relationships, an extremely helpful practical guide is Gay & Kathlyn Hendricks, 1992. (B9)

Pages 94-7. Feelings are vital

The Betty Reardon reference is to *Sexism and the War System*, 1985, page 88. (B6)

The Anne Baring and Jules Cashford reference is to *The Myth of the Goddess*, 1991, page 678, (B3).

The Jean Shinoda Bolen quotation is from *Goddesses in Every Woman*, 1985, page 284, (B3).

The information on *kundalini* is taken from: John White, 1990, (B11); Swami Sivananda Radha, 1978, (B11); and Swami Rama, Rudolf Ballentine & Swami Ajaya, 1976, (B9).

Chapter 5

Page 98
The opening quotation is about women's spirituality and is from John
White, 1990, page 183, (B11).
Pages 99-102. Sexual attraction and power
I am grateful to Gerard Fairtlough for help with the section on sexual
attraction. Some of the sentences used come directly from his com-
ments.

Those interested in finding out more could consult Osho, 1994,
(B10), and Margot Anand, 1992, (B10). Details of workshops on the
subject can be obtained from Skydancing UK, John Hawken, Lower
Grumbla Farm, Newbridge, Cornwall, TR20 8QX. Tel: 01736 788304.
A video entitled *Sacred Sex* is available from Zenith Distribution.
Pages 102-106. Liberation from sexual guilt
Anthropologist Peggy Reeves Sanday studied 156 tribal societies and
found revealing differences in their relationship to nature, which was
reflected in the role of men and women. Sanday depicts societies in
terms of their relationship with nature, both from a physical point of
view, ie how food is provided, and from a more cultural stance, looking at the societies' world views, in other words the way they see themselves as fitting in with their environment. Those societies in which
most food comes from the earth or water, where nature is regarded as
a partner rather than as a force to be dominated, and where women are
regarded as representatives of nature's power, are defined as operating
according to an 'inner orientation'. Fathers play a nurturing role in
child-rearing, and rape is a rare occurrence. In contrast, where nature
is seen as hostile, and where migration and hunting are the way of life,
Sanday identified an 'outer orientation'. Men hunt, make weapons, are
violent with one another and with women, and pursue power that is
'out there'. The sexes tend to be separate from each other, men forbid
women certain areas and practices, fathers are more distant from child-
rearing, and rape is not unusual. (Peggy Reeves Sanday, 1981. B7)

In the light of this, Charlene Spretnak comments on our own
Western society;

> Nature is not considered sacred or a partner; ultimate power resides 'out
> there' with a sky-god; and men traditionally proclaim numerous cultural
> 'spaces' (the priesthood, higher education, law, medicine, business, gov-
> ernment, the art world) to be off-limits to women. In a cultural orienta-
> tion where the elemental power of the female body – by which I mean the
> capability to grow people of either sex from her flesh, to bleed in rhythm

with the moon, to transform food into milk for infants – is considered somewhat frightening by males, a tremendous amount of effort goes into preventing women from acquiring cultural power in addition to the disquieting elemental power. (Charlene Spretnak, 1993, page 116. B11)

In England, *sheela-na-gigs* are to be found at the Church of St Laurence in Church Stretton, near Shrewsbury; the Church of Holy Trinity, Holdgate, near Shipton, which is near Shrewsbury; the Church of St Mary and St David, in Kilpeck, near Hereford; Oaksey Church, Oaksey in north Wiltshire; the Church of St Michael, on the corner of Cornmarket Street next to Ship Street, Oxford; and St Catherine's Church, Tugford, in Shropshire.

Her anomalous presence on Christian buildings seems inexplicable. Scholars still bicker about the origins and significance of sheela-na-gigs, and even the name itself is a bone of contention. The term 'sheela-na-gig' was first applied to this type of carving as recently as the 1840s, when an Irish antiquarian, cataloguing old buildings in the Tipperary countryside, asked a peasant the name of the bawdy female image on the local church. 'Sheela-na-gig,' the man is said to have replied, offering no further explanation. The antiquarian duly reported his findings to his colleagues, several of whom recalled having seen similar carvings in the course of their own research . . . Many writers, after careful analysis of the 115 surviving sheelas, are convinced that the carvings represent Celtic goddesses, particularly in their hag or crone aspect. (Anneli S Rufus & Kristan Lawson, 1990, page 105. B3)

A number of writers indicate that the traditional understanding of Mary Magdalene is barely corroborated in the gospels, and is apparent only according to a very particular interpretation. The Gnostic gospels show her to have been one of Jesus's disciples, and suggest that she was his lover. See for example Marina Warner, *Alone of All Her Sex; the Myth and Cult of the Virgin Mary*, Picador, London, 1985, page 229, (B14).

For information on the Black Madonna, see Ruth White, 'The Black Madonna' in *Caduceus*, No 11, 1990. Black Madonnas are to be found in Chartres Cathedral, in Le Puy, Marseille, and Vezelay in France, in Elnsiedely in Switzerland, in Czestochowa in Poland, in Our Lady of Guadaloupa in Mexico and in many other places. In his study, *The Cult of the Black Virgin*, 1985, Ean Begg associates them with the Queen of Sheba, as the first of many exotic women that may have inspired Black Madonnas. Robert Graves throws light on her biblical phrase, 'Though dark, I am beautiful', indicating that 'dark' has not always had the negative connotations attached to it today, as being the absence of light. Rather, Graves tells us, the Queen is saying that she is wise as a crone, and beautiful too:

> The Black Goddess is so far hardly more than a word of hope whispered among the few who have served their apprenticeship to the White Goddess. She promises a new pacific bond between men and women corresponding to a final reality of love in which the patriarchal marriage bond will fade away. Unlike Vesta, the Black Goddess has experienced good and evil, love and hate, truth and falsehood in the person of her sisters; rejecting serpent-love and corpse flesh. Faithful as Vesta, gay and adventurous as the White Goddess, she will lead man back to that sure instinct of love which he long ago forfeited by intellectual pride. (Robert Graves, 1965. B3)

Dawn French was quoted in the *Guardian*, 16 March 1994.
Jenny Saville's paintings were shown at the Saatchi Gallery, 98a Boundary Road, London NW8 ORH, and she was quoted in the *Independent*, 1 March 1994.

The story about the women in Juchitan, Mexico, is from *Elle*, September 1993.

Pages 106-111. Menstruation

The reference to Barbara Walker's *The Women's Encyclopaedia of Myths and Secrets* concerns the section on menstruation, on pages 635–45, (B5).

The description of Chalice Well is from Kathy Jones, *The Goddess in Glastonbury*, Ariadne, Glastonbury, 1990, (B3).

The Lara Owens' quotation is from *Her Blood is Gold*, 1993 on page 89, (B1). Her book also contains the following passage on page 65:

> This was the information I had needed to give me the confidence to set about healing my own gynaecological problems. It inspired me to see if I could feel the power of menstruation if I paid enough attention when I was bleeding. To think of menstruation as a source of power for women completely went against my conditioning, and yet I knew in my heart that it was true. I realised that in the dichotomy between what our culture teaches us, and my gut reaction of 'Yes! Of course!' to this ancient wisdom, there was a lot of energy. When you find the places where a culture splits from a natural truth you have found a key – a way inside the diseases of the culture. I began to understand that the split between the wisdom and power of bleeding that I was perceiving and modern society's attitudes to the womb lay at the heart of the subjugation and denial of female reality and experience.

Dr Collee's findings were reported in the *Observer*, 13 February 1994.

The Lucy Goodison reference is from *Moving Heaven and Earth*, 1992, page 264, (B10).

Pages 111-112. Birth and caring

Reading my complaint about the lack of public recognition of mothers and carers, a friend commented, 'The USSR used to give motherhood medals. Fat lot of good it did anyone there though.'

More about the 'good enough' mother can be found in D W Winnicott, *Playing and Reality*, London: Pelican, 1974, (B8).

Pages 112-113. Men and childbirth

The Carol Cohn passage about images of male birth in the atomic bomb project is from 'Sex and Death in the Rational World of Defense Intellectuals', 1987, (B6).

Michel Odent dissents from the idea that fathers should be present during childbirth. See his *Primal Health*, Century Hutchinson, Oxford, 1993, pages 138–43.

Really being with children is described by Rachel Pinney in *Creative Listening*, available from the Children's Hour Trust, 28 Wallace House, Caledonian Estate, Caledonian Road, London N7.

Pages 114-116. Wisdom and freedom

The first section draws on Barbara Walker, 1983, page 641, (B5), and the first quotation is from Lara Owen, 1993, page 97, (B1).

Pages 117-121. Understanding menopause

The quotation from Germaine Greer is from *The Change*, 1992, pages 430–1, (B1).

For some of the ideas on ritual I am indebted to Juliet Batten, 1988, (B12). When I thought about the big feast after the transition ritual, I was reminded of:

> That raucous female laughter
> is drummed from the belly.
> It rackets about kitchens,
> flapping crows
> up from a carcass.
> Hot in the mouth as horseradish, it clears the sinuses
> and the brain.
> (From 'Women's Laughter', in Marge Piercy, 1973, page 34)

Pages 122-123. Death

The paragraph on the Goddess of Death and Regeneration owes much to Marija Gimbutas, 1989, pages 187–321, (B3).

For a Buddhist approach to death, see Sogyal Rinpoche, 1992, (B11).

Chapter 6
Page 124
The quotation is from Thich Nhat Hanh, 1992, page 5. He was born
in Vietnam in 1926, and is a Zen master, poet and peace activist. He
headed the Vietnamese Buddhist Peace Delegation to the Paris Peace
Talks and was nominated by Martin Luther King for the Nobel Peace
Prize. Since 1966 he has lived in exile in France where he runs a cen-
tre to support Vietnamese refugees in France, called Plum Village.

Pages 125-26. What power from within is not
The Christian Church Association says that Church of England con-
gregations have shrunk by 21 per cent since 1975 – by 60,000 in
1992–3 (the *Guardian*, 2 November 1993). The Church of England
disputes this figure, saying that Sunday attendances are down by 8.3
per cent since 1976, and by 18,000 in the last four years for which
figures are available.

On the subject of Buddhism being non-theistic, Rita M Gross says:

> Its central teachings point out to its adherents the cause of and the cure
> for human suffering, locating both within human attitudes towards life.
> Buddhism is non-theistic, or not concerned about the existence of a
> supreme being, because a supreme being would be unable to relieve human
> suffering, as it is defined by Buddhists. A supreme being cannot cause
> human beings to give up the attitudes that produce suffering. Only human
> beings are capable of that feat. (Rita M Gross, 1993, pages 7–8)

Pages 126-27. What power from within may be
There is undoubtedly a connection between what some might refer to
as 'psychological' and what some might describe as 'spiritual'. The
newer psychotherapies recognize and work with this connection. In
both realms we are touching our deepest feelings, what we sense, what
we are capable of, our creativity, our energy – our most precious possessions, in short. The kinds of psychotherapy which work with this
are known as 'transpersonal', defined as 'experiences involving an
expansion or extension of consciousness beyond the usual ego boundaries and beyond the limitations of time and/or space.' (Stanislav Grof,
1979, page 155. B8)

John Rowan, who has written a very clear and helpful book on the
transpersonal, sees psychotherapy as a bridge between psychology and
spirituality. He says:

> Our culture has a curious attitude to spirituality, either dismissing it alto-
> gether as a primitive misunderstanding, or regarding it as something very
> religious and very special, the domain of the priest or the saint. (John
> Rowan, 1993, page 6. B9)

The Aminah Raheem quotation is from *Soul Return*, 1991, pages 6–7, (B11).

The Ardis Whitman phrase is from 'Secret Joys of Solitude' in *Reader's Digest* 122, No 732, April 1983, page 132, quoted in Jean Shinoda Bolen, 1985, page 308, note 7, (B3).

Even the Beauty Editor of *Harpers and Queen* recommends meditation – see Leslie Kenton, 1992, pages 33–34 (B1).

Pages 127-29. Things pass

The paragraph about the Buddha and awareness draws on Charlene Spretnak, 1993, pages 39–40, (B11). For an excellent brief description of the life of the Buddha, and the clearest explanation I have yet found of the central ideas of Buddhism, see her Chapter 2 – it is a delight from beginning to end.

Ram Dass wrote a book called *Be Here Now*. And he has a nice bit on being in the moment on an audio tape:

> Keep strengthening, strengthening the witness – and you understand what I mean by the witness – it's that part of your awareness that's just *noticing* how things *are*. It isn't judging and it isn't trying to change anything . . . it just notices what *is*. A part of you that's just noticing 'Ah, she wants a cup of tea' not 'Well, you've already *had* a cup of tea!!' or 'There's that tea-wanting again!' Nothing like that – just 'Ah, wants a cup of tea. Ah . . . So.' Just noticing what is 'Ah . . . So.' (Ram Dass *Sex and Spirituality*. Tape cassette available from Open Gate Tapes, 1 Woodman's Cottage, Brockham End, Bath BA1 9BZ)

The excerpt from Osho about time goes on as follows:

> If you move from the past, you never move into the present. From the past you always move into the future; there comes no moment which is present. From the present you go deeper and deeper, into more present and more present. This is everlasting life. (Osho, 1994, page 30. B10)

I am indebted to John Baldock for his comments on timelessness.

Page 129. Advantages of meditation

The Charlene Spretnak quotation is from *States of Grace*, 1993, page 45, (B11). She explains changes in the nervous system in notes to this passage as follows:

> The theory called 'Neural Darwinism', put forth by Gerald Edelman, who received the Nobel Prize in Physiology or Medicine in 1972, posits that strong reactions in the brain to certain stimuli result in the nerve cells involved with such reactions forming groups, neuronal groups that become organized into sheets or 'maps', which interact with each other.

(See Israel Rosenfeld, *The Invention of Memory: A New View of the Brain* [Basic Books, New York, 1988].) Dr Edelman believes that 'every experience in a person's life alters and shapes that individual's brain' (David Hellerstein, 'Plotting a Theory of the Brain,' *New York Times Magazine* [22 May 1988]) . . .

Regarding the structural plasticity of the nervous system, Humberto Maturana and Francisco Varela, researchers and theorists in the biology of cognition, note that structural changes occur not in the broad lines of connectivity that unite groups of neurons, which are generally the same in all individuals in a species, but in the local characteristics of those connections. 'There [in the 'final' ramifications and the synapses] molecular changes result in changes in the efficiency of the synaptic interactions that can modify drastically how the entire neuronal network functions' (*The Tree of Knowledge* [Shambhala Books, Boston, 1988],167). See also Sandra Blakeslee, 'Memory Repair', *New York Times 'Good Health' Magazine*, 8 October 1989.

Pages 130-31. Resistance
My passage about trusting our inner guidance draws on many sources, but here particularly on Merlin Stone, 'The Goddess and Evolution' in *Green Egg*, Vol XXI, No 81, Beltane 88.

Andrew Greeley is quoted in John White, (ed) *Kundalini*, 1990, page 16, (B11).

Paul McCartney has a nice comment on resistance:

> I used to think anyone doing anything weird was weird. I suddenly realised that anyone doing anything weird wasn't weird at all and it was the people saying they were weird that were weird. (quoted in Andrew Leigh & Michael Maynard 1993. B14)

Pages 131-32. The critics of spirituality
Merlin Stone analyzes the feminist critique of spirituality in 'The Word of God on the ERA', *Sojourner Newspaper*, 1980, and the quotation is from her.

I am indebted to Rosalind Armson for her test of the 'validity' of spirituality.

For some idea of the range and number of books which have appeared on the spiritual side of the women's movement, see the Bibliography.

The passage about Freud's resistance to spirituality draws on John Rowan, 1993, page 209, (B9).

Pages 133-34. Being acted through
There is a piece in Joanna Macy, 1993, pages 34–5, (B9) about being acted 'through'.

Pages 134. Bringing about change

Jane Roberts describes the point of power in the present in *The Nature of the Psyche*, 1979, page 22, (B8).

The Robert Woodson quotation is from the *International Herald Tribune*.

Pages 135-36. Finding integrity

Nelson Mandela describes how he used the period of imprisonment to go within in *Long Walk to Freedom*, 1994, (B14).

Chapter 7

Page 137

The quotation from the Gospel of Thomas is from Logion 22, quoted in Anne Baring & Jules Cashford, 1991, pages 675–6, (B3).

Page 138

On the subject of polarization, I was at a gathering once where people were enthusiastically classifying acquaintances into one of two 'types' of people. Someone said, 'There are two types of people in the world: people who classify other people into types, and people who don't.'

The passage on mind-body dichotomy draws on Betty Reardon, 1985, page 31, (B6).

Pages 138-39. We do not have to live in a world of opposites

The passage describing attributes of Neolithic deities draws on Tsultrim Allione, 1984, page 24, (B13).

The Moon Goddess reference is from M Esther Harding, 1971, page 111, (B13).

I am indebted to Anne Baring & Jules Cashford for their impeccable research in *The Myth of the Goddess*, 1991, page 660, (B3), which was the best source to be found on developments after the time of the mother goddess religions.

Linda Barlow expresses the dualistic way of thinking beautifully when she says in her unpublished MA thesis for Antioch University, entitled *Ithaca: The Journey Home* (page 60): 'The power of love (which brings elements together) becomes the love of power (which separates and dominates).'

Page 140. The split of feminine energies into dark and light

In *The Greek Myths*, 1955, (B5), Robert Graves gives a view of Medea very different from the usual one. Thomas Bulfinch also emphasizes Medea's healing capacities, telling how she rejuvenated Jason's father. (Thomas Bulfinch, *The Golden Age of Myth and Legend*, Bracken

Books, London, 1985, page 164.) As Marina Warner has pointed out in her First Reith Lecture in 1994, any retelling of such a myth as that of Medea is as valid and valuable as any other – there is no single 'truth' to be obtained. Medea challenges preconceptions of what it is to be a woman. She is remembered today primarily as the murderer of her children. This focus and outrage at a single horrifying deed, considering the culprit a fiend rather than a fallible human, echoes the findings of barrister Helena Kennedy (1993, B6), who shows that for the same crimes women receive much harsher sentences than men.

Pages 141-42. The swing of the pendulum

The Marie-Louise Von Franz quotation is from *The Feminine in Fairytales*, 1993, pages 186–7, (B5).

The sources in the section on the exploitation of nature include the *Green Globe Yearbook* (Oxford University Press, Oxford, 1993), Friends of the Earth, the Worldwide Fund for Nature and the World Conservation Maintenance Centre.

It is interesting to note that the protagonists of the 17th century scientific revolution explicitly saw their goal and duty as being the exploitation of nature, which was composed of inert matter. Francis Bacon, a key player in advocating the modern scientific method, suggested that the role of science was 'the rape of nature'. See Brian Easlea, 1981, chapter 3, (B6).

Pages 142-43. Holistic thinking

The material in this section draws heavily on the Open University course in Systems Thinking by Rob Paton, Professor Jake Chapman & John Hamwee, 1985, page 7, (B14).

The section on Chinese and Western medicine owes a lot to Peter Mole, 1992, pages 4–5, (B1).

A quotation from Ervin Lazlo may help to further understanding of holistic thinking:

The specialist concentrates on detail and disregards the wider structure which gives it context. The new scientist, however, concentrates on structure on all levels of magnitude and complexity, and fits detail into its general framework. He discerns relationships and situations, not atomistic facts and events. By this method he can understand a lot more about a great many more things than the rigorous specialist, although his understanding is somewhat more general and approximate . . . To have an adequate grasp of reality we must look at things as systems, with properties and structures of their own . . . If we are to understand what we are, and what we are faced with in the social and the natural world, evolving a general theory of systems is imperative. 'Systems sciences' are springing up everywhere, as contemporary scientists are discovering organized wholes in many realms of investigation. Systems theories are applied in almost all of the natural and social sciences today, and they are coming to the forefront of the human sciences as well. (Ervin Laszlo, 1972, pages 13–14. B14)

For further reading on holistic thinking see the invaluable Open University courses, notably course T247, 'Working with Systems'.

Art and symbols can be very useful too. All our lives we have been so much steeped in polarity, in things being *either* this *or* that, that it is hard to get beyond this. This is where pictures come in. We are looking for an image of both/and, of complementarity. The best known one is the yin/yang symbol:

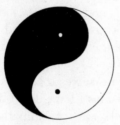

Yin/Yang symbol

Each of the two parts, though a different colour, contains some of the other in it. Each is interwoven with the other. The more substantial or 'stronger' part of each complements the finer or less substantial part of the other.

If we experiment a little with images, we could for instance represent polarity as two straight parallel lines, not meeting. Thus:

If we keep the essence of each, its separateness, but introduce fluidity, we get two wavy lines, thus:

If we then put them together, we get:

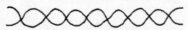

Funnily enough, when I looked this up in the encyclopedia I discovered that this is a very ancient symbol – the Greek caduceus, the sceptre of two serpents – which has re-emerged in ultra modern guise as the symbol of DNA.

In pre-Hellenic Greece the caduceus was displayed on healing temples like those of Asclepius, Hygeia, and Panacea, which is why it is still an international symbol of the medical profession. The caduceus is found also in Aztec sacred art, enthroned like a serpent-deity on an altar. North American Indians knew it too. A Navaho medicine man said his people's sacred cave once featured 'a stone carving of two snakes intertwined, the heads facing east and west'.

Hindu symbolism equated the caduceus with the central spirit of the human body, the spinal column, with two mystic serpents twined around it like the genetic double helix. (Barbara G Walker, 1983, page 131. B5)

Art knows well that things are not black or white. There are at least 20 very beautiful shades of grey. We know just from looking out of the window that there is not just darkness and light. What of twilight? And dawn? Are those not the moments when the most mysterious and moving things happen?

Pages 143-47. Bringing ourselves together
In the section on the chakras I have drawn from several sources, but relied a great deal on the lucidity of Aminah Raheem, 1991, pages 55, 64, 69, 116, 120–1, (B11). The section about the third chakra draws on Swami Rama, Rudolf Ballentine & Swami Ajaya, 1976, page 240, (B9).

Aminah Raheem (1991, page 117) also has an interesting observation on the third chakra:

> ... this centre is concerned with effective and assertive individual behaviour which will permit one to provide for one's personal needs – clothing, shelter, and the securing and digesting of food. Once again we are looking at the most primal nourishment needs. When they are met, a person will feel confident and competent and can develop an adequate personal ego. But if they are not met a person can feel inferior and develop an inferiority complex which can lead to either dominating or submissive behaviour ... Exaggerated energy in this chakra can cause one to place his own needs and ego above everyone else's. Such a person can become narcissistic, overbearing and obsessed with personal power. (B11)

Page 148. Sexuality and wholeness
The poetry of Inanna and Dumuzi is from Samuel Kramer, 1969, page 59, (B11). Such a ritual was performed throughout Mesopotamia for 2,000 years. The rite involved the sexual union of the king, representing the community, and an avatar of the great goddess Inanna – probably her chief priestess. This poetry throws a bridge for me between

present-day consciousness and the natural, unconscious, instinctive wholeness of primeval times.

Pages 148-49. The inner lover
In Carl Jung's *Memories, Dreams and Reflections*, 1983, page 414, (B8), there is the following passage:

> *Hierosgamos*. Sacred or spiritual marriage, union of archetypal figures in the rebirth mysteries of antiquity and also in alchemy. Typical examples are the representation of Christ and the Church as bridegroom and bride (sponsus et sponsa) and the alchemical conjunction of sun and moon.

Pages 150-54. Relationships
For more on why we choose the partners we do, see Harville Hendrix, 1993, (B9).

The information on Kali is from Barbara Walker, 1983, page 488, (B5).

Details of the Mastery and other courses and workshops are to be found in the section 'Going Further'.

The quotation about the branch is from Thich Nhat Hanh, 1988, pages 34–5, (B11).

Chapter 8

Page 155
The opening quotation is from the the explanation of why so many of the Dineh people refuse to cooperate with the US federal government's forced relocation order at Big Mountain in northern Arizona, given by Ruth Benally Yinishye in Anita Parlow, 1988, page 52, quoted in Charlene Spretnak, 1993, page 91, (B11).

Page 156
The phrase 'brings forth from within' is from M Esther Harding, 1971, page 111, (B13).

Pages 157-58. Chaos theory
I am indebted to John Hamwee for the paragraphs on chaos theory and thinking about complex systems. He adds:

> Unpredictable isn't the same as lack of order. One of the joys of this theory is to see the order in these complex systems. It is an order of overwhelming beauty. Perhaps the most famous order or pattern is the famous butterfly wing. It arises like this.

With certain kinds of systems, if you represent the state of that system at a particular point in time as a point on a piece of paper, you cannot predict, of course, where it will be. Nor where it will be a moment later. But you can predict the pattern, the order. You can say that after you've plotted a million points you will end up with this pattern of the butterfly wing. Always. If you speed it all up on a computer, you'll see the points all circling round the empty space on the right for a long time. Suddenly, unpredictably, the points will start to circle round the empty space on the left. (In the trade, the empty spaces are called 'strange attractors' – they seem to attract the system in some strange way.) After a while, unpredictably, they'll go back to circling round the right space again. If you do it three dimensionally and then take a cross section through one of the strands of dots (hold onto your hat!) you'll see the *same pattern* of the butterfly wing. I'll never forget the first time I saw this. It was like being one of the first people to see an insect or a leaf through a high powered microscope. This, I thought, is a glimpse of how the universe is.

One example of the ripple effect of interference is found in Gwyn Prins and Robbie Stamp, 1991, page 16:

The Beluga whales in the estuary of the St Lawrence River in north-eastern America are an endangered species. The Belugas are at the top of the aquatic food chain, feeding on eels, herring, capelin and smelt. They live in waters into which drain extensive parts of eastern and central North America. So the health of the Belugas is an index of the health of the St Lawrence system which in turn is an index of the health of the region. Since 1982, 73 dead Belugas have undergone autopsies. DDT and PCBs [pesticides] were discovered in the blubber at levels *which were among the highest ever recorded in marine animals* . . . We must interpret the fate of the St Lawrence Belugas literally. (B6)

Pages 159-60. Shamans and witches
Michael Harner is author of *The Way of the Shaman*, 1990, (B11), and I have drawn on his Introduction and pages 15–16 in particular. The piece about witches as economic rivals to the medical profession is derived from Monica Sjoo & Barbara Mor, 1987, page 203, (B3). The reference to shamans working in the realm of the feminine is from Vicki Noble, 1991, page 13, (B3).

Pages 160-61. Other healers who use energy
On the subject of modern physics discovering how energy interacts, Charlene Spretnak writes of the quote at the beginning of this chapter:

The earth knows us. Its atoms are aware of our atoms (as reflected in Bell's theorem in quantum physics). The manifestation of its wavelets and particles is affected by our presence (as reflected in Heisenberg's Uncertainty Principle in quantum physics). A people rooted in the land over time have exchanged their tears, their breath, their bones, all of their elements – oxygen, carbon, nitrogen, hydrogen, phosphorus, sulphur, all the rest – with their habitat many times over. *Here nature knows us.* (Charlene Spretnak, 1993, page 91. B11)

She explains as follows:

Bell's theorem states that reality must be nonlocal, at least partially. 'Local reality' refers to events (or microevents) occurring as the result of local causes, but it has been demonstrated that some effects occurring in one location correlate with events (or microevents) occurring elsewhere at the same moment . . . Heisenberg's Uncertainty Principle states that the results of a precise measurement of a particle's position or its velocity are affected by the intention of the person measuring. Position and velocity cannot be measured simultaneously with precision; if one decides to measure a particle's position, it will not exhibit a well-defined momentum, and vice versa. The physicist John Wheeler felt that the most important feature of quantum physics was the realization that the 'observer' is really a 'participator' (cited in Fritjof Capra, *The Tao of Physics*, Shambhala Publications, Boston, 1975, page 141)

More fascinating reflections on this subject are to be found in Danah Zohar, 1990, (B14).

Pages 161-62. Sacred places
The letter I refer to was from Ingrid Thomas, 29 June 1993.

José Alberto Rosa's experience is described in *Power Spots*, 1986, page 30, (B11).

It is worth pausing for a moment to examine what the energy in these places might be. Once again, the serpent turns up. Laurie Cabot and Tom Cowan say:

I learned that energy moves in coils like a serpent, and that DNA molecules are also spirals, and that the electromagnetic energy running along the earth's leylines moves in a similar manner. (Laurie Cabot with Tom Cowan, 1989, page 2. B13)

Monica Sjoo and Barbara Mor pick up the theme:

The spiraling force forms an energy network all over the earth's surface, affecting the germination and growth of trees and plants, as well as animals. Here is the practical side of Goddess mythology and symbolism: the moon, spirals, earth, water, all related to the right time to plant different kinds of seed, according to the moon's phases. Further, the magic earth current is known as the serpent force – or in China, the dragon current. Raising the serpent force is a common and ancient rite among Native Americans, Hindus, Asians, Africans, and the Celts of pagan Europe. These sacred serpentine paths were followed 'instinctively' by the first nomadic tribes. Australian aborigines make ritual journeys along these current-paths, 'in the steps of the gods', who created the original divine landscape. They believe that each place the gods 'stopped' became manifest reality. A spiral-center of energy. (Monica Sjoo & Barbara Mor, 1992, page 125, B3)

Pages 163-64. Sacred sexuality

For a discussion of this subject see M Esther Harding, 1973, (B13), especially pages 158–62 and 170–82. The quotations from Monica Sjoo & Barbara Mor are on pages 159, 53 and 54.

The research on religious experience conducted by James Prescott, neuropsychologist at the Institute of Humanitic Science in Los Gatos, California, is reported by Mary Long, 'Visions of a New Faith' in *Science Digest* 89 No 10, November 1981, page 41.

Pages 164-69. Sacred times

For details of Avebury see Michael Dames, 1976, (B3), and Kathy Jones, 1991, page 64. Jones says:

> The great sacred complex of stone circles and avenues at Avebury are claimed by many to represent a huge serpent in the landscape. Its head is to be found at the Sanctuary. Its body passes along the West Kennet Avenue of standing stones, through the great central henge of Avebury, and continues along the now missing Beckhampton Avenue. The serpent's tail coils, according to the dowser Brian Ashley, in the earthworks at Knoll Down. Similar representations of the Earth Serpent are to be found in the Serpent Mound of Ohio, built by the early Native Americans. (B3)

The piece about male initiation is drawn from Joseph Campbell in conversation with Fraser Boa, 1989, pages 73–6, (B5) and is in turn based by him on the letters of George Catlin, who painted portraits of the chiefs of these tribes in the 1830s.

The story about facing death in Ecuador is based on Michael Harner, 1990, pages 15–16, (B11).

Pages 169-70. Sacred knowledge

Another description of what tribal people know can be found in Marlo Morgan, 1995, and in Paula Gunn Allen, 1992, pages 22–3, (B13).

A contemporary female shaman explains the shaman as 'professional ecstatic':

> ... the direct experience of tuning in to the earth's body with our bodies, and feeling what she feels, can be *ecstasy*. Ecstasy is a physical response of the body – energy rushing through the whole system, tingling and orgasmic sensations either localized or generalized throughout. Mircea Eliade, in his germinal work called *Shamanism*, identifies the shaman as a 'professional ecstatic'. Everywhere in ancient times women were shamans. They were always connected with divination and with the movements and currents of the earth, as if they could not be separated. Women shamans and priestesses are frequently portrayed naked and grounded in the physical body, openly sexual, chanting, singing, dancing to make it rain, healing, birthing, playing musical instruments, weaving, planting, and doing the physical work of the world. These figures remain mysterious and embarrassing to the scholars, who can't make much of them, except to name them fertility figures and dancing girls. (Vicki Noble, 1991, page 51. B3)

The reference to shamans being able to talk to animals is from Mircea Eliade, 1964, (B5).

Pages 170-74. Sacred community

I am indebted to Anthony Wilson for the observation about home to an African being a group of people rather than bricks and mortar.

The James Hillman quotation is from his 1993 Recognition Award Keynote Address at the Center for Psychology and Social Change, Harvard Medical School, November 1993. Hillman is the author of many books, including (with Michael Ventura) *We've Had a Hundred Years of Psychotherapy and the World is Getting Worse*.

I am greatly indebted to Felicity Wight for writing the piece about Ladakh. The quote by Tashi Rabgyas is taken from a paper entitled 'Ecology and the Buddhist World View', presented at a conference, Ecology and Principles for Sustainable Development, September 1986.

Pages 174-78. What does this kind of power require?

The Dostoeyevsky quote is from *The Brothers Karamazov*, book V, chapter 3.

The Morris Berman quotation is from *Coming To Our Senses*, 1990, (B11).

I got the idea of 'careful, detailed feeling judgements' from Marie-Louise Von Franz, 1993, page 175, (B5).

Pages 178-79. What does this kind of power mean, in terms of living in today's world?

The piece about white and black magic draws on Elizabeth Haich, 1972, page 63, (B10).

Part III

Page 181

The piece about the distinction between knowledge and understanding draws on the Open University course, 1985, page 9.

Chapter 9

Page 182

The first quote is from Carl Jung and the second is from M K Gandhi, 1983, page 384, cited in Charlene Spretnak, 1993, page 65, (B11).

Page 183

The data on bullying in Sheffield schools is from a study led by Professor Peter Smith, Head of Psychology at Sheffield University, and funded by the Department for Education.

Pages 183-84. Acquiescence and passivity

This and the following sections owe a lot to Anne Dickson's excellent *A Woman in Your Own Right*, 1982, (B12), and Claude Steiner's *The Other Side of Power*, 1981, (B7).

The poem is part of 'Burying Blues for Janis' in Marge Piercy, 1973, (B14).

Page 185. Escalation

The Martin Luther King quotation is from Coretta Scott King, 1983, page 73, cited in Charlene Spretnak, page 61, (B11).

In David Mamet's play *Oleanna*, each of the two characters in turn bullies the other, each exercises power *over* the other. And in the end who wins? Nobody. (Royal Court Writers' Series, published by Methuen Drama, 1993. B14)

The Naomi Wolf book I refer to is *Fire with Fire*, 1993, (B7).

The quotation from Benjamin Hoff is from *The Tao of Pooh*, Mandarin, London, 1989, pages 87–8, (B14).

Page 186. Be here

The George Eliot piece is from *Daniel Deronda*, Penguin Classics, London, 1988, page 509.

Pages 187-89. State your feelings

I use the word topspin: this is when we say something which has a kick in its tail, which is actually laying blame or accusation back on the other. In this case an example would be, 'You're always threatening me like that and you make me feel hopeless.'

Jake and Eva Chapman conduct weekends for couples seeking to improve their relationships. For details, write to: The Old Manor House, Hanslope, Nr Milton Keynes, MK19 7DS.

Pages 189-90. Be vulnerable

The Marshall Rosenberg quotation is from 'A conversation with Guy Spiro' in *The Monthly Aspectarian*, April 1992, page 3.

The Ben Okri quotation is from an article entitled 'The Town of the Dying', the *Guardian*, September 1993.

The reference to the backlash to the women's movement is from Susan Faludi, 1992, page 495, (B12).

Pages 189-90

Being here, stating your true feelings, being vulnerable, being direct, being your full weight, using your symbol, expecting the positive, assuming your authority – requires that quality of sharp perception which comes with the relaxation of the ego. As I showed in chapter 6, meditation is helpful because it allows the natural luminous clarity of the self to come forth. This faculty of profound cognition is seen by Buddhists as the place for Buddha to grow in you and is therefore called 'the womb of the Buddhas'. See Tsultrim Allione, 1986, page 23, (B13).

Pages 196-98. Find the creative solution

The quotation about being preoccupied with power is from Ram Dass, *Questions and Answers* audio tape cassette, available from The Open Gate, 1 Woodman's Cottage, Brockham End, Bath, BA1 9BZ.

The description of working with a couple is from Marshall Rosenberg, 'A conversation with Guy Spiro' in *The Monthly Aspectarian*, April 1992, page 2.

The television documentary about the lack of parliamentary debate was Channel 4's 'A Farewell to Arms', *Dispatches*, 27 May 1988.

Pages 200-202. Sex

This section draws on Ros Coward, 1993, page 150, (B12).

Pages 202-204. Violent assault

Good authors on the subject of rape include Susan Brownmiller, 1975, (B12) and Pauline B Bart and Patricia H O'Brien, 1985, (B12). The latter is a study on how women respond differently to threats, and how effective different strategies are in avoiding rape. The quotation is from page 114 and refers to a book by Frederick Storaska entitled *How to Say No to a Rapist and Survive*, Random House, New York, 1975.

Pages 204-206. Feminism and power

For examples of liberal feminism see Betty Friedan, 1974, (B6), and Zillah Eisenstein, 1981, (B12).

A good summary of socialist feminism is to be found in chapter 6 of Alison M Jaggar, 1983.

For further reading on radical feminism see for example Koedt, Levine & Rapone, 1973, (B12), Mary Daly, 1978, (B12); and Adrienne Rich, 1986, (B12).

Evelyn Fox Keller is quoted in Shere Hite, 1993, page 377, (B6), as follows:

> We began by asking a few simple questions about equality, and it was like unraveling a ball of knitting, the more we looked for the beginning, the more we unraveled, until finally we are undoing the whole thing.

The Rosemary Radford Ruether quotation is from *Gaia and God*, 1993, page 9, (B11).

The following are some examples of what contemporary feminists have to say on the issue of power.

Germaine Greer is now such a household name that some people forget the extraordinary role she has played in marking out the territory and the principles of feminism since the 1960s. She is fearless, eloquent and clear. On page 114, (B6), of *The Female Eunuch*, 1985, she says:

> If women understand by emancipation the adoption of the masculine role then we are lost indeed. If women can supply no counterbalance to the blindness of male drive the aggressive society will run to its lunatic extremes at ever-escalating speed. Who will safeguard the despised animal faculties of compassion, empathy, innocence and sensuality? . . . Most women who have arrived at positions of power in a men's world have done so by adopting masculine methods which are not incompatible with the masquerade of femininity.

Camille Paglia embraces a black, hectic world of cruelty, sexual turbulence, lewdness, Dionysian pleasure; disdains warmth, tranquillity, all things blurry and kind. 'If civilisation had been left in women's hands we would still be living on grass roots.' She reckons prostitutes are sexually exposed but in control; she likes streetwise feminism, loathes the prissiness of political correctness, thinks Madonna is the embodiment of 'women's cosmic sexual power'. (Camille Paglia, 1994. B14)

Ros Coward, through interviewing dozens of women, came to the conclusion that women still give over privilege and power to their male partners, in spite of three decades of feminism. She examines women's collusion with male domination and concludes:

> Female complicity consents to many things. Sometimes it consents to extreme forms of abuse, like violence, sexual abuse and sexual exploitation. But more commonly it is a hidden complicity, a way of living our personal lives that protects men and reinforces their habitual ways of doing things. (Ros Coward, 1993, page 10. B12)

Susan Faludi is impressive in her demolition of a decade of stories in the US and British media suggesting that feminism has made women unhappy. She traces a historical pattern of regular backlashes whenever women's rights and status advance. But she notes, as does Naomi Wolf, how women in the 1980s did not take advantage of the power they already held. See Susan Faludi, 1992, (B12).

Nancy Kline is concerned mostly with the 'glass ceiling' which impedes women's progress to positions of power, and with providing training and insight for potential women leaders. So far, so good. But her entire approach is based on women developing and using their thinking faculties inside an environment defined by men. She does not seriously question the values that underpin those structures, nor address them. See Nancy Kline, 1993, (B7).

Shere Hite, through her revolutionary research on female and male sexuality, contributes in a serious way to the kind of fundamental change we are talking about. Her surveys show that:

> . . . Women are faced with having to redesign the whole system. Many, as seen, solve the problem (temporarily?) by living double lives – bisecting themselves to keep things going. But, while many women are in fact trying to see which values are workable in both systems, most men are not trying to fit in with women's 'ideology'. Nor do they see why they should. They feel women are supposed to adapt to *their* ideology. (Shere Hite)

Naomi Wolf is at first sight quite exciting – she shows convincingly how women can 'no longer be afraid to wrest power'. However it gradually dawns that the very power game she is urging women to be as good as men at is the same old male power game. And many of the tactics and attitudes she exhorts women to use are the same old male ones that got us into this mess in the first place, with the exception of her two glorious pages on the 'bad girl's route to equality'. See Naomi Wolf, 1993, pages 334–7, (B7).

When Marilyn French published *Beyond Power* in 1985, I thought, 'This is it.' At last a woman was showing that out of the roots of patriarchy have grown the violence, war and poverty which lead our world towards self-destruction:

> There is no question that the 'masculine' drive to power has achieved great power. Through intellectual structures, patriarchal ideas have come to dominate the Western mind so totally that many of us do not comprehend that there are other ways of thinking; through mechanical structures, patriarchal methods have been able to dominate most of the globe. But the morality that lies beneath patriarchy is reflected directly in the present state of the globe. On the one hand there are machines of conquest so powerful that they threaten human extinction; on the other, nature lies

defeated, its air polluted, water poisoned, trees, plants, fish and animals dying everywhere. (Page 262. B7)

She described the alternative in the transformation of society through female values, and the replacement of the power ethic with that of pleasure:

> The great end is pleasure, which unlike power is truly an end, an experience that is not simply a step to a further end. It includes all the values we presently entertain; it excludes nothing. (Page 542. B7)

But, to my great distress, the book fell off the edge of a cliff – the final chapter wasn't there; Marilyn French never told us *how* this was to happen! That is what I've been trying to work out ever since.

For other feminist writers on power, see for example Goodrich, 1991, (B12); Betty A Reardon, 1985, (B6); Kathleen Newland, 1979, (B6); Monica Sjoo & Barbara Mor, 1987, (B3); Anne Dickson, 1982, (B10); Carol Gilligan, 1982, (B8); Deborah Tannen, 1991, (B14).

Chapter 10

Page 207
The opening quotations are from Aung San Suu Kyi, 1991, page 185, and Andrew Leigh & Michael Maynard, 1993, page 21, (B14).
Pages 209-10. Realism
Freud came to believe that life is ruled by two passions, love and destruction, and called them the life instinct and the death instinct – thus further cementing the idea of human destructiveness being innate. See Erich Fromm, 1977, pages 1–10, (B6). By contrast, a Buddhist believes that human consciousness is by nature completely pure, and only becomes defiled by reaction to experiences; and therefore that whatever defilements others may have, we may have too.

When Soviet Communism was at its height it was easier to rationalize the idea of the enemy; now the enemy is more nebulous, in the form of vague 'rogue dictators'.

The Bertrand Russell quotation is from *Power*, 1975, page 201, (B7).

Kenneth E Boulding (1990, page 241. B7) doubts the effectiveness of threat power.
Pages 210-12. Why the realist position is untenable
The paragraph about the cyclical nature of power draws on Hugh

Miall, 1992, page 35. I am indebted to Hugh Miall for his description of the realist position, which forms the basis of my first paragraph on the subject.

Page 213. Ju-jitsu

Koichi Tohei is the author of *This is Aikido: With Mind and Body Coordinated*, Japan Publications, San Francisco and Tokyo, 1975. He is quoted in Shale Paul, 1987, page 116, (B7).

Pages 213-14. Non-violent direct action

Martin Luther King is quoted in Joseph Fahey, 'Conflict Creation' in *Peace Review*, Vol 5, No 4, Winter 1993, pages 414–15.

The paragraph about *satyagraha* draws on Charlene Spretnak, 1993, page 68. Interestingly, Gandhi said he learned the lessons of non-violence from his wife.

> Her determined resistance to my will on the one hand, and her quiet submission to the suffering my stupidity involved on the other hand, ultimately made me ashamed of myself and cured me of my stupidity in thinking I was born to rule over her; and in the end she became my teacher in non-violence. (Geoffrey Ashe, 1968, page 182, (B14), quoted in Spretnak, 1993, page 66. B11)

The piece about the Bontoc women stopping the dam-building is from a report I edited entitled *The Role of Women in Peace Movements, in the Development of Peace Research, and in the Promotion of Friendly Relations between Nations*. It was presented by UNESCO to the World Conference of the United Nations Decade for Women, Copenhagen, 1980.

For material on non-violence see Adam Roberts, 1969, (B2); H A Bedau, 1969, (B7); Gene Sharp, 1973, (B2), and many more.

Pages 214-19. Points of leverage for the powerless

The 'knowing where to hit it' story is from the Open University Faculty of Technology course, 1991, page 45. The story about the Oxford Research Group is an adapted version of that appearing on pages 19–26 of the same course, and the quotation at the end is from page 77.

Page 219. The means must be the same as the end

The quotation is from Anne Naess, 1965, page 37, (B14), citing from *Young India* 26 December 1924, and quoted in Charlene Spretnak, 1993, page 70, (B11).

The story of the Vietnamese nun is from Chan Khong, 1993, pages 198–9, (B14).

Pages 220-21. Get beyond the way of thinking . . .

The first paragraph owes much to Adam Curle's *Another Way: Positive Response to Contemporary Violence*, Jon Carpenter, Oxford, 1995.

Dispute resolution has expanded fast in recent years in the USA into community justice, education, policy development and so on. The techniques of dispute resolution assume that disputants can be equalized, that formal mechanisms should settle disputes, and that disputes are compatible between cultures. This approach can mean in practice that larger problems go unaddressed because they are reframed into individual issues. According to some critics, dispute resolution:

> . . . is a brainwashing that uses elaborate psychological mechanisms to make people deny or forget their real needs. The mechanisms create an illusion of justice to force co-existence and stability. The risk, then, is that a dispute will become a source of second-class justice for the poor and disempowered. Stronger powers will be able to co-opt dispute resolution as a control mechanism. (Colin Rule, 'Questioning Dispute Resolution' in *Peace Review*, Vol 5, No 4, Winter 1993, page 411)

The paragraph on UN peace-keepers draws on A B Fetherston 'UN Peacekeepers and Culture of Violence' in *Cultural Survival Quarterly*, Vol 10, No 1, 1995.

The work of the Transnational Foundation for Peace and Future Research is reported by Jan Oberg in 'Conflict Mitigation in Former Yugoslavia' in *Peace Review*, Vol 5, No 4, Winter 1993, page 428.

Pages 221-23. Inform yourself

For the neighbourhood fact bank see Tony Gibson, 1979, page 21, (B2) and the whole of his part II for examples.

The Celltech story and quotation are from Gerard Fairtlough, 1994, pages 16–17, (B14).

Pages 224-25. Give it away

The Jean Baker Miller quotation is from 'Women and Power: Reflections Ten Years Later' in Thelma Jean Goodrich, *Women and Power: Perspectives for Family Therapy*, W W Norton & Company, New York, 1991, page 39, (B12).

Pages 225-27. Are all conflicts two-sided?

The long Adam Curle quotation is from *True Justice*, 1981, page 45, (B2), and the terms yin and yang obviously connect with what has been said earlier about bringing the masculine and feminine sides of ourselves together.

The piece which follows on transformationist thinking draws heavily on Oliver Ramsbotham's *The Missing Defence Debate*, Current Decisions Report No 6, Oxford Research Group, 1991, page 10.

Pages 227-30. How can conflicts be prevented or resolved?
The steps in problem-solving and Quaker mediation were taken from Hugh Miall's *New Conflicts in Europe: Prevention and Resolution*, Current Decisions Report Number 10, Oxford Research Group, 1992.

The Adam Curle book referred to is *Another Way: Positive Response to Contemporary Violence*, Jon Carpenter, Oxford, 1995.

The piece about women reporters draws on Anne Sebba, 1993.

Elise Boulding is:

a Quaker and author of many books including *The Underside of History: A View of Women Through Time*. She served on President Carter's National Peace Academy Commission, laid the groundwork for a program in Conflict Resolution Studies at Dartmouth while she chaired the sociology department there, and developed with Warren Ziegler a process for Imaging A World Without Weapons. (Annie Cheatham & Mary Clare Powell, 1986, pages 216–17.)

The information about the Philippines women's organization is from Network Information Project, 30 Westwood Road, Southampton, SO2 1DN.

Details of the resources offered by Marshall Rosenberg are given in the 'Going Further' section.

Pages 230-31. Can structural conflict only be resolved by structural change?
The first three paragraphs in the section on structural conflict draw on Hugh Miall, 1992, page 27, (B6).

Pages 232-34. Donkey lean
If the good of all is not enticing enough, it may be interesting to know that it can be shown experientially that each individual is better off too. The XY game, developed from game theory, gives each pair of players the opportunity of co-operating or defecting at any one of a series of decisions. For over a decade thousands of students have been playing it at summer school and coming away stunned to learn that if they co-operate they actually do better for themselves than if they compete (see Robert Axelrod, 1984. B2).

I am indebted to Jim Howard for the account of Tanzanian workers' devotion and co-operation in the face of the needs of Rwandan refugees. International relations experts are also recognizing the same thing in terms of how countries can deal with each other. Catherine Kelleher was foreign policy adviser to the Carter Administration and is now lecturing at the Brookings Institute. She writes:

What is needed . . . is a process of basic cooperation and transparency, to develop a commitment on the part of each state to some level of joint action, responsibility and accountability in areas critical to the lives of citizens. The end result may be the integration of a political union – analogous to the nation-building process, or simply a loose confederation or treaty community. In the military field the minimum is to regulate effectively the military capabilities that pose uncertainty – in essence, to deny the means to commit aggression swiftly and with overwhelming force. (Catherine Kelleher, 'A New Definition of Security' from *Proceedings of the Forty-First Pugwash Conference on Science and World Affairs*, 1991.)

The economist Kenneth Boulding understood the world in terms of three kinds of power: threat power, economic power and integrative power. Integrative power is something akin to hara power but expressed in more intellectual terms. The last section of his book on power has the sort of heading which immediately makes one want to turn to that page: 'The world as a total system with nobody in charge'. For a world organization such as the UN, he concludes, integrative power alone is not enough: the UN has not enough money to do what it needs to do, nor has it the (coercive) power to tax. There is also, he says:

> . . . the problem of the use of threat in the form of sanctions. This is an important aspect of law. Situations can arise in which the behaviour of an individual or an individual nation may imperil the world community. Under these circumstances, legitimated sanctions have a place, although there is a constant problem of the method by which these are legitimated. The ideal situation is where sanctions are regarded as legitimate by the person or nation against whom they are applied.
>
> Integrative power, then, involves bringing the dissident back into the community again. Sanctions alone, threat alone, will not do this. Here again, unless threat is allied with integrative power, which it often destroys, it will be ineffective. (Kenneth E Boulding, 1990, pages 249–50. B7)

Page 234. Link
For details of how Western interest in Tibetan culture affects it, see *The Tibetan Review*, January 1994.

The Irina Tweedie quotation is from *The Chasm of Fire*, 1979, page 202, (B11).

Pages 235-36. Bear
One of Carol Gilligan's interviewees said:

Morality involves realizing that there is an interplay between self and other and that you are going to have to take responsibility for both of them. I keep using that word *responsibility*; it's just sort of a consciousness of your influence over what's going on.

At the end of her book, she says:

> In the different voice of women lies the truth of an ethic of care, the tie between relationship and responsibility, and the origins of aggression in the failure of connection. (Carol Gilligan, 1982, page 19. B8)

The anti-nuclear actions I refer to were listed originally by Sue Scott of the Women's Peace Alliance UK. Her list shows 34 significant actions, ie from 300 to 1 million women involved. It appears in Seager and Olson (eds), *Women in the World*, Pan/Pluto, London, 1986, page 39. There have been many more such actions since 1986.

For a description of links between Soviet and American women, see Annie Cheatham & Mary Clare Powell, 1986, chapter 11, (B12). For a description of the network of women from Eastern and Western Europe, see chapter 4 and for information contact NATO Alerts Network, 115 Rue Stevin, Brussels 1040.

The International Symposium on Women, Politics and Environmental Action, June 1994, was jointly organized by Russian and American women's organizations to identify ways of addressing post-nuclear pollution in both countries.

There are at least five East/West women's organizations working in Croatia and Bosnia to aid refugees, provide counselling for survivors and set up self-help projects.

The Starhawk quotation is from *Truth or Dare*, 1990, pages 268–70, (B11).

Page 236. Be (clarity)
I am paraphrasing Christina Feldman & Jack Kornfeld (eds) *Stories of the Spirit, Stories of the Heart*, HarperCollins, San Francisco, 1991, pages 358–9. For more on the notion of 'being peace' see Thich Nhat Hanh, *Peace is Every Step*, Bantam, New York, 1992, (B11). Older women may be particularly able in this area, because one of the things we can learn in menopause is to become accustomed to not being the focal point. To repeat my favourite Germaine Greer quote:

> When you are young, everything is about you. As you grow older . . . you begin to realise that everything is not about you, and that is the beginning of freedom. (Germaine Greer, 1992, page 423. B1)

Pages 237-38. Saving the world singlehanded
The Joanna Macy quotation is from *World as Lover, World as Self*, 1993, page 44, (B9).
Page 238. Overwork and the activist
I can't find where the Thomas Merton quotation is from but it could be *New Seeds of Contemplation*, 1972, (B11).

Chapter 11

Pages 248-49 The man with hara power
This section was developed from a contribution to fresh thinking by John Hamwee.

Going Further

This section provides names and addresses, and in some cases descriptions, of ways in which the ideas in this book can be followed up. There are now so many paths available, for example in the quest for self-knowledge, that choosing the right one is a matter of personal preference and personal style. What I can do is to sketch the outlines of some ways of going about it, give an airing to different approaches, offer descriptions of books which serve as introductions to these different ways, and include addresses which will be helpful in the first step on a particular path. In making these suggestions I cannot hope to cover all that is available. What I do hope to do is to suggest the kind of paths which will empower rather than disempower – the therapies and techniques which are respectful of an individual's own movement towards health and autonomy.

Chapter 3

The address of Forward is: Africa Centre, 38 King Street, London WC2 8JT, Tel: 0171 379 6889

Chapter 4

For more information on *Kahuna* traditions and bodywork, contact Nicholas Janni, 43 Brookville Road, London SW6 7BH. Tel: 0171 386 8382.

Self-knowledge can basically be gained in three ways: working by one's self, with another person, or in a group.

By oneself

Some of the greatest pioneers in self-knowledge did it on their own. But they are the first to point out the dangers. Carl Jung, who took himself into the darkest realms of the unconscious, warns of the terrors to be encountered.

> An incessant stream of fantasies had been released, and I did my best not to lose my head but to find some way to understand these strange things. I stood helpless before an alien world; everything in it seemed difficult and incomprehensible. I was living in a constant state of tension; often I felt as if gigantic blocks of stone were tumbling down upon me. One thunderstorm followed another. My enduring these storms was a question of brute strength. Others have been shattered by them – Nietzsche, and Holderlin, and many others. But there was a demonic strength in me, and from the beginning there was no doubt in my mind that I must find the meaning of what I was experiencing in these fantasies. When I endured these assaults of the unconscious I had an unswerving conviction that I was obeying a higher will, and that feeling continued to uphold me until I had mastered the task. (Carl Jung, 1983, pages 200–1. B8)

This extract and the fascinating pages which follow act as a warning of the danger of going into the unconscious alone, without a guide and companion.

Having said this, a good start to the process of self knowledge, if one wants to work alone *or* with others, is to keep a journal. To get the best out of a journal, try:

The Practice of Process Meditation, Dialogue House Library, New York, 1980, which is about keeping a journal as a way to spiritual experience.

A Life of One's Own was written by psychoanalyst Marion Milner to try to answer the question, 'What do I really want from life?' Using her own intimate diaries, kept over many years, she discovers ways of attending, of looking, of moving that bring surprising joy – ways that can be practised by anyone. She summarizes her discoveries in terms of a psychic bisexuality in all of us, realizing that she

> had not understood at all that a feminine attitude to the universe was really just as legitimate, intellectually and biologically, as a masculine one...and just as necessary for both men and women. (London: Virago, 1987)

One of the best ways to release imagination and creativity is through myth, symbol and art. There are three books on this which are so exciting, so endlessly stimulating that I would want to take them on a desert island. The first is C G Jung, *Man and His Symbols*. Get the best illustrated edition you can afford – it is worth it. Some of the pictures will stay with you for life. In it, Jung explains to the general reader his significant contribution to our knowledge of the human mind, that is, the theory of symbolism – particularly as revealed in dreams.

The second book is Marie-Louise Von Franz, *The Feminine in Fairytales*. This book shows how the feminine reveals itself in fairy tales of German, Russian, Scandinavian, and Eskimo origin, including familiar stories such as 'Sleeping Beauty,' 'Snow White and Rose Red' and 'Rumpelstiltskin'. Marie-Louise Von Franz points out that some tales offer insights into the psychology of women, while others reflect the problems and characteristics of the anima, the inner femininity of men. She discusses the archetypes and symbolic themes that appear in fairy tales as well as dreams and fantasies, draws practical advice from the tales, and demonstrates its application in case studies from her analytical practice.

The third is Fraser Boa, *This Business of the Gods*. It is based on the documentary film series of the same title featuring Joseph Campbell in conversation with Fraser Boa Campbell, a scholar of mythology, discusses the truth inherent in myth and legend, and how this can help and enhance the lives of individuals. It's extremely readable.

There are seven general books on self-knowledge which, depending on one's temperament and situation, can prove to be an invaluable guide:

* Thomas Harris, *I'm OK – You're OK* is the multi-million best seller introduction to Transactional Analysis, which has proved a turning point for many people and which brings a refreshingly practical approach to the problems we all encounter in day-to-day relationships with ourselves and other people. In sensible, non-clinical language Thomas Harris tells how to gain control of your life and be responsible for your future – no matter what happened in the past.
* José Stevens's book, *Transforming Your Dragons*, is a mixture of practicality and brilliant insight. It shows precisely how we can identify and transform the pervasive patterns of resistance which block us from being who we really are. Written without a trace of jargon or pomposity, this is an engaging, funny book which is based on a deep understanding of where we are as human beings in our world today.
* Mary Elizabeth Marlow, *Handbook for the Emerging Woman – A Manual for Awakening the Unlimited Power of the Feminine Spirit* (Virginia: the

Donning Company Publishers, 1988; and Shaftesbury: Element Books, 1994). Marlow uses the archetypes of the Greek goddesses and the elements to 'awaken, activate or direct those qualities or aspects of ourselves that have been dormant'. She uses visualization techniques to heal or reconcile those experiences or parts of ourselves that are particularly painful.

* Franklin Abbott (ed) *New Men, New Minds*, The Crossing Press, California, 1987, shows how men can support each other in overcoming their separateness, their fears and their need for control; how they can touch their deepest longings; how they can best communicate with each other and with themselves; and how they can create, equally with women, a safe and peaceful home on earth.

* Lucy Goodison's book *Moving Heaven and Earth* contains several useful exercises for working on yourself.

* There is also a book on what happens in families which is so well written and wise and funny that every household should have one: Robin Skynner & John Cleese, *Families and How to Survive Them*. Using the most modern experiences of family therapy, it shows how understanding can lead to progress, taboos can be broken down, and development of healthy relationships and families can take place.

* If you are learning about yourself through your relationship, one of the most powerful and helpful books I have ever come across is *Conscious Loving* by Gay & Kathlyn Hendricks. It contains a clear understanding of how we can either block ourselves or empower ourselves through our intimate relationships, and teaches through exercises how to get out of our traps.

Obviously, these suggestions are my personal choice, and you may well find something more suited to your own particular path by browsing through a bookshop which stocks this particular kind of book. One word of warning: be wary of those that promise instant anything. We need to do the work ourselves, but often the right book drops into our hand at the precise moment we need it.

Working with another person

Here it depends on personal preference, and money, whether you choose to work with someone like yourself, in co-counselling, or with someone professionally trained, in some kind of therapy.

Co-counselling

The techniques of co-counselling are now well recognized as a useful way for people who do not want or cannot afford therapy to learn more about themselves in safety.

There are one or two basic ground rules:

* The other person must want to engage in co-counselling as much as you and you must commit yourselves for an agreed period of working together.
* There must be absolute confidentiality between you.
* You must find a quiet place to work where you will not be disturbed and sit comfortably facing each other.
* In each session, each of you should speak for a given period of time, perhaps only five minutes at first, but building up to longer periods. The key factor is that the other not only does not interrupt, but does not react in any way – no nodding, encouragement or disapproval.
* All the other person may do is give feedback afterwards of what they have understood from what you have said which you may then correct if it is wrong.

The idea is for each of you to push yourselves into going further into the problems and issues that you are facing and to find your own solutions. Silence is quite all right. Often it comes before something really important.

Co-counselling addresses:
Jean Trewick, Westerly, Prestwick Lane, Chiddingford, Godalming, Surrey GUA 4XW. Tel: 01428 682882.
Karen Horney Psychoanalytic Counsellors, 12 Nassington Road, London NW3.
Association of Humanistic Psychology, 62 Southwark Bridge Road, London SE1 0AU.
International references: Harvey Jackins, 719 Second Avenue North, Seattle, WA 98109, USA

Therapy

Most procedures in psychotherapy may be placed on a scale having to do with power and control. At one end of the scale stand orthodox Freudians and orthodox behaviourists, believing in a politics of authoritarian or elitist control of persons 'for their own good', either to produce better adjustment to the status quo or happiness or contentment or productivity or all of these. In the middle are most of the contemporary schools of psychotherapy, confused, ambiguous, or paternalistic in the politics of their relationships (though they may be very clear regarding their therapeutic strategies). At the other end of the scale is the client-centered, experiential, person-centered approach, consistently stressing the capacity and autonomy of the person, her right to choose the directions she will move in her behaviour, and her ultimate responsibility for herself in the therapeutic relationship, with the therapist's person playing a real but primarily catalytic part in that relationship. (Carl Rogers, 1986, pages 20–21. B7)

The key thing to remember is that you can only change when you want to. For you to be pushed or to push yourself is dangerous, and in any case you will just have to come back and do it again if you were not ready. Psychologist and teacher Ram Dass has a good image here. Forcing change, he says, is like tearing the skin off a snake – better to wait until it sloughs it off naturally.

Clearly some sort of guide to the various therapies is needed. The best I have found is John Rowan & Windy Dryden (eds) *Innovative Therapy in Britain*, Open University Press, Milton Keynes, 1988. This book draws together descriptions of the more established innovative therapies which have gained considerable prominence this decade. They are characterized by their active styles of approach and engage the client in experiencing and exploring those difficulties which have prompted him or her to seek help. Each therapy is presented by a specialist practitioner, looking at the theoretical assumptions underpinning the therapy.

How do I find a therapist or counsellor?

The UK Council for Psychotherapy has developed a register which lists the names of about 3,800 qualified psychotherapists and their qualifications. The register costs £20 and can be obtained from the UK Council for Psychotherapy, Regents College, Inner Circle, Regents Park, London NW1 4NS, tel: 0171 487 7554, or consulted in a library.

A cost-free service is available from the British Association for Counselling, 1 Regent Place, Rugby, Warwickshire, CV21 2PJ, tel : 01788 578328. If you can send them an A4 size s.a.e, they will supply you, free of charge, with a 3-4 page printout of counsellors and therapists in your area, listing their qualifications, membership of professional bodies, type of approach and fees. This does not give the same attestation of training and certification as the register above, but it is a good start, and will tell you a little about each person. The BAC also publishes a *Counselling and Psychotherapy Resources Directory*, priced at £22, which is a nationwide list of 2000 practitioners, commercial and charitable counselling services and professional bodies.

Those living in continental Europe may like to contact the European Association for Psychotherapy, Rosembursenstrasse 8/3/7, A– 1010 Wien, Austria. Tel: 43 222 5127090, fax: 43 222 512 7091.

In the USA each state is governed by different regulations, so enquiries should start with the state health services regulatory body.

In a group

Group therapy by its very nature is an intense experience, condensed into a few hours or days. If the facilitators are skilled, and group members are 'held' in a loving and safe environment, it can be a quick way of travelling far on one's path, and getting through blocks. But if the atmosphere is unsupportive and the facilitators badly trained, it can be a damaging experience. Check thoroughly on the credentials of the facilitators; ask how many years of personal therapy or analysis they have done (because it is essential that they should have done enough work on themselves to prevent their own 'stuff' becoming involved in the group). Check also on their orientation and belief system, to make sure it is acceptable to you.

The same scale as Rogers's on pages 305–6 can be applied to the interpersonal relationships in intensive groups. There are so many different kinds – consciousness-raising groups, workshops, support groups, encounter groups, sensitivity training, sensory awareness groups, Gestalt groups and so on – that generalization is impossible. The main issue is that group leaders vary enormously in the way of relating. Some are authoritarian and directive. Others make maximum use of exercises and games to reach goals they have chosen. Others feel little responsibility toward group members – 'I do my thing and you do your thing.' Others endeavour to be facilitative rather than controlling.

Whichever route you choose, time and energy invested in self-knowledge will be time and energy saved.

> I walk down the street.
> There is a deep hole in the sidewalk
> I fall in.
> I am lost . . . I am hopeless.
> It isn't my fault.

It takes forever to find a way out.
I walk down the same street.
There is a deep hole in the sidewalk.
I pretend I don't see it.
I fall in again.
I can't believe I'm in the same place.
But it isn't my fault.
It still takes a long time to get out.

I walk down the same street.
There is a deep hole in the sidewalk.
I see it is there.
I still fall in . . . it's a habit.
My eyes are open
I know where I am
It is my fault.
I get out immediately.

I walk down the same street.
There is a hole in the sidewalk
I walk around it.

I walk down another street.

(This poem appears in 'Autobiography in Five Chapters' from Sogyal Rinpoche, 1992; it is thought to be by Portia Nelson.)

Chapter 5

There are many different routes available now, both to prevent illness and to heal the body, including osteopathy, shiatsu, massage, aromatherapy, herbalism, homoeopathy, reflexology and nutritional therapy. It would be impossible to describe them all, so I will confine myself to a description of those I personally have found helpful.

Acupuncture

Acupuncture is a holistic therapy which originated in China over 5,000 years ago and is now widely practised in the Western world. By inserting very fine needles into specific points on the body, or by burning a herb called moxa on these points, the life force or '*chi*' in the body is stimulated, enabling it to return to health, balance and harmony in body, mind and spirit. In the UK contact: The British Acupuncture Council, Park House, 206–8 Latimer Road, London W10 6RE, tel: 0181 964 0222. In the USA contact: The Traditional Acupuncture Institute, American City Building, Columbia, MD 21044, tel: 1 301 997 3770.

Zero Balancing

Zero balancing is an innovative body-work technique. Using gentle finger pressure and held stretches, it invites the release of tension accumulated in the deep structures of the body. The work takes place at the interface between a person's physical structure and their energy, harmonizing the relationship between the two. Zero balancing provides a point of stillness, around which the body can relax and let go of unease and pain. In the UK contact the Zero Balancing Association, 36 Richmond Road, Cambridge CB4 3PU, tel & fax: 01223 315480. In the USA contact the Zero Balancing Association, PO Box 1727, Capitola, CA 95010, tel: 1 408 476 0665. Fax: 1 408 462 6662.

Yoga

There are at least five different types of yoga in India, of which the best known in the West are Raja Yoga (a yogic meditation system based on dualist principles), and Hatha Yoga (balancing 'Ha' or sun with 'Tha' or moon, masculine and feminine).

In the West, integral yoga incorporates elements from all five systems, and is described as follows by Sissel Fowler of the Oxford Yoga Group:

> Yoga is an ancient system of self-improvement: a way to growth and self-knowledge as well as to better health. Integral Yoga aims to integrate and harmonise all levels of the being – physical, psychological, spiritual – and also to create a harmonious relationship with one's surroundings and other people. Yoga awakes potential and unlocks energy, leading to a fuller, more 'whole' life.

Contact the British Wheel of Yoga, 1 Hamilton Place, Boston Road, Sleaford, Lincolnshire NG34 7ES, tel: 01549 306851, or buy a copy of *The Yoga Journal*, PO Box 469018, Escondido, CA 92046-9018, USA. This journal regularly prints contact addresses for around the world.

McTimoney Chiropractic

The aim of a McTimoney chiropractic treatment is to remove any interference with the body's nerve supply. If a nerve is compressed or stretched, however subtly, the information passing along the nerve fibre will be distorted, giving false information to the organ or muscle it serves. Once these distortions are removed the body can function correctly. McTimoney chiropractors check and subtly adjust bones of the skull, thorax, spine, pelvis and limbs, relieving distortions throughout the entire structure. For a list of practitioners, contact the McTimoney Chiropractic School Ltd, 14 Park End St, Oxford OX1 1HH, tel: 01865 246786.

How to find a practitioner or teacher

In all disciplines of medicine and therapy there are some great healers and many good ones. There are also some who are less developed, and a very few who are charlatans.

When you have found out more and decided which way of working attracts you most, phone or write for a list of qualified practitioners in or near your area. At the same time, ask for a leaflet describing what you can expect in treatment. Your relationship with the practitioner is of great importance, and it is worth taking trouble to find a person you feel really comfortable with. After all, you are entrusting this person with your most important possession – your well-being. If there is a choice of practitioners in your area, it is worth speaking to several on the phone just to see how they sound before you make a first appointment. It is difficult to know in one session exactly whether you have found the 'right' person or not, and there are some questions you can ask yourself which may clarify and deepen your first impressions (it is wise to pay more attention to what your intuition says than to your brain).

* Do you feel comfortable telling this person about yourself? Do you feel safe?
* Does the practitioner strike you as someone who is 'together' and there for you – i.e. is there a sense of order and purpose?
* Do you feel the treatment is designed for and responds to you personally?
* Was the discussion of payment direct and straightforward?
* If you showed your pain, did the practitioner have compassion? Did you feel genuinely listened to and acknowledged?

* Do you feel this practitioner is capable of seeing the potential you, the you that you are aspiring to be?

If the answer to all these is a firm yes, you've probably found a practitioner who suits you. If it's less clear, try the following questions:

* Was there any sense in which you felt the practitioner was trying to impress you?
* Did you get the sense that the practitioner was anxious to have you as a patient?
* Was he/she telling you what to think instead of helping you to find your own path?
* Did you ever feel defensive?
* If touch was involved in the treatment, did it ever feel creepy?

If the answer to any of these questions is yes, then it may be a good idea to try someone else.

Hara-strengthening through yoga

Here are some yoga exercises which are useful for hara-strengthening, offered by Sissel Fowler of the Oxford Yoga Group.

Hara breathing

Sit in a kneeling position (*vajrasana*), using a cushion or meditation stool between the buttocks and the heels. Lengthen your spine, keep your elbows wide and your hands on top of your hara. Relax your shoulders. Fix your gaze on a point. Exhale, slowly making a soft sighing sound. Pause, relax. Let your in-breath be reflexive. You could count exhalations from 1 to 10.

Hara rocking

Sitting in the same position, close your eyes. Exhale as before, but tuck your tailbone under so that your back becomes convex. Pause and relax, especially your shoulders. The reflexive in-breath straightens the pelvis and back. Use slow, rhythmic movements.

Pelvic contraction (mula bandha)

Stand relaxed with your feet hip-width apart and your hands on your hara. Squeeze the muscles at base of your buttocks. Inhale and contract the pelvic floor (perineum) in an upward movement. Exhale and release. Feel the hara while doing this from five to ten times.

Dragon breath

Stand with your knees bent and your hands on your hara. Tuck your tailbone under and do *mula bandha*. Inhale and raise your arms. Hold your breath. Be wide awake. Exhale strongly lowering the arms and return to the starting position. Hold your breath out and feel the energy in your hara.

Chapter 6

Once again, the contacts I am able to offer below represent only a fraction of those available, and are those which I have found useful.

The Society of Friends, or Quakers as they are more generally known, have meeting houses in many towns. The telephone number will usually be listed in your local directory, and meetings for worship are held on Sunday mornings. The meetings are without liturgy, hymns or clergy, and are generally silent except when someone present feels moved spontaneously to speak or 'minister'.

Ram Dass' teaching schedule, books and tapes are available from the Hanuman Foundation, Suite 203, 524 San Anselmo Ave, San Anselmo, CA 94960, tel: 1 415 4535111.

Enlightenment Intensives provide participants with a good and safe opportunity to experience the change of state of consciousness known as 'enlightenment'. For an initial three-day period, participants work on a question such as 'Who am I?' or 'What is life?' The aim is not to find an answer to the question but to directly experience the truth of who one is or what life actually is. For details, contact Jake and Eva Chapman, The Old Manor House, The Green, Hanslope, Milton Keynes, MK19 7LS, tel: 01908 510 548, fax: 01908 5113 59. In

Australia, contact Lawrence Noyes, PO Box 10279, Gouger Street, Adelaide, South Australia 5000.

Plum Village is the community in south-western France set up by Thich Nhat Hanh to support education projects in Vietnam. Each year two main retreats are offered, one in summer for families, and a longer one in winter given in Vietnamese. Another retreat involves an intensive three week course in English and is given in even numbered years. Contact Plum Village, Meyrac, Loubes-Bernac, 47120 France, tel: 3353 94 75 40.

The Community of Interbeing organizes UK retreats and local contacts for those interested in the teachings of Thich Nhat Hanh. Contact Martin Pitt, 42 Hanging Royd Road, Hebden Bridge, West Yorkshire, HX7 6AH.

The Meridian Trust was set up in 1985 to document in film and video the traditions and teachings of various Buddhist cultures. Contact the Meridian Trust, 330 Harrow Road, London W9 2HP, tel: 0171 2895443.

The Gaia Centre runs courses in meditation and retreats especially for women. Brochure available on request from the Gaia Centre, Woodland Road, Denbury, Nr Newton Abbot, Devon TQ12 6DY, tel: 01803 813188.

The Schumacher College is an international centre for ecological and spiritual studies. 'It encourages individuals of all ages, cultures and educational backgrounds to spend time in an atmosphere of reflection and discussion, stimulated by the most exciting of contemporary thinking and by a respect for wisdom both ancient and modern.' For details and availability of bursaries contact Hilary Nicholson, The Old Postern, Dartington, Totnes, TQ9 6EA, tel: 01803 865934, fax: 01803 866899.

Several specialist bookshops have an extensive list of books and tape cassettes available by mail order, including: **The Bodhi Tree Book Store** in Los Angeles; **Wisdom Books**, 402 Hoe Street, London; **Compendium Bookshop**, 234 Camden High St, London NW1 8QS, tel: 0171 485 8944; and **Silver Moon Women's Bookshop**, 64-68 Charing Cross Road, London WC2H 0BB, tel: 0171 8367906.

Books, meditation tapes and details of retreats in the UK are available from **The Open Gate**, 1 Woodman's Cottage, Brockham End, Bath BA1 9BZ, tel: 01225 428557.

Chapter 7

Details of the Mastery and other courses and workshops can be obtained from the Actors' Institute, Carpenters Mews, North Road, London N7 9EF, tel: 0171 609 9221. There are also two extraordinarily helpful courses, entitled *Performing with Presence* and *Dramatic Shift*, presented by Maynard/Leigh Associates, Marvic House, Bishop's Rd, London SW6 7AD, tel: 0171 3852588.

Chapter 9

Nonviolent Communication

A list of publications, audio and tape cassettes can be obtained from the Center for Nonviolent Communication, 3229 Bordeaux, Sherman, TX 75090, USA, tel: 1 903 893 3886, fax: 1 903 893 2935.

Physical self-defence resources

There is a video made by Penny Gulliver entitled *Self Defence for Women*, available from Video Seven Dimensions, 18 Armstrong Street, Middle Park, Victoria 3206, Australia.

The following books may also be useful:
Denise Caignon & Gail Groves (eds) *Her Wits about Her: Self-defence Success Stories by Women*, The Women's Press, London, 1989, which lists many local resources and addresses on self-defence.
Cheryl Reimold, *The Woman's Guide to Staying Safe*, Cloverdale Press/Monarch Press, 1985.
Kathleen Hudson, *Every Woman's Guide to Self Defence*, St Martin's Press, New York, 1978.
Susan Smith, *Fear or Freedom: A Woman's Options in Social Survival and Physical Defence*, Mother Courage Press, 1986.
Pauline Bart & Patricia O'Brien, *Stopping Rape: Successful Survival Strategies*, Pergamon Press, Oxford, 1985.

Chapter 10

Marshall Rosenberg offers the following resources (details of both are given in the Bibliography): *A Model for Nonviolent Communication*, a model whose purpose is to empower people to prevent violence and inspire compassion, containing exercises which will help readers to check their understanding of the material presented; and *Nonviolent Communication Workbook*, which is designed for those who want to introduce non-violent communication to people who have not attended a workshop. The latter can be used by individuals or groups and contains exercises and written materials to help develop skills in applying this process in real-life situations. *Introduction to a Model for Nonviolent Communication* is a 60-minute audio cassette introducing the model for nonviolent communication through discussion, stories, and music. All the above are available from the Center for Nonviolent Communication, 3229 Bordeaux Street, Sherman, TX 75090, tel: 903 893 3886, fax: 903 893 2935.

Starhawk, in her book *Truth or Dare*, provides a good section on the steps needed to build a movement for change, including clarifying vision, withdrawing consent and building networks and coalitions (see pages 336–8).

Quaker Peace and Service offers a programme of workshops, consultancies and training to help groups working for positive social change. This programme uses well-established experience and includes: understanding different forms of power; naming goals and developing strategies; manageable objectives; releasing creativity; and building groups. Contact Catharine Sherman Perry, Turning the Tide, Quaker Peace and Service, Friends House, Euston Road, London NW1 2BJ, tel: 0171 387 3601, fax: 0171 388 1977.

Woodbroke Quaker Study Centre runs an Alternatives to Violence project offering weekend and short courses. It is at 1046 Bristol Road, Birmingham B29 6LJ, tel: 0121 4725171, fax: 0121 4725173.

Bibliography

1 The Body

Dalton, Katharina, *Once a Month*, Fontana, London, 1982.

Dorkenoo, Efua, *Cutting the Rose*, Minority Rights Group, London, 1994.

Dorkenoo, Efua, and Elworthy, Scilla, *Female Genital Mutilation: Proposals for Change*, Minority Rights Group, London, 1992.

Goldsworthy, Joanna (ed) *A Certain Age: Reflecting on the Menopause*, Virago, London, 1993.

Greer, Germaine, *The Change; Women, Ageing and the Menopause*, Penguin, London, 1992.

Hosken, Fran, *The Hosken Report – Genital and Sexual Mutilation of Females*, Women's International Network News, Lexington, USA, 1982.

Kenton, Leslie, *10 Day Clean-Up Plan; De-toxify Your Body for Natural Health and Vitality*, Vermillion, London, 1992.

Mole, Peter, *Acupuncture; Energy Balancing for Body, Mind and Spirit*, Element Books, Shaftesbury, Dorset, 1992.

Owen, Lara, *Her Blood is Gold: Reclaiming the Power of Menstruation*, The Aquarian Press, London, 1993.

Phillips, Angela & Rakusen, Jill, *Our Bodies Ourselves*, 5th edition, Penguin, Harmondsworth, 1986.

Shreeve, Caroline M., *Overcoming the Menopause Naturally; How to Cope Without Artificial Hormones*, 4th edition, Arrow Books, London, 1990.

Shuttle, Penelope, & Redgrove, Peter, *The Wise Wound: Menstruation & Everywoman*, 2nd edition, Penguin, London, 1980.

2 Conflict Prevention and Resolution

Axelrod, Robert, *The Evolution of Cooperation*, Basic Books, New York, 1984.

Curle, Adam, *True Justice*, Swarthmoor Lecture, 1981.

De Bono, Edward, *Conflicts, A Better Way to Resolve Them*, Penguin, London, 1985.

Gandhi, M K, *Satyagraha in South Africa*, Tanam Press, New York, 1983.

Gibson, Tony, *People Power: Community and Work Groups in Action*, Penguin,

Harmondsworth, 1979.

Olson, Mancur, *The Logic of Collective Action and the Theory of Groups*, Harvard University Press, Cambridge, Massachusetts, 1965.

Roberts, Adam (ed), *Civilian Resistance as a Natural Defence*, Penguin, London, 1969.

Rosenberg, Marshall B, *A Model for Nonviolent Communication*, New Society Publishers, Philadelphia, Pa.,1983.

Rosenberg, Marshall B, *Nonviolent Communication Workbook*, New Society Publishers, Philadelphia, Pa.,1983.

Sandole, Dennis, & van der Merwe, Hugo (eds), *Conflict Resolution Theory and Practice*, Manchester University Press, Manchester, 1993.

Sharp, Gene, *The Politics of Nonviolent Action*, Extending Horizons Books, Boston, 1973.

Wilbee, Brenda, *Taming the Dragons: Christian Women Resolving Conflict*, HarperCollins, New York, 1992.

3 The Goddess

Baring, Anne and Cashford, Jules, *The Myth of the Goddess: Evolution of An Image*, Viking Arkana, London, 1991.

Bolen, Jean Shinoda, *Goddesses in Everywoman*, Harper & Row, New York, 1987.

Condren, Mary, *The Serpent and the Goddess: Women, Religion and Power in Celtic Ireland*, HarperCollins, San Francisco, 1989.

Dames, Michael, *Silbury Treasure: the Great Goddess Rediscovered*, Thames and Hudson, London, 1976.

Daniel, GE & Crawford, OGS, *The Eye Goddess*, Phoenix House, London, 1957.

Edwards, Carolyn McVickar, *The Storyteller's Goddess*, HarperCollins, New York, 1991.

Eisler, Riane, *The Chalice and the Blade*, Harper and Row, San Francisco, 1987.

Fleming, Andrew, 'The Myth of the Mother Goddess' in *World Archaeology* Vol 2, October 1969.

Frothingham, A L, *Medusa*, 'Apollo and the Great Mother' *AJA* 15, no 3, 1911.

Frothingham, A L, 'Medusa' 11 *AJA* 19, no 1, 1915.

Gadon, Elinor, *The Once and Future Goddess*, HarperCollins, San Francisco, 1989.

George, Demetra, *Mysteries of Dark Moon: The Healing Power of the Dark Goddess*, HarperCollins Publishers, New York, 1992.

Getty, Adele, *Goddess: Mother of Living Nature*, Thames & Hudson, London, 1990.

Gimbutas, Marija, *The Goddesses and Gods of Old Europe 6500–3500 BC,* Thames & Hudson, London, 1974, 1982.

Gimbutas, Marija, *The Language of the Goddess,* Thames & Hudson, London, 1989.

Graves, Robert, *The White Goddess,* Faber & Faber, London, 1961.

Graves, Robert, *Mammon and the Black Goddess,* 4th edition, Cassell & Co Ltd., London, 1965.

Johnson, Buffie, *Lady of the Beasts: Ancient Images of the Goddess and her Sacred Animals,* HarperCollins, New York, 1990.

Jones, Kathy, *The Ancient British Goddess; Her Myths, Legends and Sacred Sites,* Ariadne Publications, Glastonbury, 1991.

Matthews, Caitlín, *Voices of the Goddess; A Chorus of Sibyls,* Aquarian Press, Wellingborough, 1990.

Matthews, Caitlín, *The Elements of the Goddess,* 3rd edition, Element, Shaftesbury, 1993.

Mookerjee, Ajit, *Kali The Feminine Force,* Thames and Hudson, London, 1991.

Noble, Vicki, *Shakti Woman,* HarperCollins, New York, 1991.

Pepper, Elizabeth, & Wilcock, John, *Magical and Mystical Sites,* Harper & Row, New York, 1977.

Perera, Sylvia Brinton, *Descent to the Goddess: a Way of Initiation for Women,* Inner City Books, Toronto, 1981.

Rufus, Anneli S & Lawson, Kristan, *Goddess Sites: Europe,* HarperCollins Publishers, New York, 1990.

Sjoo, Monica, *New Age and Armageddon: The Goddess or the Gurus? Towards a Feminist Vision of the Future,* The Women's Press, London, 1992.

Sjoo, Monica & Mor, Barbara, *The Great Cosmic Mother; Rediscovering the Religion of the Earth,* HarperCollins, New York, 1987.

Stone, Merlin, *When God Was a Woman,* Dorset Press, New York, 1976.

Ucko, Peter, *Anthropomorphic Figurines,* Andrew Smidla, London, 1968.

Von Cles-Reden, Sibylle, *The Realm of the Great Goddess,* Thames & Hudson, London, 1961.

Whitmont, Edward C, *Return of the Goddess,* Arkana, London, 1987.

Wombwell, Felicity, *The Goddess Changes,* Mandala, London, 1991.

4 Men's Issues

Jukes, Adam, *Why Men Hate Women,* Free Association Books, London, 1993.

Kimmel, Michael S, *Changing Men; New Directions in Research on Men and Masculinity,* Sage Publications, California, 1987.

Lederer, Wolfgang, *The Fear of Women,* Harcourt Brace Jovanovich, New York, 1968.

Monick, Eugene, *Phallos,* City Books, Inner City Books, Toronto, 1987.

Moore, Robert & Gillette, Douglas, *The King Within,* Anon Books, New York, 1992.

Rowan, John, *The Horned God; Feminism and Men as Wounding and Healing*, Routledge & Kegan Paul, London, 1987.

5 Myth and Symbol

Birkhauser-Oeri, Sibylle, *The Mother: Archetypal Image in Fairy Tales*, Canada, Toronto, 1988.

Boa, Fraser, *This Business of the Gods . . . Joseph Campbell in Conversation with Fraser Boa*, Windrose Films Ltd, Ontario, Canada, 1989.

Campbell, Joseph, *The Mythic Image*, Princeton University Press, Princeton, 1974.

Campbell, Joseph, *The Hero with a Thousand Faces*, Paladin, London, 1988.

Campbell, Joseph with Moyers, Bill, *The Power of Myth*, Doubleday, New York, 1989.

Cassell Encyclopedia of Myths and Legends, Cassell, London, 1992.

Eliade, Mircea, *Images et Symboles*, Paris, 1952.

Fraser, James, *The Golden Bough*, Macmillan, New York, 1922.

Graves, Robert, *The Greek Myths* (2 vols), Penguin, London: 1955.

Hays, H R, *The Dangerous Sex: The Myth of Feminine Evil*, London, 1966.

Hooke, S H, *Middle Eastern Mythology*, Penguin, Harmondsworth, 1963.

Joines, K, *Serpent Symbolism in the Old Testament*, Haddonfield House, Haddonfield, 1974.

Jung, Carl, *Man and His Symbols*, Doubleday, New York, 1964.

Langdon, S H, *Semitic Mythology*, vol 5 of Gray, L H (ed), *Mythology of All Races*, Marshall Jones, Boston, 1931.

Larousse Encyclopedia of Mythology, Hamlyn, London, 1968.

Noonuccal, Oodgeroo and Oodgeroo, Kabul, *The Rainbow Serpent* Australian Government Publishing Service, Canberra, 1988.

Slater, Philip, *The Glory of Hera: Greek Mythology and the Greek Family*, Beacon Press, Boston, 1968.

Von Franz, Marie-Louise, *The Feminine in Fairytales*, Shambhala, Boston, Massachusetts, 1993.

Walker, Barbara G, *The Woman's Encyclopedia of Myths and Secrets*, HarperCollins, New York, 1983.

6 Political Issues

Barnett, L & Lee, I (eds) *The Nuclear Mentality*, Pluto Press, London, 1989.

Burke, Patrick, *The Nuclear Weapons World: Who, Where and How*, Pinter, London, 1988.

Cohn, Carol, 'Sex and Death in the Rational World of Defense Intellectuals' in *SIGNS: Journal of Women in Culture and Society*, Vol 12, No 4, 1987.

Commission on Global Governance, Open University Press, Oxford, 1995.

Dinnerstein, Dorothy, *The Rocking of the Cradle and the Ruling of the World*, The Women's Press, London, 1987.

Dixon, Norman, *Our Own Worst Enemy*, Jonathan Cape, London, 1976.

Easlea, Brian, *Science and Sexual Oppression: Patriarchy's Confrontation With Woman and Nature*, Weidenfeld and Nicolson, London, 1981.

Elshtain, Jean Bethke, *Women and War*, The Harvester Press, Brighton, 1987.

Elworthy, Scilla, *British Nuclear Weapons Policy: Why it has not Changed with the End of the Cold War*, unpublished, PhD thesis.

Freidan, Betty, *The Feminine Mystique*, Dell, New York, 1974.

Fromm, Erich, *The Anatomy of Human Destructiveness*, 2nd edition, Penguin, Harmondsworth, 1977.

George, Susan, *How the Other Half Dies: The Real Reason for World Hunger*, Penguin, London, 1976.

Greer, Germaine, *The Female Eunuch*, Paladin, London, 1971.

Hall, Catherine, *White, Male and Middle Class: Explorations in Feminism and History*, Polity Press, London, 1992.

Hite, Shere, *Women as Revolutionary Agents of Change 1972-1993*, Bloomsbury, London, 1993.

Howard, Michael, *The Causes of War*, Counterpoint, London, 1983.

Isaksson, Eva (ed), *Women and the Military System*, Harvester Wheatsheaf, London, 1988.

Jeffreys, Stella, *Anticlimax; A Feminist Perspective on the Sexual Revolution*, The Women's Press, London, 1993.

Jones, Squadron Leader E G, 'Women in Combat – Historical Quirk or the Future Cutting Edge?' Trench Gascoigne Prize Essay, in *RUSI Journal*, August 1993.

Jones, Lynn (ed) *Keeping the Peace*, London, Women's Press, 1983.

Kennedy, Helena, *Eve Was Framed: Women and British Justice*, Vintage, London: 1993.

McLean, Scilla, Elworthy, Scilla (ed), *The Role of Women in Peace Movements in the Development of Peace Research, and in the Promotion of Friendly Relations between Nations*, presented by UNESCO to the World Conference of the United Nations Decade for Women, Copenhagen, 1980.

McLean, Scilla (later Elworthy), (ed), *How Nuclear Weapons are Made*, Macmillan, London, 1986.

Miall, Hugh, *Nuclear Weapons: Who's in Charge?*, Macmillan, London, 1987.

Miall, Hugh, *The Peacemakers; Peaceful Settlement of Disputes Since 1945*, Macmillan in association with the Oxford Research Group, London, 1992.

Newland, Kathleen, *The Sisterhood of Man: The Impact of Women's Changing Roles on Social and Economic Life Around the World*, W W Norton, New York, 1979.

Oxford Research Group *Current Decision Reports Nos 6, 1991 and 10, 1992.*

Prins, Gwyn & Stamp, Robbie, *Top Guns and Toxic Whales: The Environment and Global Security*, Earthscan, London, 1991.

Proceedings of the Forty-First Pugwash Conference on Science and World Affairs, Beijing, China, 17–22 September 1991.

Reardon, Betty A, *Sexism and the War System*, Teachers College Press, New York, 1985.

Roberts, Yvonne, *Mad About Women: Can There Ever be Fair Play Between the Sexes?*, Virago Press, London, 1992.

Robie, David, (ed), *Tu Galala: Social Change in the South Pacific*, Pluto Press, Australia, 1992.

Rosenau, James N, *Turbulence in World Politics: A Theory of Change and Continuity*, Harvester Wheatsheaf, Hertfordshire, 1990.

Seager, Joni, (ed), *The State of the Earth*, Unwin Hyman, London, 1990.

Thompson, Dorothy, *Over Our Dead Bodies: Women Against the Bomb*, Virago Press, London, 1983.

United Nations, *The World's Women: Trends and Statistics 1970–1990*, United Nations, New York, 1992.

Vickers, Jeanne, *Women and War*, Zed Books, London, 1993.

Warnock Kitty, Bexley, Jo and Bennett, Olivia, (eds), *Arms to Fight: Arms to Protect*, Panos, London, 1995.

Women and Girls: The Key to Development, UK Committee for UNICEF, London, 1994.

7 Power

Bedau, H A, (ed), *Civil Disobedience: Theory and Practice*, Pegasus, New York, 1969.

Beetham, David, *The Legitimation of Power*, Macmillan Education, London, 1991.

Boulding, Kenneth E, *Three Faces of Power*, Sage Publications, Newbury Park, 1990.

Dahl, Robert, 'The Concept of Power' in *Behavioural Science*, 2, 1957.

French, Marilyn, *Beyond Power: Women, Men and Morals*, Jonathan Cape, London, 1985.

Kline, Nancy, *Women and Power: How Far Can We Go?*, BBC Books, London, 1993.

Lukes, Stephen, *Power*, Basil Blackwell, Oxford, 1986.

Mackenzie, W J M, *Power, Violence, Decision*, Penguin, Harmondsworth, 1975.

McClelland, David, *Power: the Inner Experience*, Irvington, New York, 1976.

Paul, Shale, *The Warrior Within: A Guide to Inner Power*, Delta Group Press, Colorado, 1987.

Pearson, Vida, *Women and Power: Gaining Back Control*, Pavic Publications, Sheffield, 1992.

Rogers, Carl, *On Personal Power: Inner Strength and its Revolutionary Impact*,

5th edition, Constable, London, 1986.

Russell, Bertrand, *Power: A New Social Analysis*, Unwin, London, 1975.

Sanday, Peggy Reeves, *Female Power and Male Dominance: On the Origins of Sexual Inequality*, Cambridge University Press, Cambridge, 1981.

Snow, C P, *Corridors of Power*, Penguin, London, 1964.

Spender, Dale, *Man Made Language*, 2nd edition, Routledge and Kegan Paul, London, 1985.

Steiner, Claude M, *The Other Side of Power: How to Become Powerful without being Power-Hungry*, Grove Press, New York, 1981.

Toffler, Alvin, *Power Shift: Knowledge, Wealth, and Violence at the Edge of the 21st Century*, 2nd edition, Bantam Books, London, 1991.

Wolf, Naomi, *Fire with Fire: The New Female Power and How it will Change the 21st Century*, Chatto & Windus, London, 1993.

Wrong, Dennis, *Power: Its Forms, Bases and Uses*, Blackwell, Oxford, 1979.

8 Psychology

Gilligan, Carol, *In a Different Voice: Psychological Theory and Women's Development*, Harvard University Press, Cambridge, Massachusetts, 1982.

Grof, Stanislav, *Realms of the Human Unconscious*, Souvenir Press, London, 1979.

Hunt, Heather, *An Example of Early Intervention Mental Health Project within the National Health Service*, paper presented to the First International Seminar for Mental Disorders of Women, Rome, June 1988.

Jacobi, Jolande, *The Psychology of C G Jung*, Routledge and Kegan Paul, London, 1975.

Rowman & Allanheld, Jaggar, Alison M, *Feminist Politics and Human Nature*, Totowa, New Jersey, 1983.

Jung, Carl, *Memories, Dreams and Reflections*, Fontana, London, 1983.

Jung, Emma, *Animus and Anima*, Spring Publications, New York, 1978.

Lasch, Christopher, *The Minimal Self: Psychic Survival in Troubled Times*, Pan Books, London, 1985.

Mankowitz, Ann, *A Change of Life: A Psychological Study of Dreams and the Menopause*, Inner City Books, Toronto, 1984.

Miller, Alice, *Breaking Down the Wall of Silence: To Join the Waiting Child*, Virago, London, 1990.

Miller, Alice, *For Your Own Good: The Roots of Violence in Child-Rearing*, Virago, London, 1987.

Peck, M Scott, *The Road Less Travelled: A New Psychology of Love, Traditional Values and Spiritual Growth*, Rider, London, 1985.

Roberts, Jane, *The Nature of the Psyche: Its Human Expression*, Prentice Hall, New York, 1979.

Rogers, C R, *Carl Rogers on Encounter Groups*, Harmondsworth, Penguin, 1973.

Winnicott, D W, *Playing and Reality*, Pelican, London, 1974.

Woodman, Marion, *The Pregnant Virgin: A Process of Psychological Transformation*, Inner City Books, Toronto, 1985.

9 Self-knowledge

British Association for Counselling, *Counselling and Psychotherapy Resources Directory*, BAC, Rugby, 1993.

Chapman, Jake, *Tell Me Who You Are*, Chapman, Hanslope, 1988.

Cooper, Diana, *The Power of Inner Peace*, Judy Piatkus, London, 1994.

De Castillejo, Irene Claremont, *Knowing Woman: A Feminine Psychology*, Shambala, Boston, 1990.

Dowling, Colette, *The Cinderella Complex: Women's Hidden Fear of Independence*, Summit Books, USA, 1981.

Field, Joanna, (Marion Milner) *A Life Of One's Own*, Virago, London, 1987.

Hall, Nor, *The Moon and The Virgin: A Voyage Towards Self-Discovery and Healing*, The Women's Press, London, 1980.

Harding, Mary Elizabeth, *Handbook for the Emerging Woman: A Manual for Awakening the Unlimited Power of the Feminine Spirit*, the Donning Company, Norfolk, Virginia, 1988.

Harris, Amy and Thomas, *Staying OK*, Pan Books, London, 1968.

Harris, Thomas, *I'm OK You're OK*, Pan Books, London, 1970.

Hendricks, Gay & Kathlyn, *Conscious Loving*, Bantam, New York, 1992.

Hendrix, Harville, *Getting the Love You Want*, Pocket Books, London, 1993.

Henley, Nancy M, *Body Politics; Power, Sex and Nonverbal Communication*, Simon & Schuster, New York, 1977.

Johnson, Bob, 'Knowing Why' in *The Friend*, 22 October, 1993.

Knight, Lindsay, *Talking to a Stranger: A Consumers Guide to Therapy*, Fontana, London, 1986.

Kubler-Ross, Elisabeth, *On Death and Dying*, Tavistock Routledge, London, 1989.

Leonard, Linda Schierse, *The Wounded Woman: Healing the Father-Daughter Relationship*, Shambala, Boston, 1985.

Macy, Joanna, *World as Lover, World as Self*, Rider, London, 1993.

Marlow, Mary Elizabeth, *Handbook for the Emerging Woman: Manual for Awakening the Unlimited Power of the Feminine Spirit*, Element, Shaftesbury, 1994.

Martz, Sandra, (ed), *When I Am an Old Woman I Shall Wear Purple*, Papier Maché Press, San Francisco, 1987.

Rama, Swami, Ballentine, Rudolf, & Ajaya, Swami, *Yoga and Psychotherapy: the Evolution of Consciousness*, Himalayan International Institute of Yoga Science and Philosophy of USA, 1976.

Rogers, Natalie, *Emerging Woman*, Personal Press, Point Reyes, 1980.

Rowan, John, *The Transpersonal: Psychotherapy and Counselling*, Routledge,

London, 1993.

Rowe, Dorothy, *Wanting Everything; the Art of Happiness*, Fontana, London, 1992.

Skynner, Robin and Cleese, John, *Families and How to Survive Them*, Methuen, London, 1985.

Steinem, Gloria, *Revolution From Within*, Bloomsbury, London, 1992.

Stevens, José, *Transforming Your Dragons – How to Turn Fear Patterns into Personal Power*, Bear & Co, Santa Fé, 1994.

Swan, Bonita L, *Thirteen Steps: An Empowerment Process for Women*, Spinsters/Aunt Lute, San Francisco, 1989.

Whitfield, Charles, *Healing the Child Within*, Health Communications, Deerfield Beach, 1989.

10 Sexuality

Anand, Margot, *The Art of Sexual Ecstasy*, Aquarian Press, London, 1992.

Dickson, Anne, *The Mirror Within: A New Look at Sexuality*, Quartet Books, London, 1985.

Goodison, Lucy, *Moving Heaven and Earth: Sexuality, Spirituality and Social Change*, Pandora, London, 1992.

Haich, Elizabeth, *Sexual Energy and Yoga*, 2nd edition, George Allen & Unwin, London, 1972.

Henderson, Julie, *The Lover Within*, Station Hill Press, New York, 1986.

Hite, Shere, *The Hite Report on Female Sexuality*, Macmillan, New York, 1976.

Hite, Shere, *Women and Love*, Penguin, London, 1989.

Jolan Chang, *Le Tao de l'Art d'Aimer*, Calmann-Levy, Paris, 1977.

Leroy, Margaret, *Pleasure: The Truth about Female Sexuality*, HarperCollins, London, 1993.

Lowen, Alexander, *Betrayal of the Body*, Collier Books, New York, 1976.

Osho, *Tantra, Spirituality and Sex*, Chidvilas, Boulder, 1994.

Qualls-Corbett, Nancy, *The Sacred Prostitute: Eternal Aspect of the Feminine*, Inner City Books, Toronto, 1988.

Rawson, Philip, *The Art of Tantra*, New York Graphic Society, Greenwich, Connecticut, 1973.

Rawson, Philip, *Erotic Art of the East*, G P Putnam's Sons, New York, 1968.

Sadock, B J, Kaplan, H I, & Freedman, A M., *The Sexual Experience*, Williams & Wilkins, Baltimore, 1976.

White, Ruth, *Sexuality and Spirituality* (ed by Lorna St Aubyn),

11 Spirituality and Religion

Anderson, Bernard, *The Living World of the Old Testament*, 4th edition, Longman Group, London, 1978.

Armstrong, Karen, *The End of Silence: Women and Priesthood*, Fourth Estate, London, 1993.

Bancroft, Anne, *Weavers of Wisdom: Women Mystics of the Twentieth Century*, Penguin, London, 1989.

Begg, Ean, *The Cult of the Black Virgin*, Arkana, Penguin, London, 1985.

Berman, Morris, *Coming To Our Senses: Body and Spirit in the Hidden History of the West*, 2nd edition, Unwin Paperbacks, London, 1990.

Burkert, Walter, *Greek Religion Archaic and Classical*, 2nd edition, Basil Blackwell, Oxford, 1985.

Christ, Carol, *Diving Deep and Surfacing: Women Writers on a Spiritual Quest*, Beacon Press, Boston, 1980.

Christ, Carol & Plaskow, Judith, (eds), *Womanspirit Rising: a Feminist Reader in Religion*, Harper & Row, San Francisco, 1979.

Dowell, Susan & Hurcombe, Linda, *Dispossessed Daughters of Eve: Faith and Feminism*, SCM Press, London, 1981.

Eliade, Mircea, *Shamanism: Archaic Techniques of Ecstasy*, Pantheon, Bollingen Series 76, New York, 1964.

Ereira, Alan, *The Heart of the World*, Jonathan Cape, London, 1990.

Freud, Sigmund, *Moses and Monotheism*, Random House, New York, 1955.

Gross, Rita M, *Buddhism after Patriarchy: A Feminist History, Analysis, and Reconstruction of Buddhism*, State University of New York Press, Albany, 1993.

Harner, Michael, *The Way of the Shaman*, HarperCollins, New York, 1990.

Kramer, Samuel, *The Sacred Marriage Rite*, Indiana University Press, Bloomington, 1969.

Kroll, Una, *Women as Spiritual Guides*, Guild Lecture No 19: June 1978.

Merton, Thomas, *New Seeds of Contemplation*, New Directions, New York, 1962.

Moore, Thomas, *Care of the Soul*, Judy Piatkus, London, 1992.

Morgan, Marlo, *Mutant Message Down Under*, Thorsons, London, 1995.

Needham, Joseph, *The Three Masks of the Tao*, Teilhard Centre for the Future of Man, London, 1979.

Plaskow, Judith & Christ, Carol P, *Weaving the Visions: New Patterns in Feminist Spirituality*, HarperCollins, New York, 1989.

Radha, Swami Sivananda, *Kundalini Yoga for the West*, Timeless Books, Spokane, 1978.

Raheem, Aminah, *Soul Return: Integrating Body, Psyche and Spirit*, Aslan Publishing, California, 1991.

Rodegast, Pat & Stanton, Judith, *Emmanuel's Book: A Manual for Living Comfortably in the Cosmos*, Bantam Books, New York, 1987.

Rodegast, Pat & Stanton, Judith, *The Choice For Love*, Bantam, New York, 1989.

Rosa, José Alberto, with Altman, Nathaniel, *Power Spots: A Shamanic Way to Finding Personal Power*, Aquarian, Wellingborough, 1986.

Ruether, Rosemary Radford, *Gaia and God: An Ecofeminist Theology of Earth*

Healing, SCM Press, London, 1993.

Sharma, Arvind, (ed), *Women in World Religions*, State University of New York Press, Albany, New York, 1987.

Sogyal Rinpoche, *The Tibetan Book of Living and Dying*, Harper, San Francisco, 1992.

Spretnak, Charlene, (ed), *The Politics of Women's Spirituality: Essays on the Rise of Spiritual Power Within the Feminist Movement*, Anchor Books, New York, 1982.

Spretnak, Charlene, *States of Grace: The Recovery of Meaning in the Postmodern Age*, HarperCollins, San Francisco, 1993.

Starhawk, *Truth or Dare: Encounters with Power, Authority, and Mystery*, HarperCollins, New York, 1990.

Strachan, Elspeth & Gordon, *Freeing the Feminine*, Labarum Publications, Dunbar, 1985.

Thich Nhat Hanh, *The Sun My Heart*, Rider, London, 1992.

Thich Nhat Hanh, *The Heart of Understanding*, Parallax Press, 1988.

Thich Nhat Hanh, *Peace is Every Step*, Bantam, New York, 1992.

Trevett, Christine, *Women and Quakerism in the 17th Century*, Sessions Book Trust, York, 1991.

Tweedie, Irina, *The Chasm of Fire: A Woman's Experience of Liberation through the Teachings of a Sufi Master*, Element Books, Wiltshire, 1979.

Weil, Simone, *Gravity and Grace*, 3rd edition, Routledge and Kegan Paul, London, 1972.

White, John, (ed), *Kundalini: Evolution and Enlightenment*, Paragon House, New York, 1990.

Wilhelm, Richard, *The Secret of the Golden Flower*, Kegan, Trench and Tubner, London, 1965.

Williamson, Marianne, *A Return to Love*, Aquarian, London, 1992.

Williamson, Marianne, *A Woman's Worth*, Rider, London, 1993.

12 Women's Issues

Aberdene, Patricia & Naisbitt, John, *Megatrends for Women*, Random House, London, 1993.

Bart, Pauline B & O'Brien, Patricia H, *Stopping Rape: Successful Survival Strategies*, Pergamon Press, Oxford, 1985.

Batten, Juliet, *Power from Within: A Feminist Guide to Ritual-Making*, Ishtar Books, Auckland, 1988.

Brownmiller, Susan, *Against Our Will*, Martin Secker & Warburg, London, 1975.

Brownmiller, Susan, *Femininity*, Paladin, London, 1986.

Cheatham, Annie & Powell, Mary Clare, *This Way Day Break Comes: Women's Values and the Future*, New Society Publishers, Philadelphia, 1986.

Coward, Ros, *Our Treacherous Hearts: Why Women Let Men Get Their Way*, Faber & Faber, London, 1993.

Daly, Mary, *Beyond God the Father*, Beacon Press, Boston, 1973.

Daly, Mary, *Gyn/Ecology: The Metaethics of Radical Feminism*, Women's Press, London, 1978.

De Beauvoir, Simone, *The Second Sex* (trans & ed. H M Parshley) Penguin, Harmondsworth, 1984.

Dickson, Anne, *A Woman in Your Own Right: Assertiveness and You*, Quartet Books, London, 1982.

Eisenstein, Zillah, *The Radical Future of Liberal Feminism*, Longmans, New York, 1981.

Faludi, Susan, *Backlash; The Undeclared War Against Women*, Vintage, London, 1992.

Figes, Eva, *Patriarchal Attitudes: Women in Society*, Virago, London, 1978.

Foerstal, Lenora, (ed), *Women's Voices on the Pacific: The International Pacific Policy Congress*, The Maisonneuve Press, Washington, 1991.

Goldenberg, Naomi M, *Returning Words to Flesh; Feminism, Psychoanalysis, and the Resurrection of the Body*, Beacon Press, Boston, 1990.

Goodrich, Thelma Jean, (ed), *Women and Power; Perspectives for Family Therapy*, W W Norton & Company, New York, 1991.

Koedt, Levine & Rapone, (eds), *Radical Feminism*, Quadrangle, New York, 1973.

Morgan, Robin, (ed), *Sisterhood is Powerful: An Anthology of Writings from the Women's Liberation Movement*, Vintage Books, New York, 1970.

Phelps, Stanley and Austin, Nancy, *The Assertive Woman*, Impact Publishers, California, 1975.

Rich, Adrienne, *Of Woman Born: Motherhood as Experience*, W W Norton, New York, 1986.

Ryan, Jo, '*Feminism and Therapy*', Pam Smith Memorial Lecture, Department of Applied Social Sciences, Polytechnic of North London, 1983.

Spender, Dale, *For the Record: The Making and Meaning of Feminist Knowledge*, Women's Press, London, 1985.

13 Women's Traditions

Allen, Paula Gunn, *Grandmothers of the Light*, Women's Press, London, 1992.

Allione, Tsultrim, *Women of Wisdom*, Arkana, London, 1986.

Boulding, Elise, *The Underside of History: a A View of Women Through Time:* Westview Press, Boulder, 1976.

Briffault, Robert, *The Mothers*, Macmillan, New York, 1927.

Cabot, Laurie, with Cowan, Tom, *Power of the Witch: A Witch's Guide to her Craft*, Penguin, Harmondsworth, 1989.

Cameron, Anne, *Daughters of Copperwoman*, Women's Press, London, 1984.

Feldman, Christina, *Woman Awake: A Celebration of Women's Wisdom*, Arkana, London, 1989.

Harding, M Esther, *Woman's Mysteries: Ancient and Modern*, Rider, London, 1971.

Hope, Murry, *Essential Woman: Her Mystery, Her Power*, HarperCollins, London, 1991.

O'Faolain, Julia & Martines, Lauro, (ed), *Not in God's Image: A History of Women in Europe from the Greeks to the Nineteenth Century*, Harper & Row, New York, 1973.

Rahesha, Namua, *The Serpent and the Circle*, Judy Piatkus, London, 1994.

14 General Reading

Ashe, Geoffrey, *Gandhi: A Study in Revolution*, William Heinemann, London, 1968.

Aung San Suu Kyi, *Freedom From Fear and Other Writings*, Viking Penguin, New York, 1991.

Avalon, Arthur, *Shakti and Shakta*, Dover Publications, New York, 1978.

Barr, Roseanne, *Roseanne: My Life As A Woman*, Collins, London, 1990.

Bello, W & Rosenfeld, S, 'Dragons in Distress: The Economic Miracle Unravels in South Korea, Taiwan, and Singapore', in *Food First Action Alert*, Spring/Summer, 1990.

Budge, Sir E A Wallis, *Egyptian Magic*, Dover Publications, New York, 1971.

Budge, Sir E A Wallis, *Gods of the Egyptians*, (2 vols), Dover Publications, New York, 1969.

Bullough, Vern L, *The Subordinate Sex*, University of Illinois Press, Chicago, 1973.

Carr, E H, *The Twenty Years' Crisis 1919–1939*, Macmillan, London, 1939.

Chan, Khong, *Learning True Love: How I Lived and Practised Social Change in Vietnam*, Parallax Press, Berkeley, 1993.

Charlesworth, Kate & Cameron, Marshall, *All That: the Other Half of History*, Pandora Press, London, 1986.

Dawkins, Richard, *The Selfish Gene*, Granada, St Albans, 1978.

Dawkins, Richard, *The Blind Watchmaker*, Penguin Books, London, 1986.

Dillard, Annie, *A Pilgrim at Tinker's Creek*, Harper & Row, New York, 1974.

Douglas, Mary, *Purity and Danger: An Analysis of the Concepts of Pollution and Taboo*, Arc Paperbacks, London, 1966.

Evans, Arthur, *The Palace of Minos Vol III*, Macmillan, London, 1930.

Fairtlough, Gerard, *Creative Compartments: A Design for Future Organisation*, Adamantine Press, London, 1994.

Harvey, Andrew, *A Journey in Ladakh*, Pan Books, London, 1983.

Hawkes, Jacquetta & Woolley, Leonard, *Prehistory and the Beginnings of Civilisation*, History of Mankind: Cultural and Scientific Development, London, 1963.

Hawkes, Jacquetta, *Dawn of the Gods*, Chatto & Windus, London, 1968.

Hildegard of Bingen, *Illuminations*, Bear & Co, Santa Fé, 1985.

Hinde, Robert, 'Aggression and War: Individuals, Groups and States' in *Behaviour, Society and International Conflict*, Vol 3, 1993.

Hoff, Benjamin, *The Tao of Pooh*, Mandarin, London, 1989.

Huffington, Arianna, *The Fourth Instinct*, Judy Piatkus, London, 1995.

Khanna, Summa, *Ghandi and the Good Life*, Gandhi Peace Foundation, Delhi, 1985.

King, Coretta Scott, (ed), *The Words of Martin Luther King, Jr.*, Newmarket Press, New York, 1983.

Kirsta, Alex, *Deadlier Than The Male*, HarperCollins, London, 1994.

Laszlo, Ervin, *The Systems View of the World*, Basil Blackwell, Oxford, 1972.

Leigh, Andrew & Maynard, Michael, *Ace Teams: Creating Star Performance in Business*, Butterworth Heinemann, Oxford, 1993.

Mahanirvanatantra (trans. Sir John Woodroffe), Dover Publications, New York, 1972.

Mamatoto – A Celebration of Birth, Virago, London, 1991.

Mamet, David, *Oleanna*, Methuen Drama, London, 1993.

Mandela, Nelson Rohihlahla, *Long Walk to Freedom*, Little Brown, New York, 1994.

Marcuse, Herbert, *Eros and Civilisation*, Vintage Books, New York, 1955.

Mead, Margaret, *Male and Female*, 10th edition, Penguin, London, 1978.

Mead, Margaret, *Culture and Commitment: A Study of the Generation Gap*, 2nd edition, Panther Books, St Albans, 1977.

Mehta, Ved, *Mahatma Gandhi and his Apostles*, Penguin, London, 1977.

Mill, John Stuart, *The Subjugation of Women*, Prometheus Books, New York, 1986.

Moir, Anne & Jessel, David, *Brainsex: The Real Difference between Men & Women*, Mandarin, London, 1991.

Montagu, Ashley, *The Natural Superiority of Women*, Collier Macmillan, London, 1968.

Naess, Anne, *Gandhi and the Nuclear Age*, Bedminster Press, Totowa, 1965.

National Institute of Economic and Social Research, *Discussion Paper No.50*, October 1993.

Norberg-Hodge, Helena, *Ancient Futures; Learning from Ladakh*, Rider, London, 1991.

Open University, Rob Paton, Professor Jake Chapman & John Hamwee *T244 Technology: A Second Level Course: Managing in Organizations, Block V: Wider Perspectives*, The Open University Press, Milton Keynes, 1985.

Open University, *T247 Technology: A Second Level Course Block 7 Working with Systems; Decision Making*, The Open University, Milton Keynes, 1991.

Paglia, Camille, *Sexual Personae: Sex, Art and American Culture*, Penguin, London, 1994.

Parlow, Anita, *Cry, Sacred Ground*, The Christic Institute, Washington, 1988.

Piercy, Marge, *To Be of Use*, Doubleday and Company, New York, 1973.

Radcliffe Richards, Janet, *The Sceptical Feminist*, Penguin, Harmondsworth, 1980.

Ramage, Janet, *Energy: a Guidebook*, Oxford University Press, Oxford, 1988.

Roux, George, *Ancient Iraq*, Allen & Unwin, London, 1964.

Scarf, Maggie, *Unfinished Business*, Ballantine Books, New York, 1980.

Sebba, Anne, *Battling for the News: The Rise of the Woman Reporter*, Hodder & Stoughton, London, 1993.

Simpson, G G, *The Meaning of Evolution*, Yale University Press, New Haven, 1949.

Tannen, Deborah, *You Just Don't Understand; Women and Men in Conversation*, Virago, London, 1991.

Tauroa, Hiwi & Pat, *Te Marae: A Guide to Customs and Protocol*, Heinemann Reed, Auckland, 1987.

Taylor, Bridget, Brook, Lindsay & Jowell, Roger (eds), *British Social Attitudes: the 8th Report*, Dartmouth, 1991.

Waddington, C H, *Tools for Thought*, Paladin, Frogmore, 1977.

Walker, Alice, *Possessing the Secret of Joy*, Vintage, London, 1992.

Warner, Marina, *Alone of All Her Sex*, Picador/Pan, London, 1976.

Weber, Max, *Economy and Society*, University of California Press, Los Angeles, 1978.

Woolf, Virginia, *A Room of One's Own*, The Hogarth Press, London, 1978.

Zohar, Danah, *The Quantum Self: A Revolutionary View of Human Nature and Consciousness Rooted in the New Physics*, Bloomsbury, London, 1990.

Index